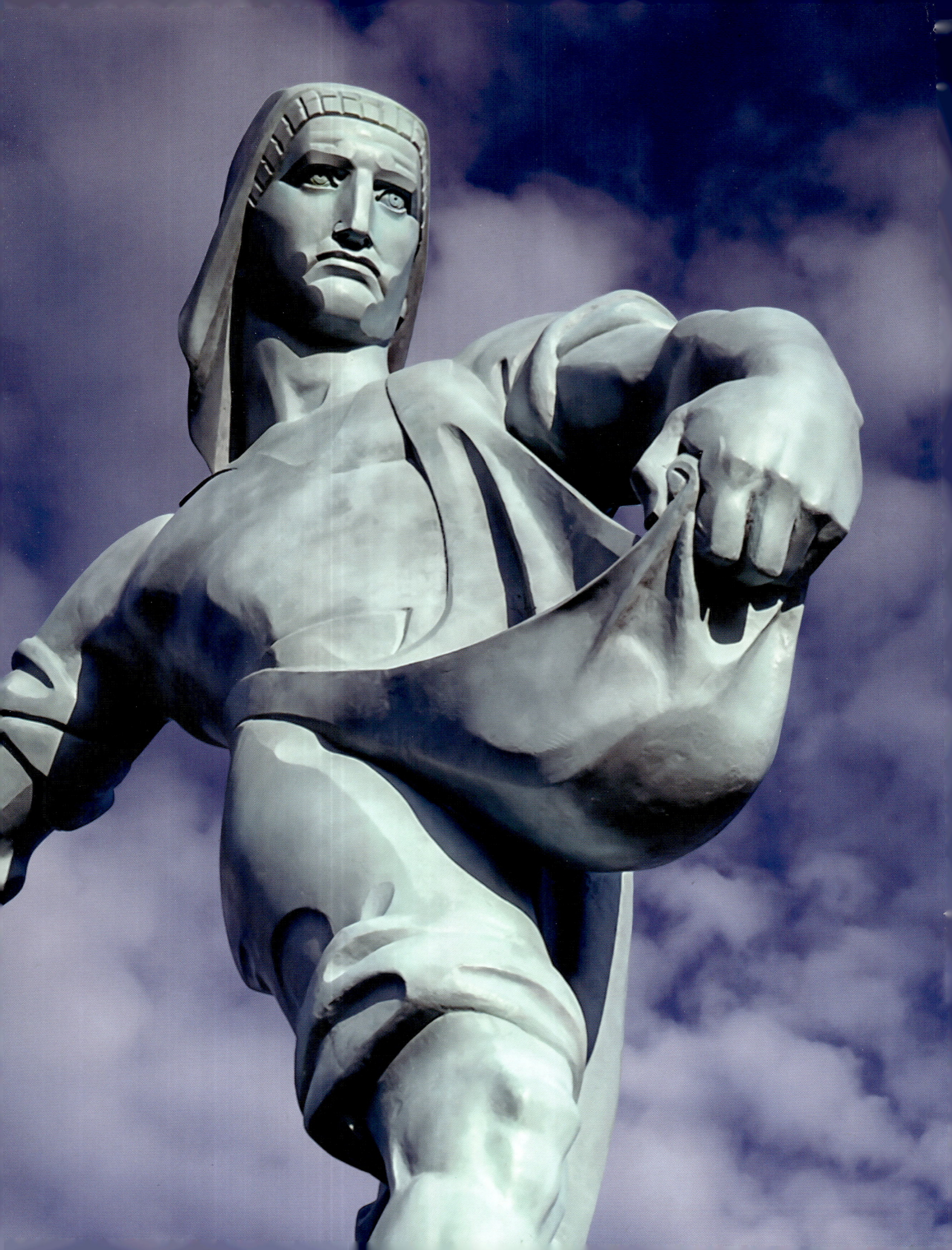

CREATIVE GENIUS:
THE ART OF THE NEBRASKA CAPITOL

SUSANNE SHORE
KEVIN MOSER
DREW DAVIES

UNIVERSITY OF NEBRASKA PRESS   LINCOLN

Acknowledgments for the use of copyrighted material appear on page 210, which constitutes an extension of the copyright page.

The University of Nebraska Press is part of a land-grant institution with campuses and programs on the past, present, and future homelands of the Pawnee, Ponca, Otoe-Missouria, Omaha, Dakota, Lakota, Kaw, Cheyenne, and Arapaho Peoples, as well as those of the relocated Ho-Chunk, Sac and Fox, and Iowa Peoples.

Library of Congress Control Number: 2023942831

Set in DTL Nobel and Garamond Premier Pro.
Designed by Drew Davies / Oxide.

GRATITUDE

As with most big endeavors in life, it's best not to know what you are getting into until you have jumped in fully. The three of us did just that when we committed to one another to complete a book showcasing a building that we love and cherish.

This book originated from our collaboration on the Nebraska state license plate. Drew's design using the *Genius of Creative Energy* mosaic in the Capitol led Kevin and Susanne to the realization that no complete collection of high-quality, high-resolution photos of the Capitol's artwork existed. We were focused on the surprisingly complex task of photographing every piece of artwork in the Capitol when a friend suggested producing a coffee table book to share the images with the public (thank you, Justin Petersen).

"Creating a book should be easy enough," we thought when we signed the publishing agreement; turns out we were wrong. When reality hit us, we found ourselves relying on the kindness of friends and strangers for help.

To all of those who lent us support and advice, we give our heartfelt thanks. This would have been impossible without you.

We need to begin by thanking Matthew Hansen who took our meeting and then jumped right in with us, agreeing to edit many of the sections of the book. He also unwittingly played the role of parent, as in, "We need to get this done because Matthew is getting involved soon."

So many people within the Capitol assisted us along the way. Thank you to the office of the Nebraska Capitol Commission, especially Bob Ripley, who outstandingly ran the show at the Capitol for more than four decades.

Thanks also to the entire staff in the Governor's Office for allowing us to invade their workspace multiple times and to Governor Pete Ricketts for saying "yes" when we asked to fly drones in the Capitol — an unprecedented request unpopular for some.

To the Legislature, we send our appreciation for allowing access to their chambers. A special thank you to Patrick O'Donnell for heading that effort.

To the International Hildreth Meière Association, and especially Hildreth Meière Dunn, a note of appreciation for providing advice, connections, and images to help us complete this book.

Also to the amazing partners who helped us push this to the end: the University of Nebraska Press for their expertise and patience; Jay Davis Photography for not only the amazing images provided but for the extra time he spent getting the perfect shot; and to Digital Sky and MTD Aerial for the fantastic drone images (also for not crashing the drones into the building because we would have been in so much trouble).

Finally, a special note to the greatest ambassador for the Capitol we could hope for — Roxanne Smith, who spent hours helping us gain access to all of the spaces and assisting us in understanding the significance of every piece of art in the building. There just are not enough words to express our gratitude for all of the time she spent answering our questions, pointing us in the right direction, and opening doors we were sure would never be accessible.

They say "it takes a village," but we found it takes a state. This book is dedicated to all Nebraskans. Whether you've lived in the state forever, or keep it in your heart while living elsewhere — the Nebraska Capitol is a building that connects us all. We hope you enjoy the artwork and the stories within this book.

Susanne Shore, Kevin Moser, and Drew Davies

FOREWORD
ROBERT C. RIPLEY, FAIA

Does anyone ever fall in love with a building or a place? After all, they exist mainly for our use and enjoyment. In the summer of 1953, I did.

It happened when my mother, Donna, first walked my brother David and me from our home near 25th and J Streets, west to the Nebraska Capitol. I was absolutely awestruck. It might seem odd that someone so young could appreciate a remarkable building, but working in the Capitol for 40 years has taught me the Nebraska Capitol touches each visitor, no matter their age.

For many Nebraskans, the Capitol is the largest and tallest building they have ever seen. For everyone, it is an impressive combination of art and architecture opening their eyes to a Nebraska story beyond their expectations. The richly decorated floors and ceilings by Hildreth Meière and the exterior and interior sculpture by Lee Lawrie take visitors on a visual journey using ancient and modern artistic techniques. Together, they transform the building from a seat of government to an inspirational monument. Capitol architect Bertram Goodhue's design seamlessly integrates art and architecture; the building uplifts Nebraska's story and inspires thoughtful contemplation of what it means to be a citizen in a democracy.

Children explore the building with sight and sound. On the floor, they are fascinated by the mosaics with images they know, geometric shapes and prehistoric animals. Small children walk the black-and-white curving bands encircling the four elemental spheres in the rotunda. They point at the prehistoric creatures, unaware they are experiencing an art form thousands of years old. As they move through the vaulted spaces, they make sounds just to hear the echo, unaware they are experiencing architectural forms originating a thousand years ago to glorify the human voice. Their first interaction with the Capitol's art and architecture may even inspire them to become an artist or architect. That's what it did for me. Preserving the Capitol for future generations became my life's work.

When Nebraskans come back as adults, they are awestruck by the magnitude of the building and its artwork. Years of sharing the Capitol with national and international visitors and architects have only reinforced what I knew as a child: Nebraska's Capitol is remarkable.

The Capitol was completed in the early 1930s during the Great Depression. Nebraskans sacrificed to achieve their dream of a Capitol worthy of the state they loved, but had to leave murals unrealized. Those hard times provided Nebraskans with the subsequent opportunity to participate in the addition of the 20 wall murals that were part of the original artistic program. National competitions for the murals on the second floor in the 1950s and 1960s brought new artistic styles into the Capitol.

Those of us who were first introduced to the Capitol as children — a Capitol then with gray, blank spaces on the Memorial Chamber walls — felt a thrill, and a sense of accomplishment, when Nebraska artist Stephen Roberts's murals were hung in the chamber in 1996, completing the original mural program.

I am grateful for the efforts of former First Lady Susanne Shore to create and publish *Creative Genius: The Art of the Nebraska Capitol,* which will allow Nebraskans and everyone else to see why the Nebraska Capitol is considered an art-and-architecture masterpiece. As you leaf through this book and try to choose a favorite mosaic or mural, you might find, as I have, that it is impossible. The Nebraska Capitol demonstrates the adage that the whole is greater than the sum of its parts.

Robert C. Ripley, FAIA
Former Capitol Administrator,
Office of the Nebraska Capitol Commission,
1983–2023

PROLOGUE

The Nebraska State Capitol may be the most beautiful capitol building in the United States.

From the day it opened, it's been recognized as an outlier relative to its 49 rivals. The influential leaders of *American Architect* certainly thought so, choosing to feature the Nebraska Capitol in the October 1934 issue soon after the building opened. In the introduction, they wrote:

> "From the engineering standpoint, the building embodies the cumulative results of American energy, inventive skill and organizing ability; and from all combined points of view, it stands as a remarkable interpretation of innumerable events that have shaped the progress of American art, industry and democratic government."

Nebraska's Capitol manages to stand out not only for its impressive architecture but also for its unique artwork. While other capitol buildings contain art, none incorporated it into the building design from the very first step of planning. The Nebraska Capitol's architects focused on art as a crucial part of the building — every bit as important to its planning as its walls, shape, or iconic dome.

Each piece of art has meaning. Together it tells a larger story about Nebraska. This is artwork that shows us how we live, how we thrive, how we govern, where we came from, and a path forward. The result: The mythology of Nebraska, brought to life throughout the building.

Two men, Bertram Goodhue and Hartley Burr Alexander, conjured and drove this artistic vision. Goodhue, picked as the lead architect for the Nebraska Capitol, was already well-versed in using ornamentation to elevate architecture. He was also something of a romantic when it came to art and architecture. He once wrote:

> "Beautiful architecture is just as much in my mind a matter of inspiration as poetry, painting, or sculpture. In fact, I believe all art to be a varied expression of the one great impulse towards beauty."

He also viewed the study of art as crucial for architecture, arguing that "the best architects have been artists first." He believed architecture is meant to inspire and tell stories.

In order to tell the story of Nebraska, he partnered with Alexander, a Nebraska-born philosopher. Alexander's task: craft a narrative that tied the building together. Alexander deeply studied democracy and the political thinking of the early 1900s. He also wrote numerous books and essays on Native cultures, becoming an expert on Native American faith, mythology, and symbolism. He harnessed elements of philosophy, history, and Native lore to develop the artistic theme he sought to set for the State Capitol. Today, Alexander's views on philosophy and democracy are omnipresent throughout the building, both in the hundreds of pieces of art and in inscriptions etched in the building's Indiana limestone walls.

Goodhue and Alexander collaborated with a multitude of talented artists to create the beauty contained in the Capitol. Most significant were muralist Hildreth Meière and sculptor Lee Lawrie. Together these visionaries created a masterpiece — one they often considered their greatest work.

This book tells the stories of the Capitol building and its art, capturing its beauty, meaning, and importance for Nebraskans today. Throughout this book you will find Alexander's theme woven into the story, often in direct quotes. His vision serves as a guide and provides deeper depth to the understanding behind each piece of art and each part of the Capitol. We've provided additional historical context to help these stories come alive.

The artwork is beautiful as photographed, but the best way to experience and appreciate this building is in person. We hope this book inspires you to make the trip to Lincoln's 1445 K Street and serves as a guide when you do.

THE
BUILDING

CONSTRUCTING
THE CAPITOL

NEBRASKA'S TERRITORIAL ERA

Picking a location for Nebraska's capital proved contentious from the start — a fight that began even before Nebraska became a state. Since the location wasn't specified, the original decision fell to Nebraska's first territorial governor, Francis Burt, a man appointed by President Franklin Pierce. Burt arrived in Bellevue by steamboat in early October 1854, already deathly ill. Upon landing in Bellevue, he stayed in his bed until October 16, when he forced himself out to take the oath of office. He died two days later — before he got the chance to choose the Nebraska capital location.

People close to Burt believed he planned to choose Bellevue as Nebraska's capital city. But after Burt's untimely demise, the position of territorial governor was handed to 25-year-old Thomas Cuming, the territorial secretary. Cuming was a member of an influential group of Iowans in Washington DC, who wanted Nebraska's capital to be located directly across the Missouri River from Council Bluffs.

Cuming made the decision to do exactly that, choosing a place then called Omaha City. It proved a decision unpopular with many. Omaha City sat north of the Platte River, but twice as many people in the Nebraska Territory lived south of the river. Despite its unpopularity, Cuming devised a steel-tight plan to cement his capital choice; he created a legislature that gave 14 seats to those living north of the Platte and only 12 to those living south. Despite much contention, plotting, and turmoil — including at least one fistfight on the House floor — the stacked territorial legislature officially chose Omaha as its capital.

The South Platte legislators, infuriated by the decision, actually attempted to secede from the Nebraska Territory and join Kansas. The effort ultimately failed, and the territorial capital remained in Omaha until Nebraska became a state in 1867.

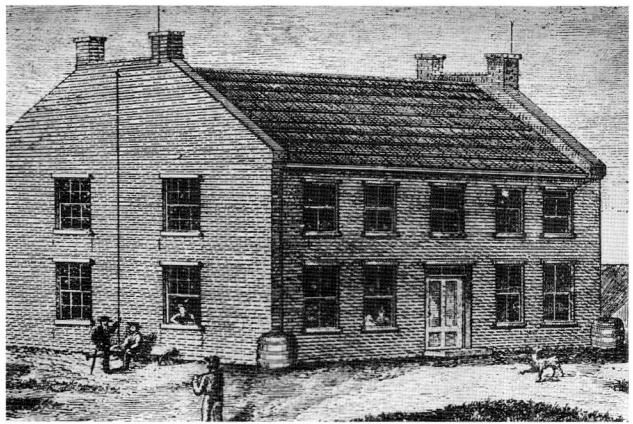

Nebraska's first territorial capitol, built in Omaha City.

LINCOLN BECOMES NEBRASKA'S CAPITAL

After Nebraska became a state in 1867, the first state legislature of Nebraska convened. One of the first votes taken called for the capital to be moved from Omaha. A potential new capital city: the tiny village of Lancaster, located on the east bank of Salt Creek.

The bill passed the House and the Senate and then was signed into law by Governor David Butler. Omaha legislators made a last-ditch effort to keep the capital in Omaha — they amended the bill to name the new capital Lincoln. The Omahans thought this might prove a poison pill, as most legislators south of the Platte were pro-slavery and thus not fond of Abraham Lincoln. But the effort to keep the capital in Omaha failed, and the newly appointed capital commissioners went to work to choose a new location. They ultimately settled on Lancaster — now named Lincoln — despite it having a population of only 30.

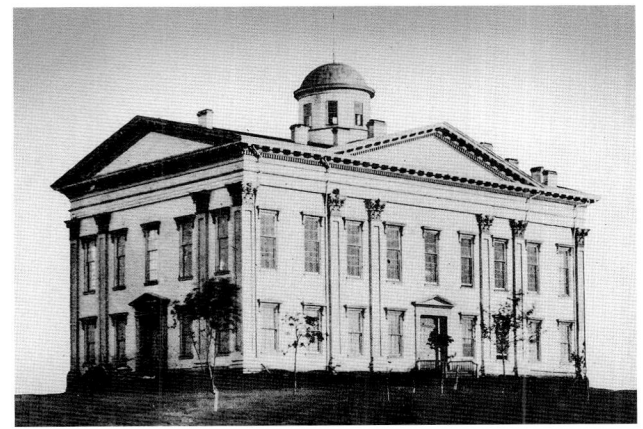

Nebraska's second territorial capitol, located in the city now known as Omaha.

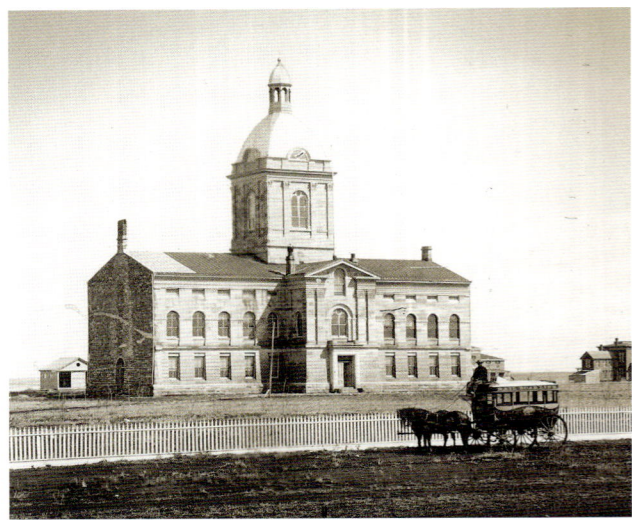

Nebraska's first state capitol, erected in Lincoln in 1868.

THE FIRST CAPITOL

Construction began on Lincoln's first capitol building in 1867 and was completed in 1868 at a cost of $75,000. It wasn't money well spent. The building proved so hastily and shoddily constructed that, a mere dozen years after it was built, Governor Silas Garber reported to the Nebraska Legislature that the building was in danger of collapse. The Omaha legislators pounced, renewing calls to move the capital out of Lincoln, potentially to a more central location like Kearney or Columbus.

THE SECOND CAPITOL

Despite efforts to move it, the capital remained in Lincoln. The next step was to tackle the problem of the ailing building. State leaders decided to proceed in phases. Wings to the east and west parts of the first building would be added and then the center portion demolished and rebuilt, all at an estimated cost of $191,000. Once the core of the first capitol had been razed, workers began construction on a new center portion of the second capitol. The complicated construction dragged on for years, and costs exploded. The building, not completed until 1889, eventually cost $450,000, the equivalent of $14.8 million today.

This piecemeal strategy resulted in a new building built better than the first — but just barely. After 20 years of use, the second building began to settle, and its limestone walls began to crumble. Leaders decided it was time for the state to construct a permanent building — one that would stand the test of time.

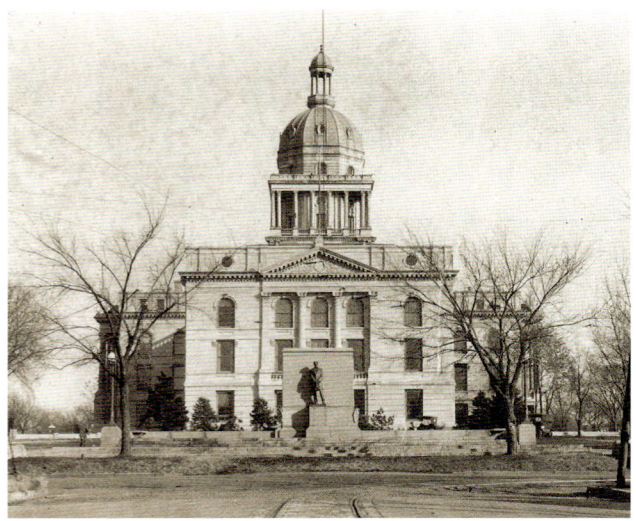

Nebraska's second state capitol, seen here with the Abraham Lincoln memorial that still stands outside the Capitol today.

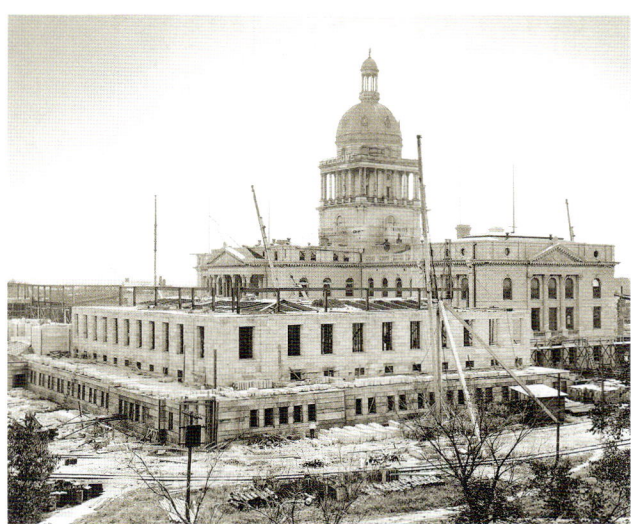

Construction of Nebraska's third state capitol, being built directly around the second capitol.

THIRD TIME'S A CHARM

In January 1919 Samuel McKelvie, a 37-year-old publisher of the *Nebraska Farmer* and a progressive who promised political reform, became governor. He urged the state to build a new capitol that would stand as a memorial to the Nebraskans who died in World War I. On February 20 he signed a bill paving the way for the construction to begin.

The law also created a capitol commission tasked with planning and executing the new building. Led by famed Nebraska architect Thomas R. Kimball, the group created a unique process for attracting submissions from the best American architectural firms. Put simply, they gave no specific requirements on the building's plan, style, or materials, unlike most competitions of the time for public buildings. This granted the architects extraordinary and immense freedom.

There were some stipulations. First, the commission set a daunting, overarching directive that the building should be "an inspiring monument worthy of the state for which it stands; a thing of beauty so conceived and fashioned to properly record and exploit our civilization, aspirations and patriotism, past, present and future."

Second, the building had to be completed without debt and at a cost "not to exceed $5,000,000."

The competition drew nationwide attention and the finalists represented some of the best-known architectural firms in the United States. In 1920 the commission selected Bertram Grosvenor Goodhue of New York. His design incorporated something unique for the time — a dramatic dome-topped tower. This tower would not only be spectacular but also practical. It would be seen for miles, providing a magnificent sight; it would also provide a large amount of useful office space without requiring more land.

Goodhue proposed an unexpected design, and he also brought a lofty goal. He wanted to create a space filled with beauty and meaning, something that would serve as a historical record and inspiring gift. To that end, he included leaders in philosophy, sculpting, painting, and mosaic to produce a masterpiece.

On April 15, 1922, ground was officially broken. Construction began around the second capitol building while it was still being used. This time, construction took ten years and cost nearly $10 million. As state leaders had required, it was paid for entirely as it was being built. Nebraska's State Capitol was constructed without a cent of debt, another attribute that sets it apart from every other state capitol, then or now.

The result was and still is lauded as a feat of architecture and art. As Charles Harris Whitaker wrote in *American Architect*:

> "The Nebraska Capitol . . . stands both as
> a significant and a challenging building.
> It is not only evidence of the genius that
> no civilization can afford to neglect,
> but it is also a legacy of one of the most
> fertile imaginative brains that the art of
> building has ever known."

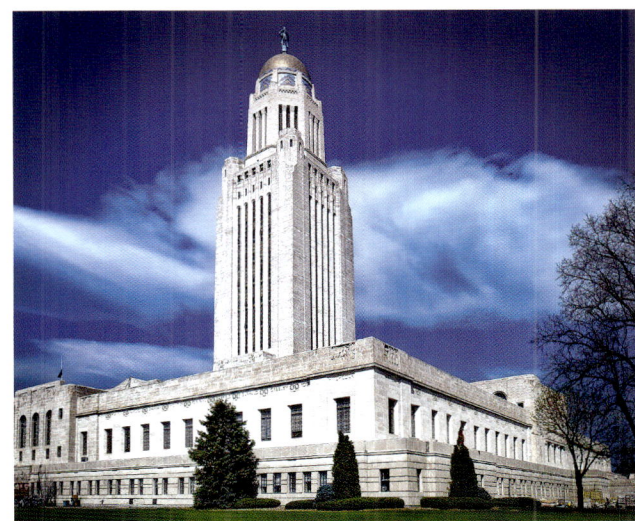

Nebraska's third state capitol, "an inspiring monument worthy of the state for which it stands."

FLOOR MOSAICS

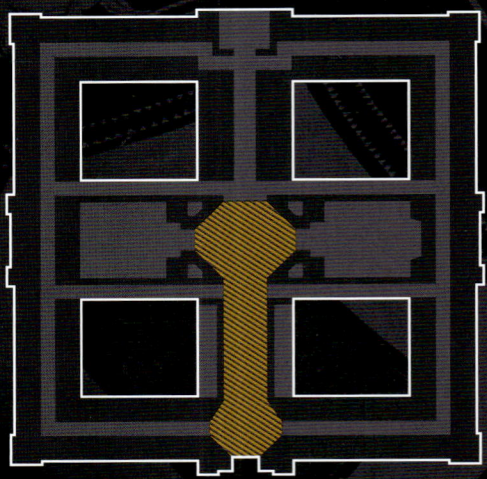

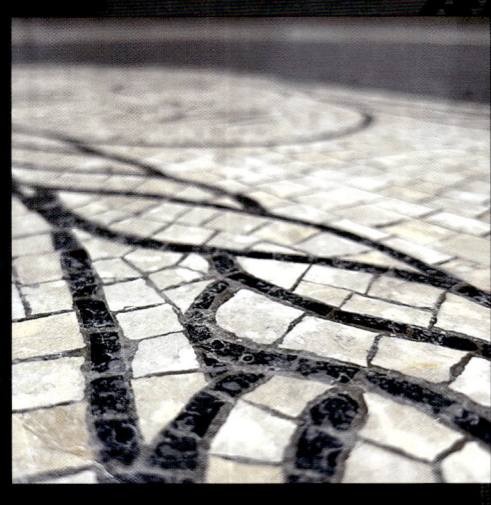

HILDRETH MEIÈRE

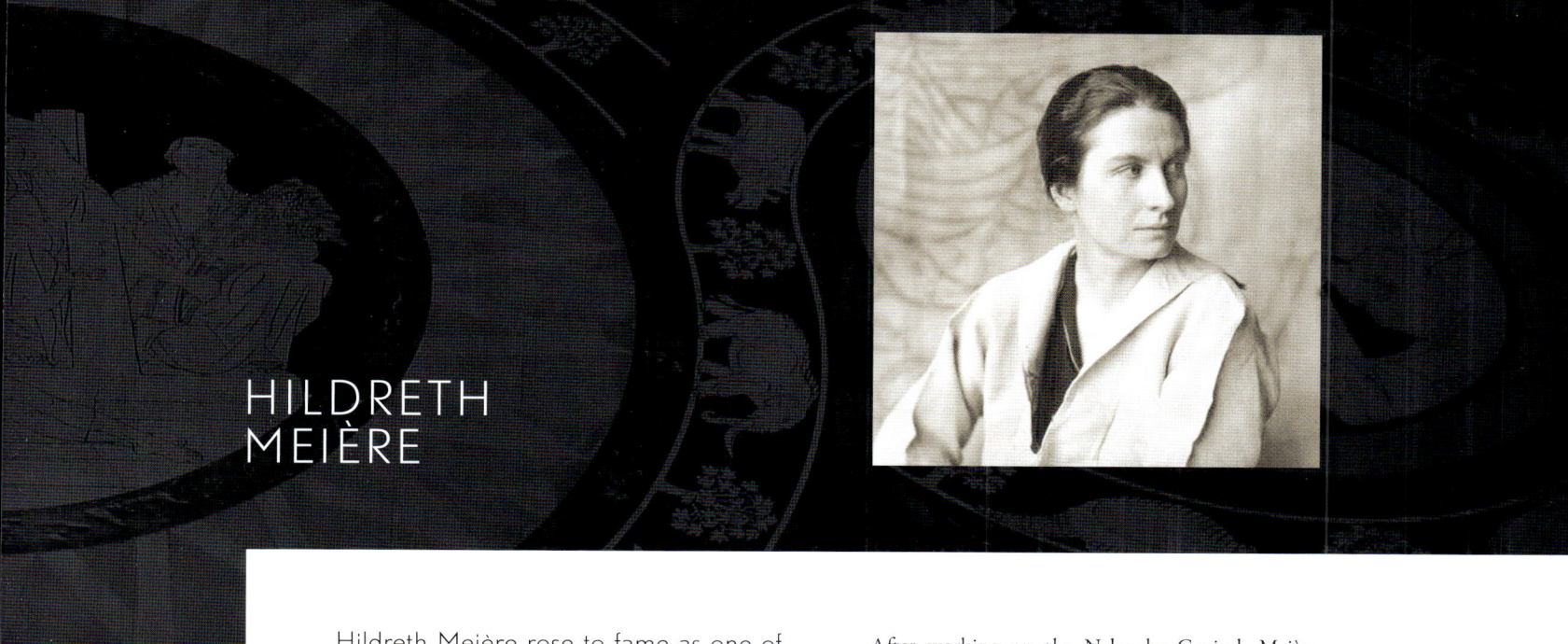

Hildreth Meière rose to fame as one of the most renowned American muralists of the 20th century, a leader in the art world dominated almost exclusively by men. But she never wanted to be known as a "female artist." She wanted to be considered "an artist" with no other qualifiers.

After studying in New York and California and traveling to Florence, Italy, Meière worked on beaux arts projects in New York City. The art style, with its emphasis on decorative flair and monumental grandeur, matched her own approach, influenced by the Italian classical and Renaissance styles. In 1922, the 29-year-old met Bertram Goodhue who asked her to design sketches for the Nebraska Capitol and assist him in decorating the Great Hall of his National Academy of Science in Washington DC.

Meière shared Goodhue's view that artwork should occupy an essential spot within a grand building. A master of considering the history and purpose of a space before creating its art, her methods complemented Goodhue's expansive vision for the Capitol. Together they used ornamentation and decoration to tell an epic tale of Nebraska.

After working on the Nebraska Capitol, Meière continued to distinguish herself as a prolific artist. Considered one of America's premier muralists, she created artwork for Radio City Music Hall, St. Bartholomew's Episcopal Church in Manhattan, and the National Academy of Sciences.

Meière also gained tremendous recognition for all of her life's work. For her designs in the Nebraska Capitol, she received the gold medal in mural decoration from the Architectural League of New York. The American Institute of Architects awarded her its Fine Arts Medal in 1956 and recognized her as a "Master of Murals." Meière held multiple leadership roles, often as the first woman, in art commissions and organizations. In a poetic twist of fate, she was named Director of the Department of Mural Painting at the Beaux Arts Institute of Design, a school that had decades before refused to accept her as a student because of her gender.

With all of her success, by the end of her life in 1961, she considered one building to be her crowning achievement — the Nebraska State Capitol.

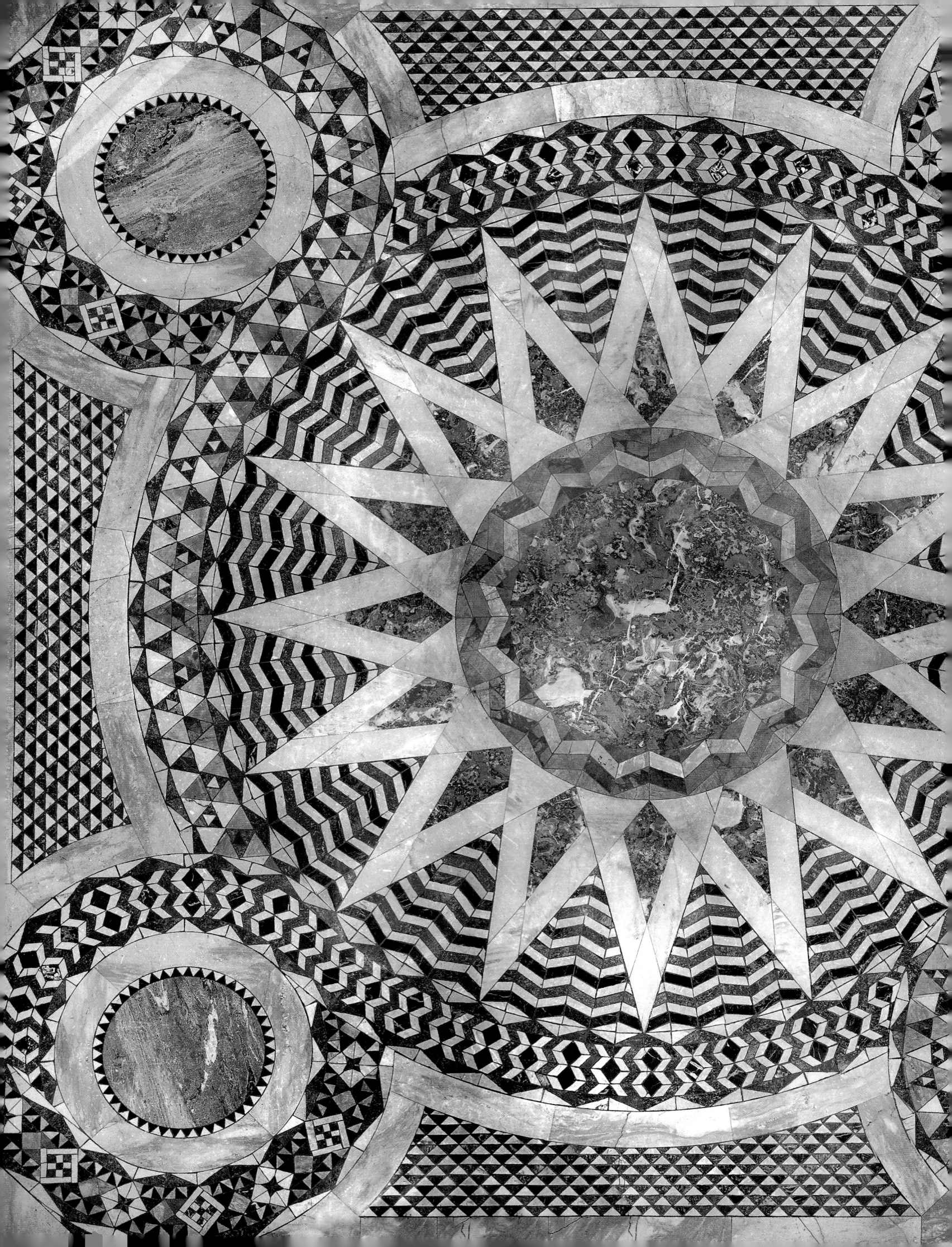

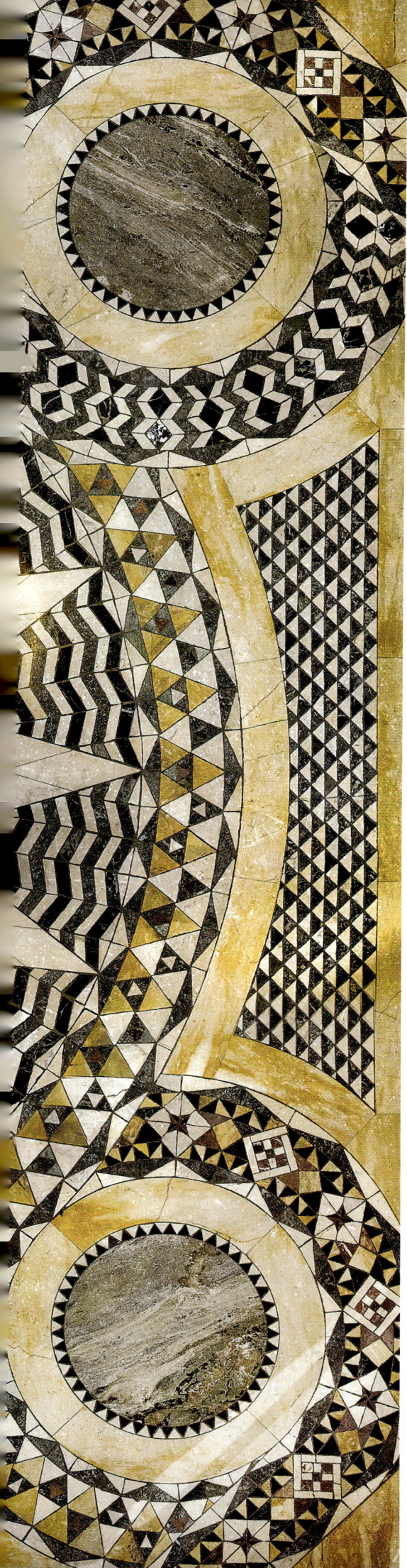

Hildreth Meière
Cosmic Sun, c.1930
approx. 21 x 21 feet
Marble mosaic set in inlaid marble

"The whole floor will be a
symbol of the Creation."

For Goodhue and Alexander, the floors of
the vestibule, foyer, and rotunda served as
a representation of the story of life, with the
Cosmic Sun at the center. While this work
appears as a simple geometric pattern of
points and spheres, it signifies all of creation
and the creative energy needed for the
universe. Surrounding the center star are four
panels, symbols of celestial forms, including
a spiral nebula, a comet, a planet of the
Saturn type, and a solar group. This work
serves as the root for the symbolism which
grows through the succeeding mosaics.

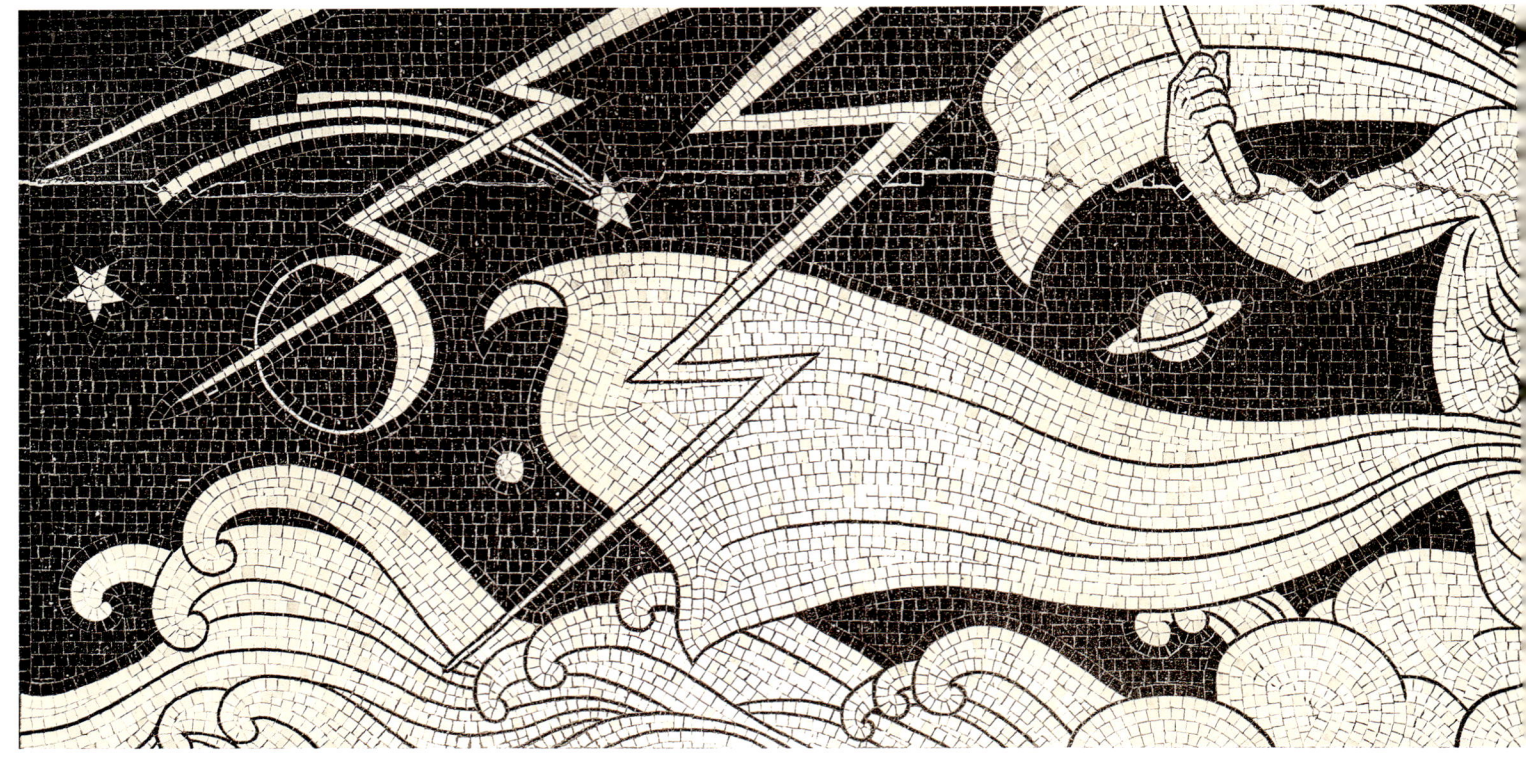

Hildreth Meière
Genius of Creative Energy, c.1930
approx. 4 x 18 feet
Marble mosaic set in inlaid marble

As he rides a cloud through the cosmos, the *Genius of Creative Energy* issues from the *Cosmic Sun* to rule over the Elements. He holds reins that extend out past the edge of the mosaic, and Alexander described him as being "propelled across the sky by an unseen force."

This, like all of the black and white floor mosaics of the Capitol, was originally intended to be created in the manner of those in Siena Cathedral in Florence, Italy. Figures were to be engraved into the surface of marble slabs and the engraved lines gilded in gold. This proved too costly, so instead they created large-scale mosaics using black and buff marble.

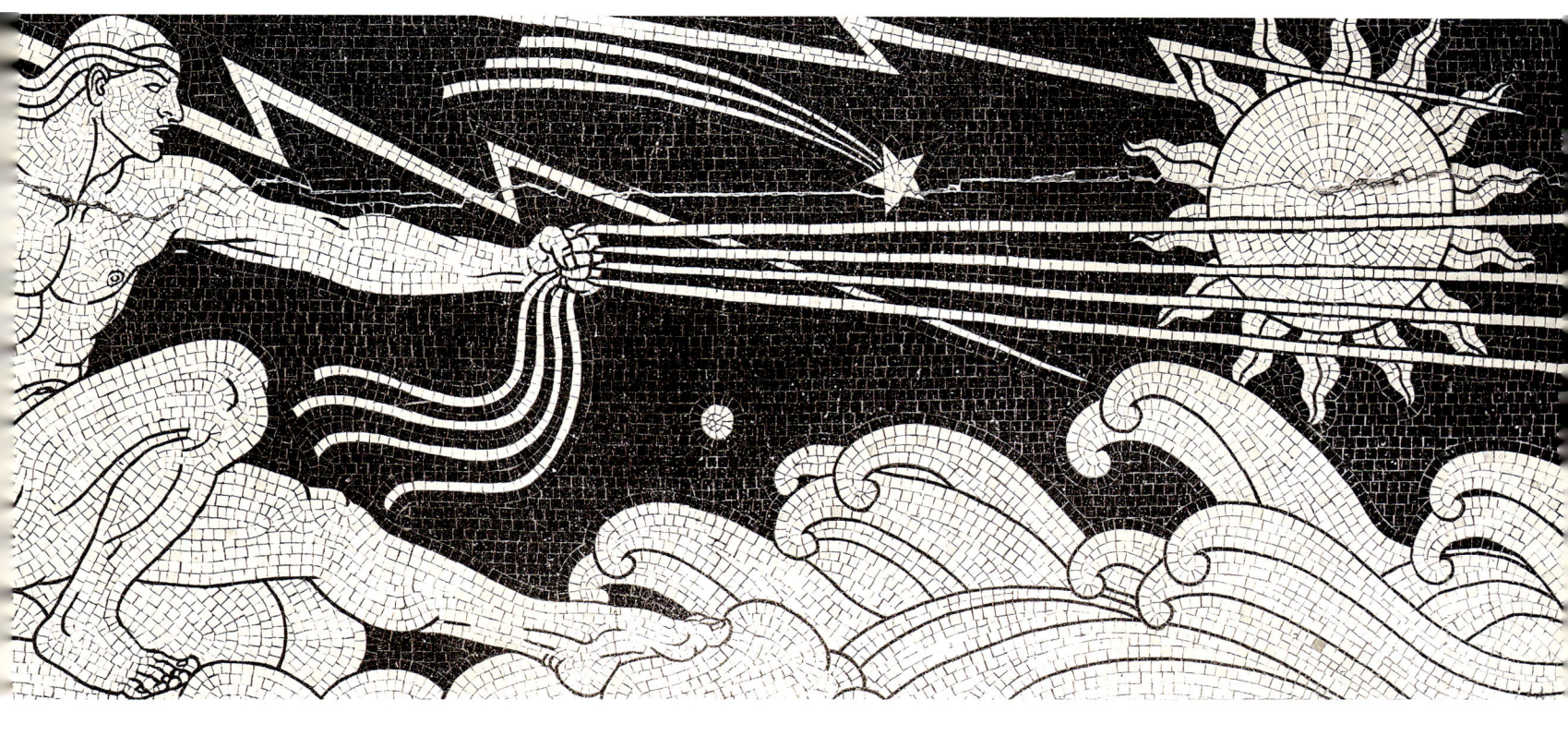

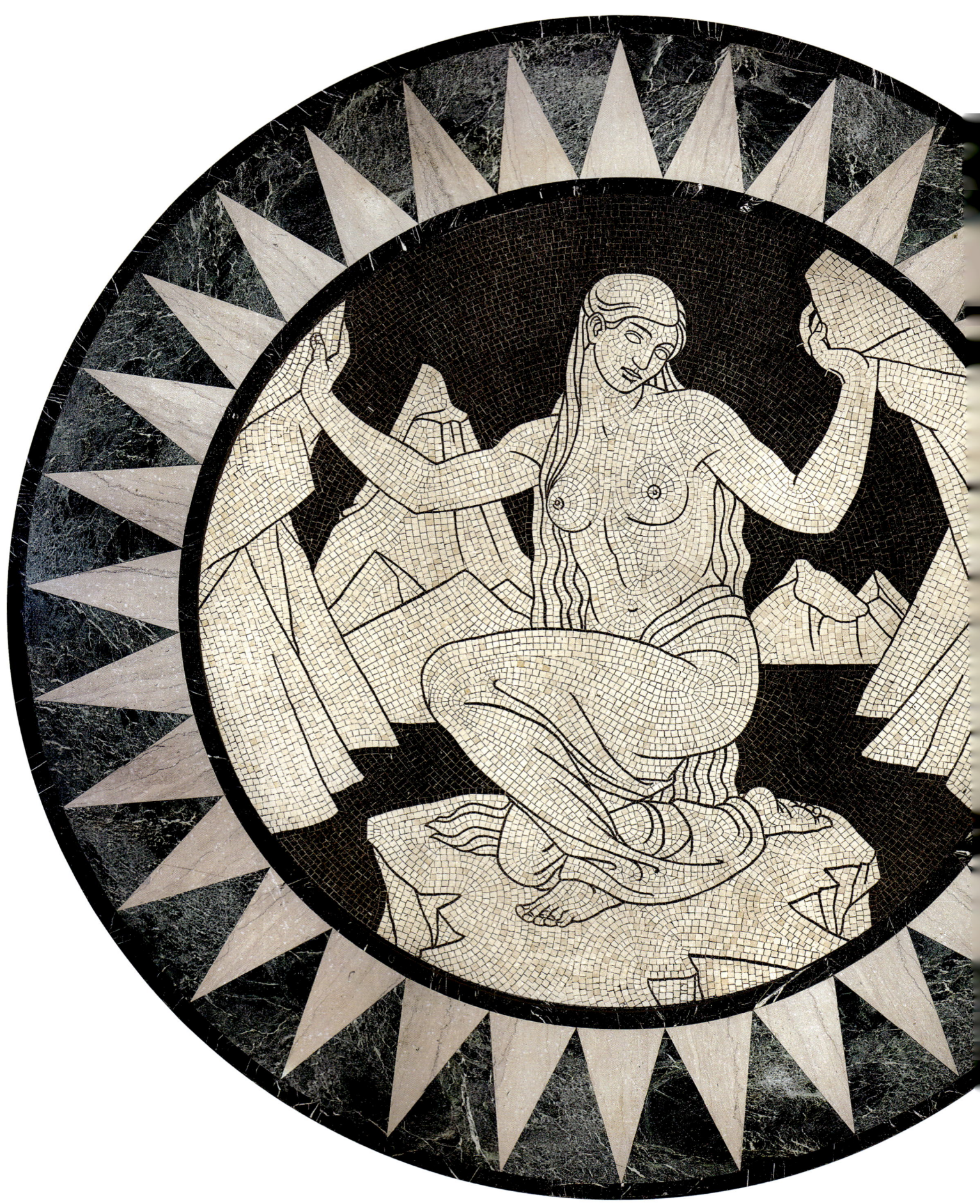

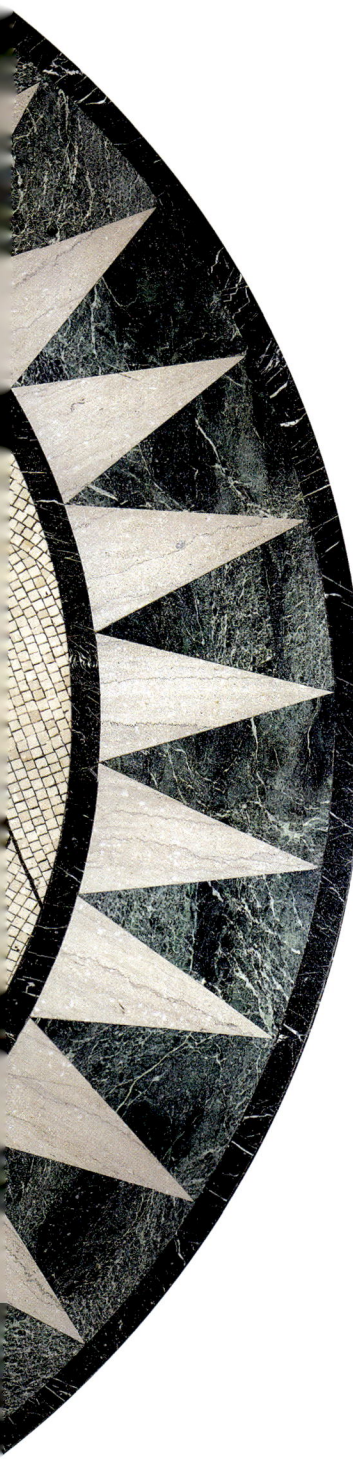

Hildreth Meière
Spirit of the Soil, c.1930
approx. 12 x 12 feet
Marble mosaic set in inlaid marble

The three "Spirit" panels of the foyer floor utilize open spaces as much as the geometric patterns. Each represents the natural foundation of human life and flows from the *Cosmic Sun* in the center of the vestibule in successive steps of creation, leading to humanity.

Spirit of the Soil depicts a Terra Mater, symbolic of the structural earth with its rock foundations, as she helps to form the land.

Hildreth Meière
Spirit of Vegetation, c.1930
approx. 12 x 12 feet
Marble mosaic set in inlaid marble

A Flora lays the foundation of the life that springs
from the earth. Surrounded by opulent trees, flowers,
and plants, she brings bounty to the world.

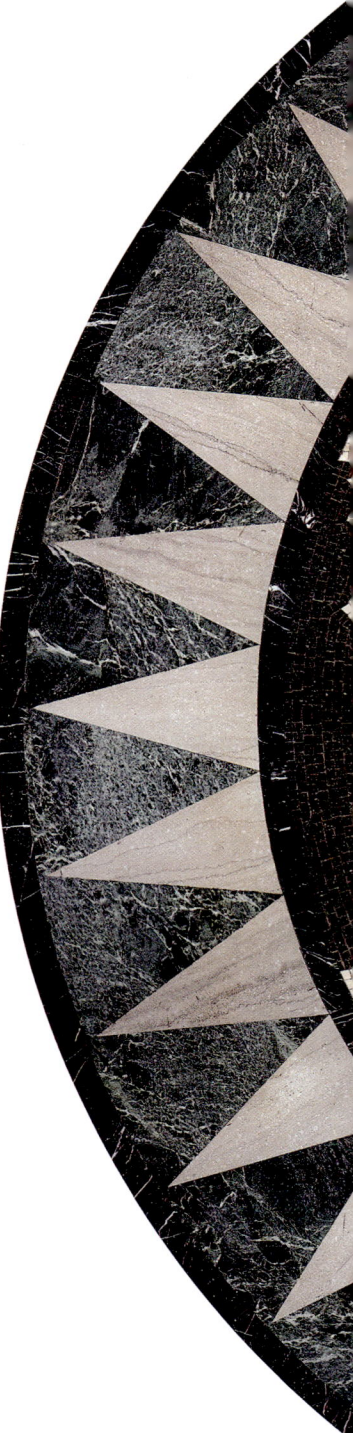

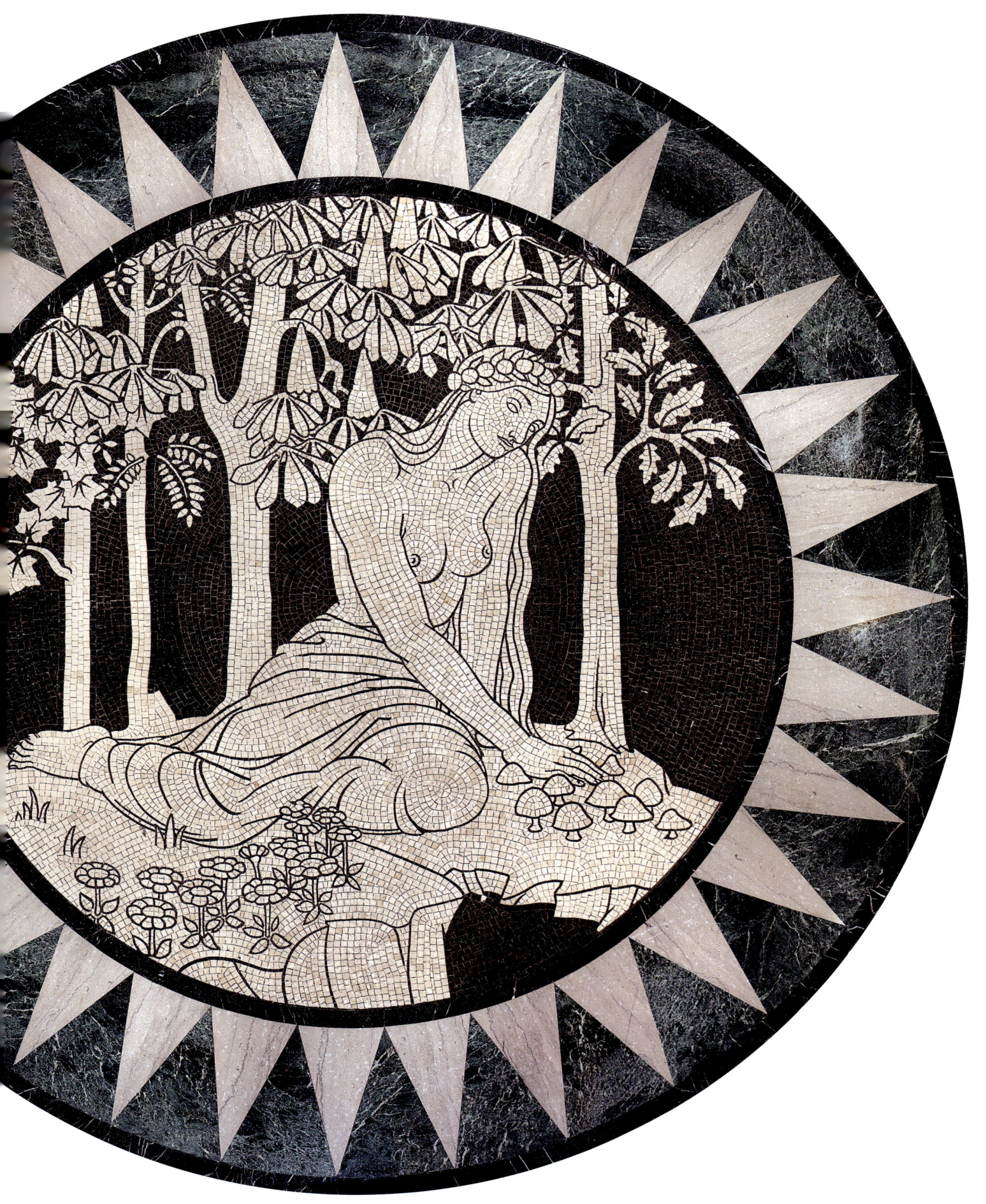

15

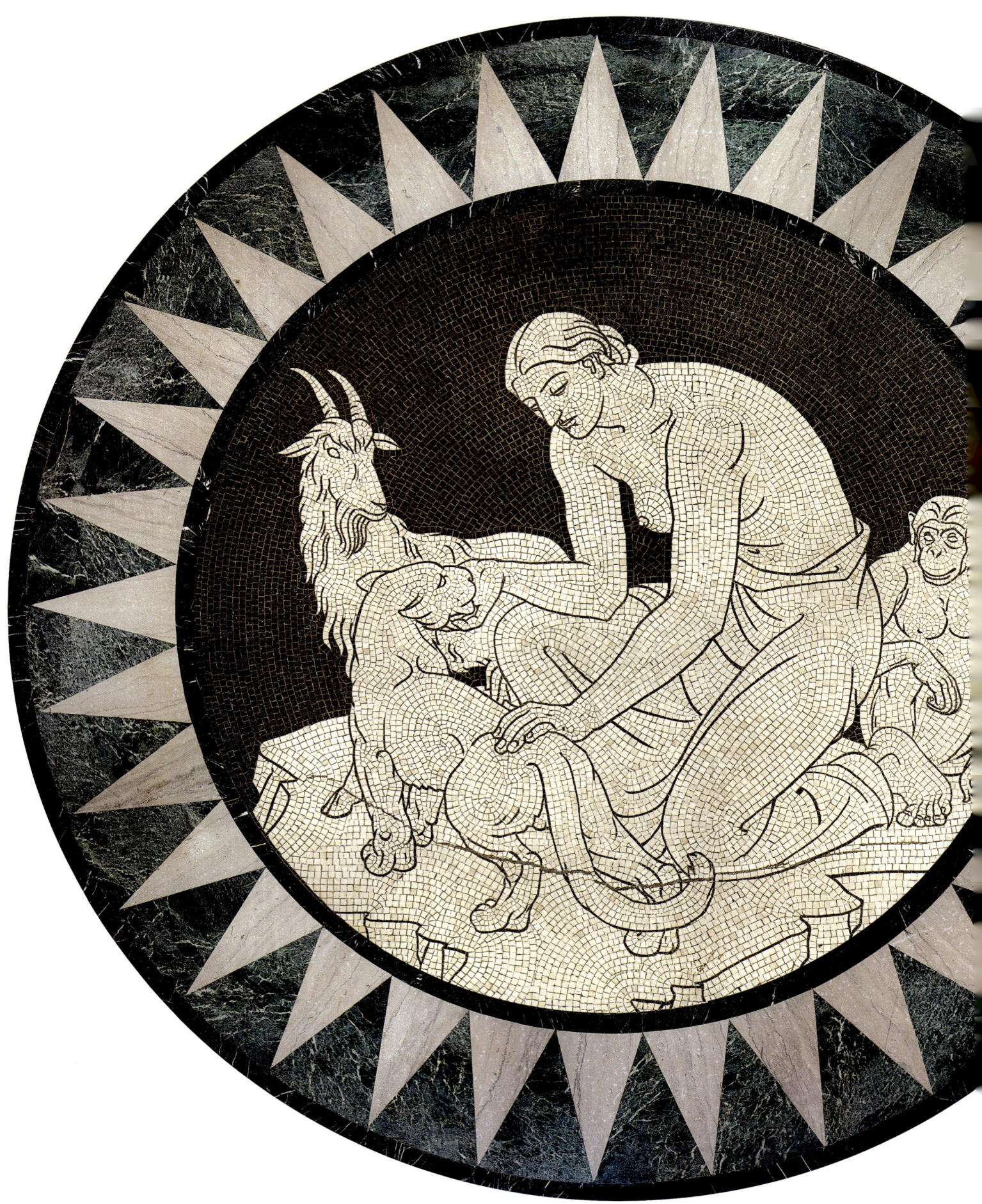

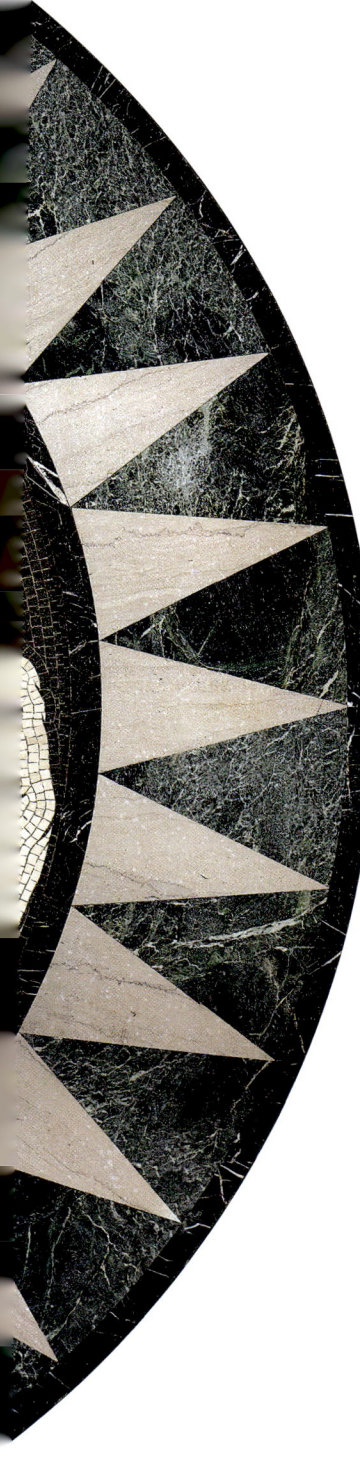

Hildreth Meière
Spirit of Animal Life, c.1930
approx. 12 x 12 feet
Marble mosaic set in inlaid marble

A Forester serves as the guardian of the animals.

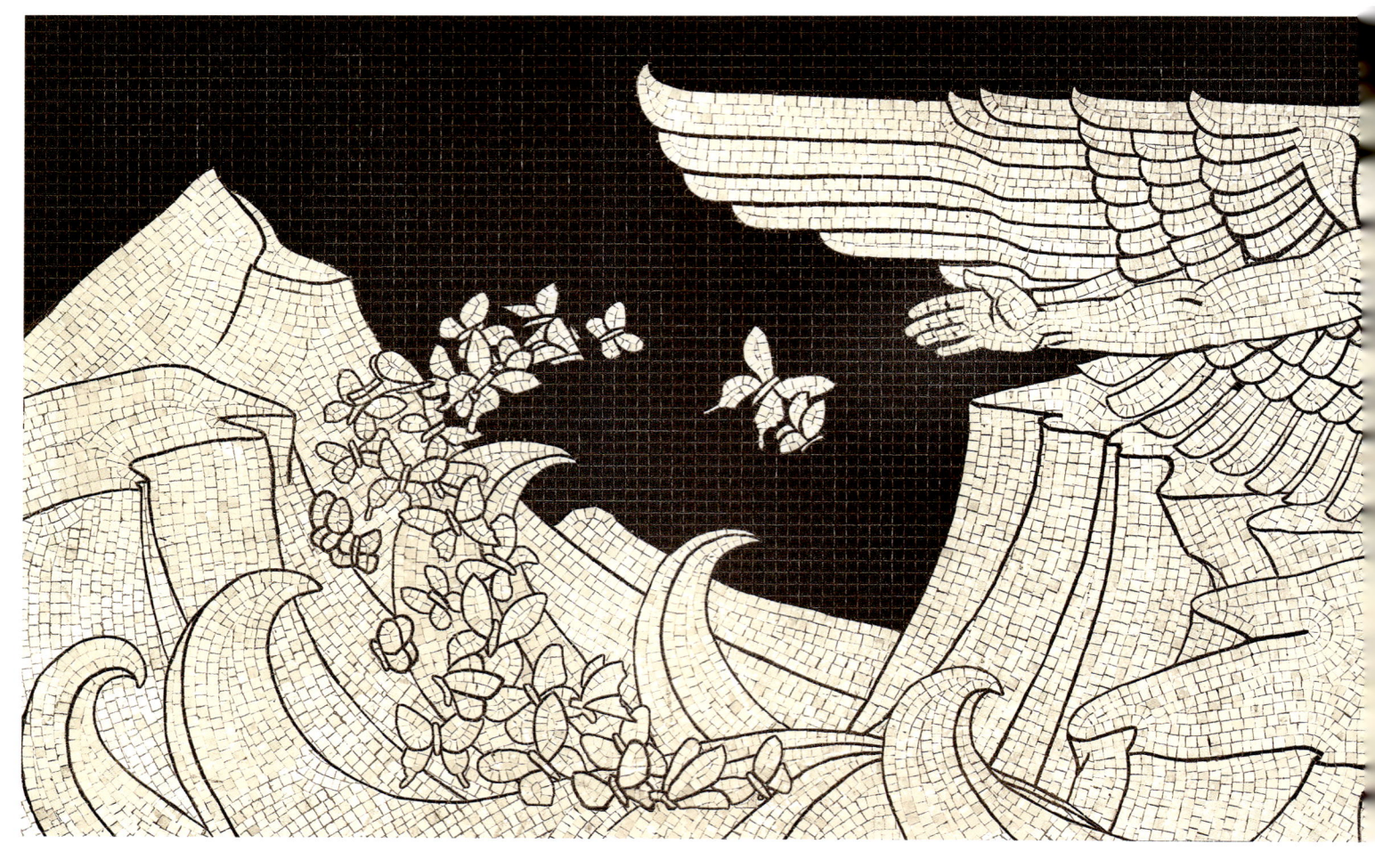

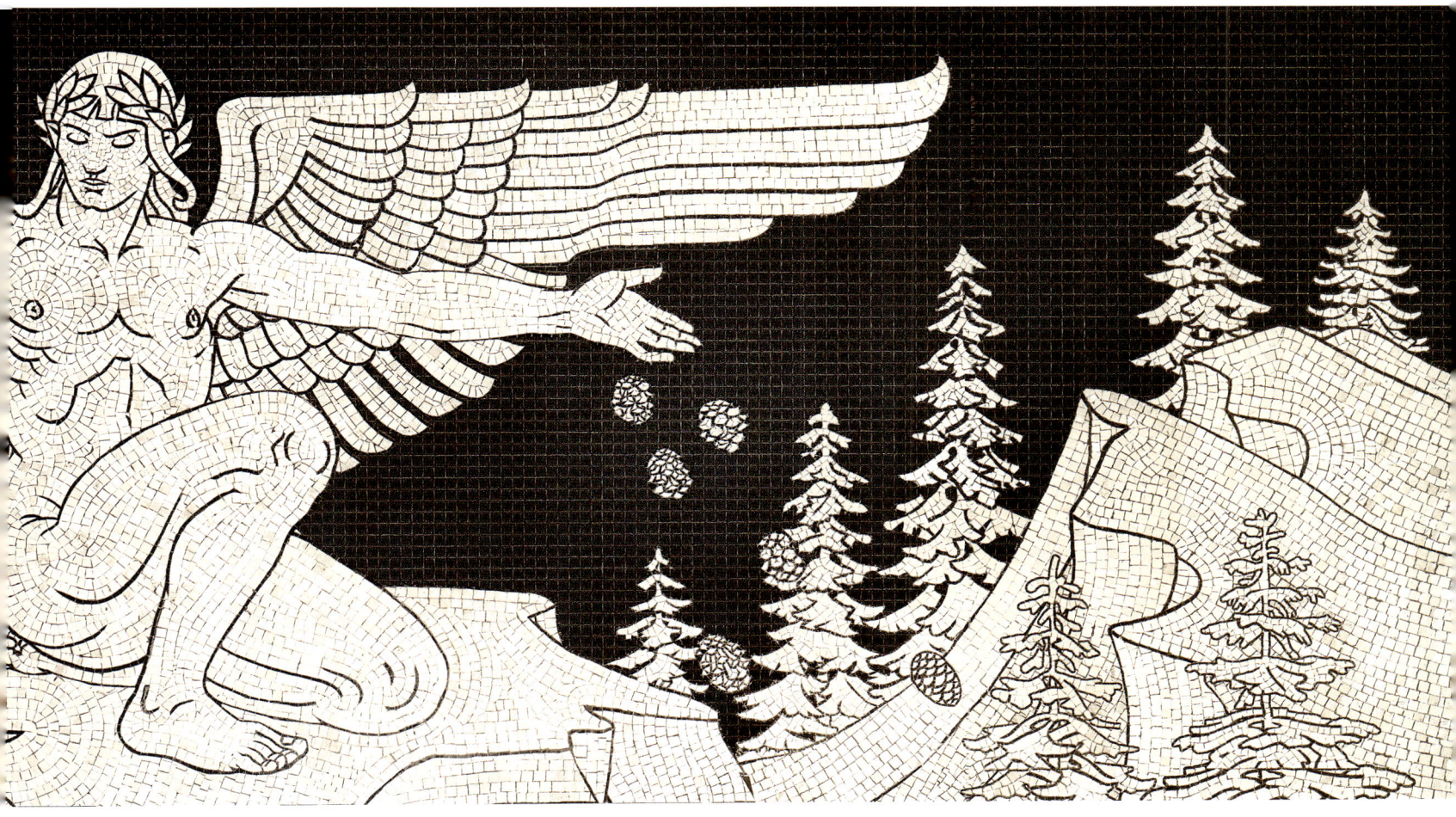

Hildreth Meière
Vital Energy, c.1930
approx. 4.5 x 17 feet
Marble mosaic set in inlaid marble

Vital Energy, the life-giving force of the universe, casts seeds and scatters flowers across the landscape. Life springs beneath him.

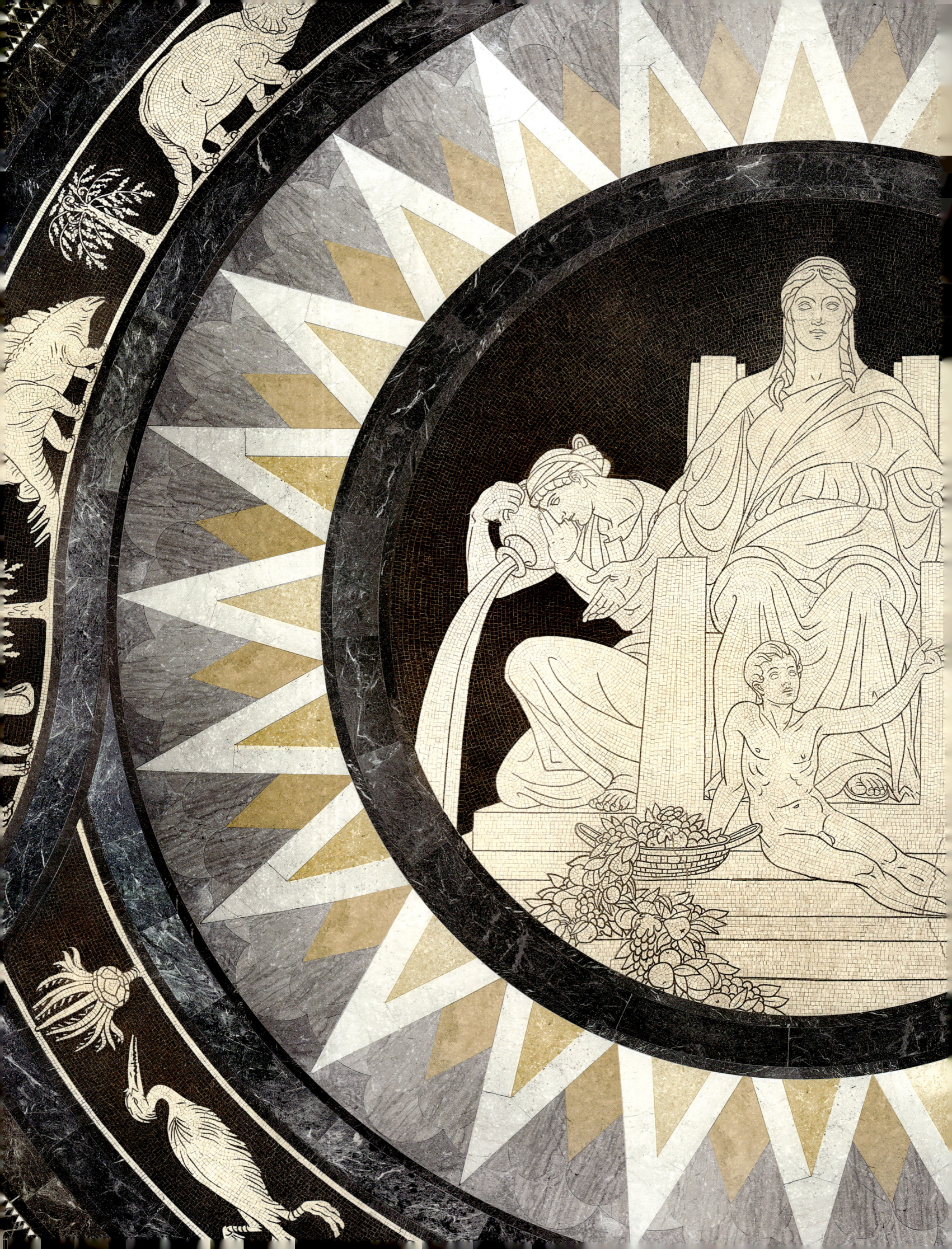

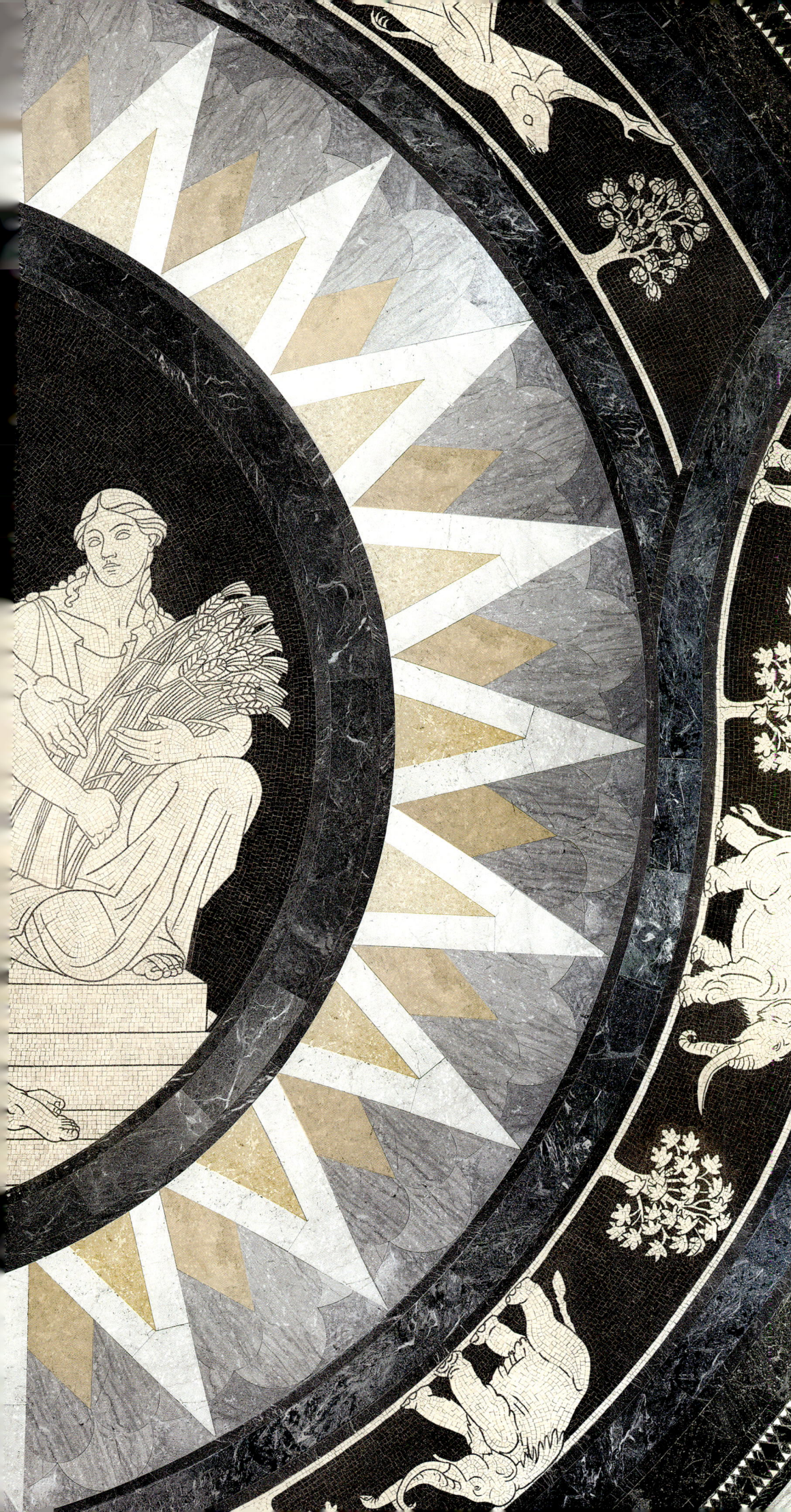

Hildreth Meière
Earth as Life Giver, c.1930
approx. 23.5 x 23.5 feet
Marble mosaic set
in inlaid marble

The mosaics of the rotunda
floor coordinate to embody
the process of life and its
bounty. In the center, *Earth as
Life Giver*, often referred to
as Mother Nature, illustrates
all that the earth provides
man, including food, water,
agriculture, and opportunity.

The rotunda mosaics include
a variety of prehistoric
animals. To accurately depict
these animals, Meière
relied on Erwin H. Barbour,
a paleontologist and
director of the University
of Nebraska Museum.

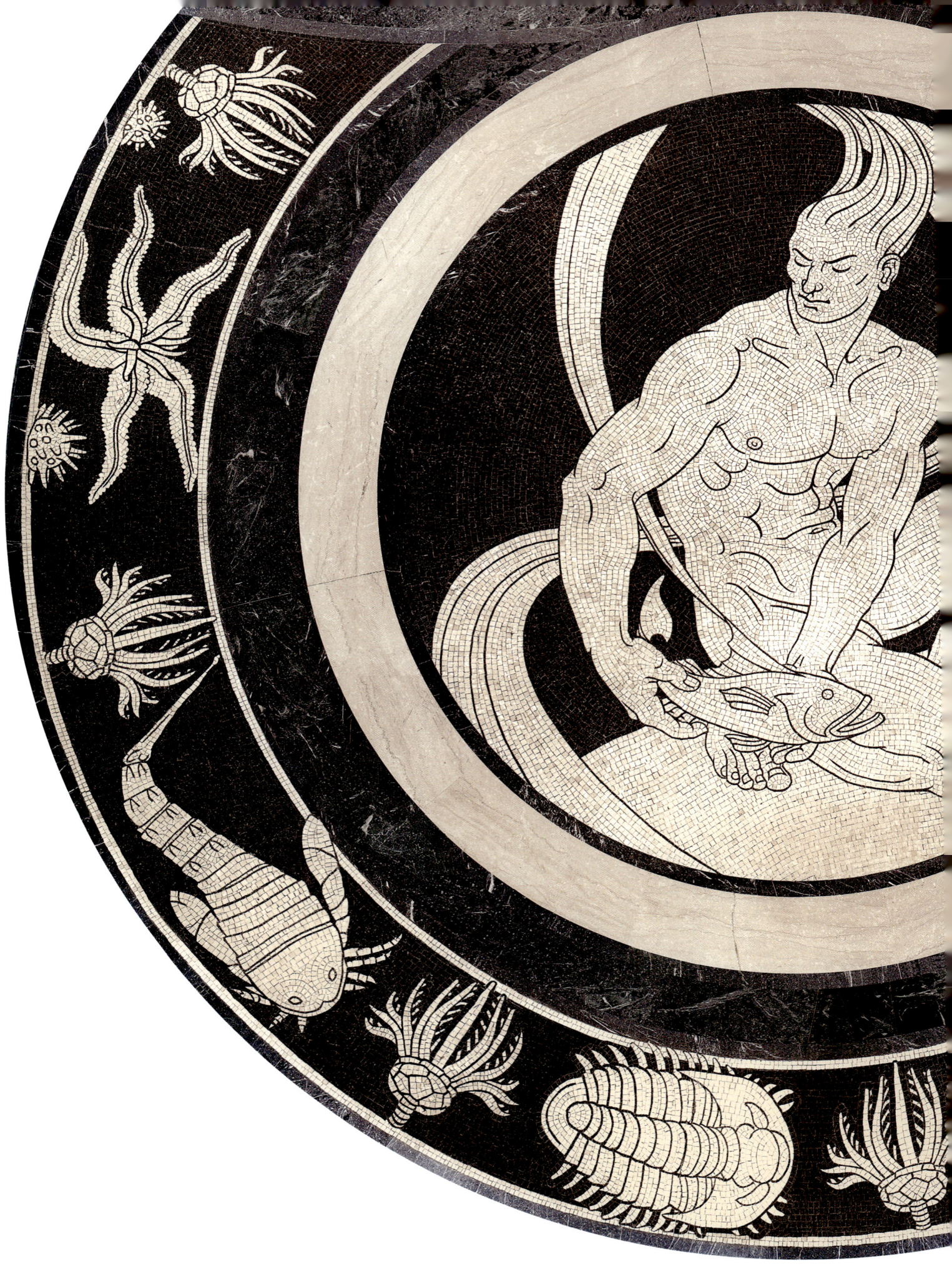

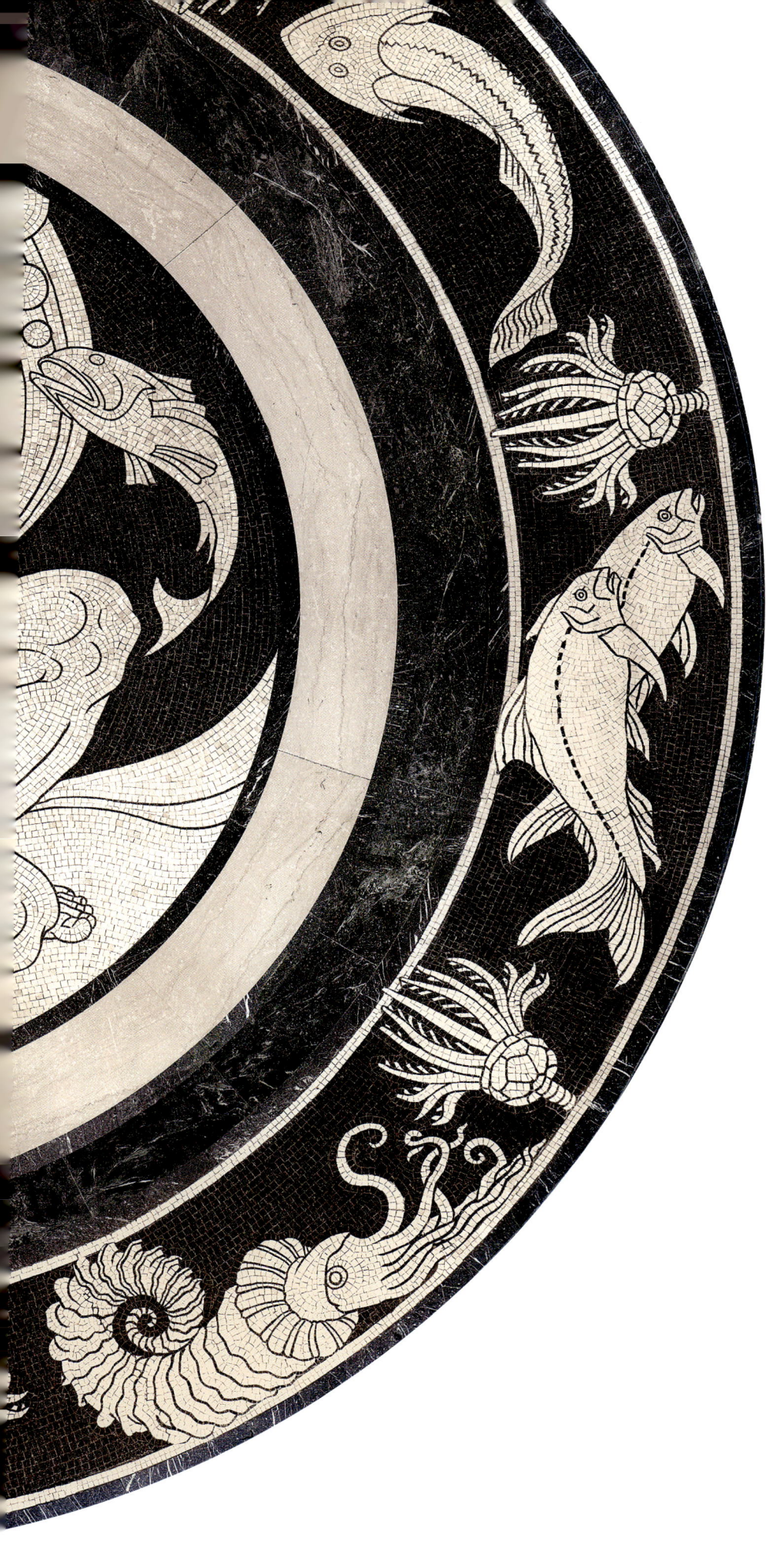

Hildreth Meière
Genius of Water, c.1930
approx. 19 x 19 feet
Marble mosaic set in inlaid marble

The panels bordering *Earth as Life Giver* symbolize the Four Geologic Ages and draw from Mother Earth's power and presence. Each is surrounded by animal forms from its corresponding realm connected by interlaced bands that display the succession of these animals through time.

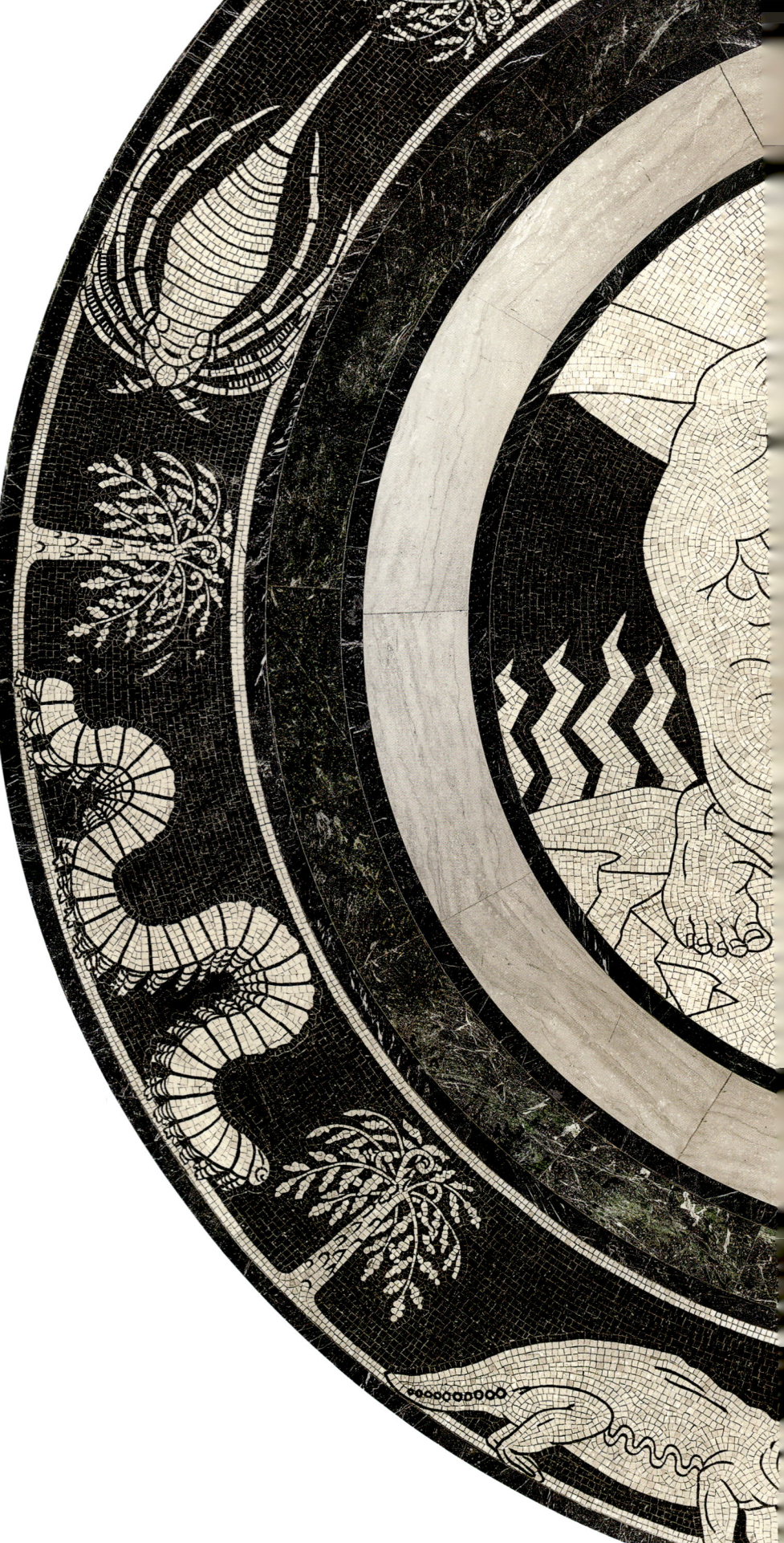

Hildreth Meière
Genius of Fire, c.1930
approx. 19 x 19 feet
Marble mosaic set in inlaid marble

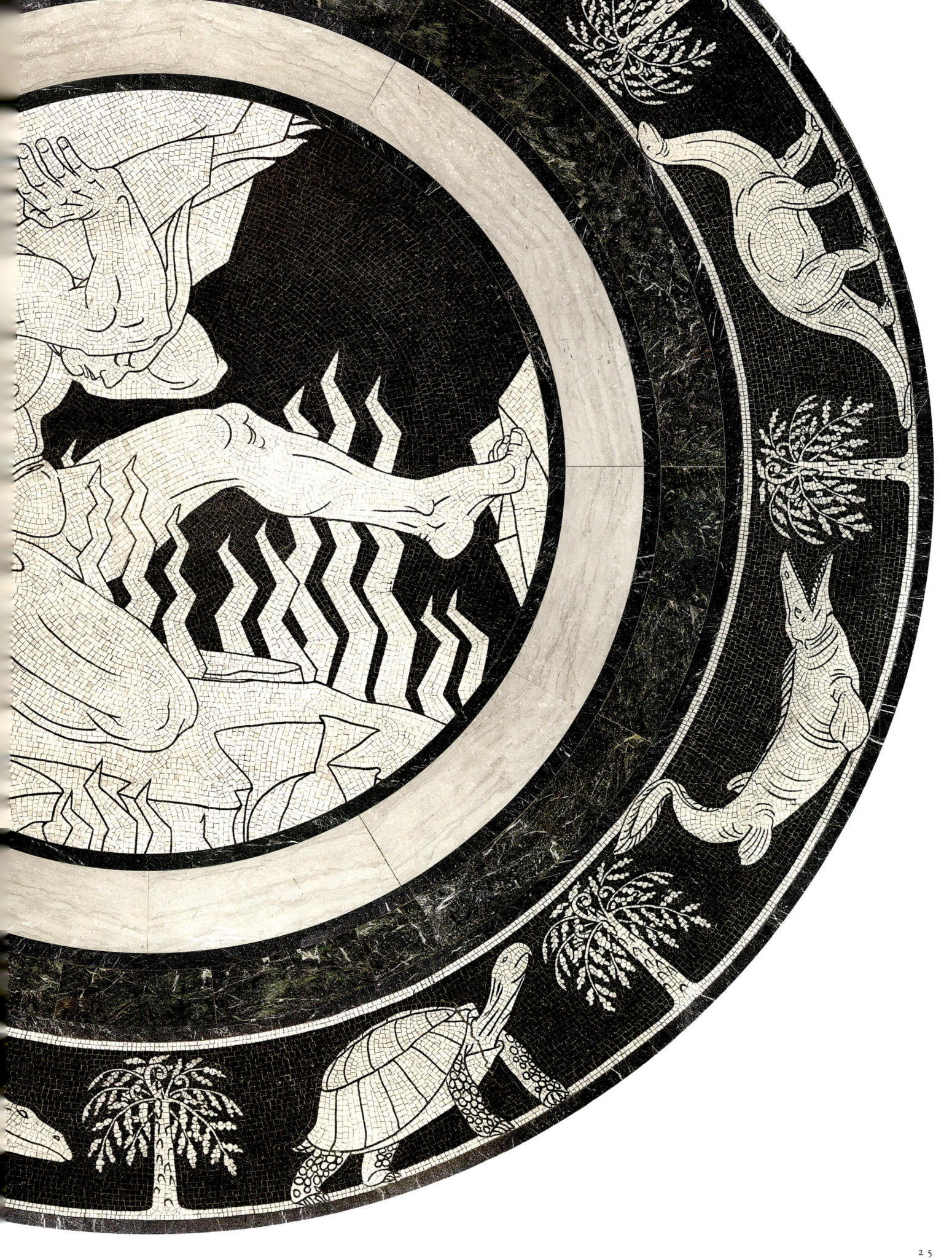

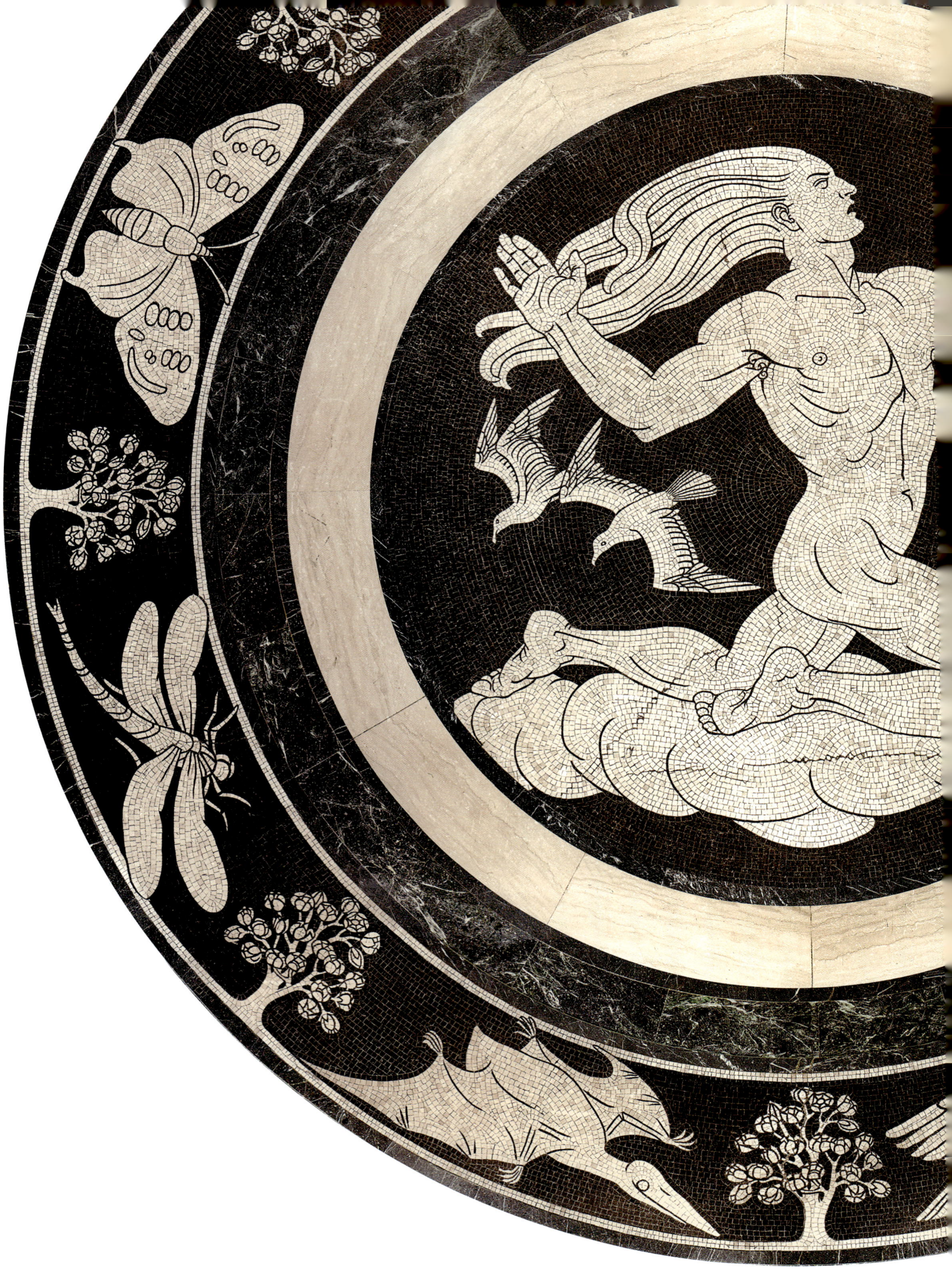

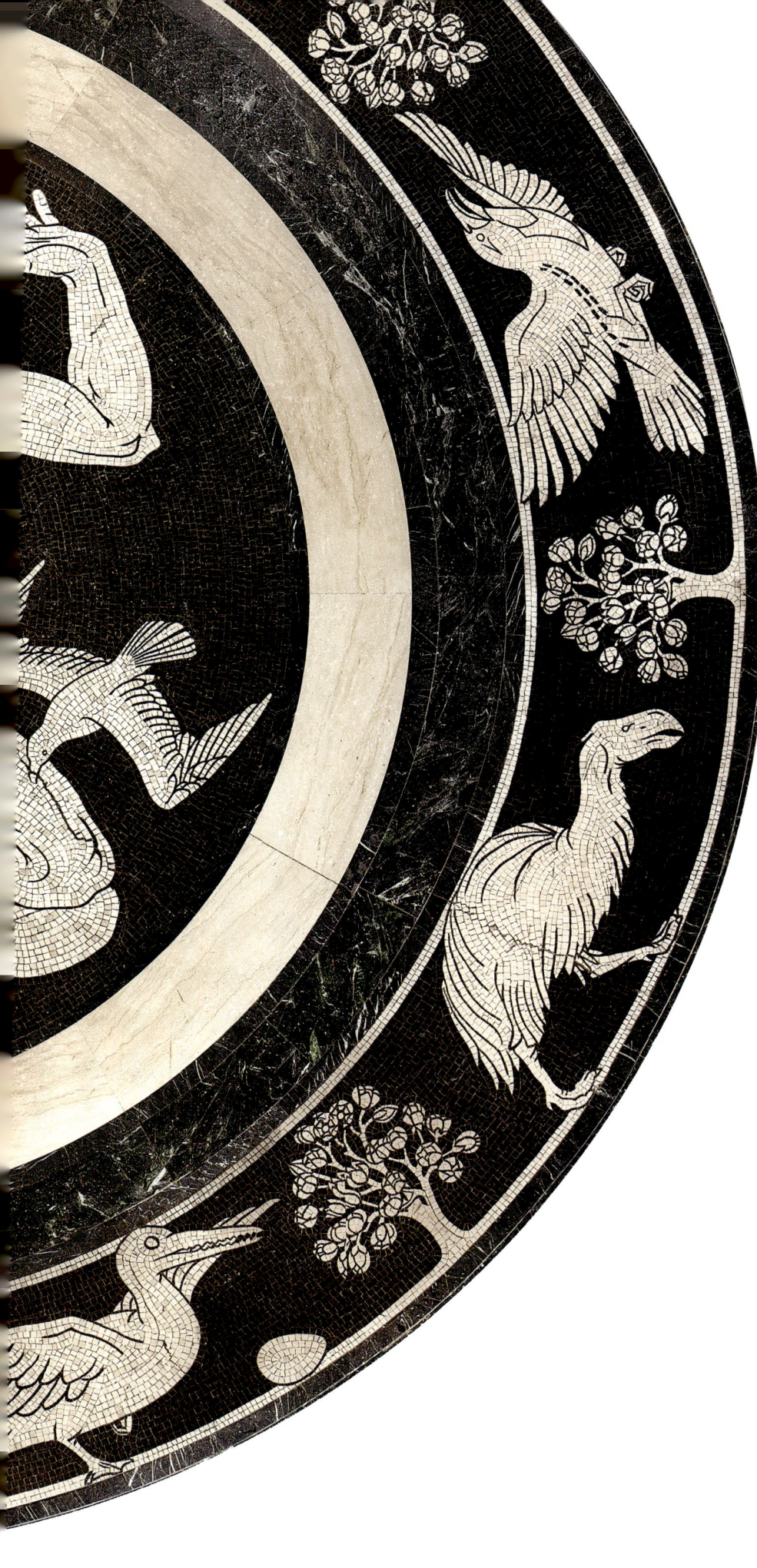

Hildreth Meière
Genius of Air, c.1930
approx. 19 x 19 feet
Marble mosaic set in inlaid marble

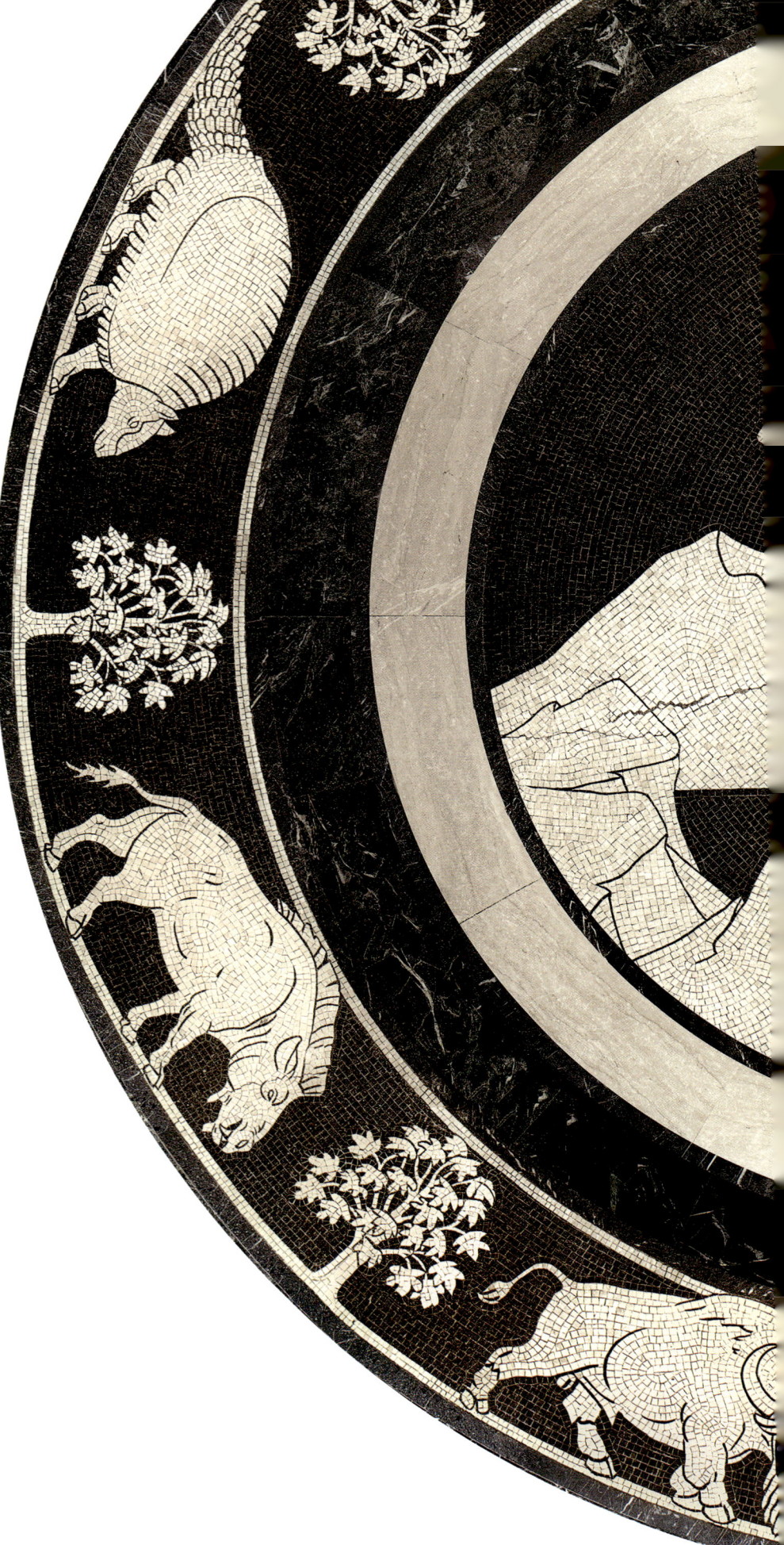

Hildreth Meière
Genius of Earth, c.1930
approx. 19 x 19 feet
Marble mosaic set in inlaid marble

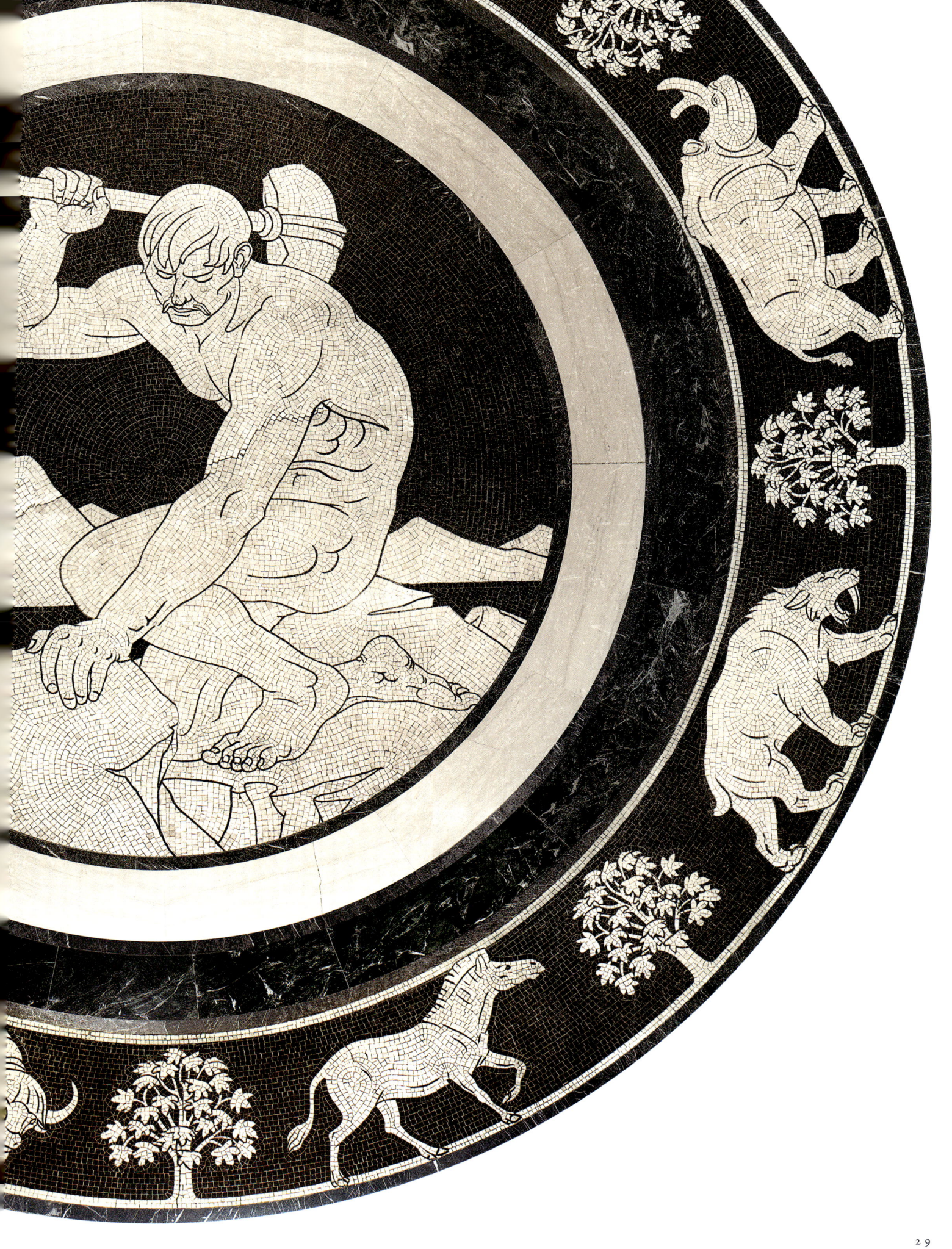

29

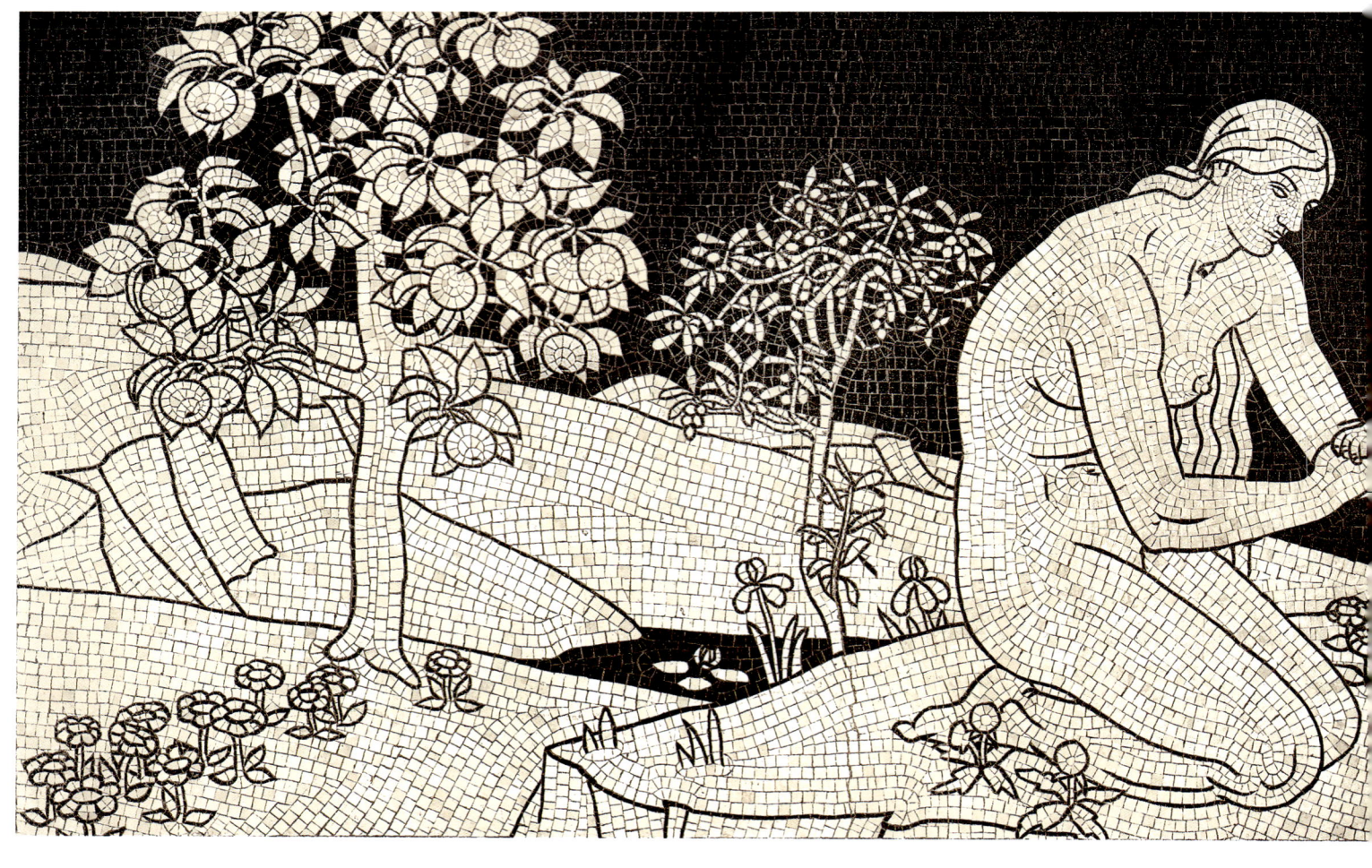

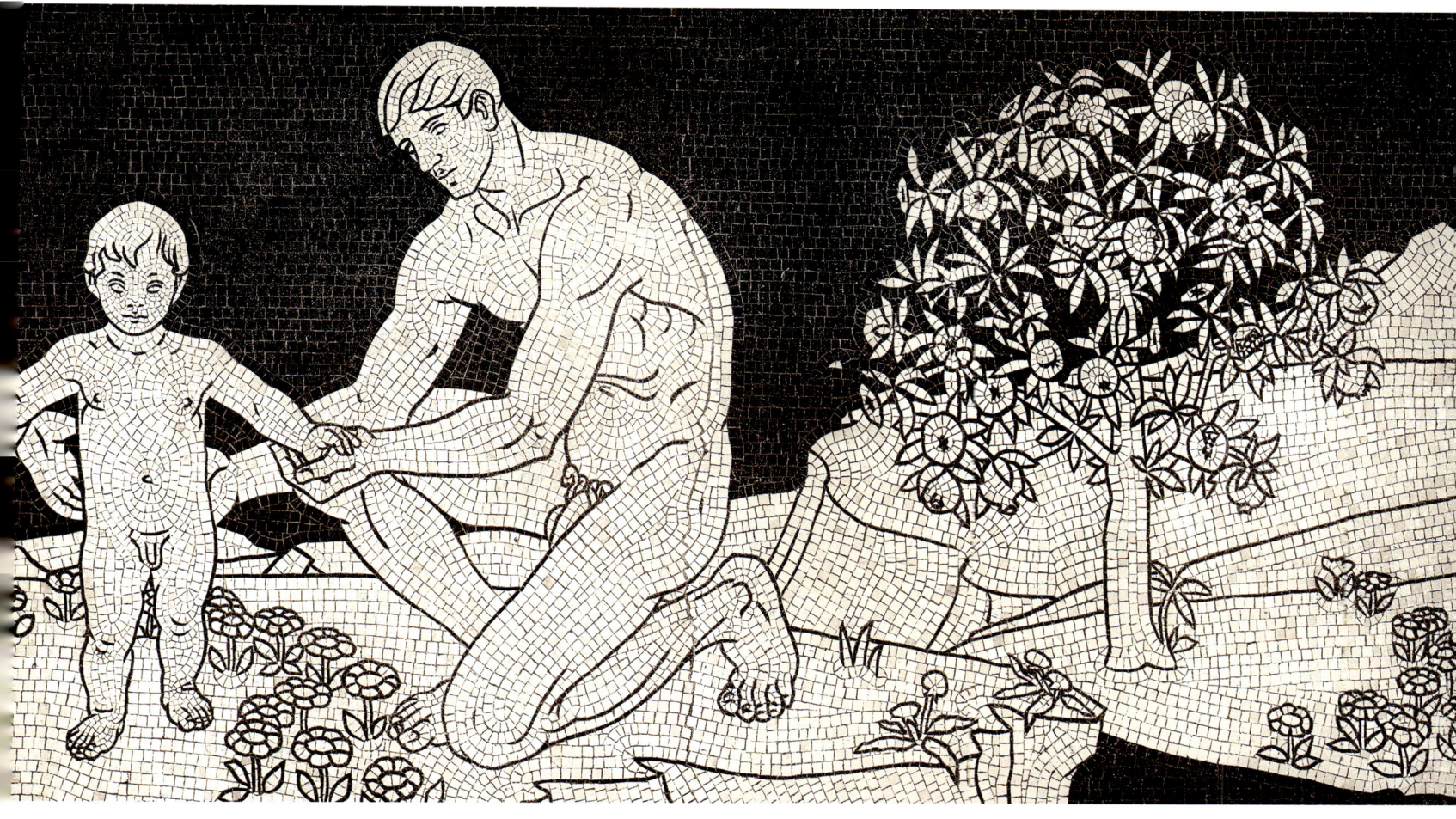

Hildreth Meière
Human Existence, c.1930
approx. 4.5 x 17 feet
Marble mosaic set in inlaid marble

The work of the *Cosmic Sun* and all of the universal forces
culminates with the creation of humans. A family grows,
and the fertile land provides support and sustenance.

VESTIBULE

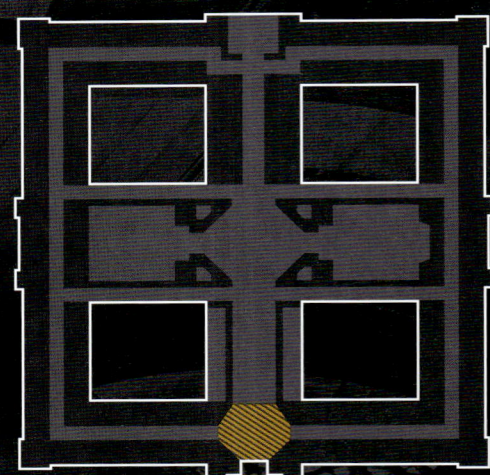

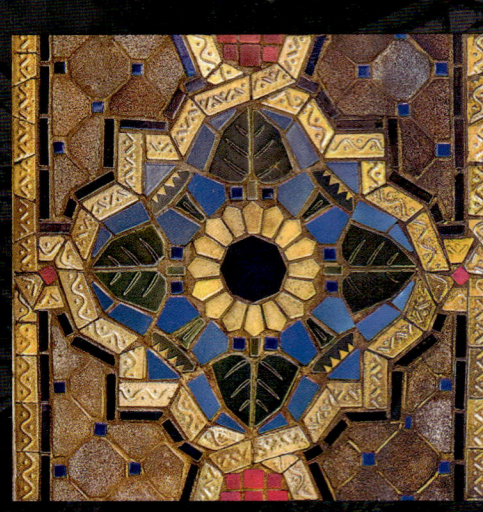

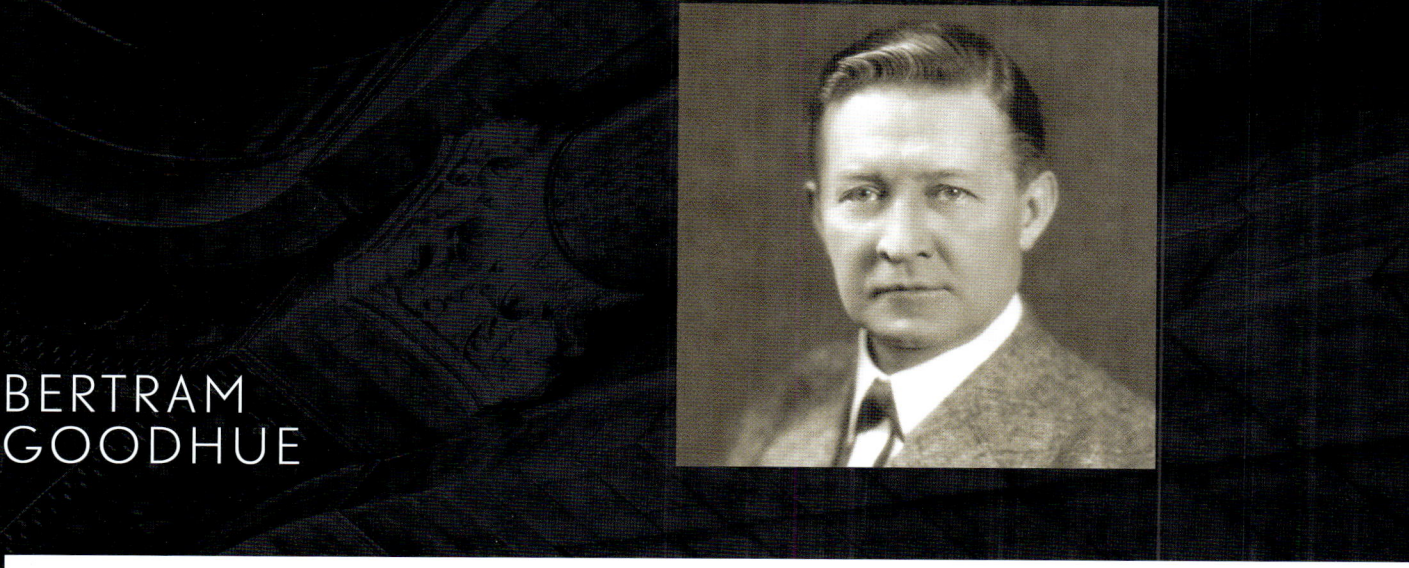

BERTRAM GOODHUE

Bertram Goodhue, the nationally prominent architect of the Capitol, largely taught himself architecture.

Born in 1869 into an old, genteel Connecticut Yankee family, he began as a draftsman at age 17. Within four years, he became the firm's chief draftsman. His apprenticeship ended when he won a design competition for Dallas's St. Matthews Church at age 22. That year, he and a partner formed a firm that would quickly become a national leader in neo-Gothic architecture.

Once leading his own firm, Goodhue's approach synthesized multiple styles including Gothic, Romanesque, and art deco. But he became best known for one style, establishing himself as a master of the Spanish Colonial Revival style of architecture. Goodhue was awarded a major commission at the 1915 Panama-California Exposition, where Frank Lloyd Wright assisted him. Many believe Goodhue's work influenced the integration of the Spanish Colonial Revival style in Southern California architecture.

American Architect in their 1934 issue featuring the Nebraska Capitol praised Goodhue: "In many ways the architectural genius of Bertram Grosvenor Goodhue dramatized in this design a peak in the history of building accomplishment. As a break from the precedent of tradition the Nebraska State Capitol did much to advance a new and more virile architectural philosophy."

Goodhue died in 1924 at only 54 years old — eight years before the completion of the Nebraska Capitol building. But his design lived on, in large part because his leadership style as a great collaborator with artists, craftsmen, and builders meant that his successors and the artists hired were able to stay loyal to his vision.

Goodhue also designed the Rockefeller Chapel at the University of Chicago, the Los Angeles Central Library, the campuses of Rice and Princeton, and St. Thomas Episcopal Church in New York City. His work on the National Academy of Science on the Mall in Washington DC began his collaborations with Hildreth Meière.

He was remembered as a great mentor, leader, and friend. Lee Lawrie, the chief sculptor for the Nebraska Capitol, created Goodhue's tomb at the Church of the Intercession in New York, one of his own commissions. The tomb includes depictions of some of Goodhue's most prominent buildings. At his tomb's center: the Nebraska State Capitol.

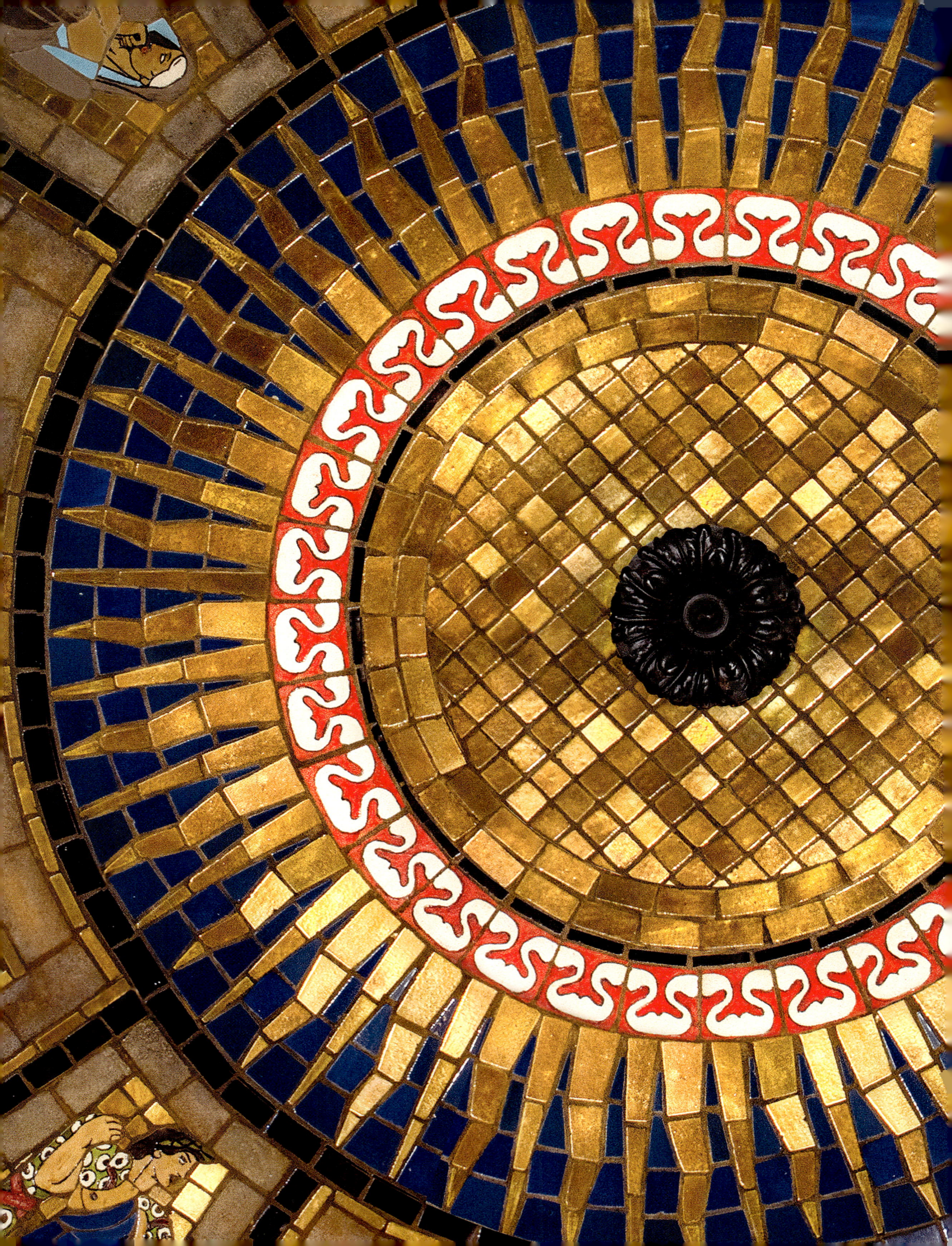

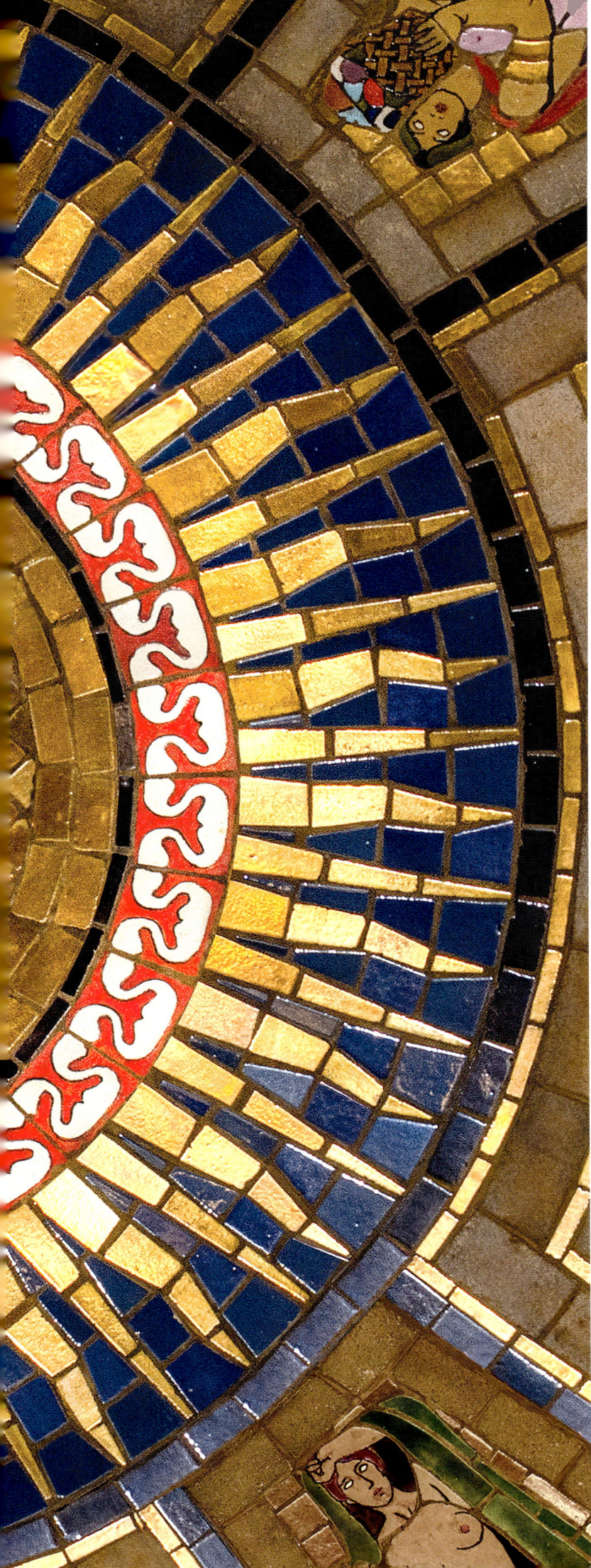

Hildreth Meière
The Sun, c.1930
approx. 6 x 6 feet
Glazed ceramic tile

Alexander's theme prescribed
that the symbolism of the
vestibule should represent
the "gifts of nature to man on
the plains of Nebraska." He
specifically called for distinct
subjects for the murals and
colors throughout—utilizing
the warm colors of the sun.

The theme of gifts of nature
given to people of the prairies
culminates with this mosaic
of *The Sun*, the ultimate
endowment of nature.

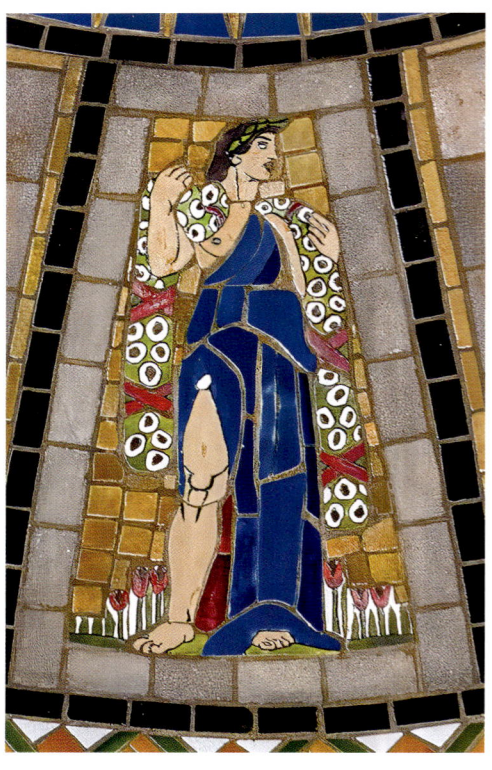

Hildreth Meière
Spring, c.1930
approx. 3 feet tall
Glazed ceramic tile

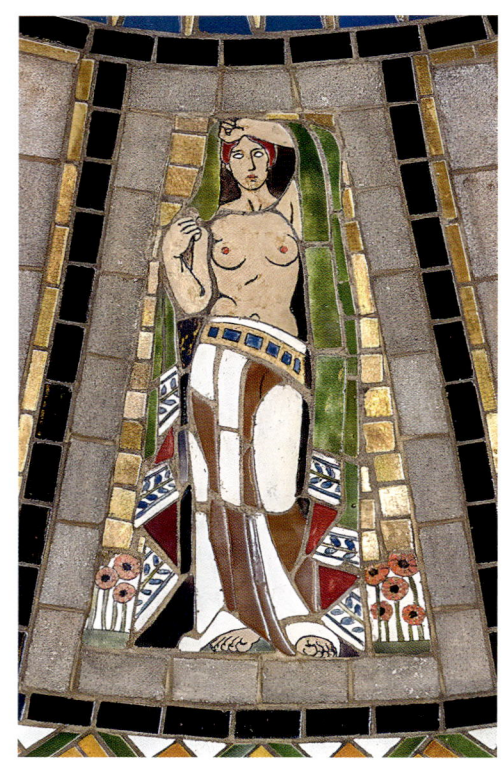

Hildreth Meière
Summer, c.1930
approx. 3 feet tall
Glazed ceramic tile

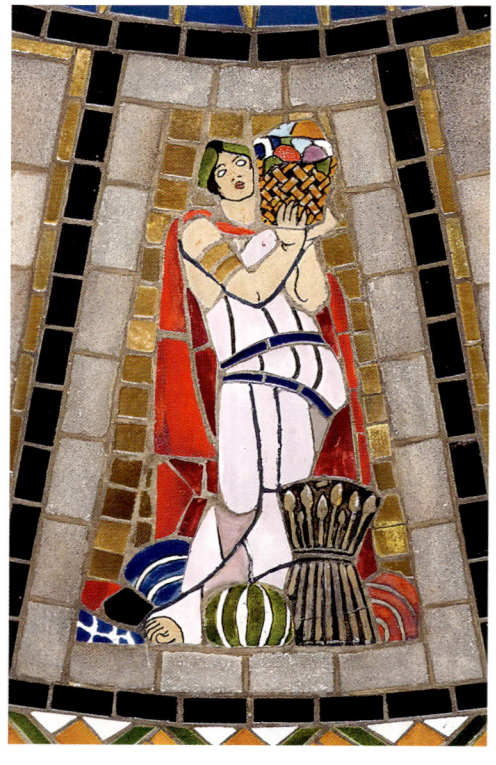

Hildreth Meière
Fall, c.1930
approx. 3 feet tall
Glazed ceramic tile

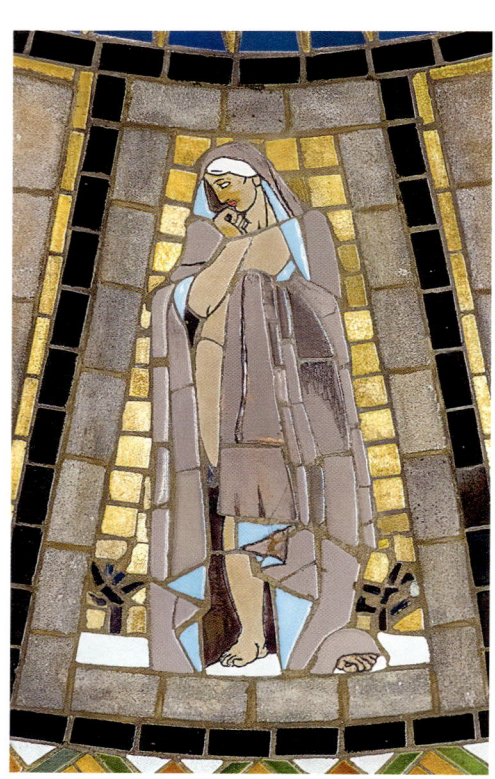

Hildreth Meière
Winter, c.1930
approx. 3 feet tall
Glazed ceramic tile

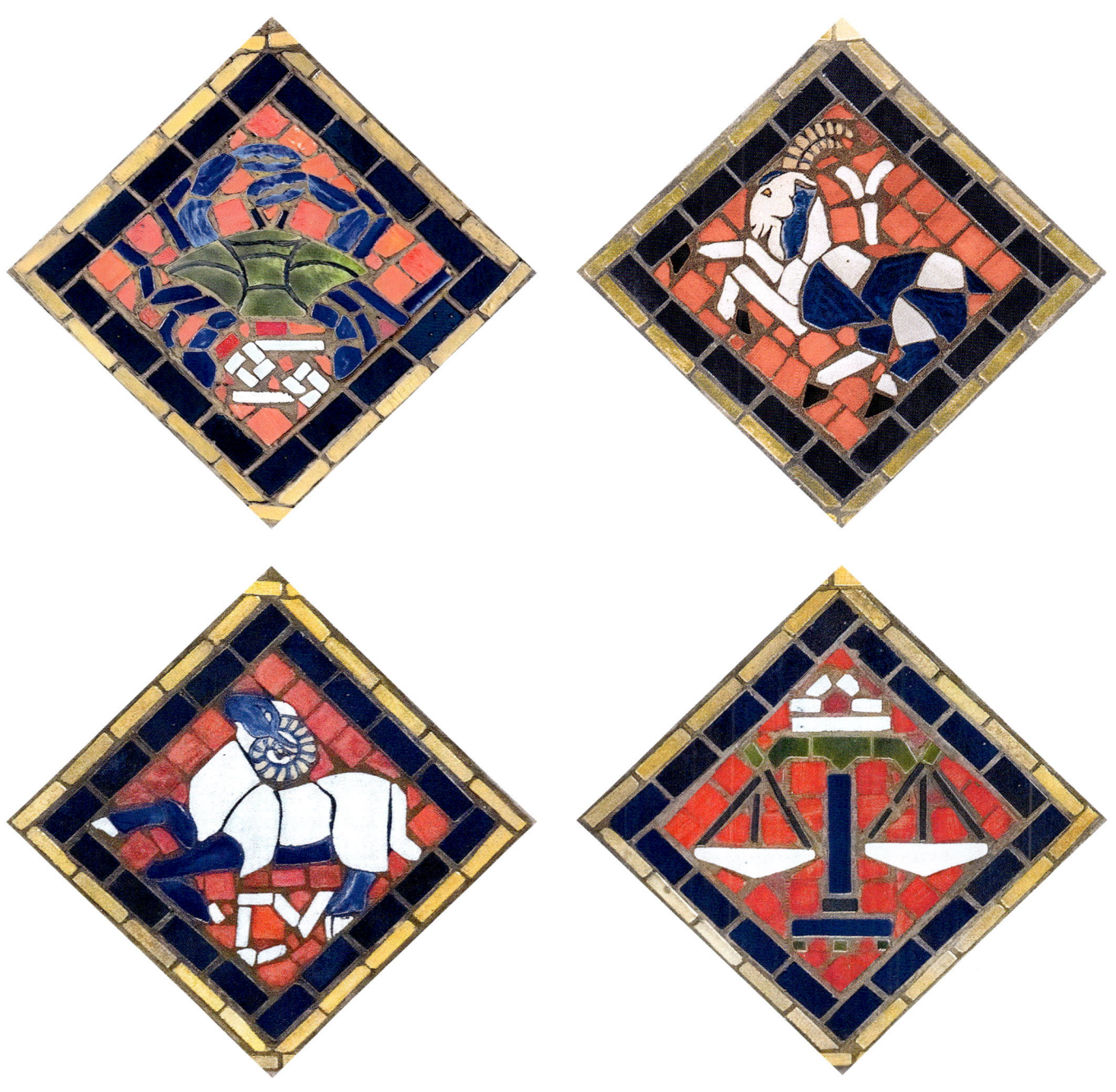

Hildreth Meière
Zodiac Signs, c.1930
approx. 2 x 2 feet
Glazed ceramic tile

The Sun is encircled by depictions of the four seasons and their corresponding signs of the zodiac, emphasizing the integral role the seasons played for the settlers on the prairie.

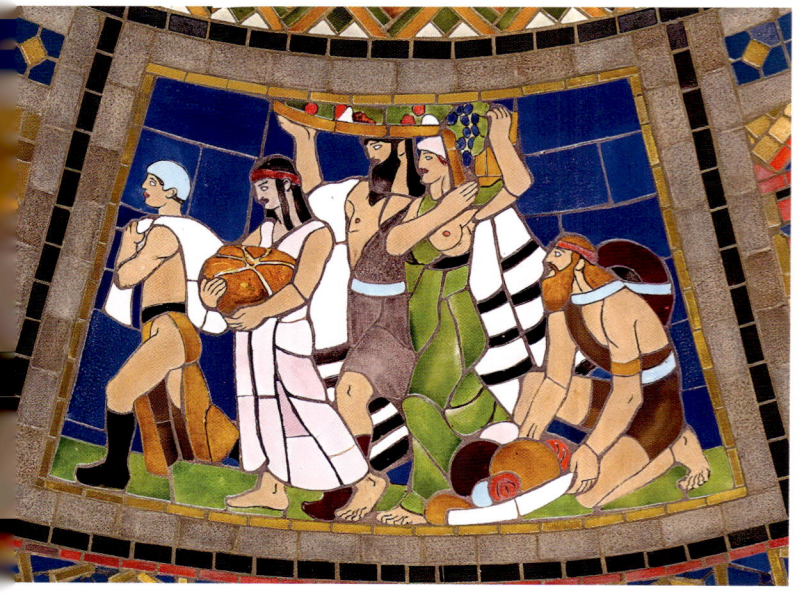

Hildreth Meière
Fruit, c.1930
approx. 4 x 5.5 feet
Glazed ceramic tile

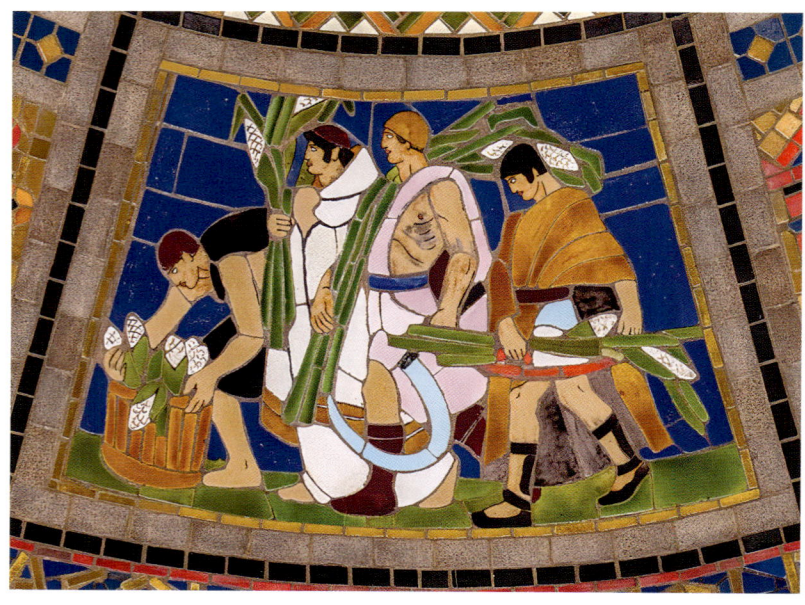

Hildreth Meière
Maize, c.1930
approx. 4 x 5.5 feet
Glazed ceramic tile

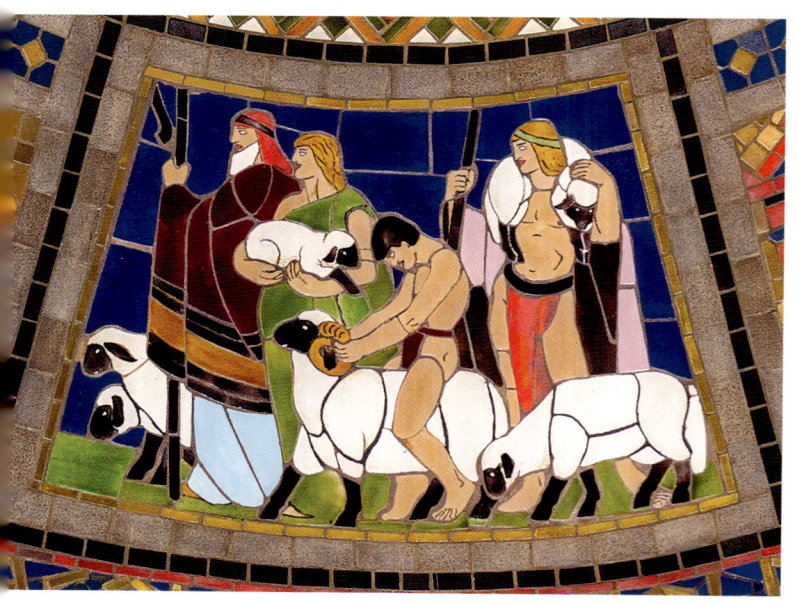

Hildreth Meière
Sheep, c.1930
approx. 4 x 5.5 feet
Glazed ceramic tile

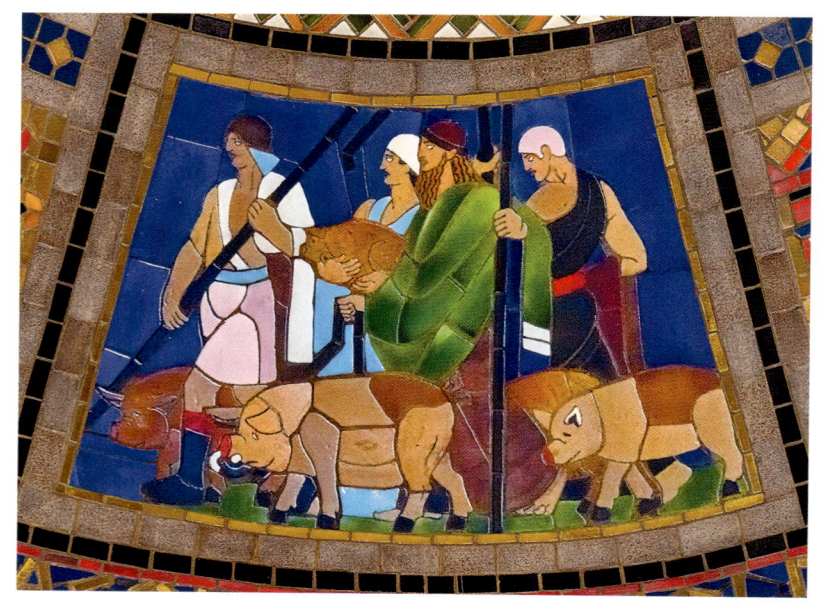

Hildreth Meière
Swine, c.1930
approx. 4 x 5.5 feet
Glazed ceramic tile

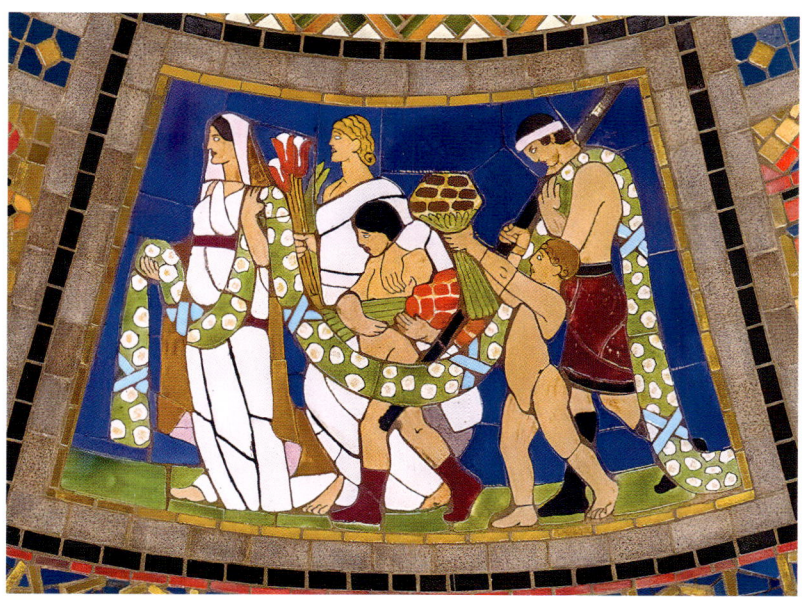

Hildreth Meière
Flowers, c.1930
approx. 4 x 5.5 feet
Glazed ceramic tile

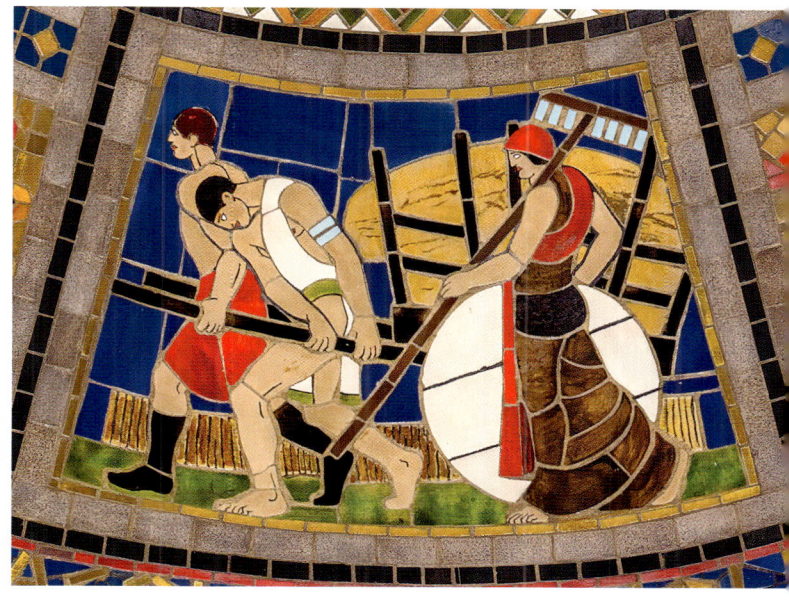

Hildreth Meière
Grasses, c.1930
approx. 4 x 5.5 feet
Glazed ceramic tile

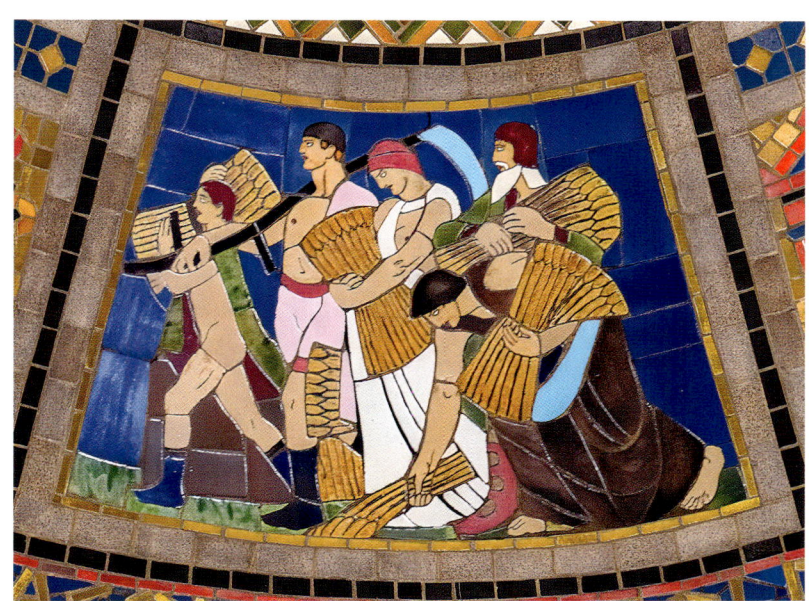

Hildreth Meière
Wheat, c.1930
approx. 4 x 5.5 feet
Glazed ceramic tile

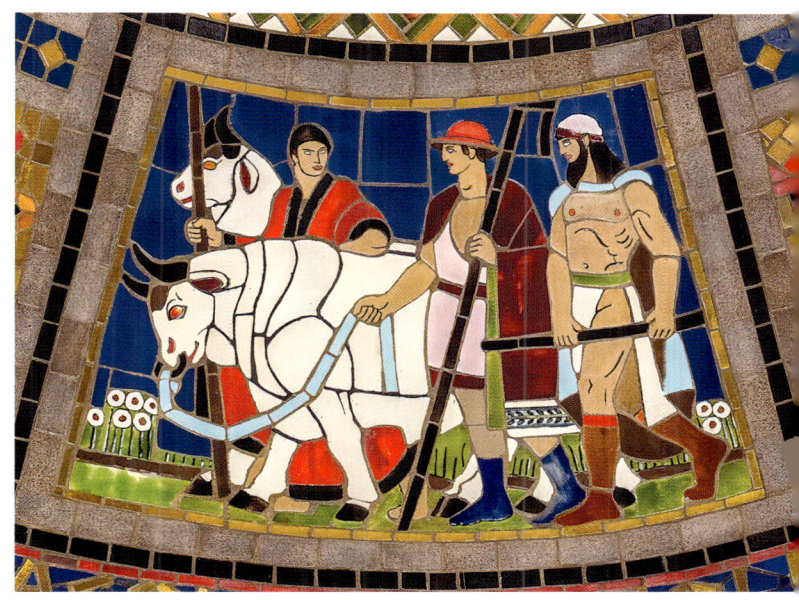

Hildreth Meière
Cattle, c.1930
approx. 4 x 5.5 feet
Glazed ceramic tile

The eight vignettes of the outer concentric circle
surrounding the dome portray the gifts of the soil. These
vignettes are encircled by a quote from Alexander
reading, "Behold they come as householders bringing
Earth's first fruits, rejoicing that the soil hath rewarded
their labors with the abundance of the season."

Hildreth Meière
Plowing, c.1930
approx. 3 x 3.5 feet
Glazed ceramic tile

Four pendentives represent
what Alexander refers to as
"Four Moments of Agriculture."

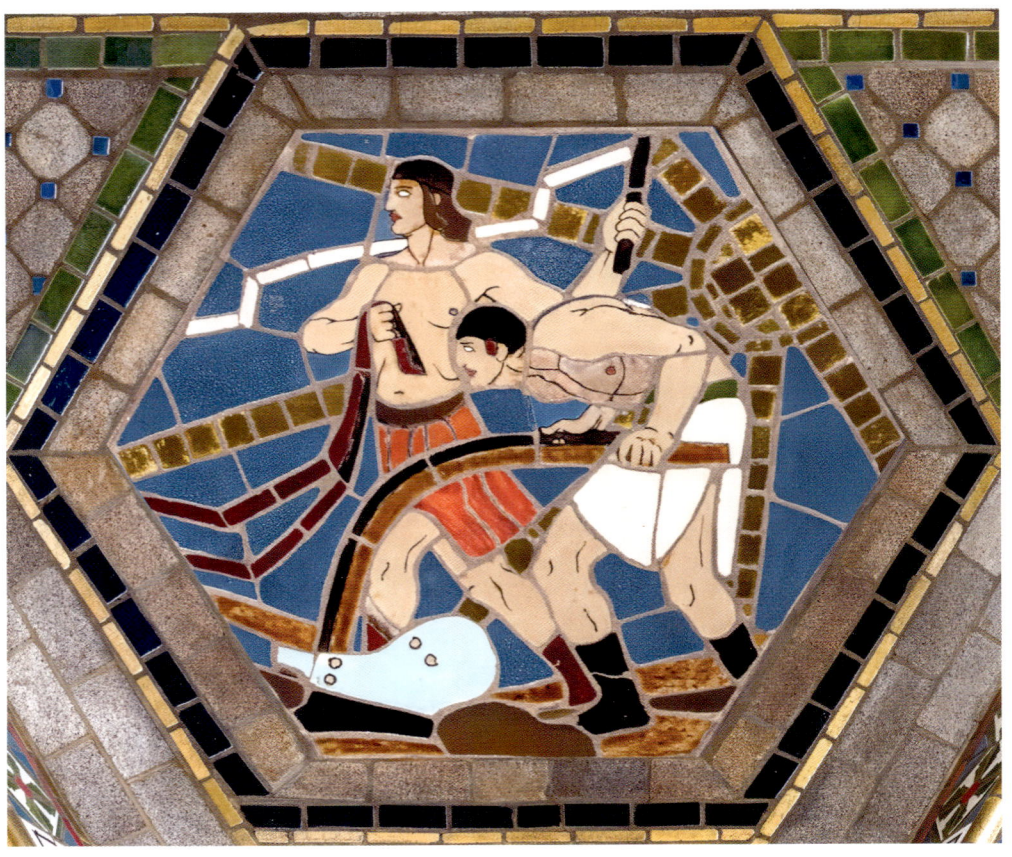

Hildreth Meière
Sowing, c.1930
approx. 3 x 3.5 feet
Glazed ceramic tile

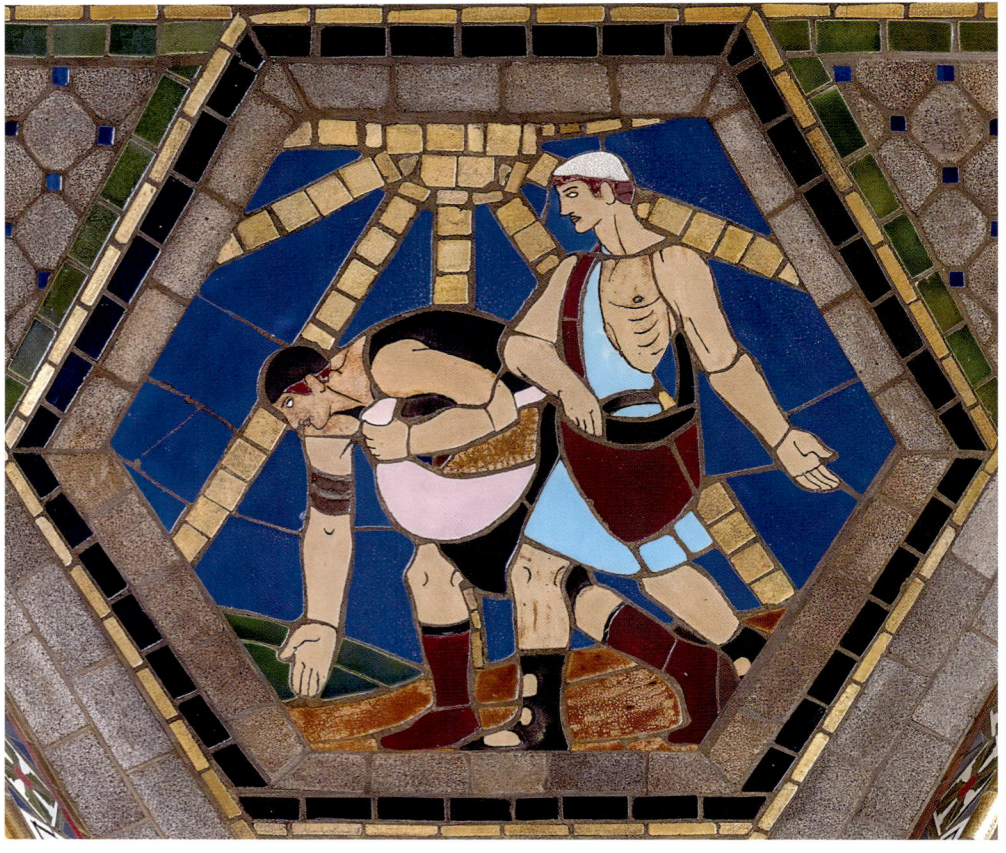

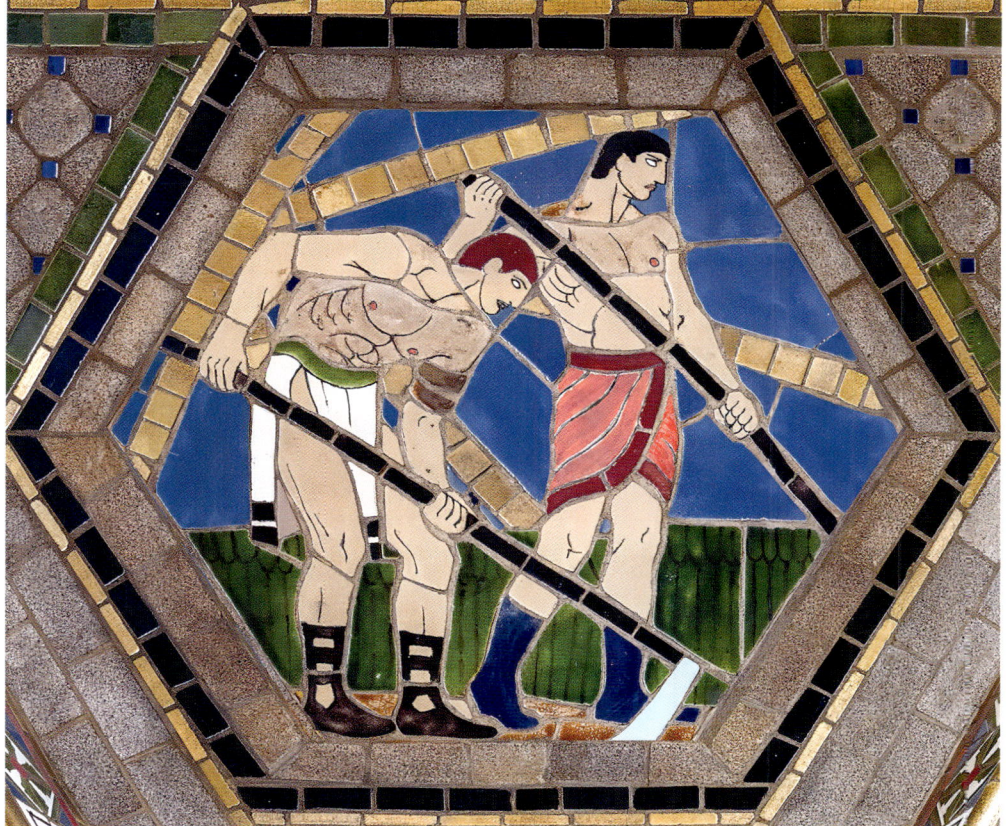

Hildreth Meière
Cultivating, c.1930
approx. 3 x 3.5 feet
Glazed ceramic tile

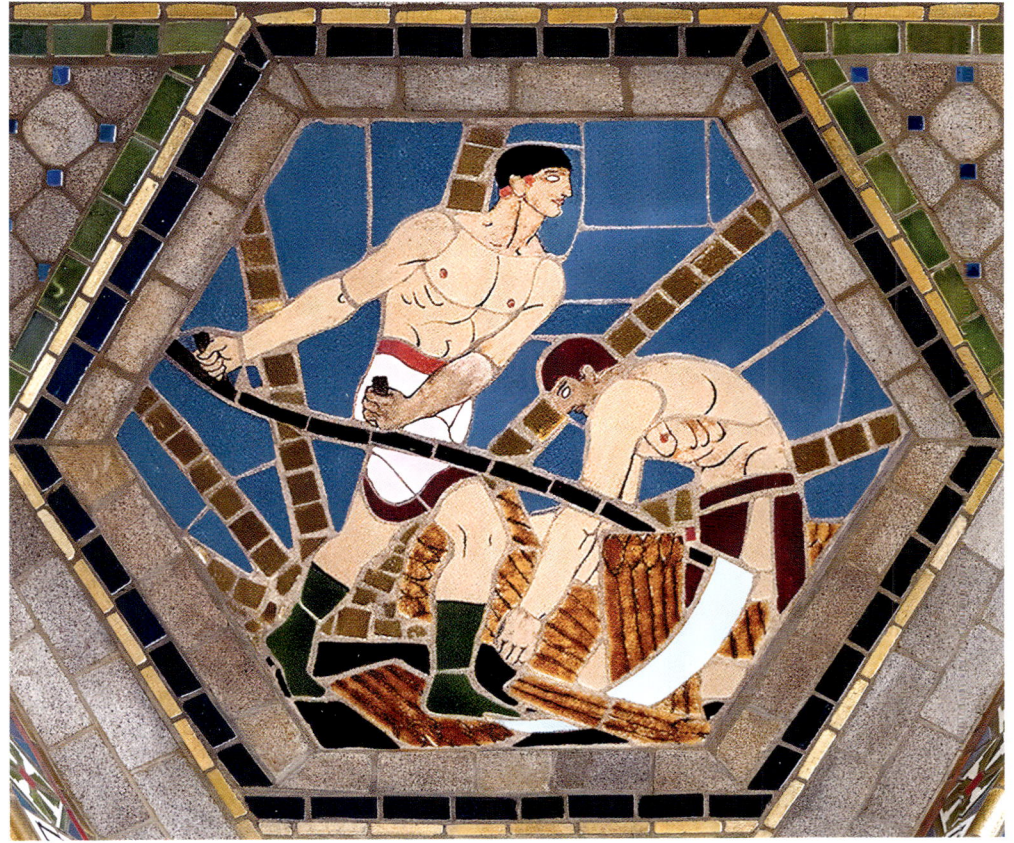

Hildreth Meière
Reaping, c.1930
approx. 3 x 3.5 feet
Glazed ceramic tile

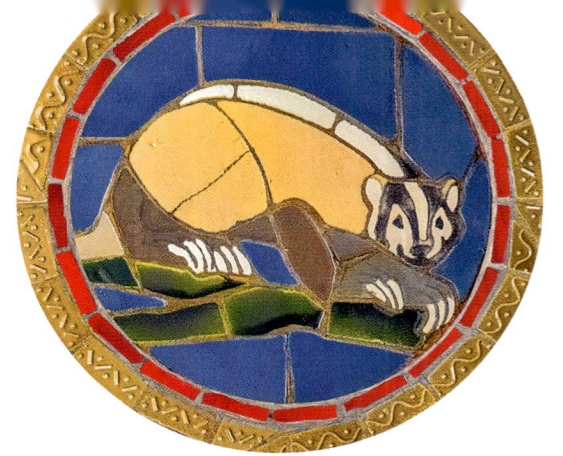
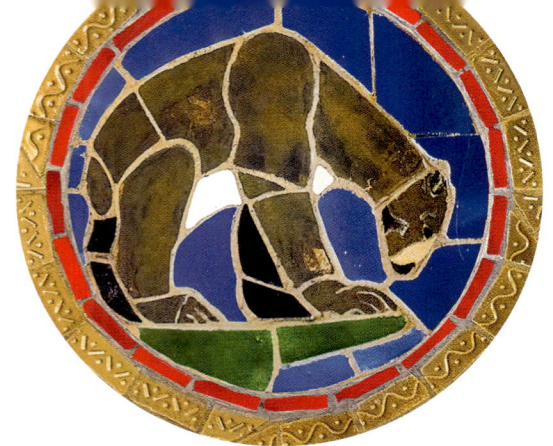
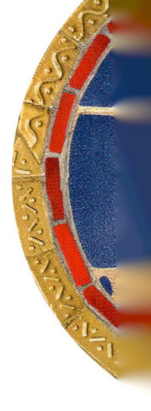
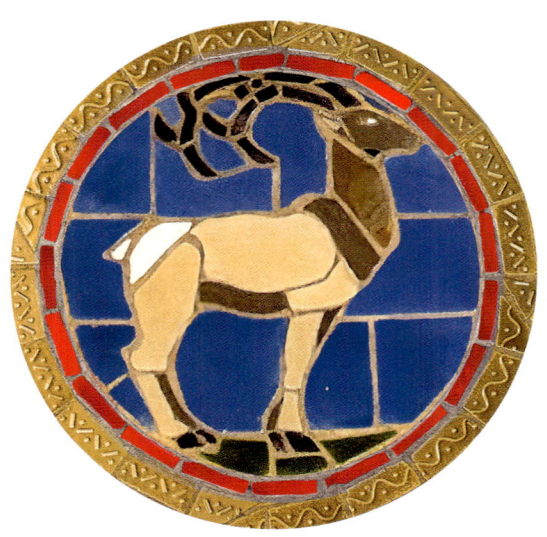
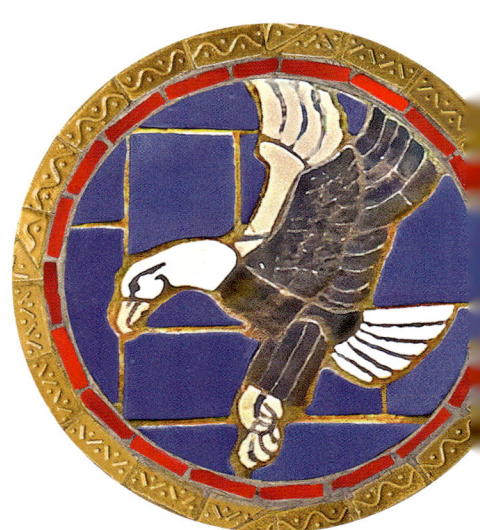
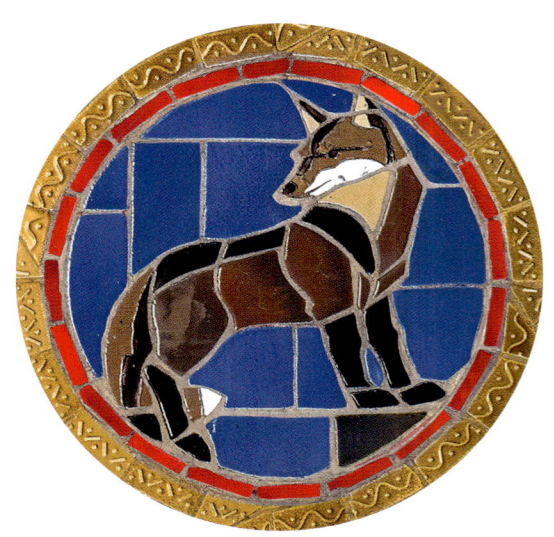
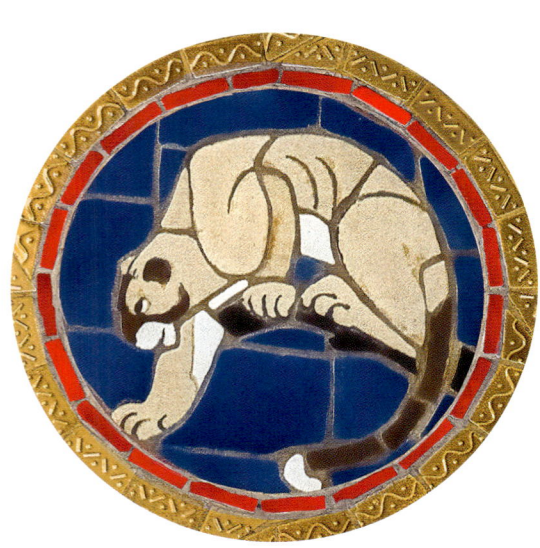
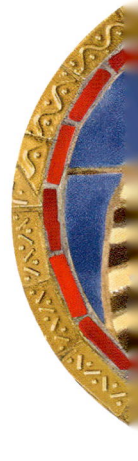

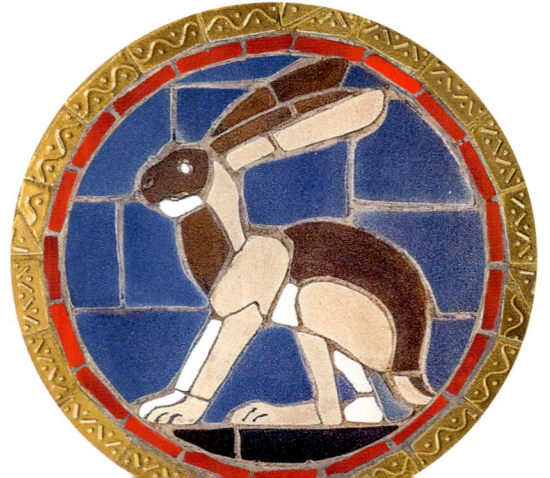
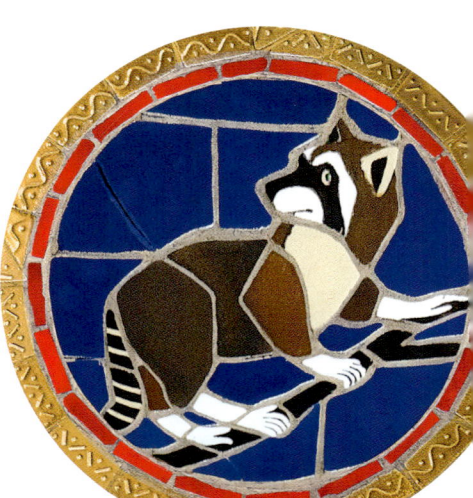

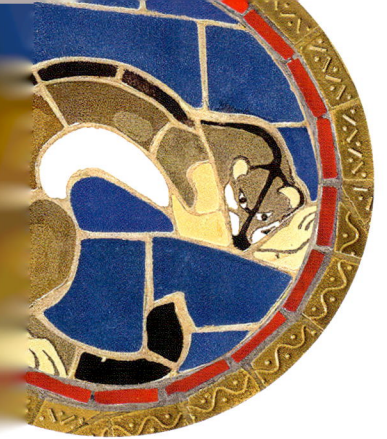
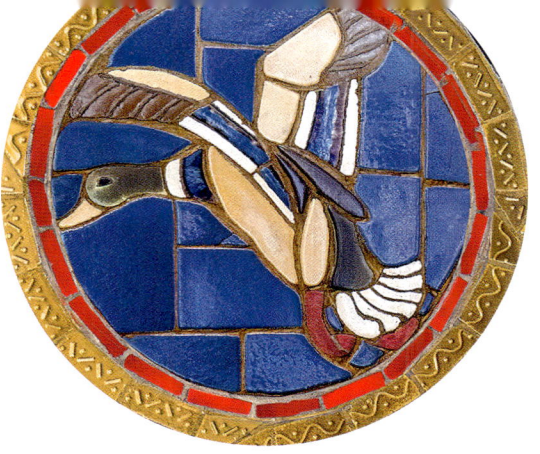

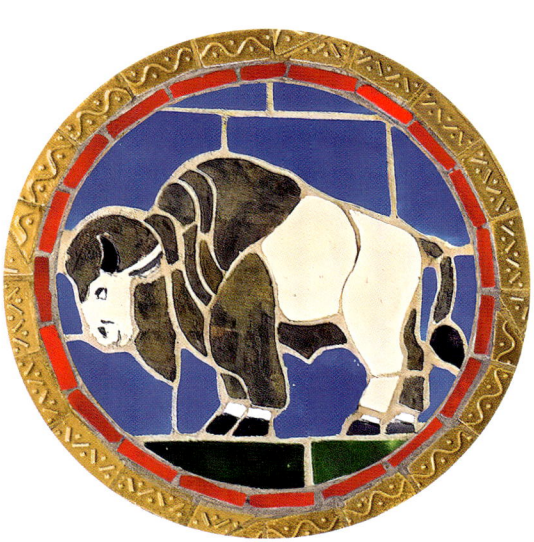

Hildreth Meière
Native Fauna, c.1930
approx. 2.5 x 2.5 feet
Glazed ceramic tile

The arch soffits adjacent to the dome include a border pattern of circular panels representing native animals, alternating with sunflowers.

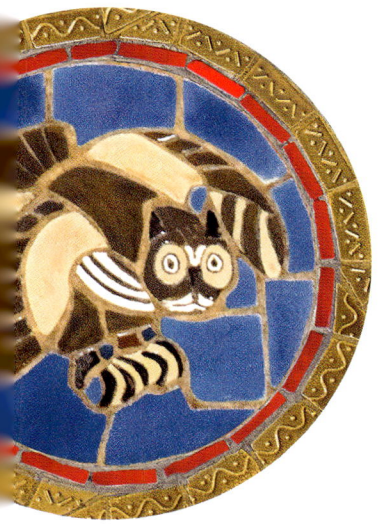
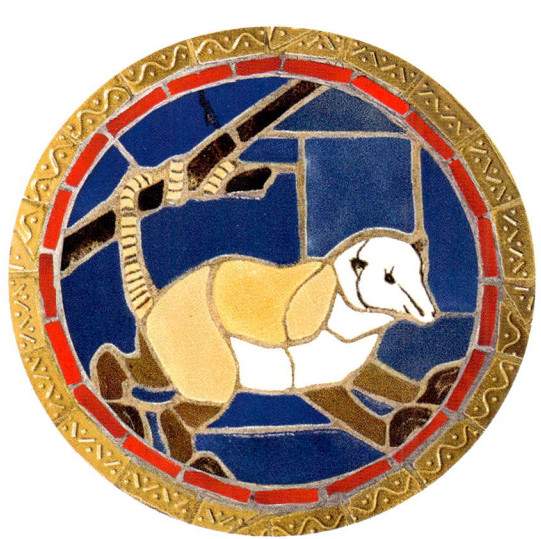

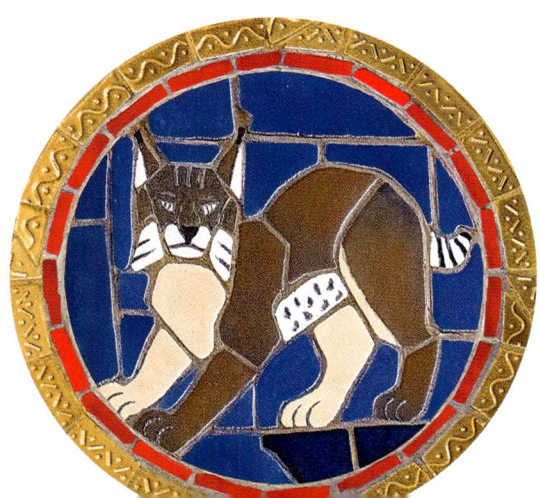
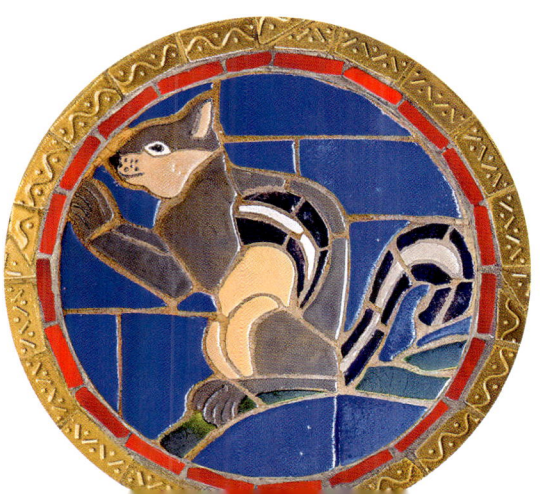

Edward F. Caldwell & Co.
Chandelier, c.1930

The chandelier of the vestibule contains symbols of corn and arrows, representing Native American culture. Weighing around 3,500 pounds, this great light fixture is carefully raised and lowered with a windlass, an apparatus using heavy weights, a crank, and ropes.

Lee Lawrie
Column Capitals, c.1930
Carved marble

The column capitals are adorned with Nebraska iconography, including cattle, corn, and wheat.

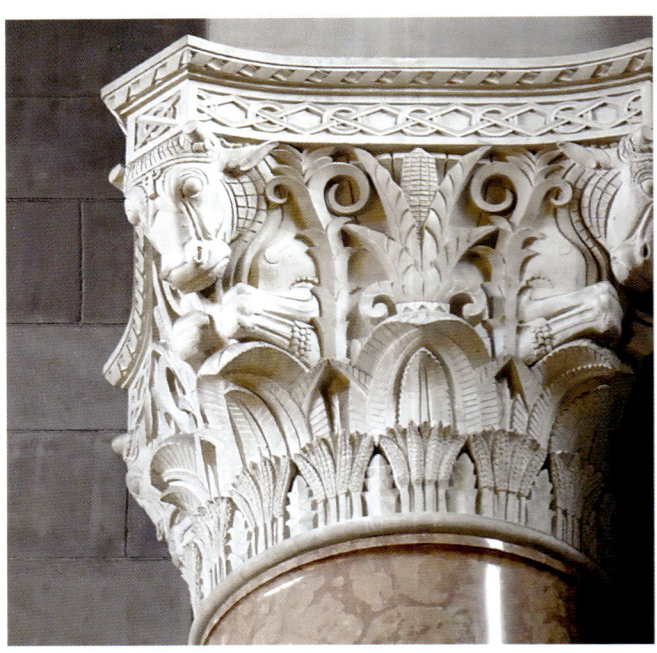

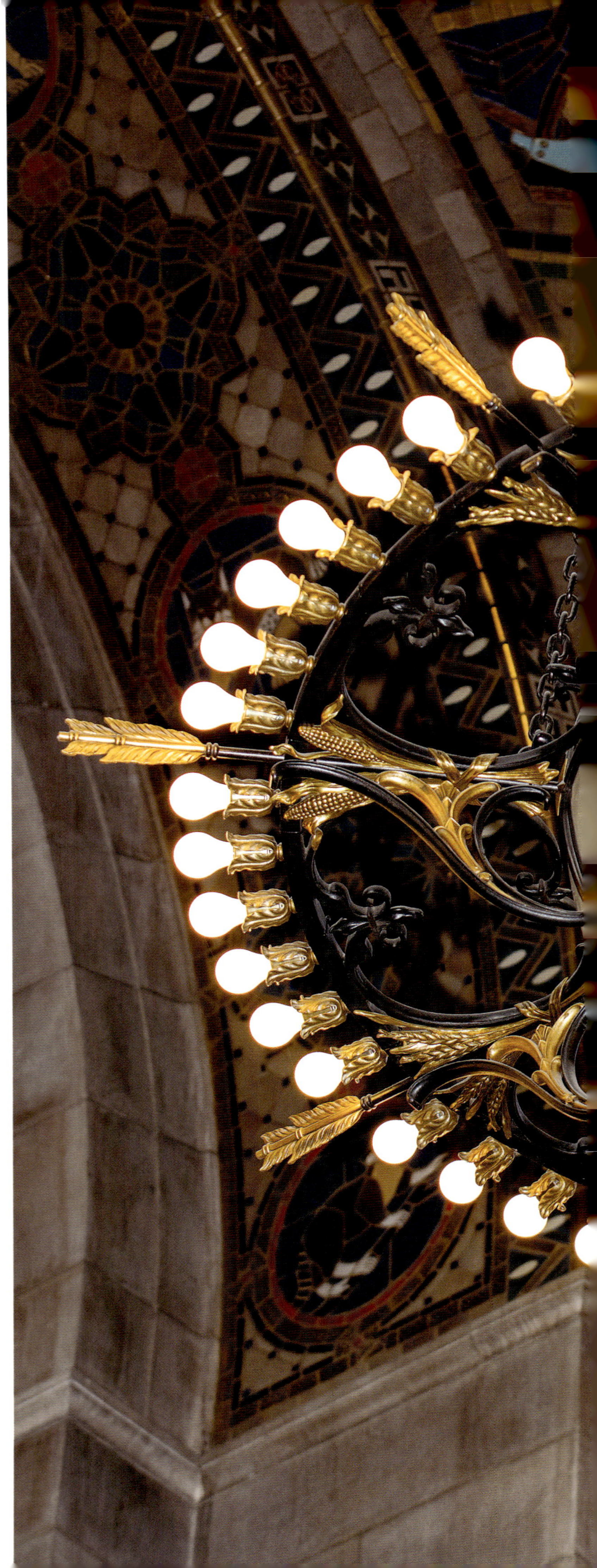

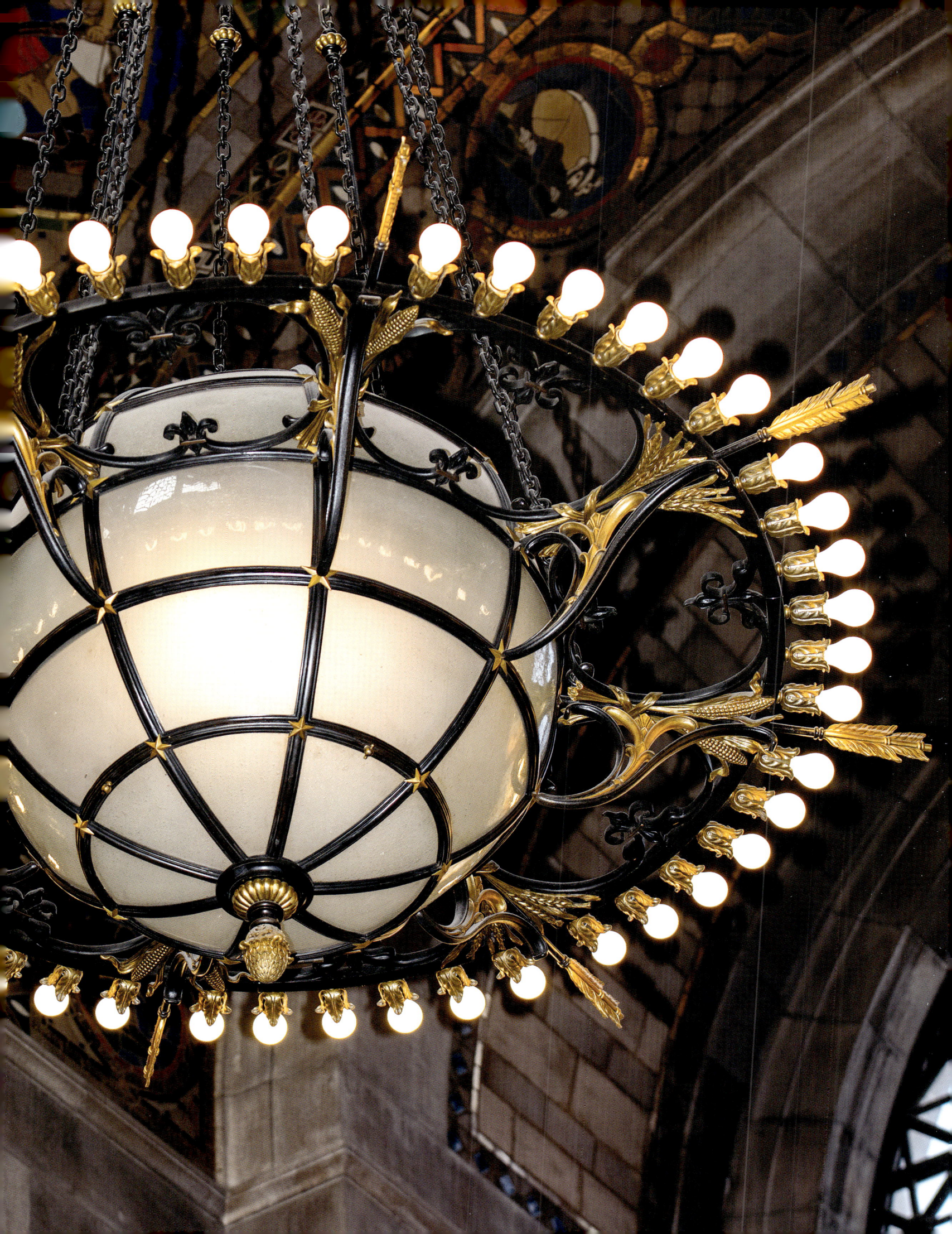

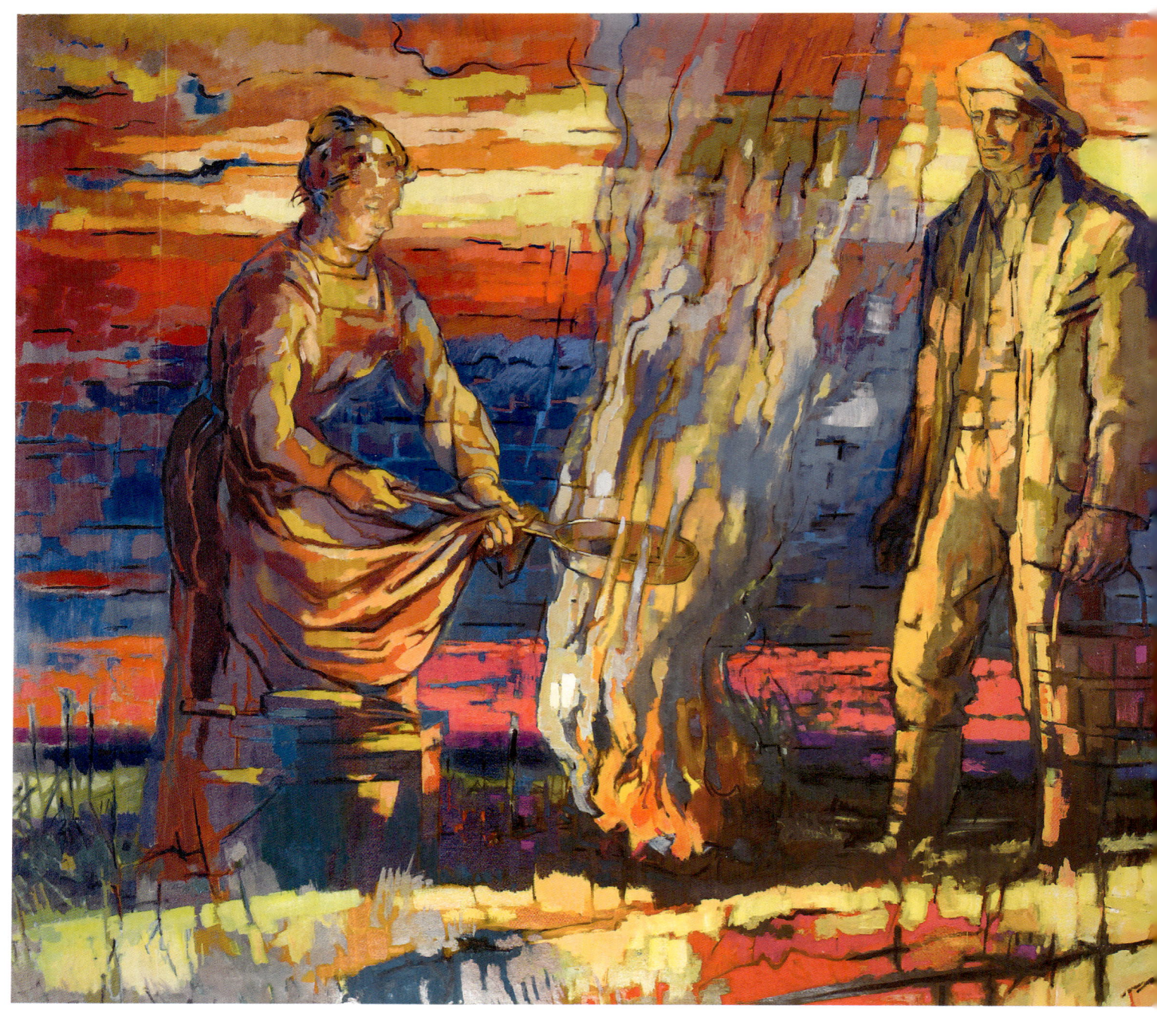

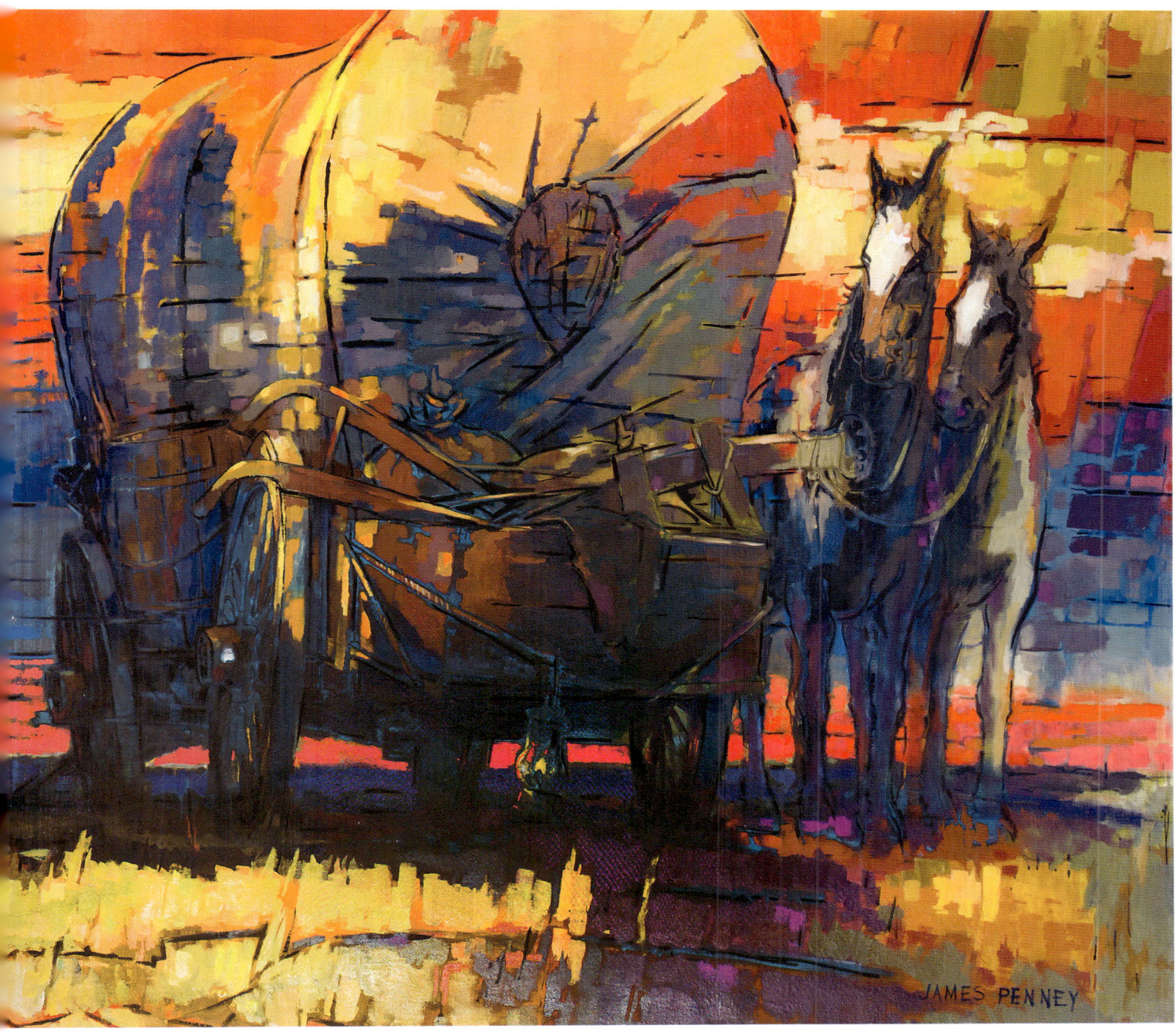

James Penney
The Homesteader's Campfire, 1963
8.5 x 19 feet
Oil on linen

The Homesteader's Campfire depicts a pioneer family, newly
arrived to the prairies. Many pioneers came to the state thanks to
the Homestead Act of 1862. The offer of free land led to a rapid
growth of new farmers coming to Nebraska and helped it to
become the first new state admitted to the union after the Civil War.

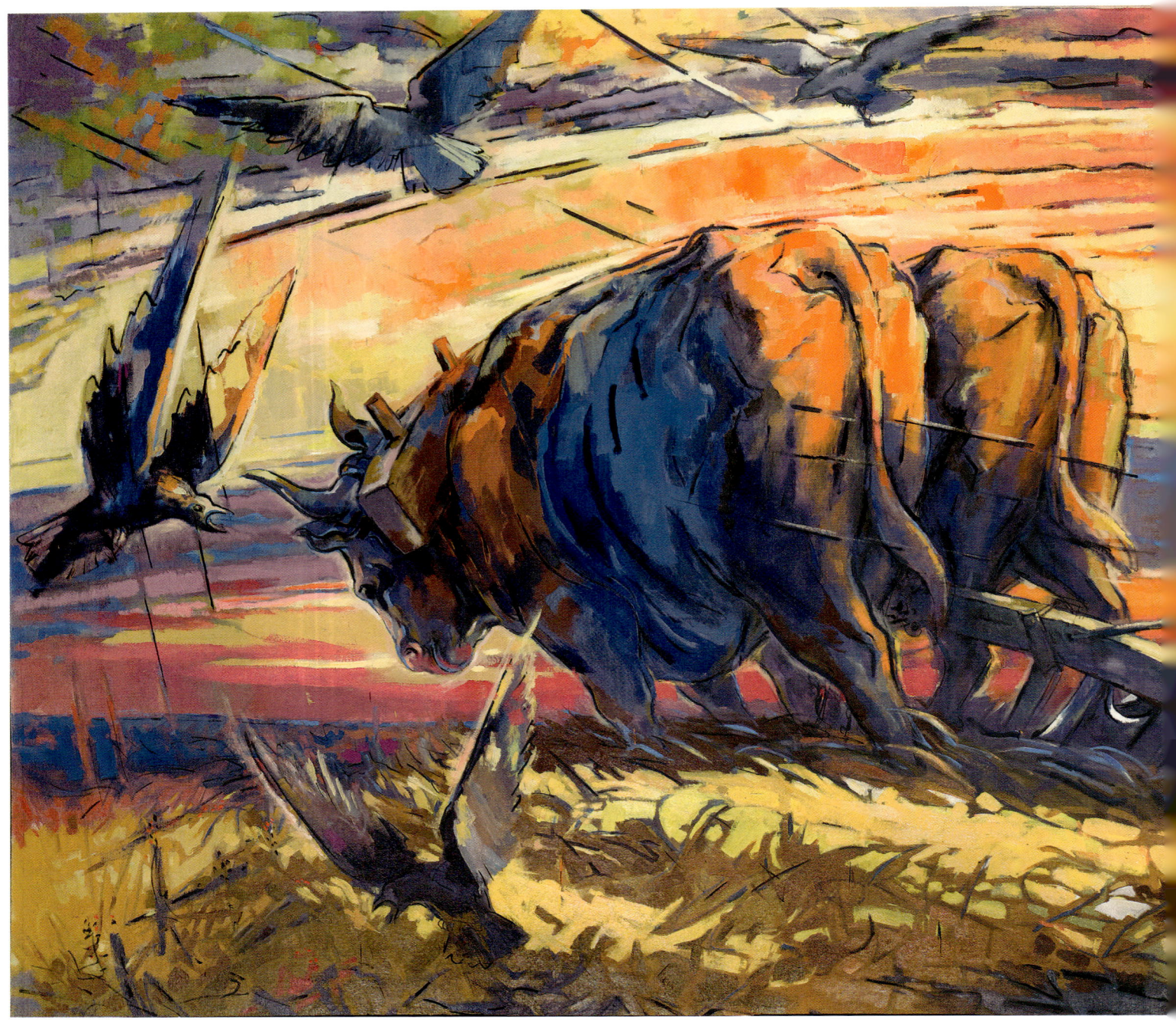

James Penney
The First Furrow, 1963
8.5 x 19 feet
Oil on linen

While the Homestead Act provided plenty of land and opportunities for farmers, it wasn't a panacea. Farmers still needed the equipment and knowledge necessary to succeed. For many, this was a slow and difficult process, and they often lacked any farming assistance. This mural highlights the challenges and opportunities presented to these farmers.

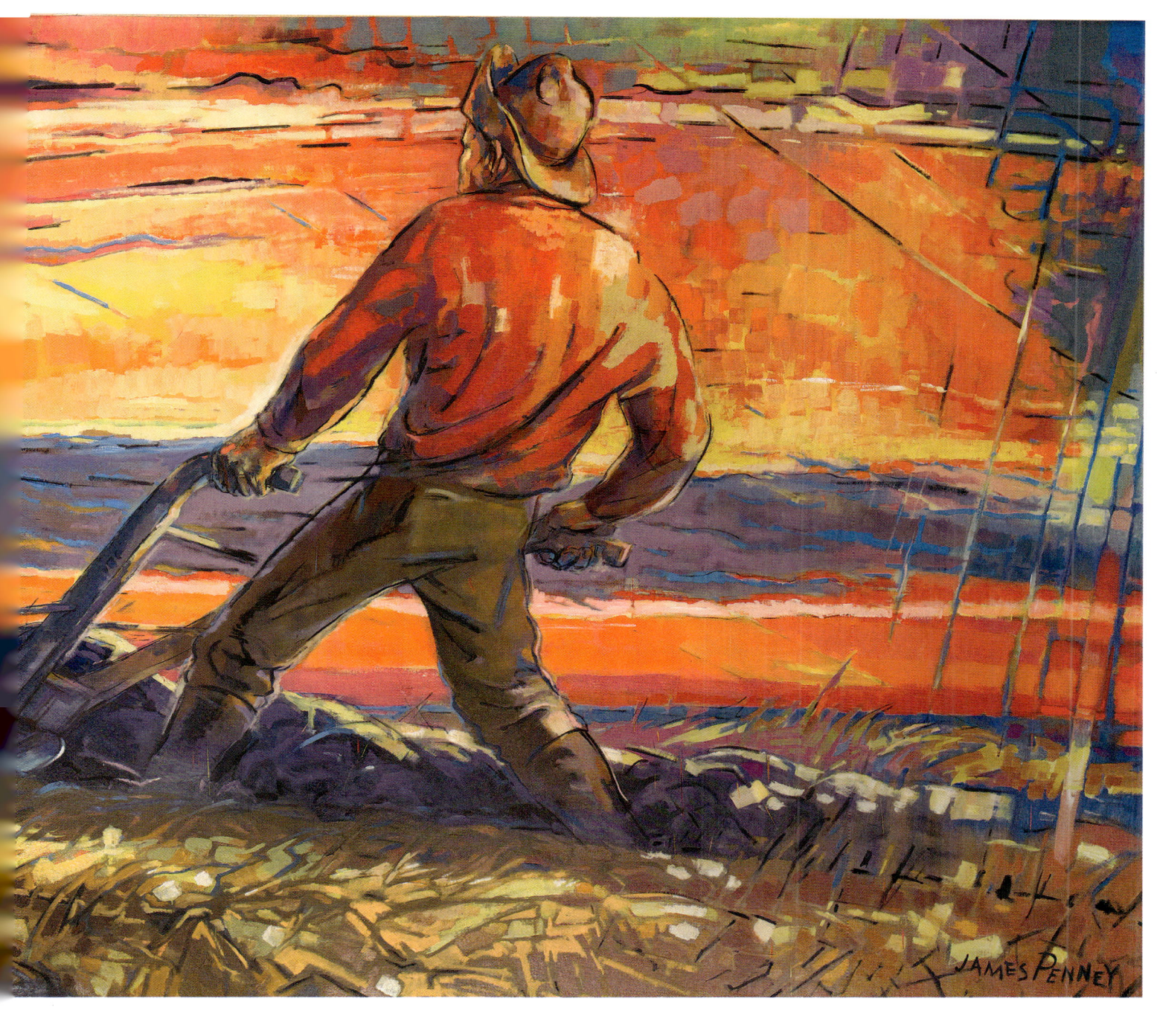

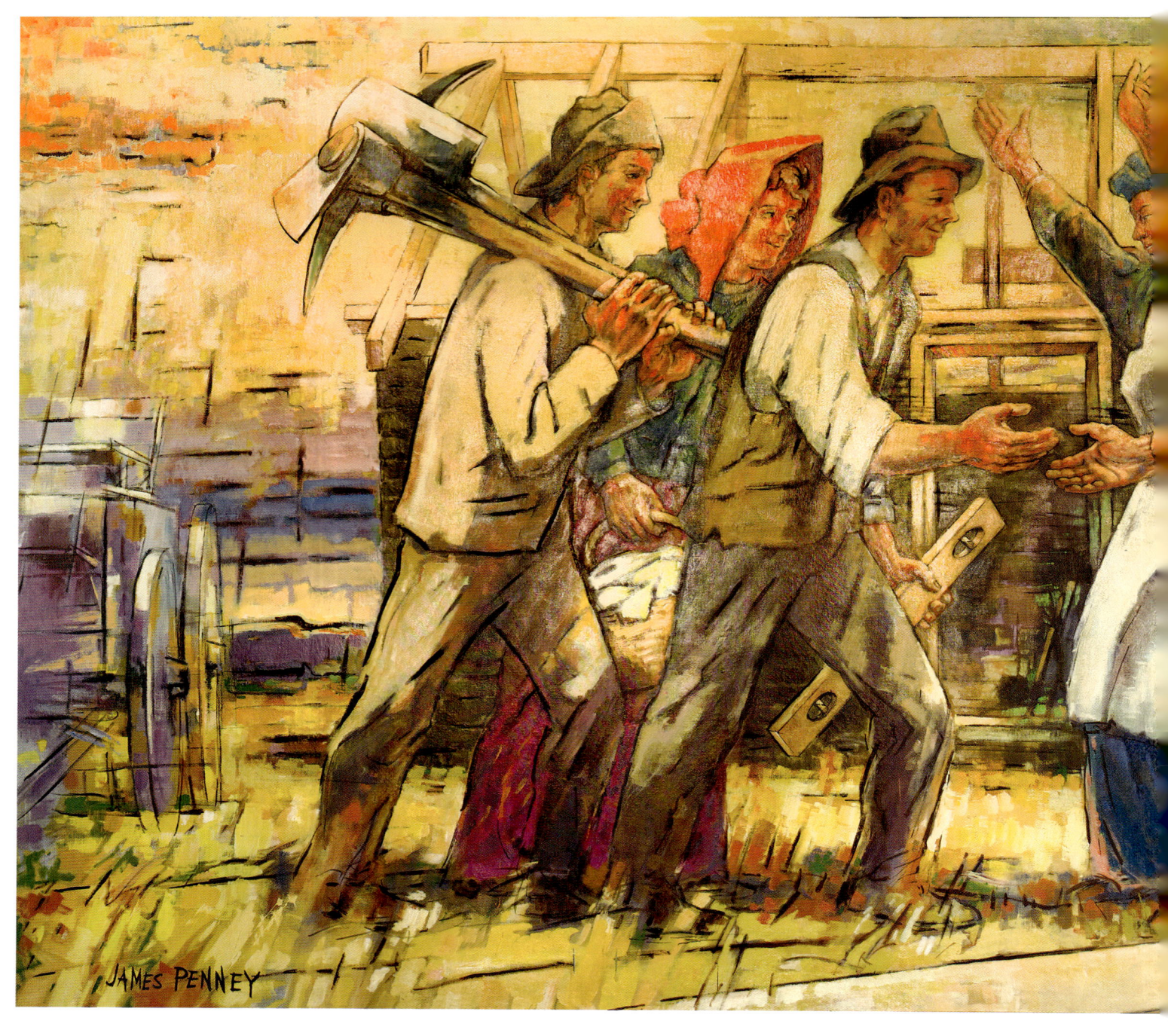

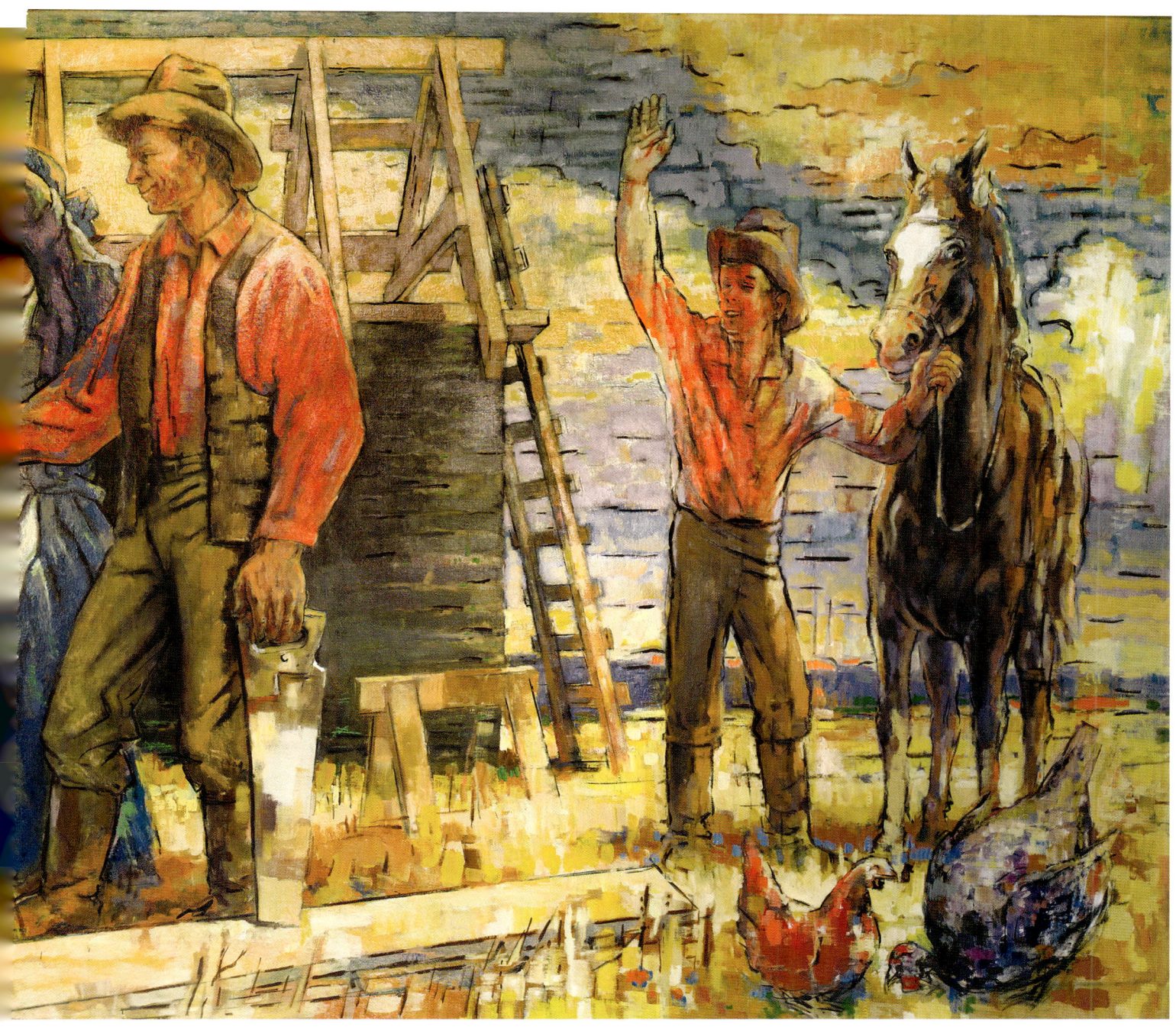

James Penney
The House Raising, 1963
8.5 x 19 feet
Oil on linen

The House Raising shows neighbors coming together to help
raise a sod home for a newly-arrived settler family. In the
early days of Nebraska, homesteaders relied on neighbors
and friends to complete large projects like home building.
Homes were often constructed with sod walls, the easiest
and cheapest way to build a home or barn on the prairie.

FOYER

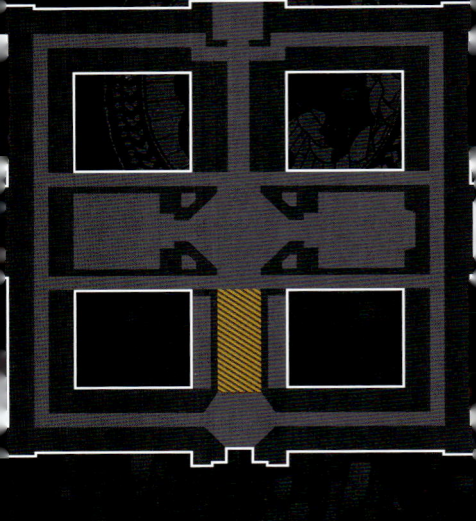

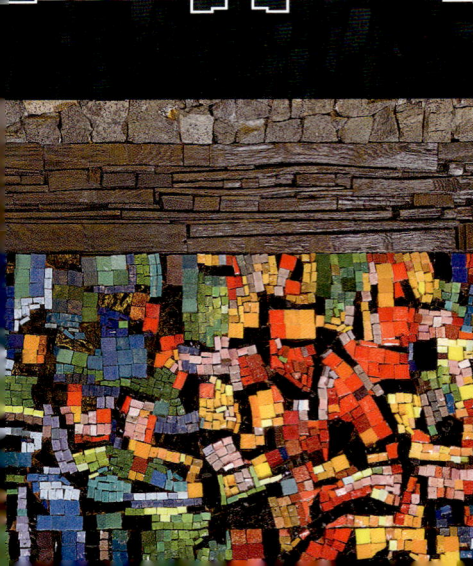

REINHOLD
MARXHAUSEN

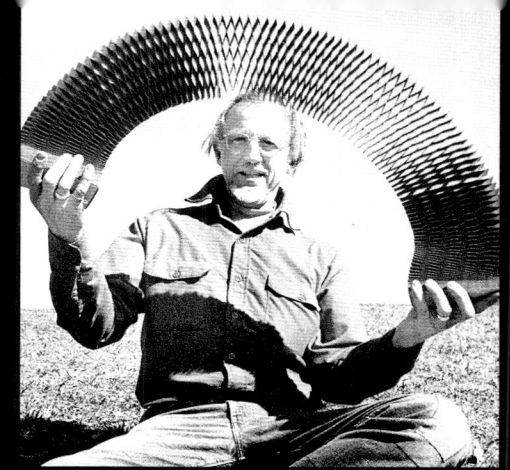

Reinhold Marxhausen's mural installations in the foyer came decades after Goodhue, Meière, and Lawrie worked on the Capitol. Yet, like his predecessors, he came to the project as a multifaceted artist who was able to integrate a unique perspective to the building.

Marxhausen worked in photography, painting, mosaic, and sculpture, mastering those different media and integrating them into original, inventive work. He utilized many of the techniques in the two murals he created for the Capitol.

Born in Minnesota in 1922, Marxhausen became an accomplished artist at a young age, opening his own painting and wallpaper business after high school. Drafted into the military during World War II, Marxhausen closed his business to serve in the Pacific Theater. Despite this career setback, he continued to make art while a soldier, turning objects he found on the Pacific Islands, including tin and plastic from destroyed aircraft, into new artwork.

After returning to the States and attending a variety of schools, Marxhausen got his big break as an artist with the Ford Motor Company, which ran a publication called the *Ford Times*.

After seeing his work in the magazine, the president of Concordia College in Seward, Nebraska, wrote Marxhausen to offer him a position to start an art program at the college. The artist was so shocked that he initially thought the letter was a practical joke. He eventually accepted and created a Concordia art program renowned to this day.

Marxhausen considered himself a sound artist as well as a visual artist, creating works he called "sound sculptures." His palm-sized sculptures called *Stardust* used wires inside stainless steel objects to create mini-symphonies of delicate sound.

He worked at Concordia College for 40 years, retiring in 1991 as a much-loved educator and mentor. Marxhausen also played a significant role in expanding access to and awareness of the arts in Nebraska.

His most well-known works include the two murals installed in the Capitol in 1967. Marxhausen, who died in 2011, considered them his proudest accomplishment.

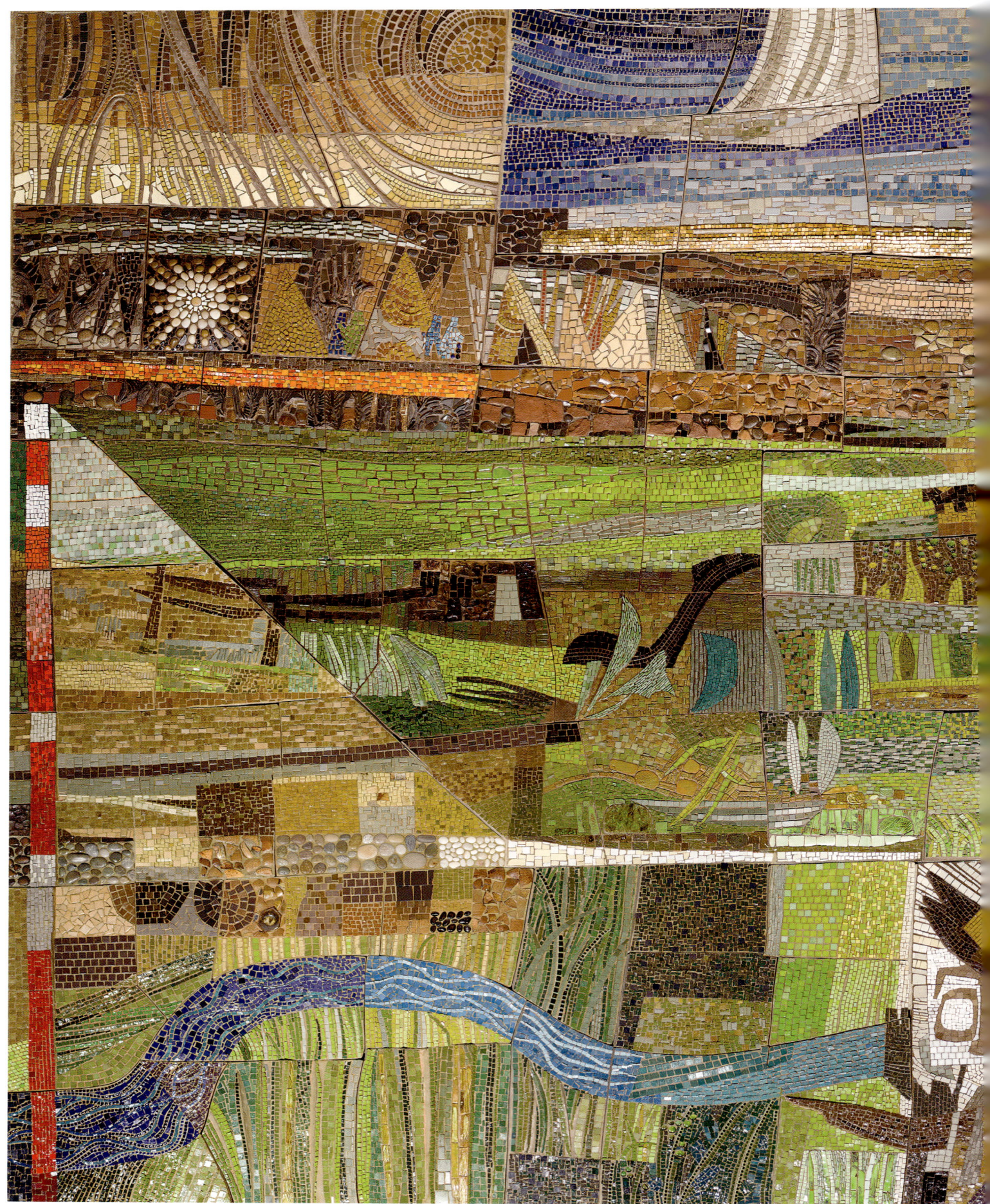

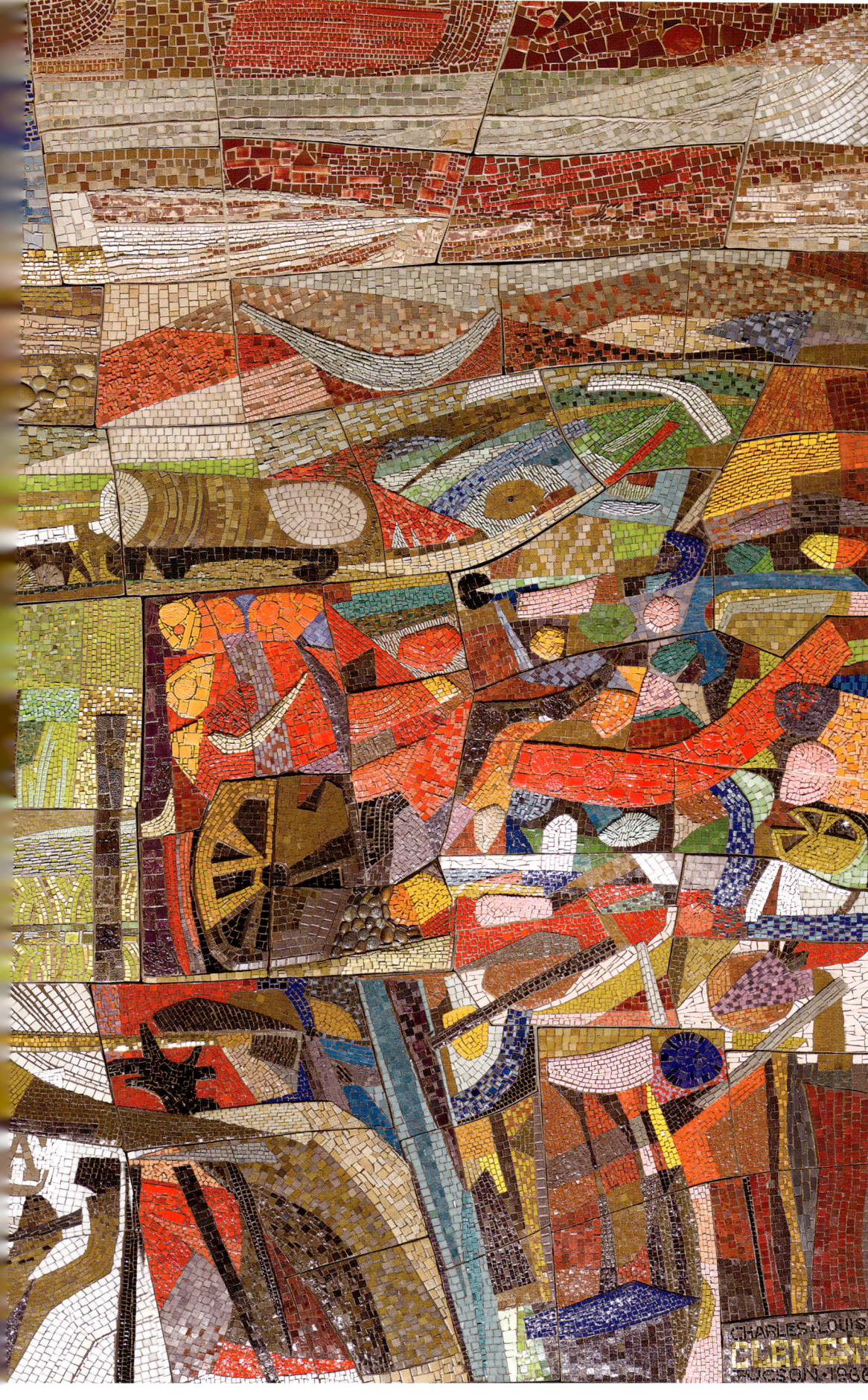

Charles Clement
United States Survey, 1966
13 x 19 feet
Gold, Japanese glass,
American glass, and
Venetian glass mosaic

The art of the foyer works
together to represent the past,
present, and future of life on
the prairies of Nebraska.

Foretelling the changes
to the state and country
that came with westward
expansion, *United States
Survey* shows to the right a
group of surveyors at work.
Behind them, a colorful
and new world advances,
including the growth of the
new Nebraska Territory. They
point to the mural's left with the
plains, bison, homesteaders,
and Native Americans.

Jeanne Reynal
Blizzard of 1888, 1966
13 x 19 feet
Venetian glass mosaic

This mural represents the
tenacious pioneer spirit of
Nebraska through the story of
Minnie Freeman, a teacher at
a prairie school who bravely
led 13 schoolchildren safely
through the Blizzard of 1888.
The golden line stretching
from the bottom right of the
mural represents the rope
Freeman used to tether the
children in a line so as not to
lose any. The larger figure on
the left side is believed to be a
great spirit guiding the group
to safety or a representation
of the great storm itself.

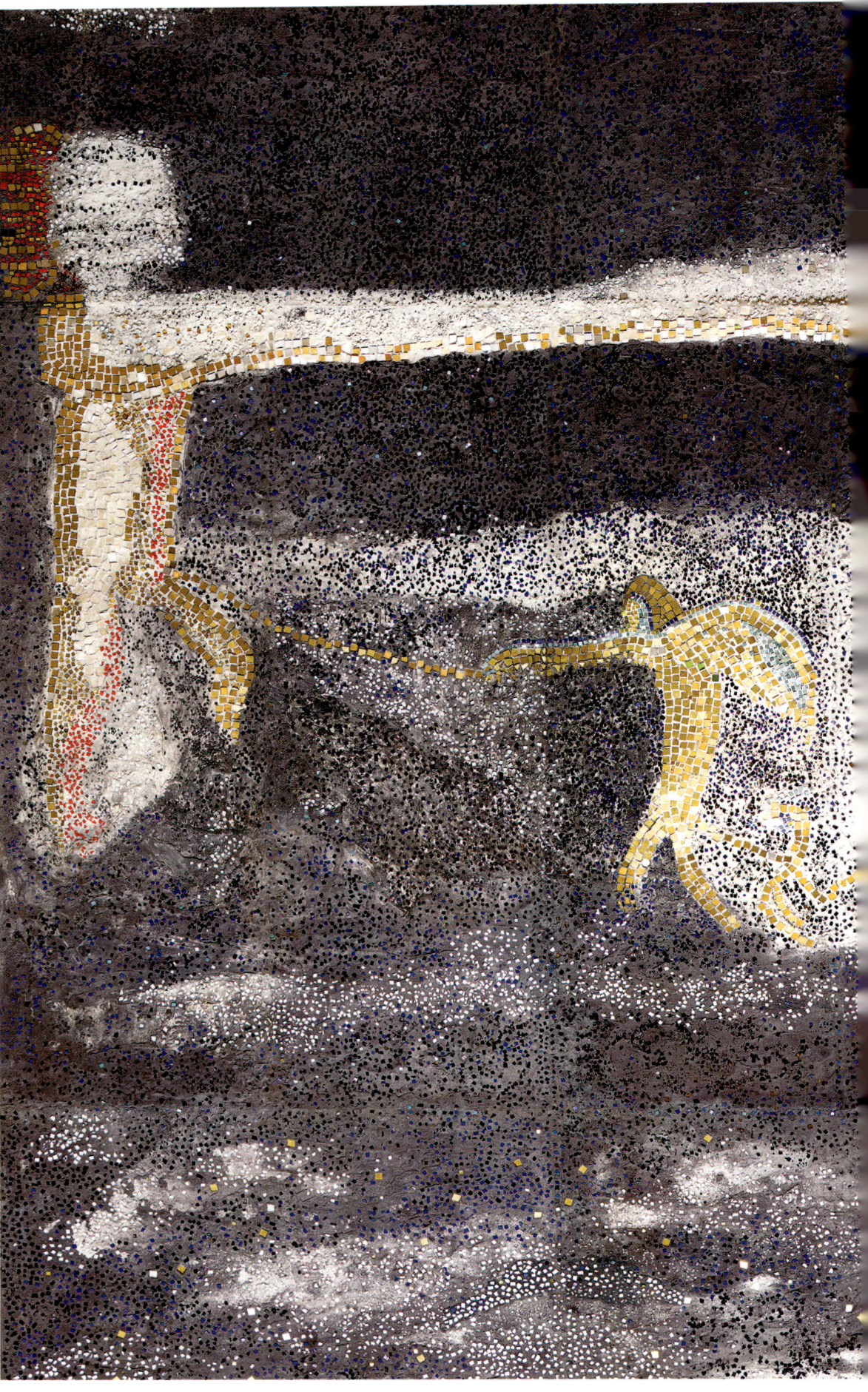

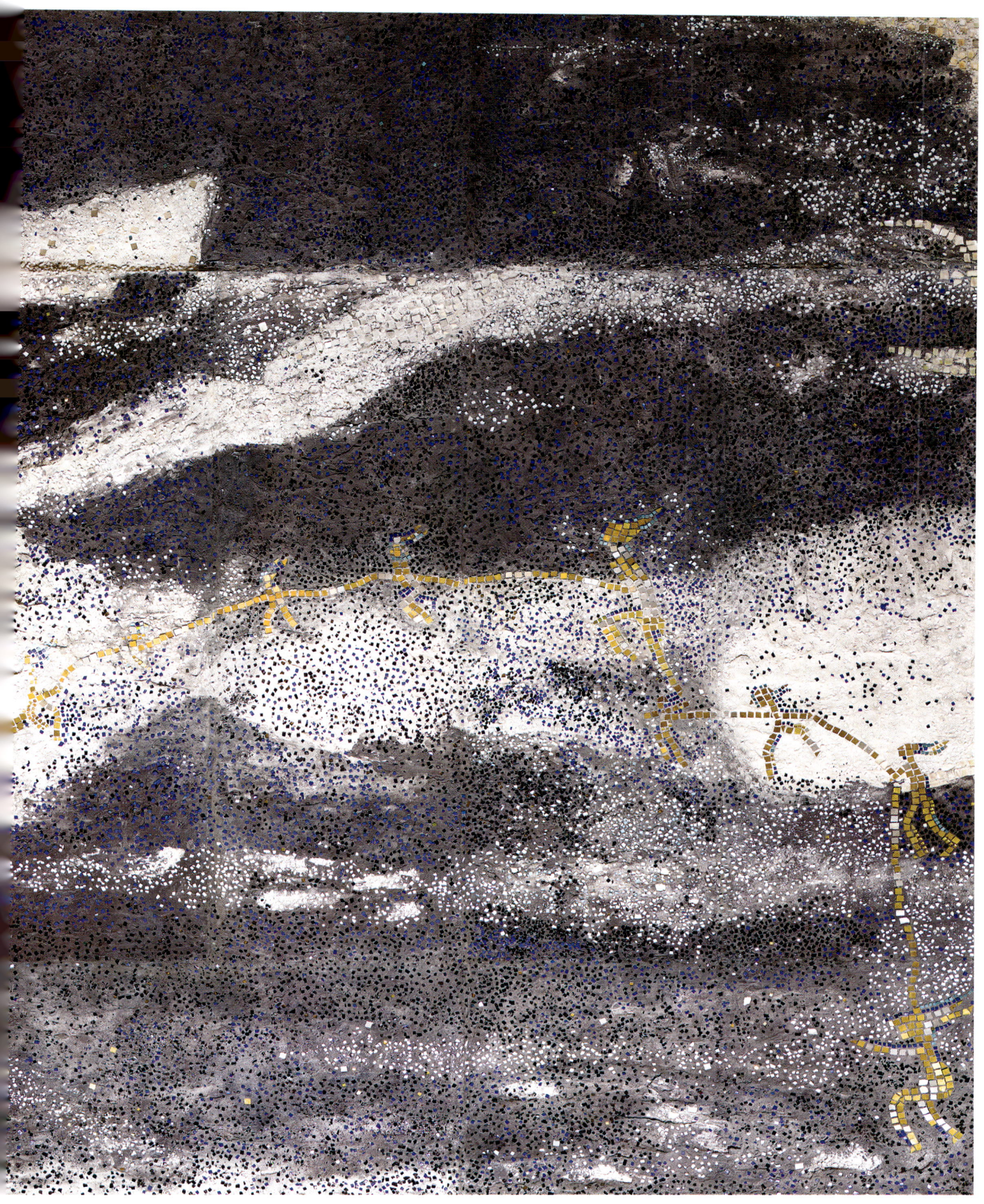

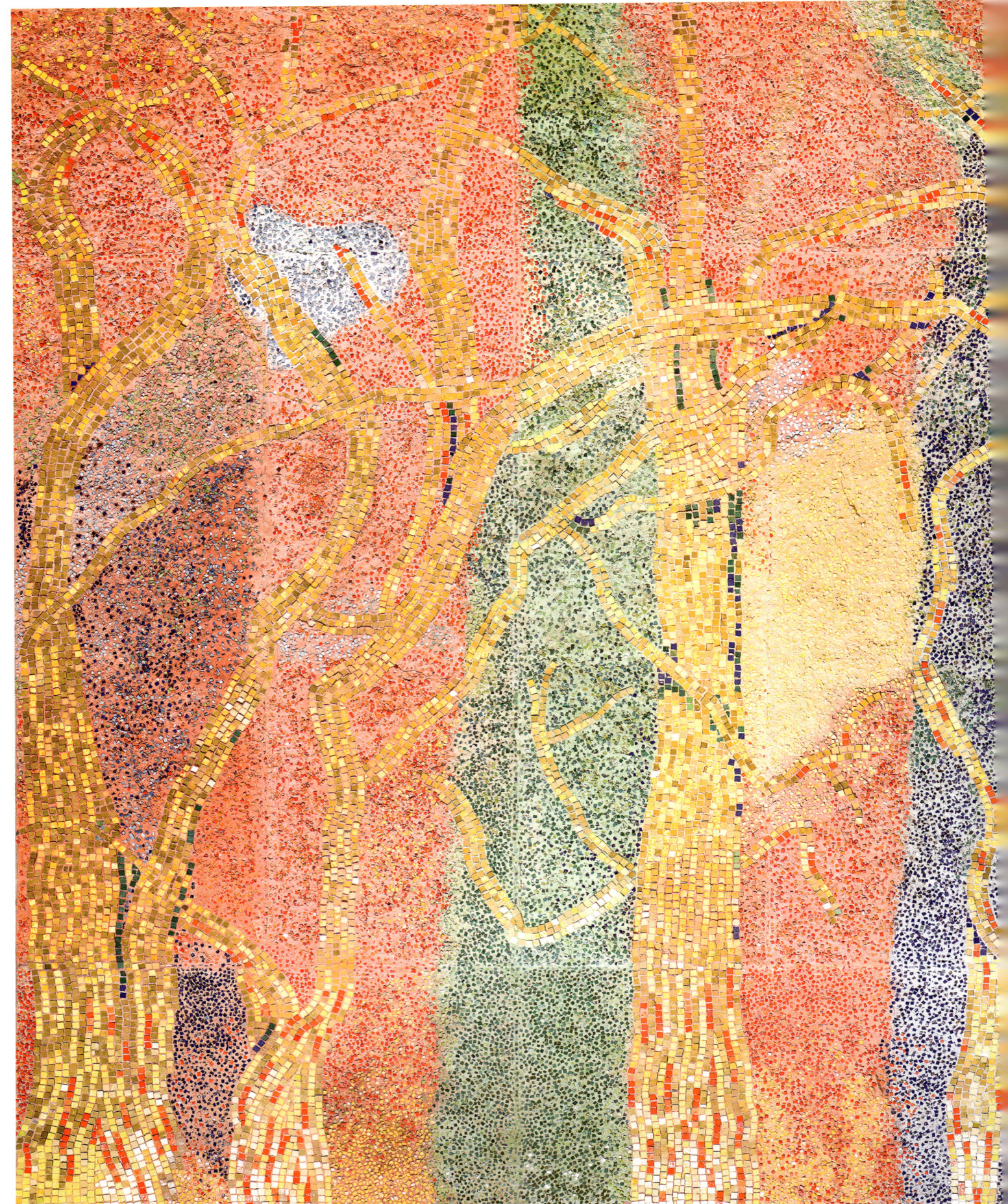

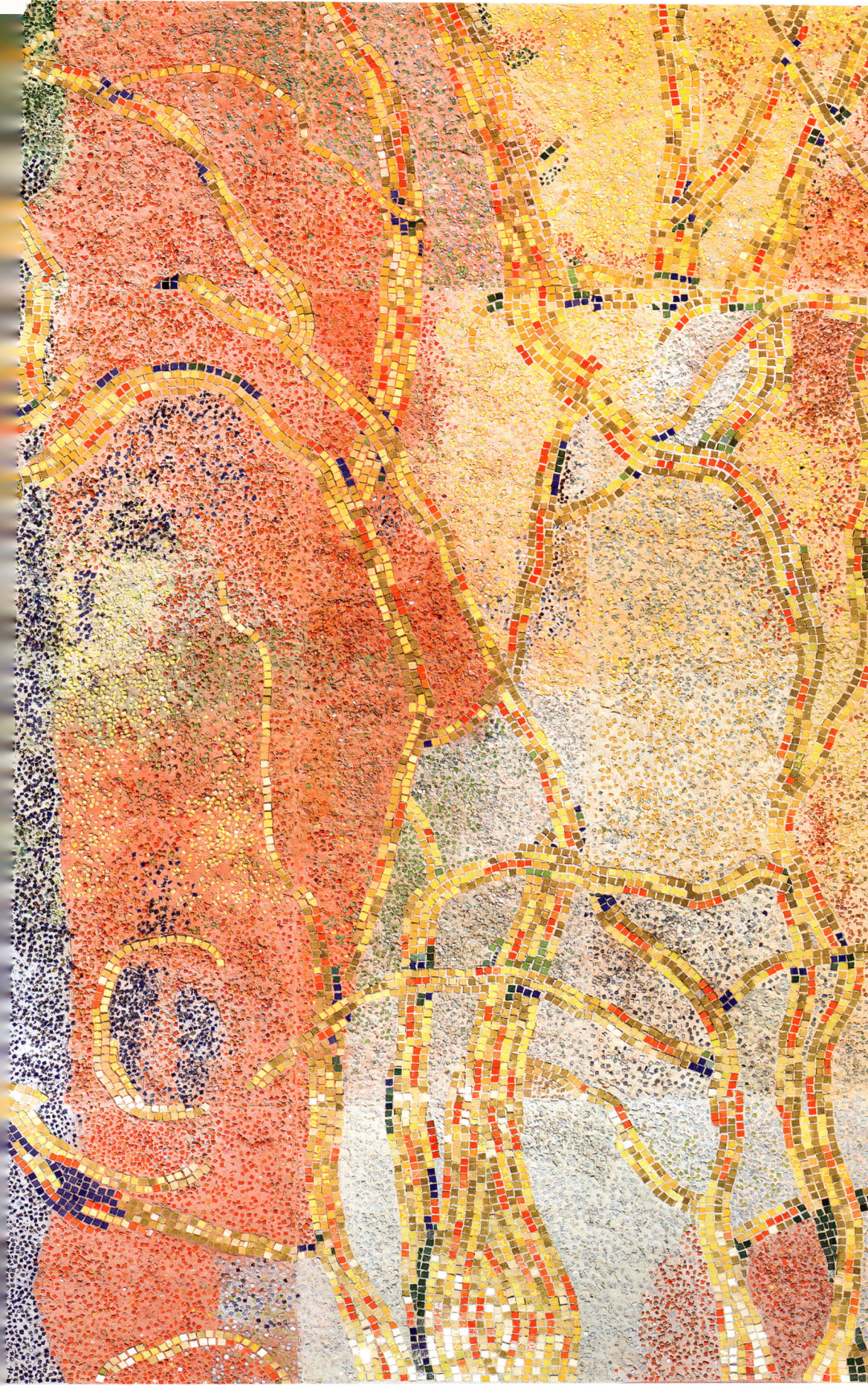

Jeanne Reynal
Tree Planting, 1966
13 x 19 feet
Venetian glass mosaic

Golden trees and branches
rise up in the foreground with
a varied, colorful background.
Tree Planting celebrates Arbor
Day and the significant role
trees play in the state. Arbor
Day, a national holiday that
celebrates and promotes the
planting of trees, originated
in the state in 1872. More
than one million trees were
planted on the first Arbor Day.

Francis John Miller
The Coming of the Railroad, 1966
13 x 19 feet
Venetian glass mosaic

This mural tells the story of the changes the railroad brought to the state, beginning with the first rails laid in Omaha in 1865. On the right sits a steam locomotive engine, ready to cross the Great Plains. To the left stands a colorful group, including a sheriff, a gambler, and a gunslinger, who have settled in the towns springing up in the railroad's path. With the advancement of the railroad came the expansion and growth of the people on the plains.

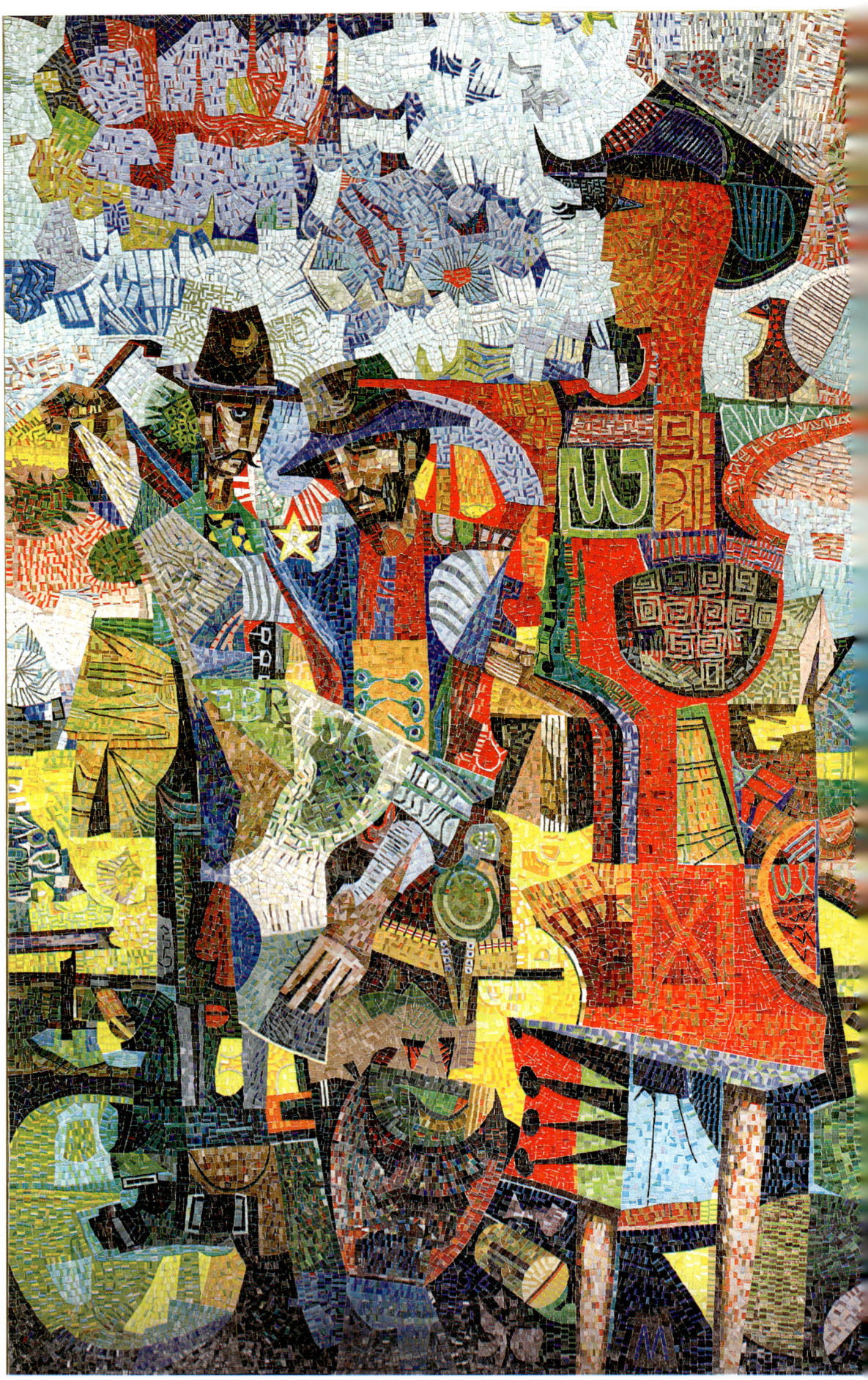

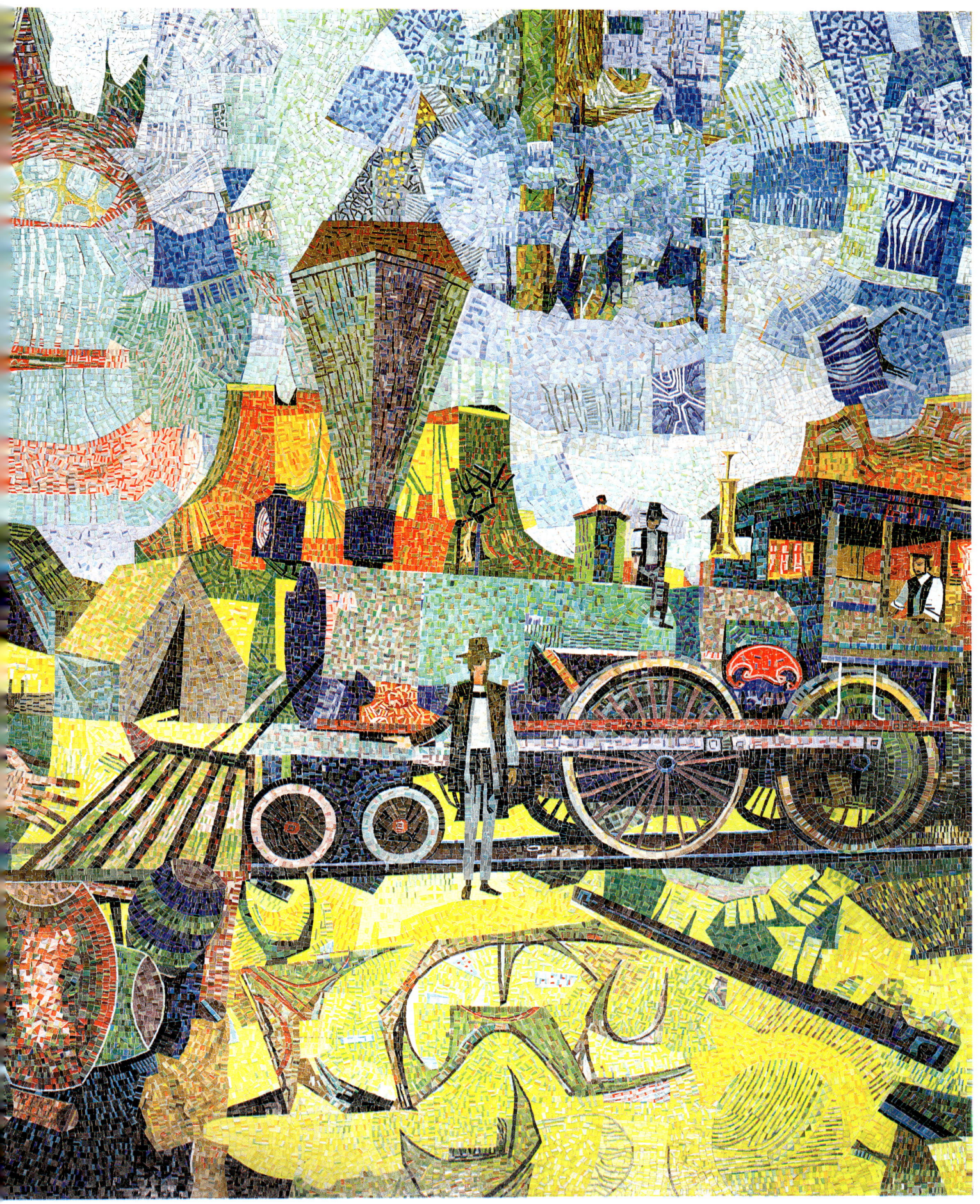

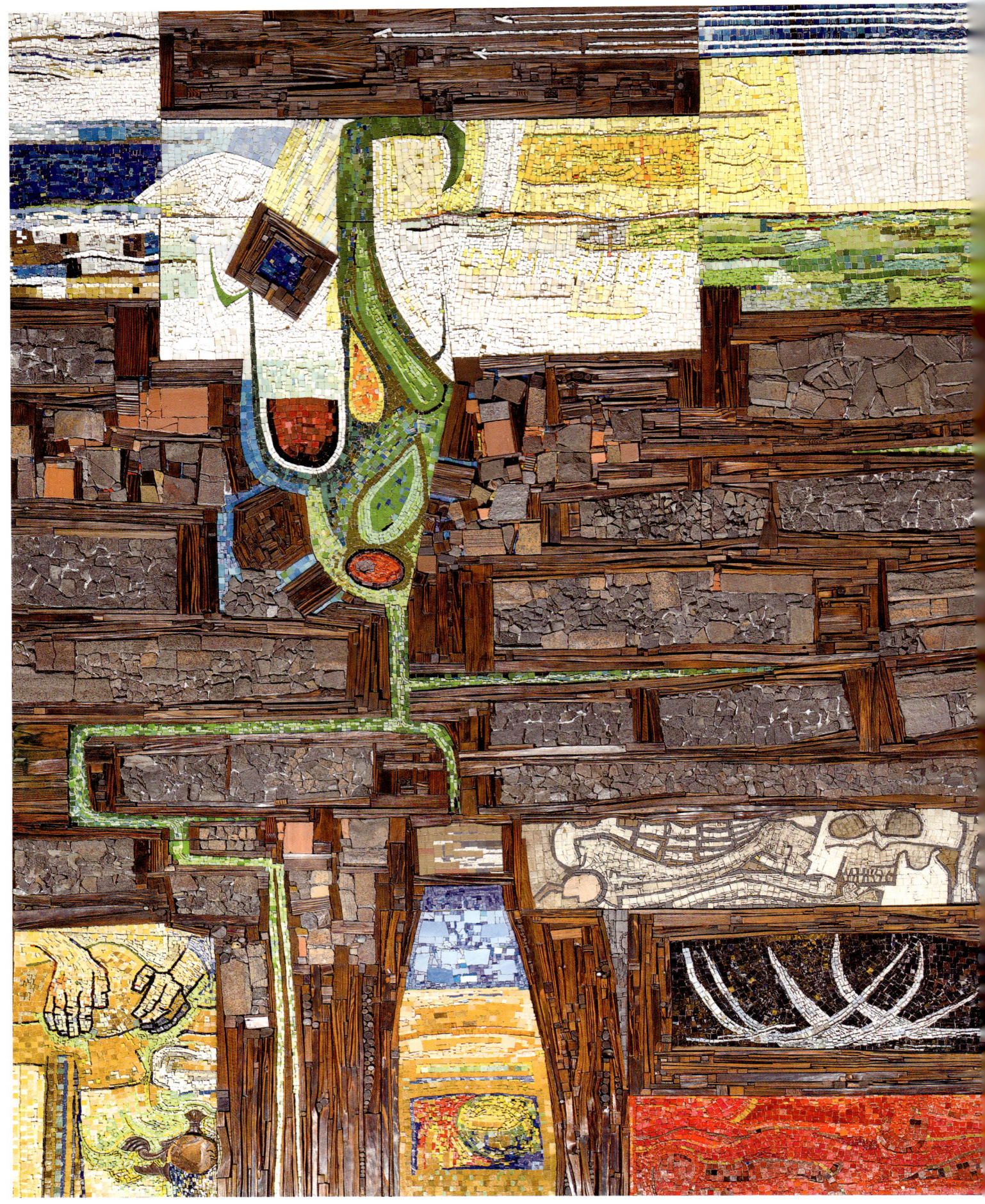

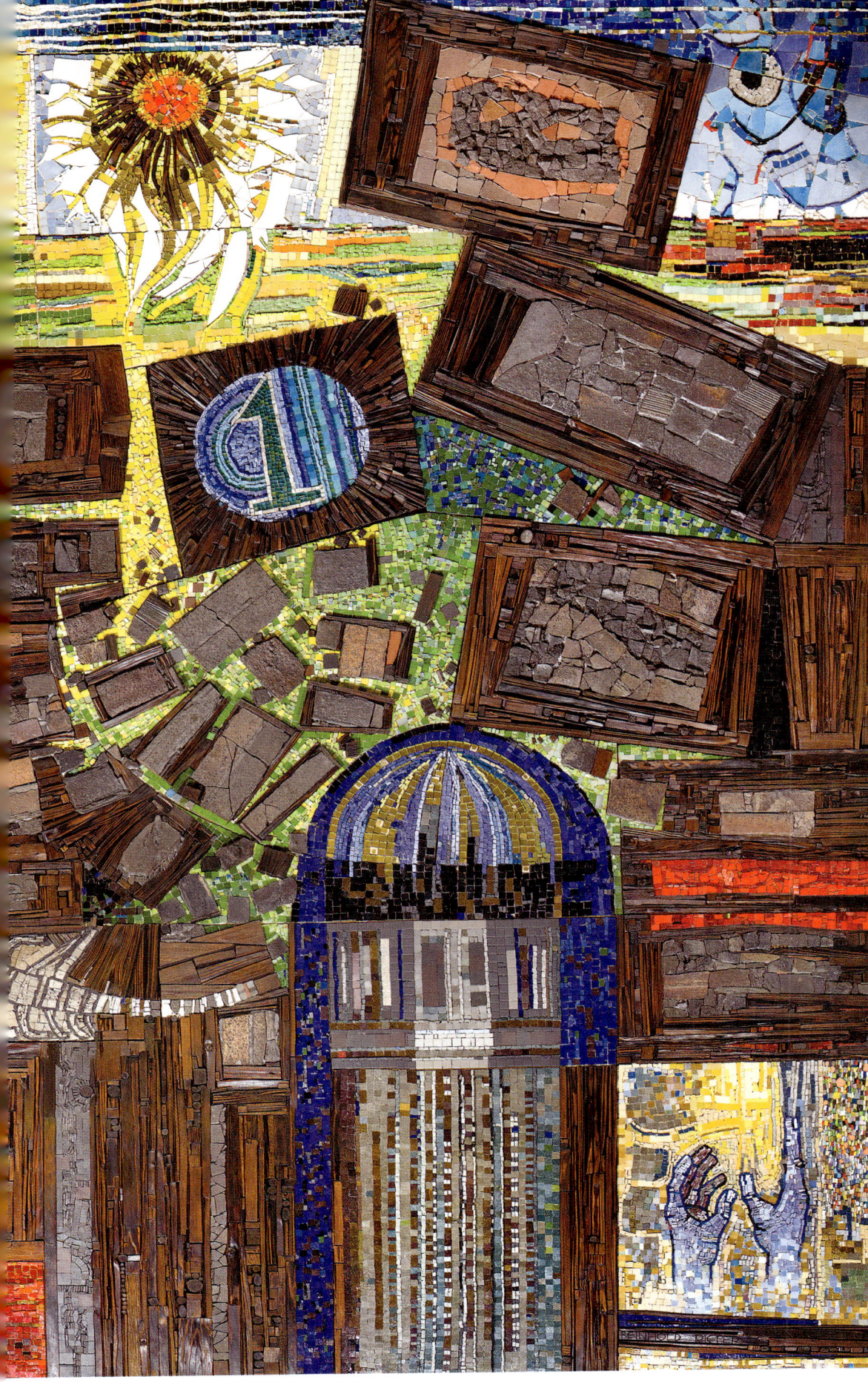

Reinhold Marxhausen
The Spirit of Nebraska, 1966
13 x 19 feet
Brick, wood, ceramic, and
Venetian glass mosaic

Marxhausen packed *The Spirit of Nebraska* with significant features of his beloved state. The lower left portion features blue, representing the Ogallala Aquifer, from which seeds sprout and plants grow above. Next to it are prehistoric fossils found in the state. The Capitol dome rises through the ground and the number "1" represents the Unicameral. Above the ground, various colors of the sky symbolize the four seasons.

Reinhold Marxhausen
The Building of the Capitol, 1966
13 x 19 feet
Brick, wood, ceramic, and
Venetian glass mosaic

Representing the construction of Nebraska's third and final capitol, the mural shows the new building being erected around the site of the second capitol without disturbing any of the existing state offices.

The capitol structure tells its own story. Goodhue believed in the power of using a building and its architectural form as a historic record and a means of symbolically proclaiming public truths. He used the architecture of the Capitol as a metaphor, with the lower square at the base representing the Earth and the historic course of human experience. The tower, with its upward sweep, symbolizes the Heavens and the abstract conceptions of life derived from experience. Together, they express the essence of all human life.

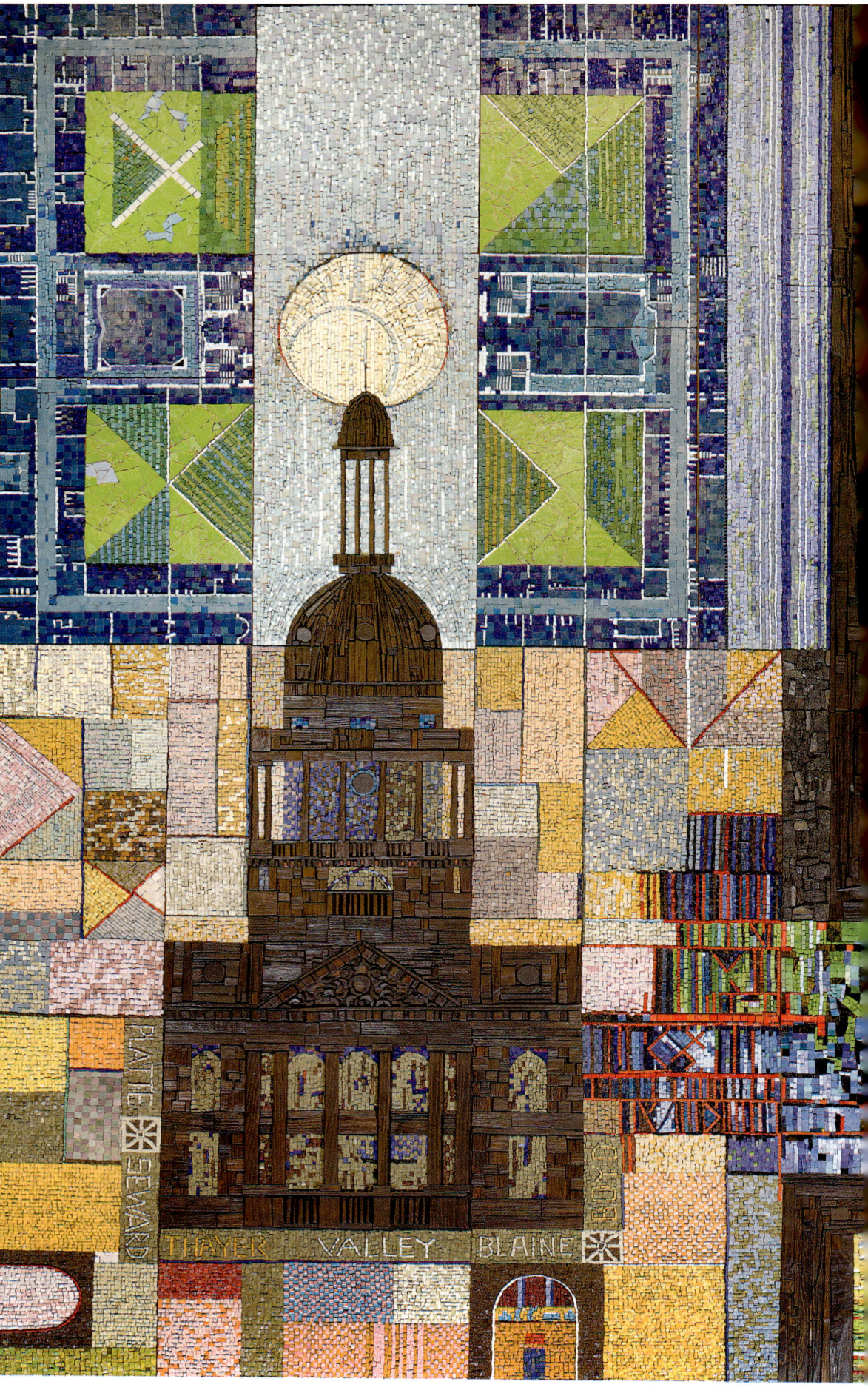

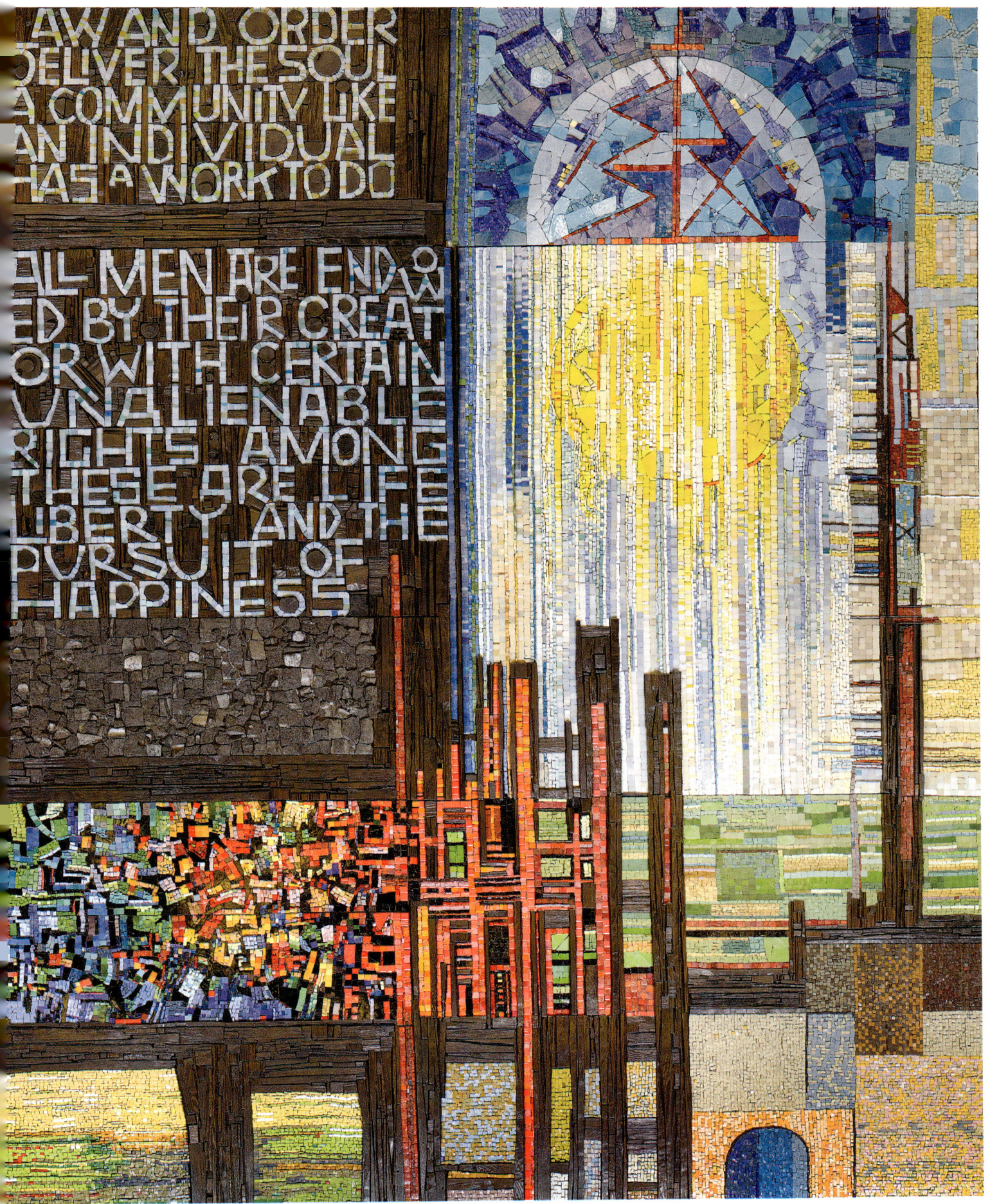

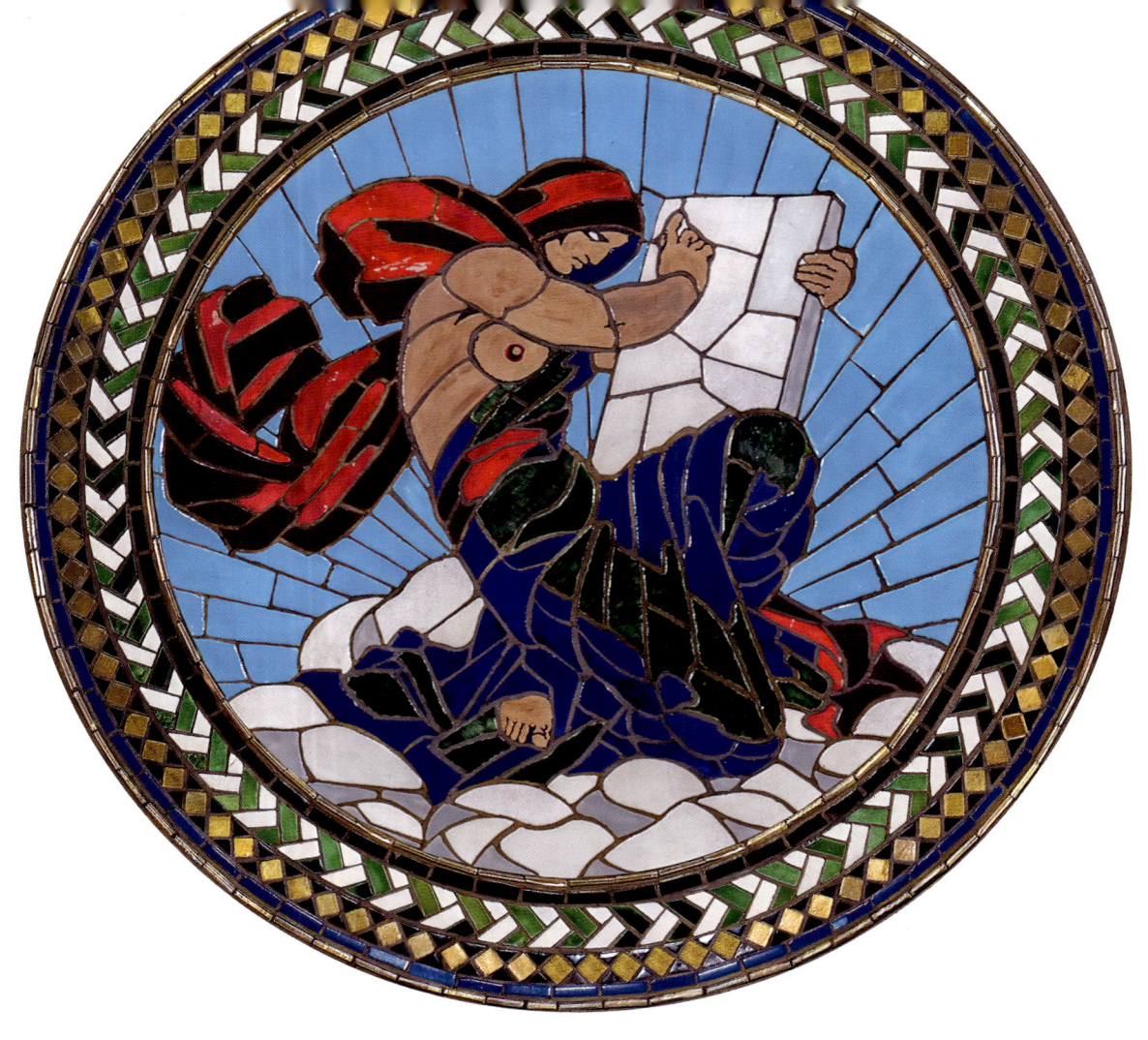

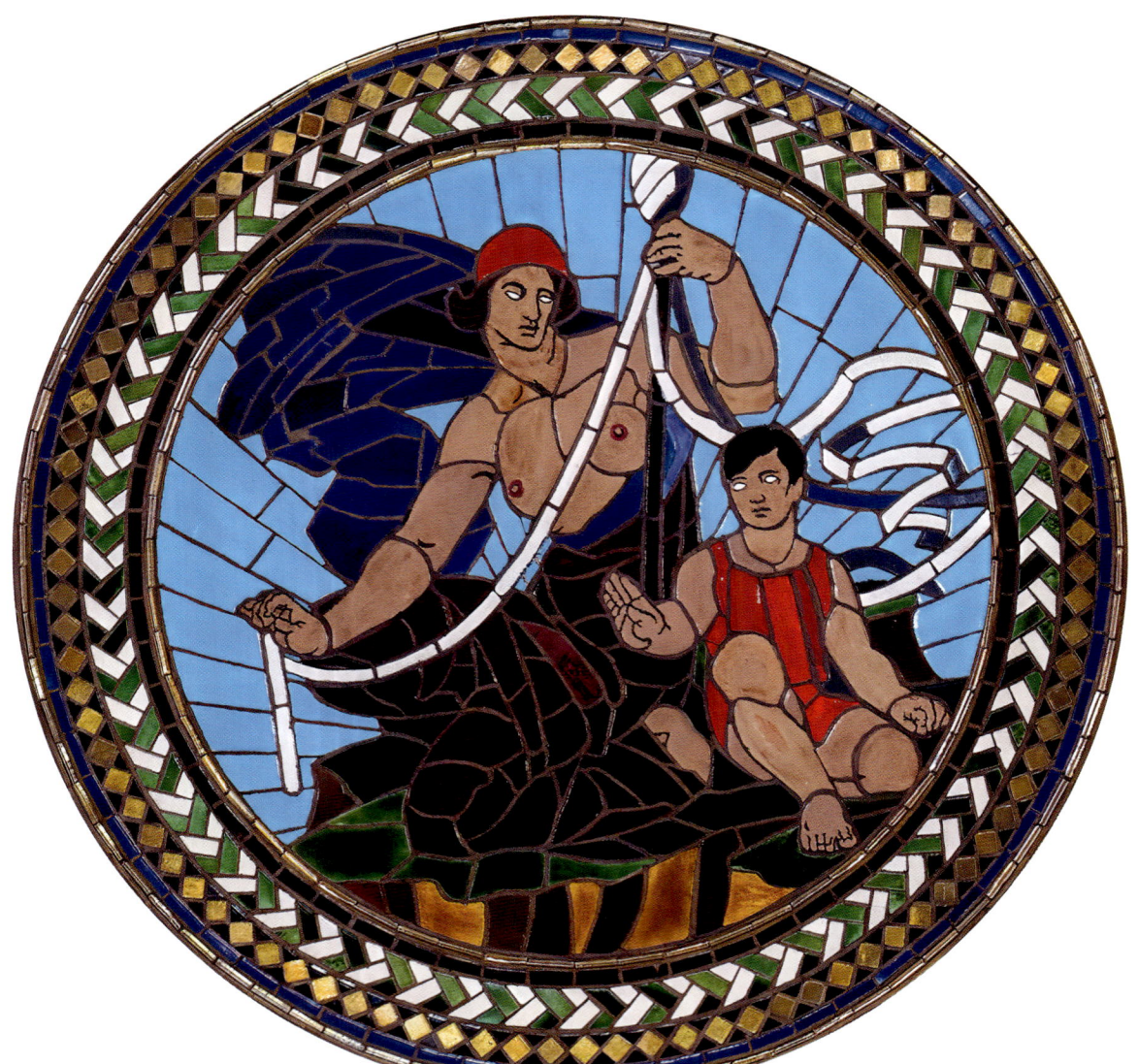

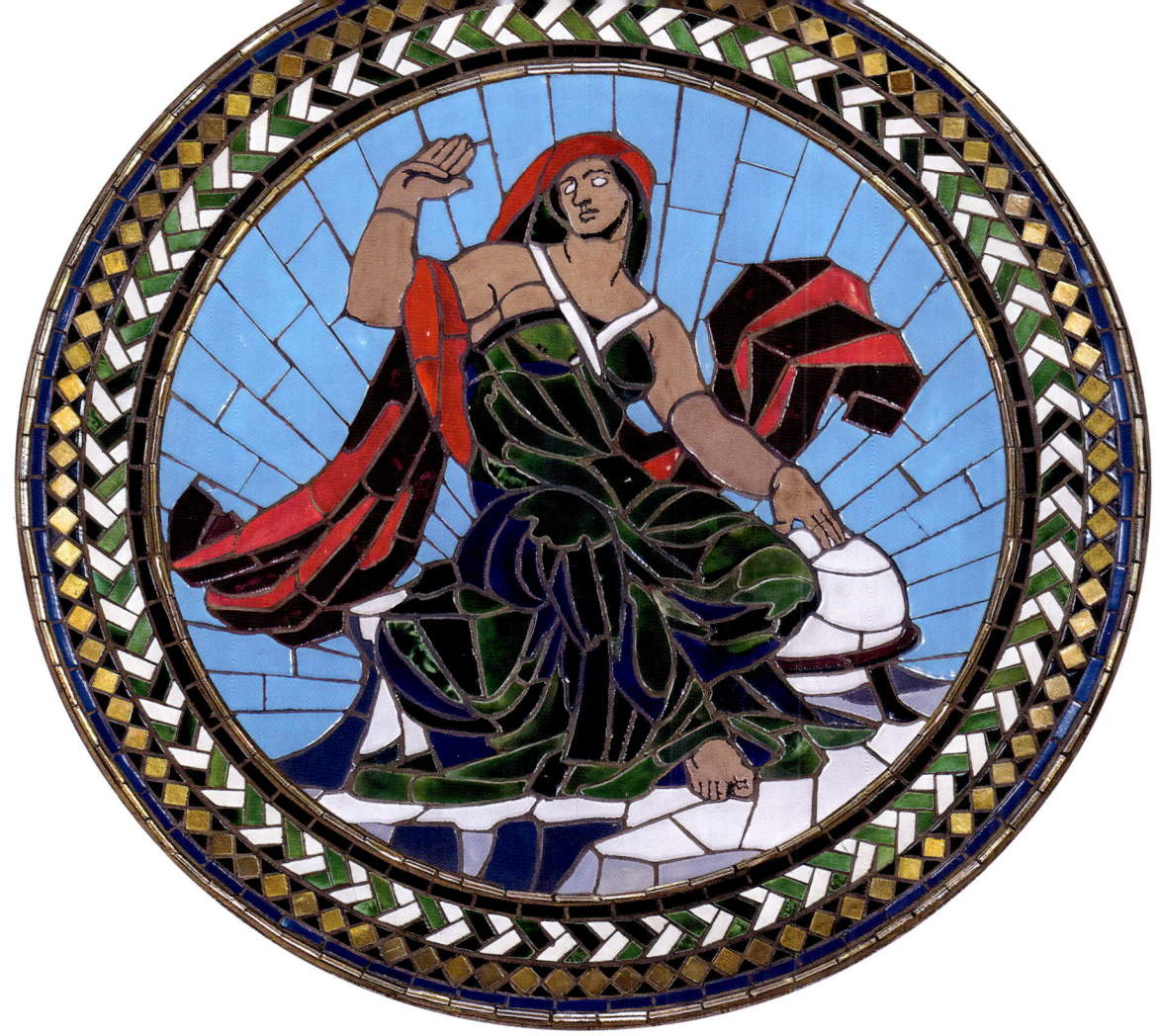

Hildreth Meière
Traditions of the Past, c.1930
approx. 8.5 x 8.5 feet
Glazed ceramic tile

Hildreth Meière
Life of the Present, c.1930
approx. 8.5 x 8.5 feet
Glazed ceramic tile

The entire foyer subdivides
structurally into three sections, each
representing the overarching motifs
of the overall space. *Traditions
of the Past* depicts the Recorder
holding a stone tablet documenting
ancient wisdom. *Life of the Present*
includes the Spinner who weaves the
fabric of time. *Ideals of the Future*
shows the Foreseer who looks
expectantly forward into the future.

Hildreth Meière
Ideals of the Future, c.1930
approx. 8.5 x 8.5 feet
Glazed ceramic tile

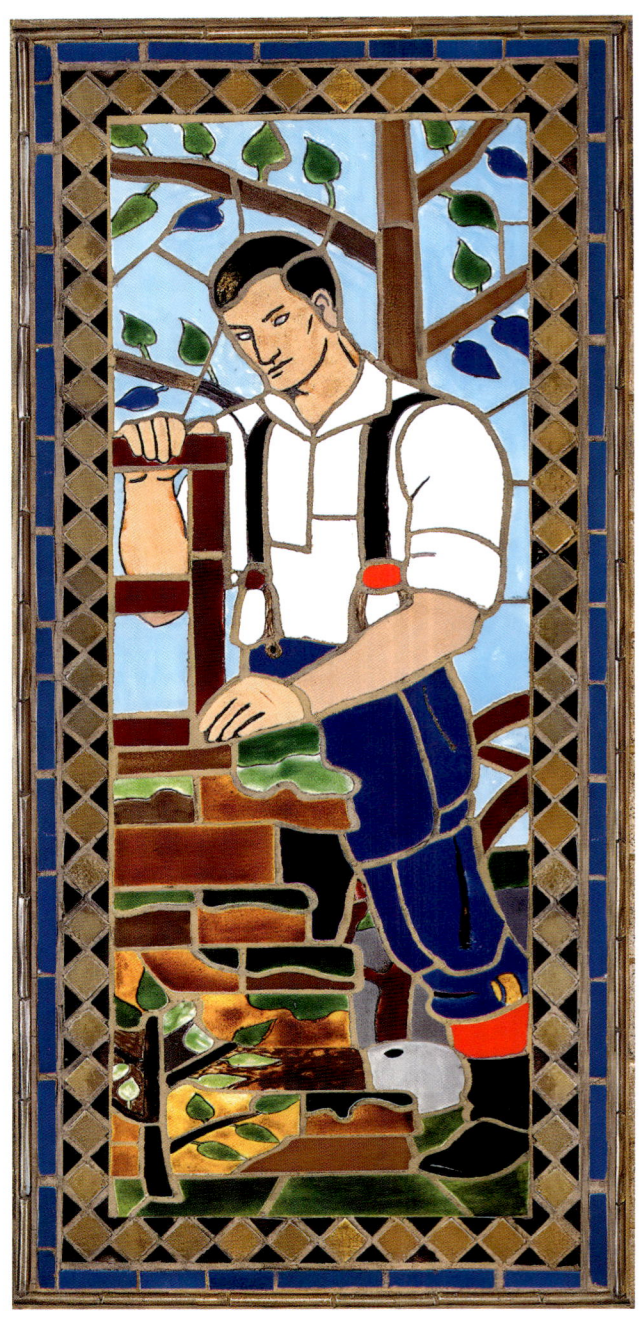

Hildreth Meière
The Homebuilder, c.1930
approx. 9.5 x 3.5 feet
Glazed ceramic tile

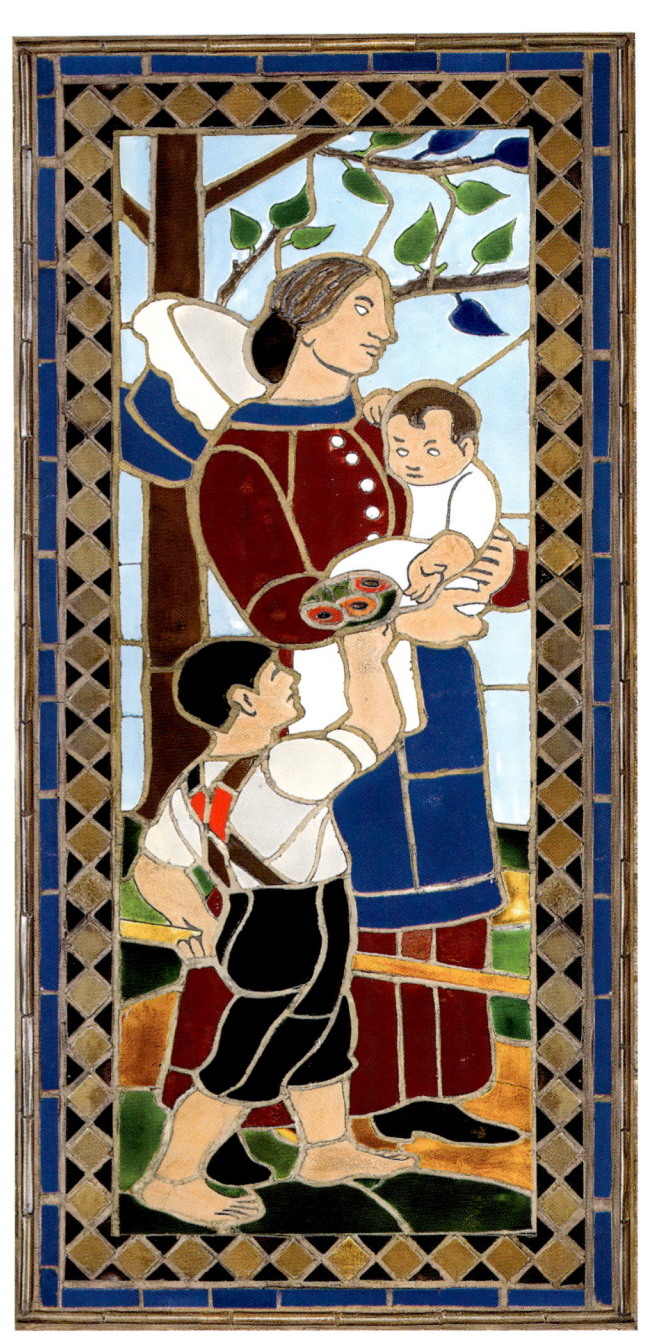

Hildreth Meière
The Pioneer Mother, c.1930
approx. 9.5 x 3.5 feet
Glazed ceramic tile

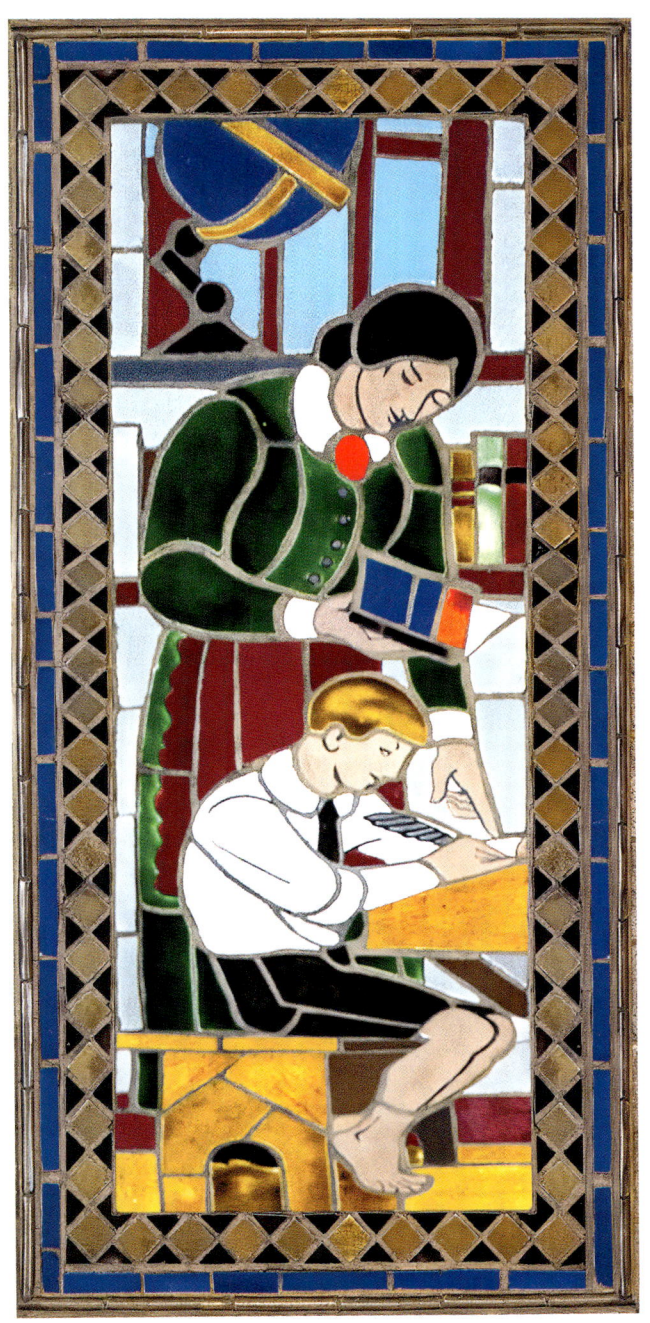

Hildreth Meière
The Teacher, c.1930
approx. 9.5 x 3.5 feet
Glazed ceramic tile

Placed in the window arches of the foyer, twelve panels
represent critical aspects of life in Nebraska, including
"family," "recreation," and "the sense of beauty."

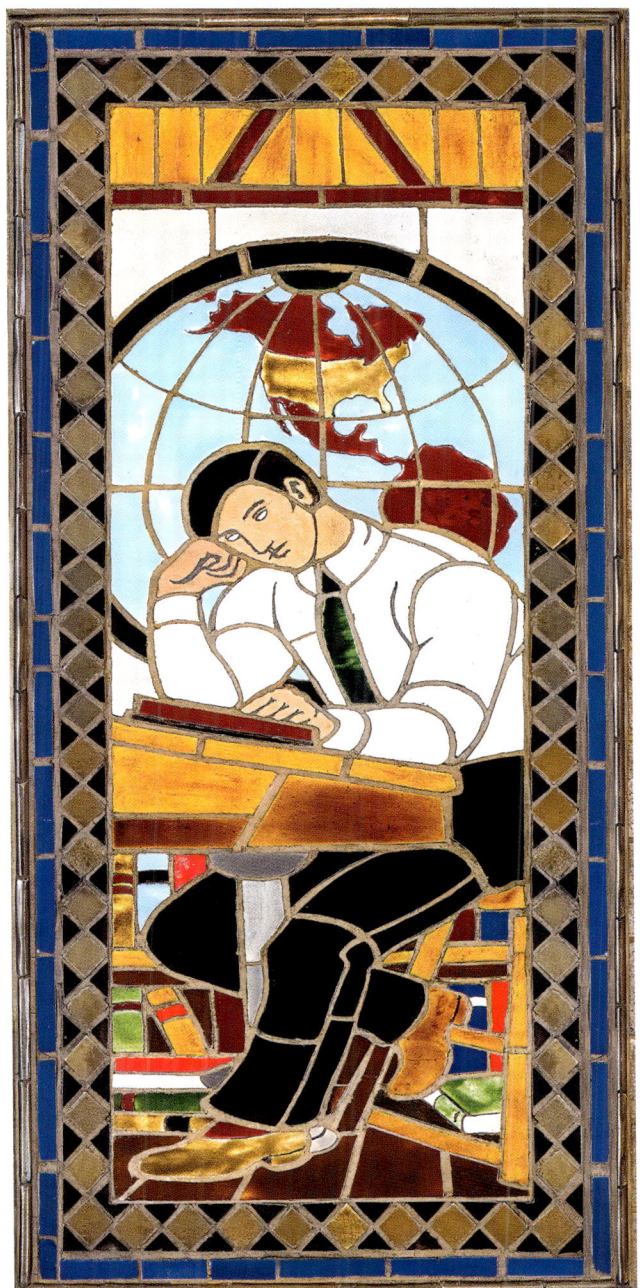

Hildreth Meière
The Pupil, c.1930
approx. 9.5 x 3.5 feet
Glazed ceramic tile

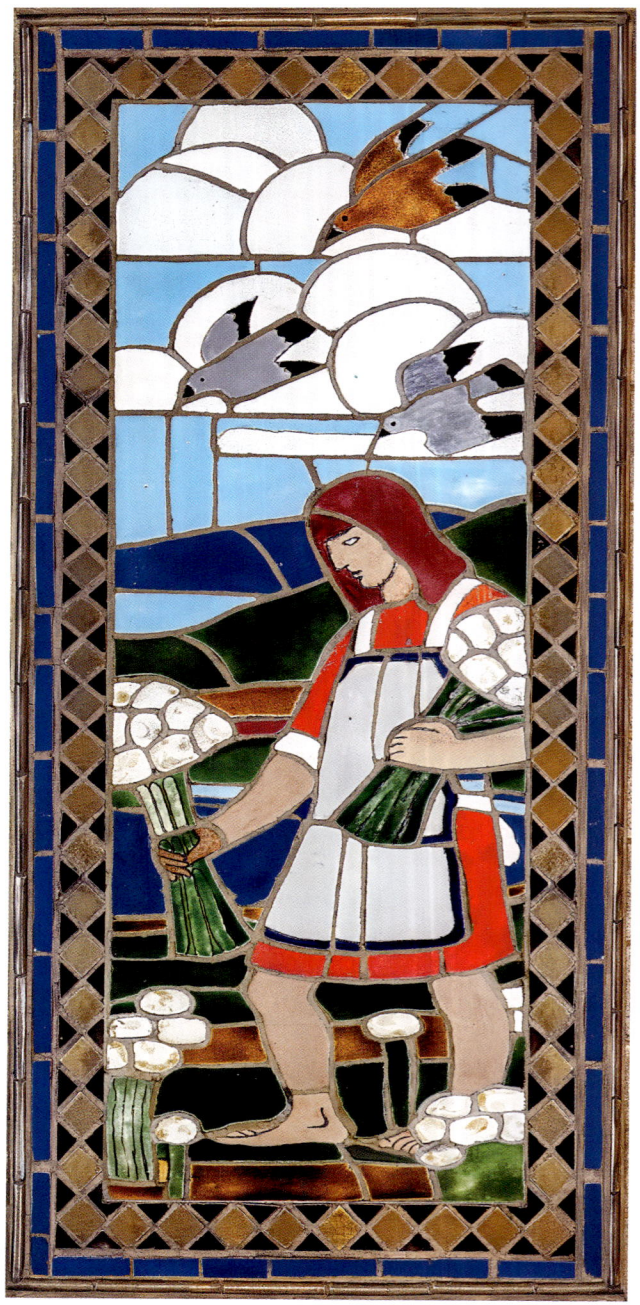

Hildreth Meière
The Flower Girl, c.1930
approx. 9.5 x 3.5 feet
Glazed ceramic tile

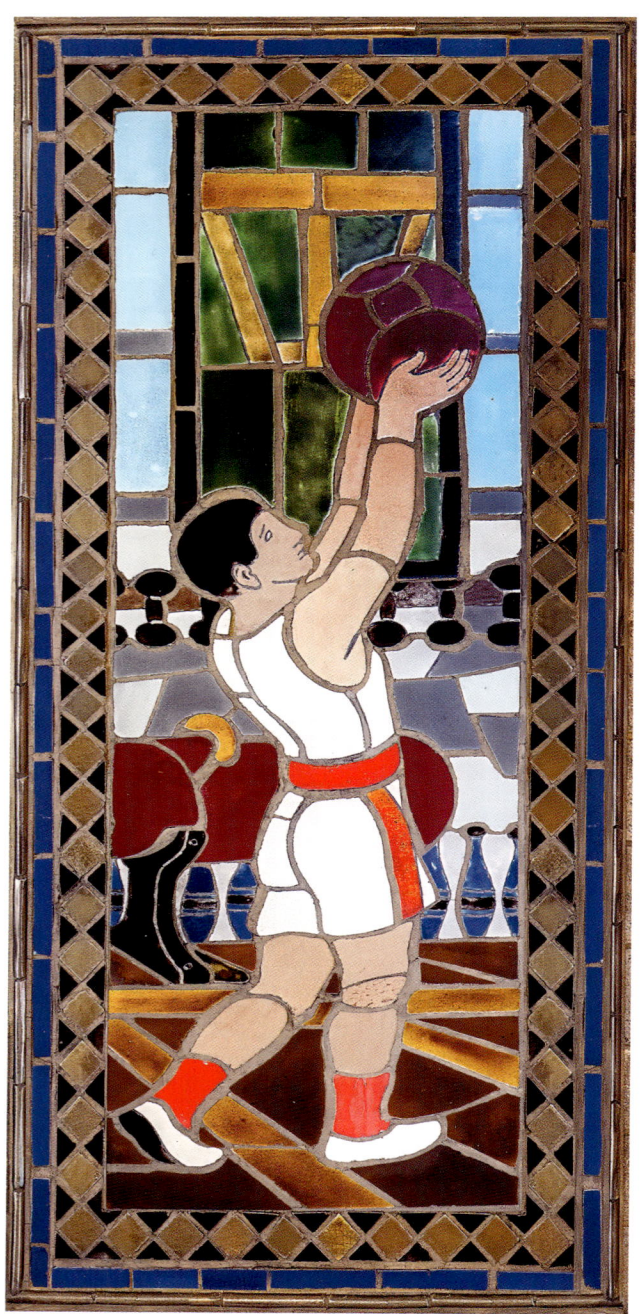

Hildreth Meière
The Ball Player, c.1930
approx. 9.5 x 3.5 feet
Glazed ceramic tile

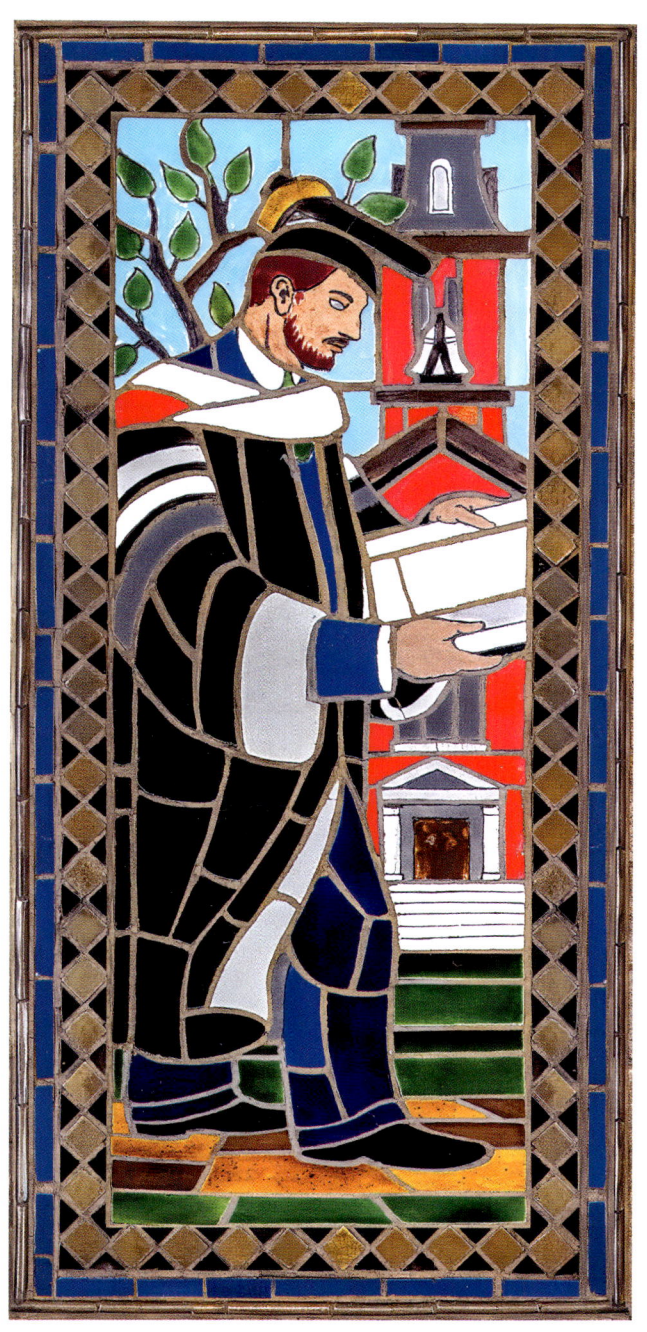

Hildreth Meière
The Scholar, c.1930
approx. 9.5 x 3.5 feet
Glazed ceramic tile

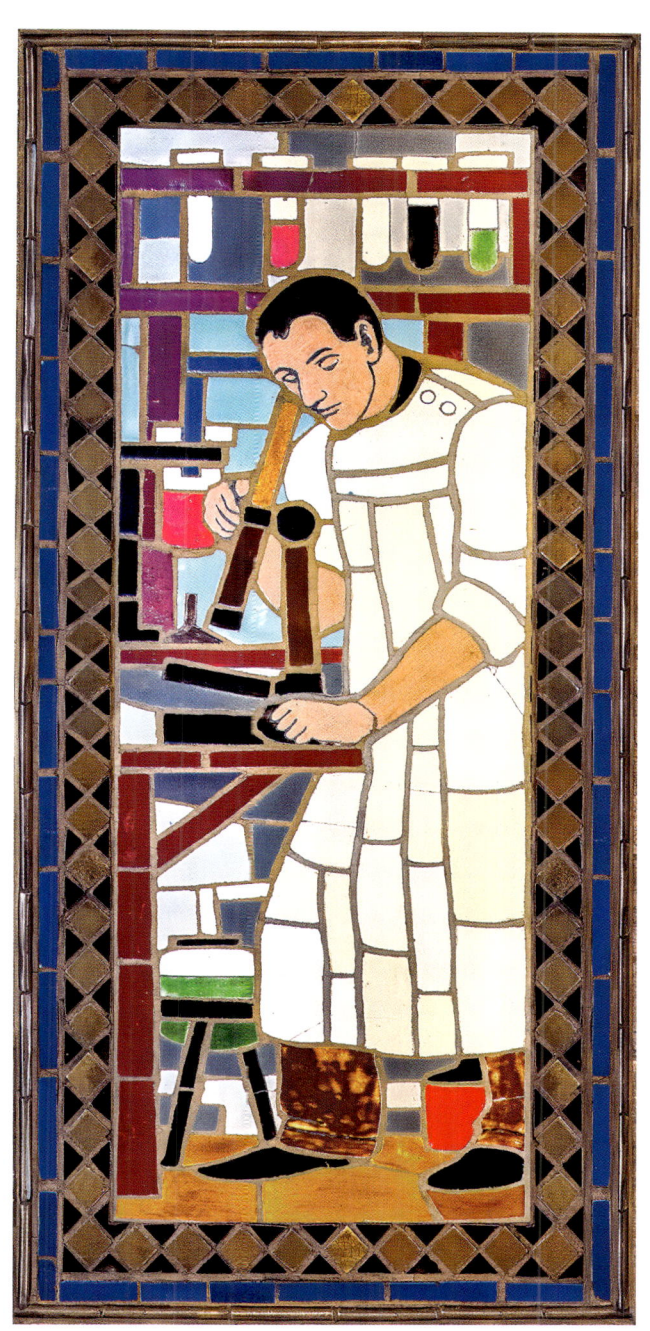

Hildreth Meière
The Scientist, c.1930
approx. 9.5 x 3.5 feet
Glazed ceramic tile

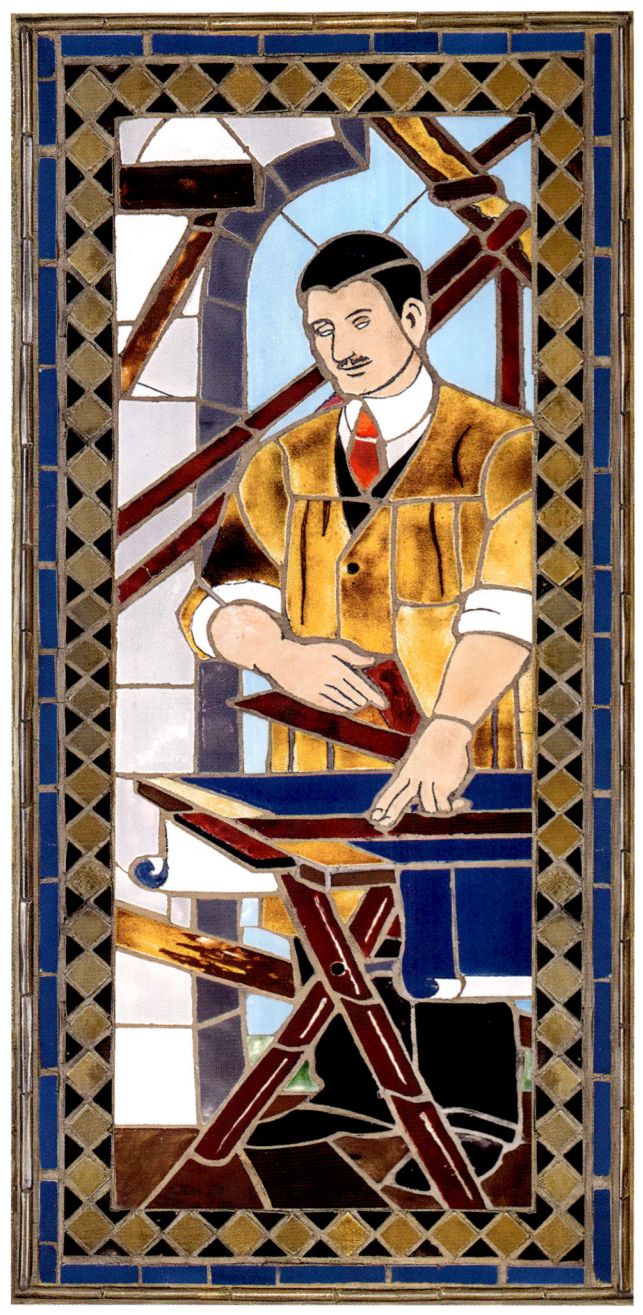

Hildreth Meière
The Architect, c.1930
approx. 9.5 x 3.5 feet
Glazed ceramic tile

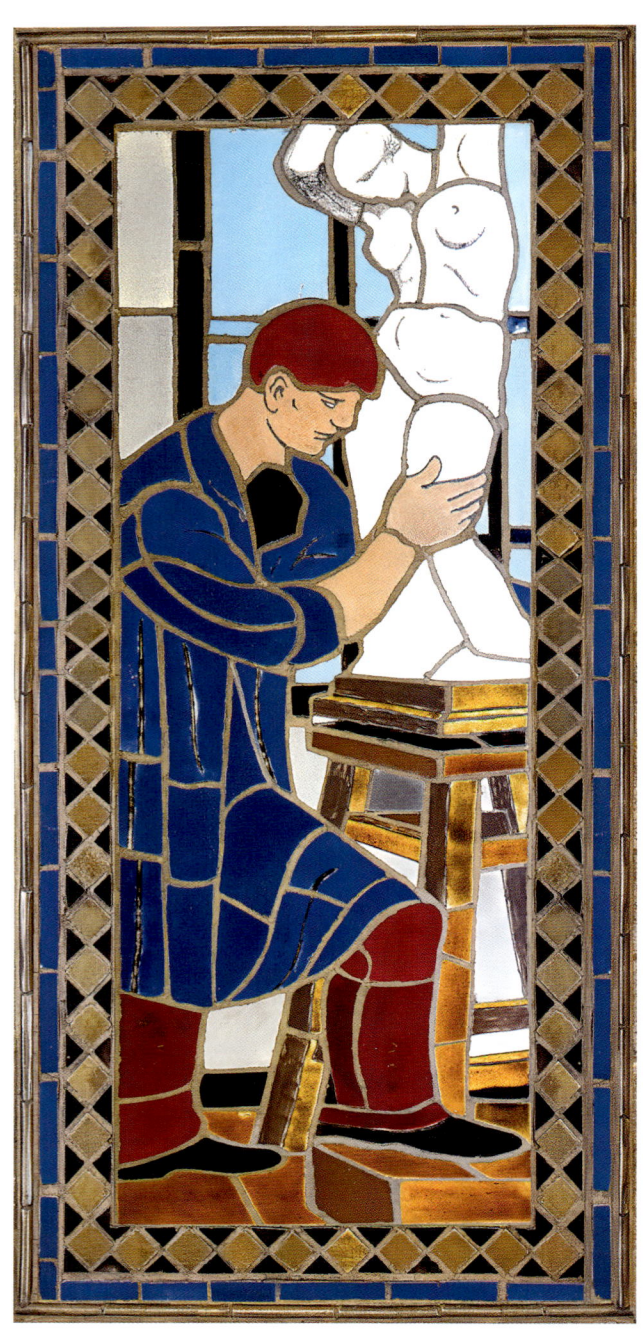

Hildreth Meière
The Artist, c.1930
approx. 9.5 x 3.5 feet
Glazed ceramic tile

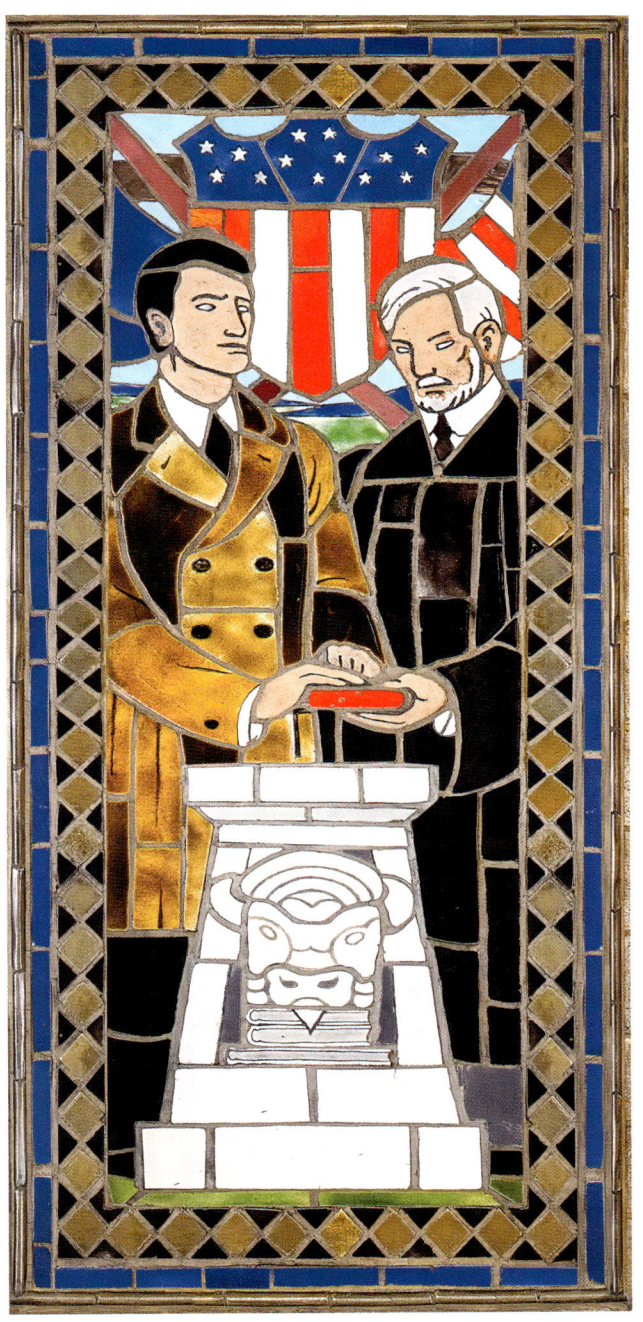

Hildreth Meière
The Statesman, c.1930
approx. 9.5 x 3.5 feet
Glazed ceramic tile

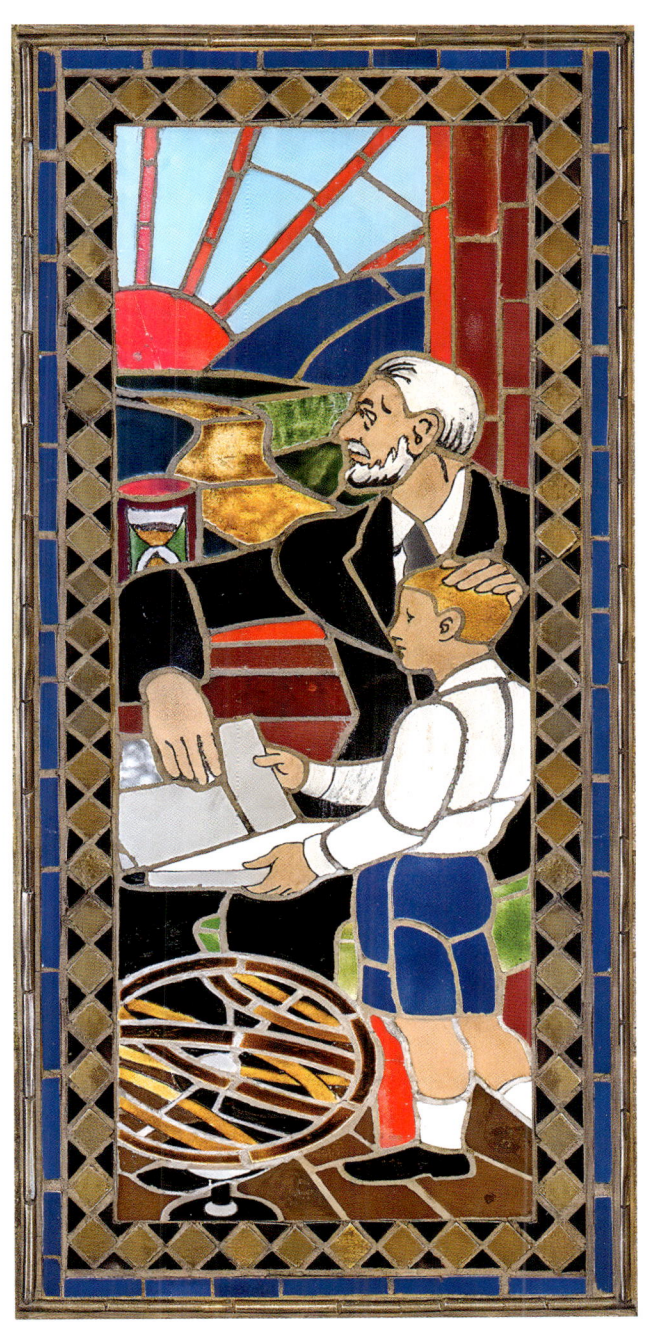

Hildreth Meière
The Philosopher, c.1930
approx. 9.5 x 3.5 feet
Glazed ceramic tile

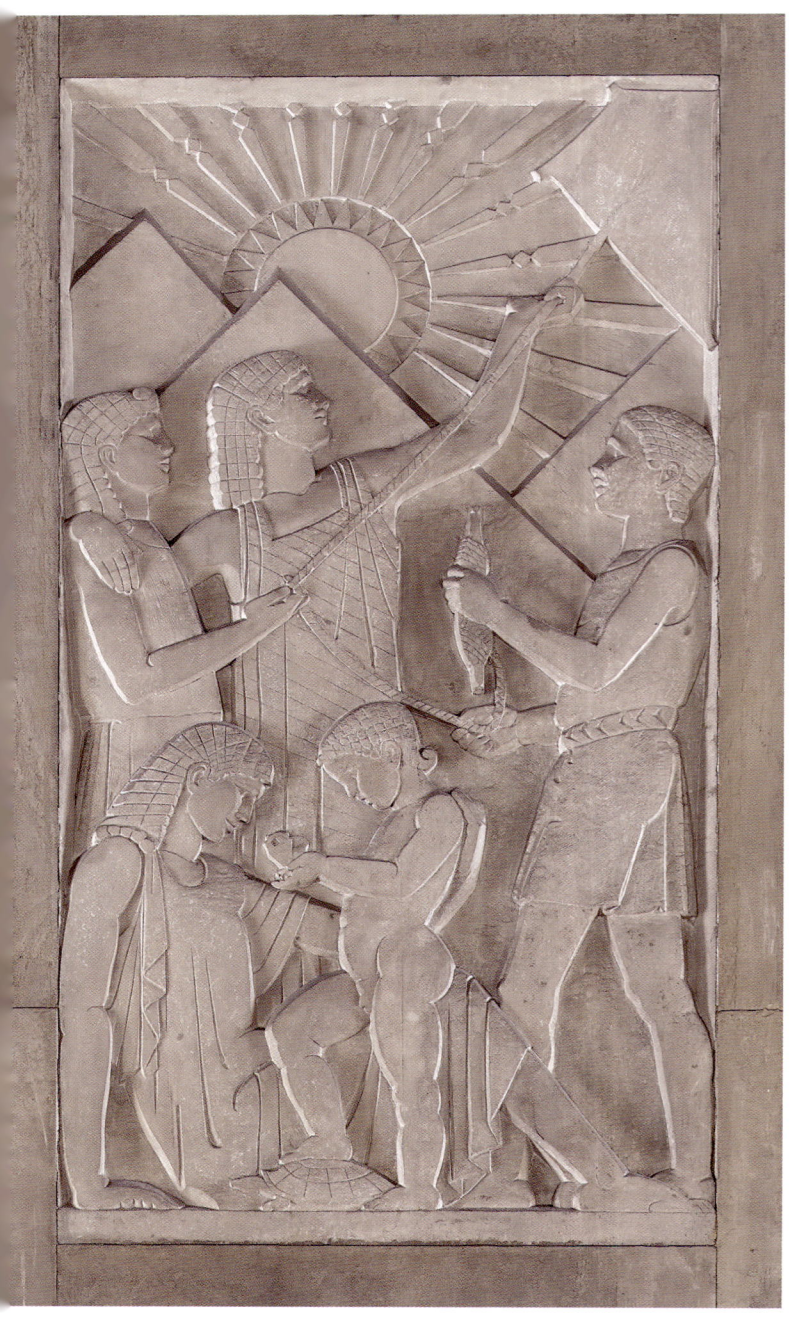

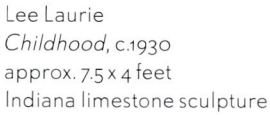

Lee Laurie
Childhood, c.1930
approx. 7.5 x 4 feet
Indiana limestone sculpture

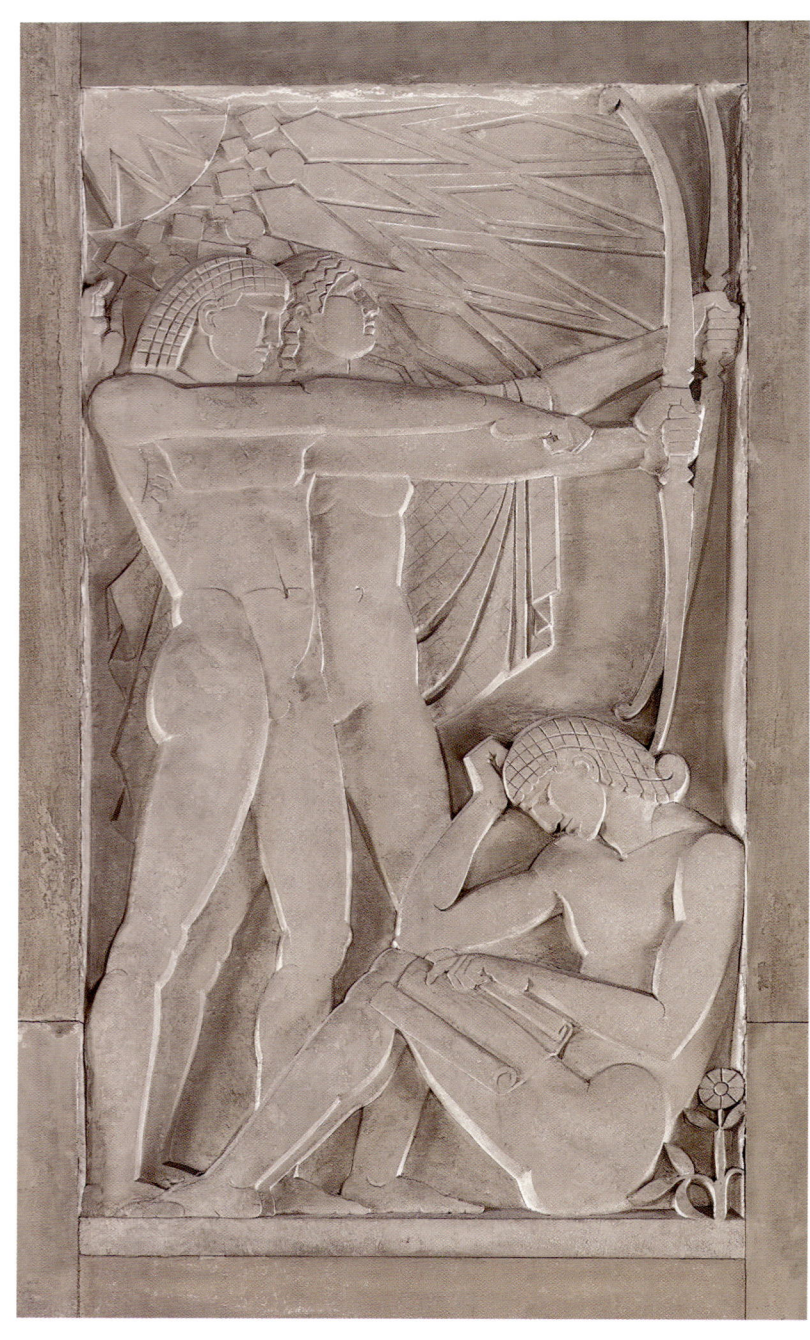

Lee Lawrie
Youth, c.1930
approx. 7.5 x 4 feet
Indiana limestone sculpture

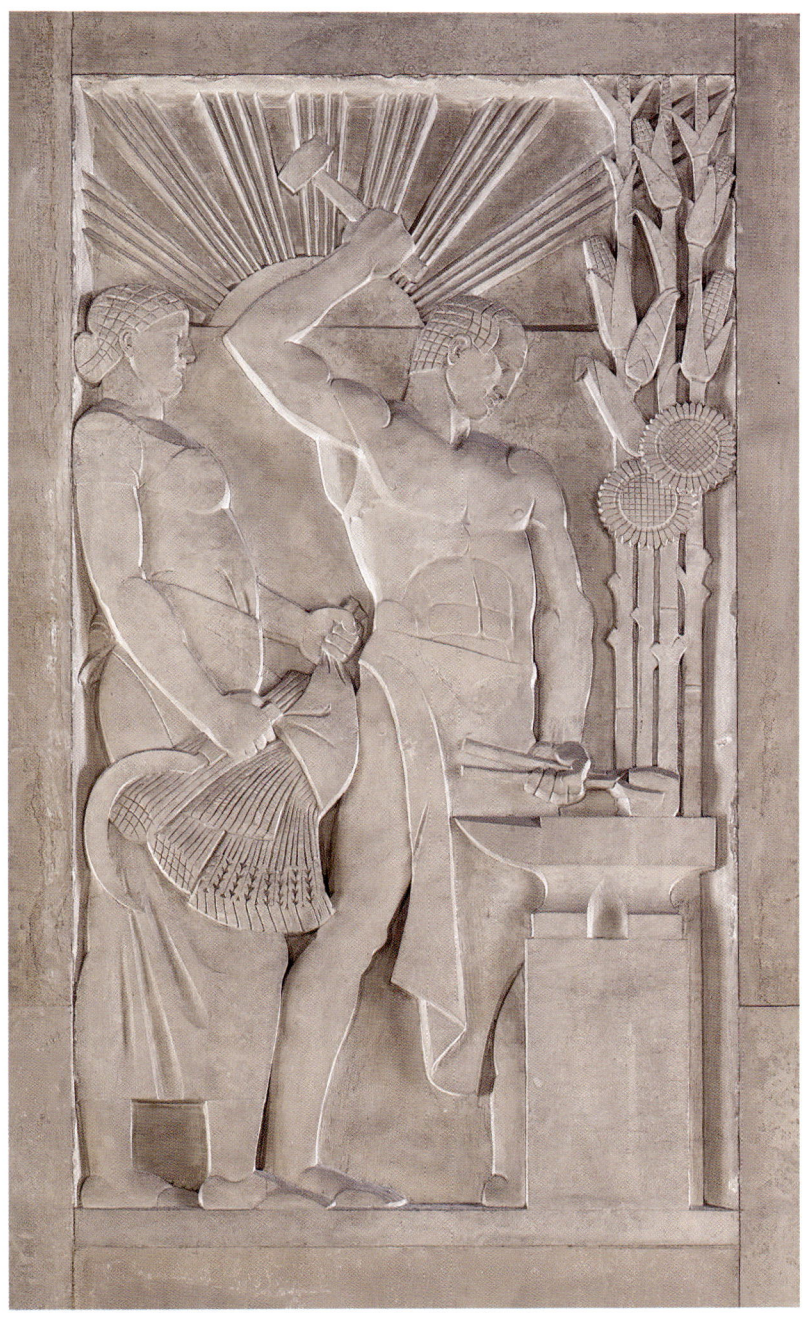

Lee Lawrie
Maturity, c.1930
approx. 7.5 x 4 feet
Indiana limestone sculpture

Four panels in bas-relief represent the phases of life.
Together they connect the several sections of the foyer to
symbolize the course of the "Life of Man." The entire section
builds to a unity representing the past and civilization; the
present with an emphasis on wisdom, work, and health;
and the future, with a cultivation of beauty and truth.

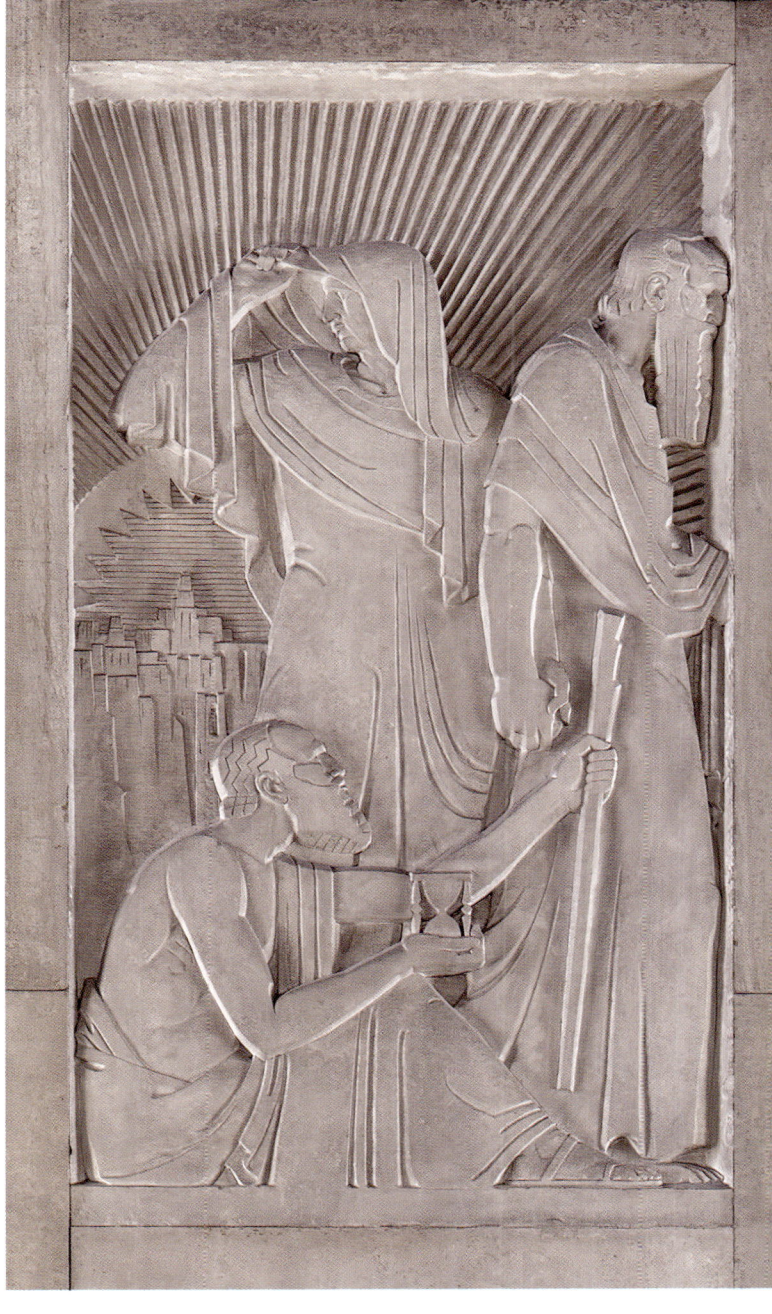

Lee Lawrie
Age, c.1930
approx. 7.5 x 4 feet
Indiana limestone sculpture

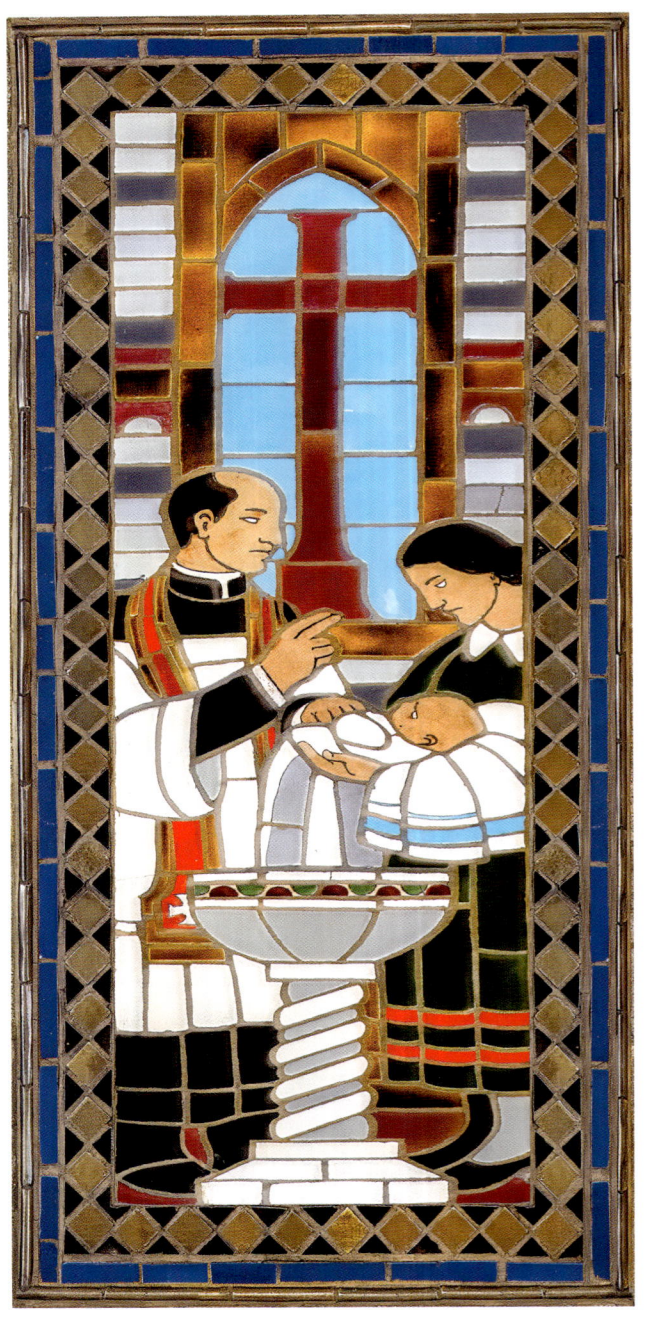

Hildreth Meière
Religion, c.1930
approx. 9.5 x 3.5 feet
Glazed ceramic tile

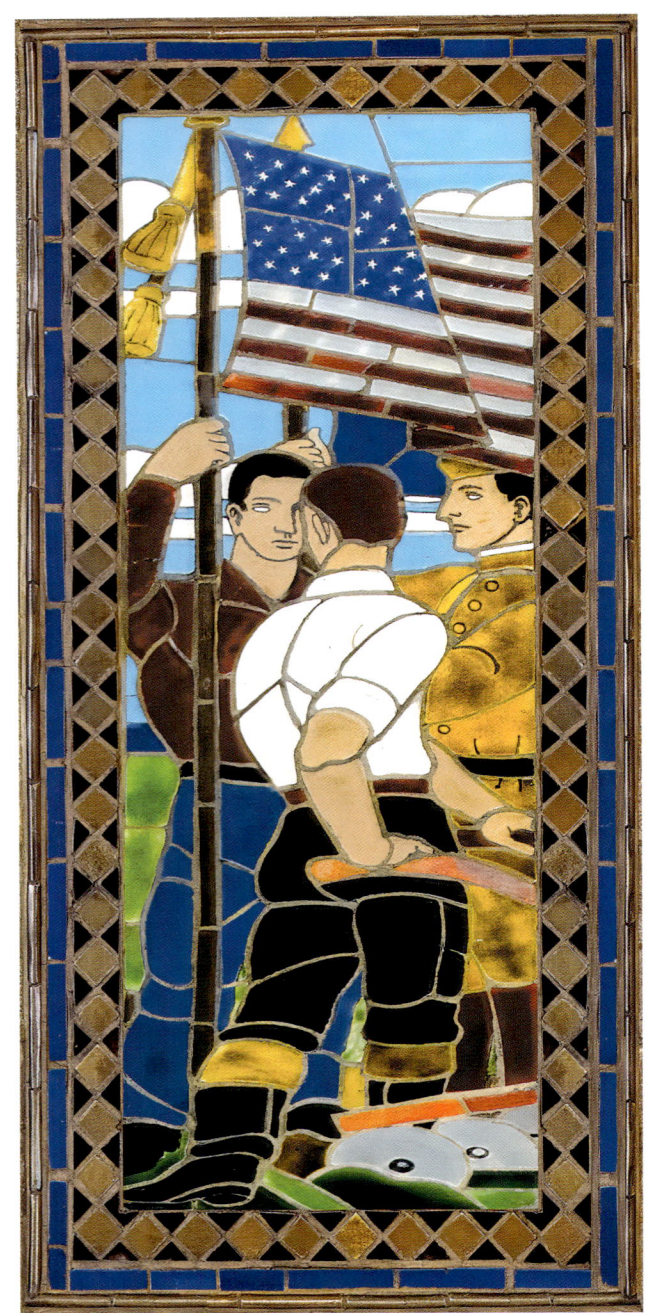

Hildreth Meière
Public Spirit, c.1930
approx. 9.5 x 3.5 feet
Glazed ceramic tile

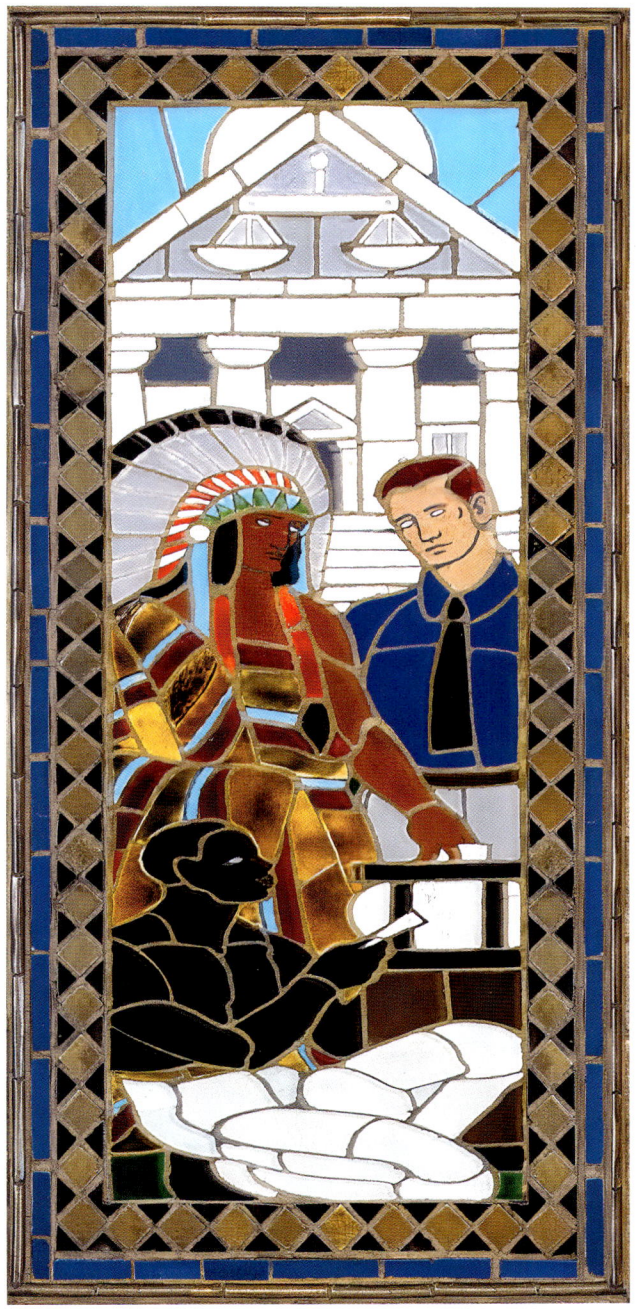

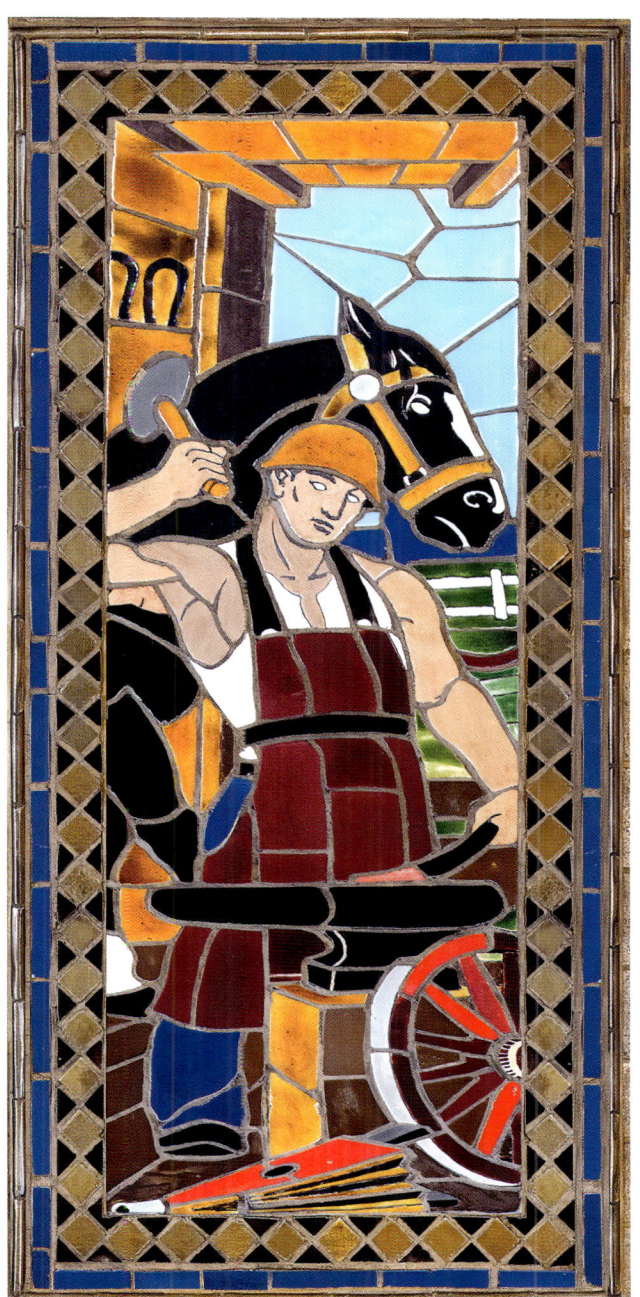

Hildreth Meière
Law, c.1930
approx. 9.5 x 3.5 feet
Glazed ceramic tile

Hildreth Meière
Labor, c.1930
approx. 9.5 x 3.5 feet
Glazed ceramic tile

Four ceiling panels devote themselves to the great activities of society and the central bonds of human life. *Labor* is represented by the Farrier. *Law* shows men of three races casting ballots. In *Public Spirit*, a citizen answers the call to the service of the state. And *Religion* is represented by a baptism.

ROTUNDA

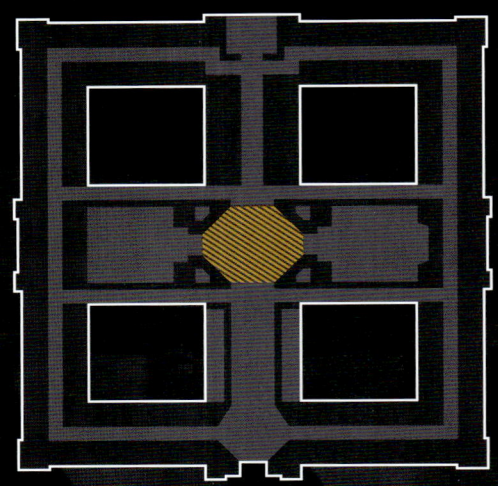

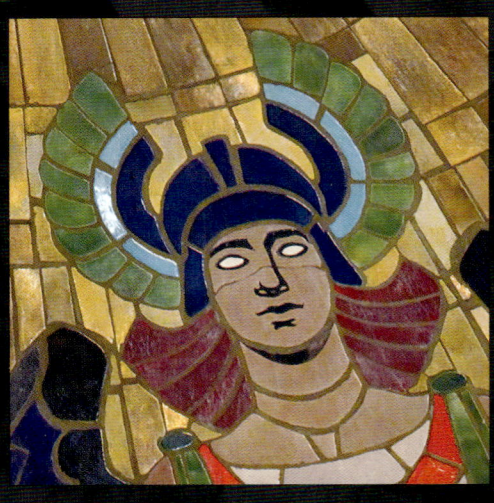

KENNETH EVETT

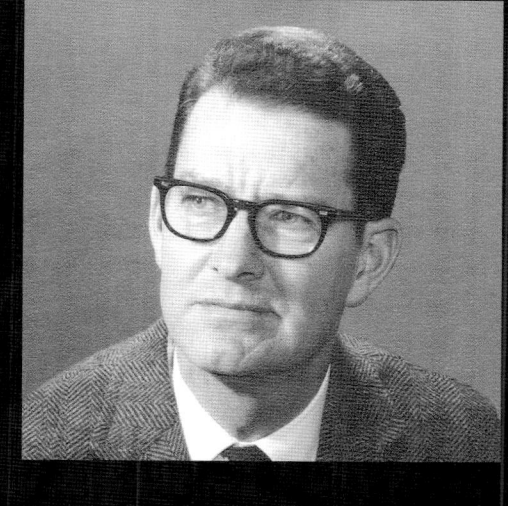

Goodhue always planned for murals in multiple areas of the Capitol. However, the commissioning and installation for some, including the three slated for the rotunda, were delayed by the Great Depression. That finally changed in 1956, when Kenneth Evett installed his three "Labors" murals.

Born in Colorado in 1913 and educated at the Fine Arts Center in Colorado Springs, he won several commissions from the Works Progress Administration's Federal Section of Fine Arts, part of the employment and infrastructure program created during the bleakest days of the Depression. Those included six murals in post offices in Colorado, Kansas, and Nebraska.

He spent many years relocating and teaching, trying to make a living through his painting. In 1948, a fortunate opportunity came his way. The New York art dealer he was meeting with received a call from the chairman of the Fine Arts Department at Cornell, who was looking for a painter to fill in for a semester. Evett's 31-year career teaching art at Cornell University began.

His recognition as a gifted artist also began. He showed his paintings at the Whitney Museum of American Art, the Metropolitan Museum of Art, and the Corcoran Museum of Art in Washington DC.

In 1954, Evett won the nationwide juried competition to paint three murals for the Nebraska Capitol. His artistic style naturally differed from those who had worked on the building decades earlier, given the amount of time that passed since the Capitol's construction; but his motif aligned with Goodhue's vision and Alexander's theme. At the time, the murals were both praised and criticized. As reported in the *New York Times* after the unveiling, one state legislator mocked the murals, calling them "modern," and complained that the figures were too "square." Others strongly supported Evett's work, saying that the murals were appropriate for the decor and that they represent ideas, "not literal illustration."

Evett continued to create artwork until his death in 2005 at the age of 91. His works stood out due to his use of bold, vibrant colors and abstract forms. He wrote that the act of painting engaged him "in the age-old all-compelling pursuit of creative life — the effort to make it all come out right."

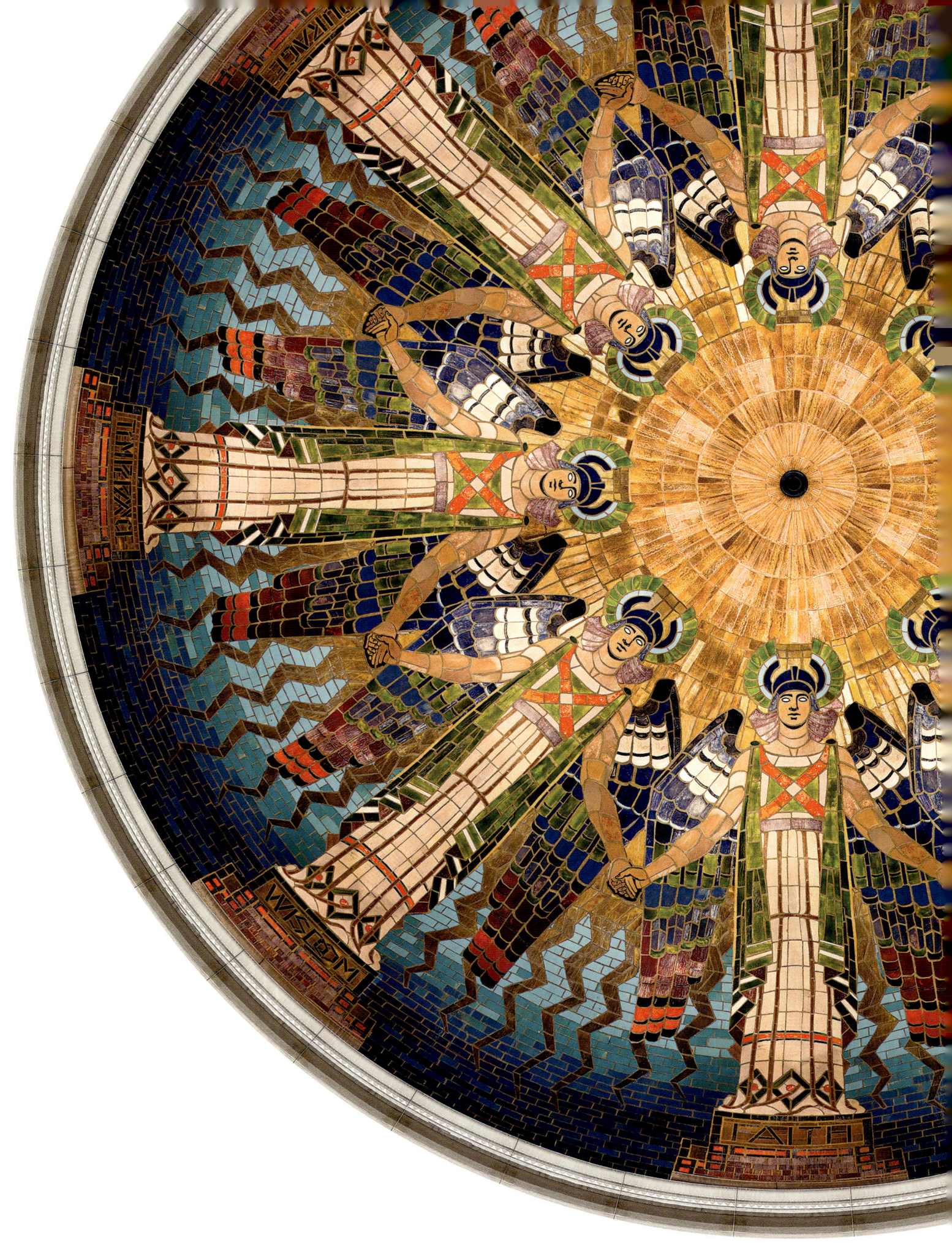

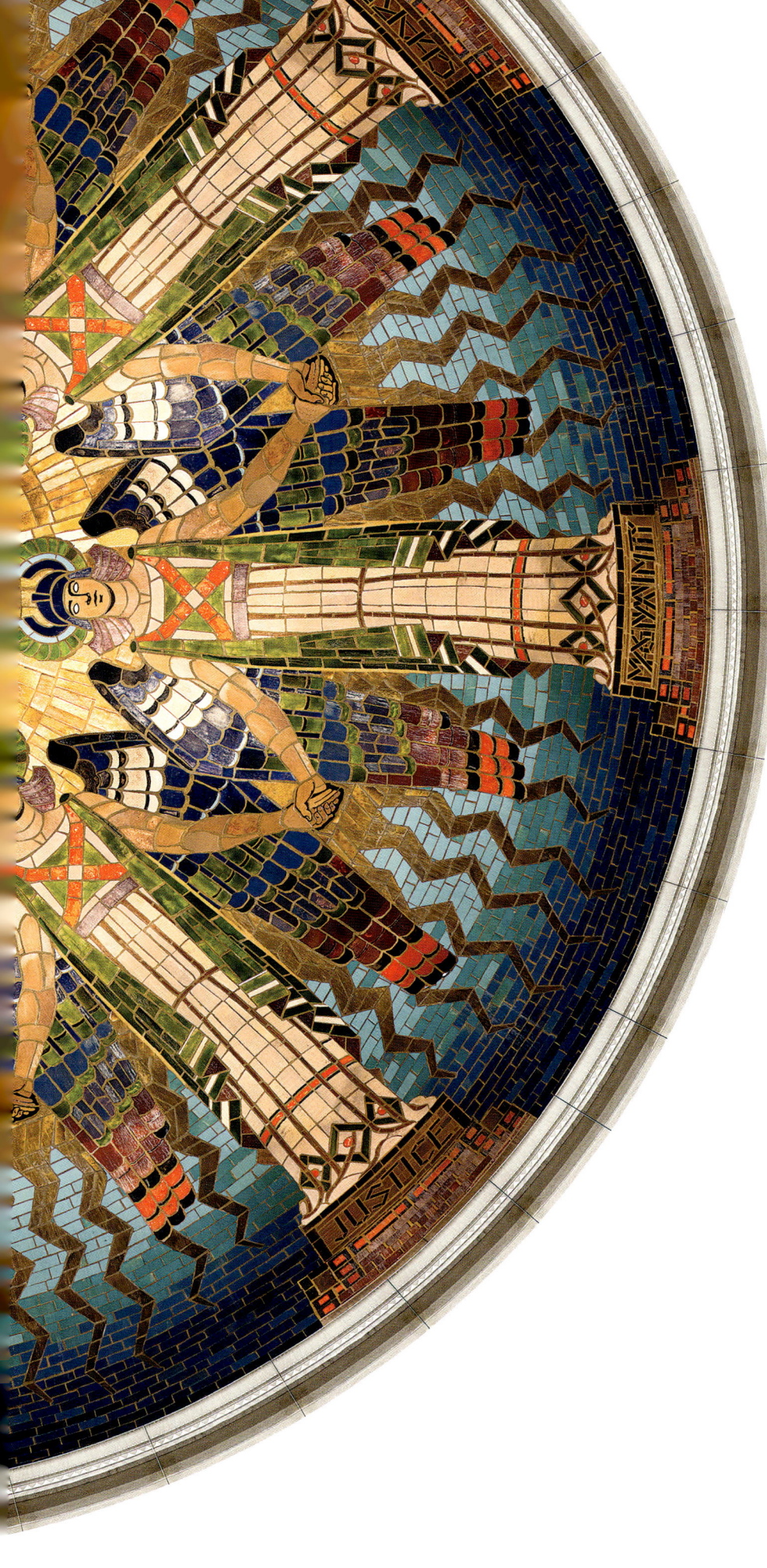

Hildreth Meière
The Virtues, 1928
approx. 38 x 38 feet
Glazed ceramic tile

Each section of the Capitol carries a
theme concerning imperative issues
for the success of the citizen. While
the vestibule focuses on the "Gifts of
Nature" and the foyer on the "Life of
Man," the message climaxes in the
rotunda, which centers on the "Virtues
of the State" and the ideals of society.

The eight winged entities in the rotunda
dome epitomize these ideals, forming
a celestial rose and representing
sacred and civic virtues. Charity, Hope,
Magnanimity, Faith, Justice, Wisdom,
Courage, and Temperance all stand
interconnected to evoke and inspire the
best in the leaders and citizens below.

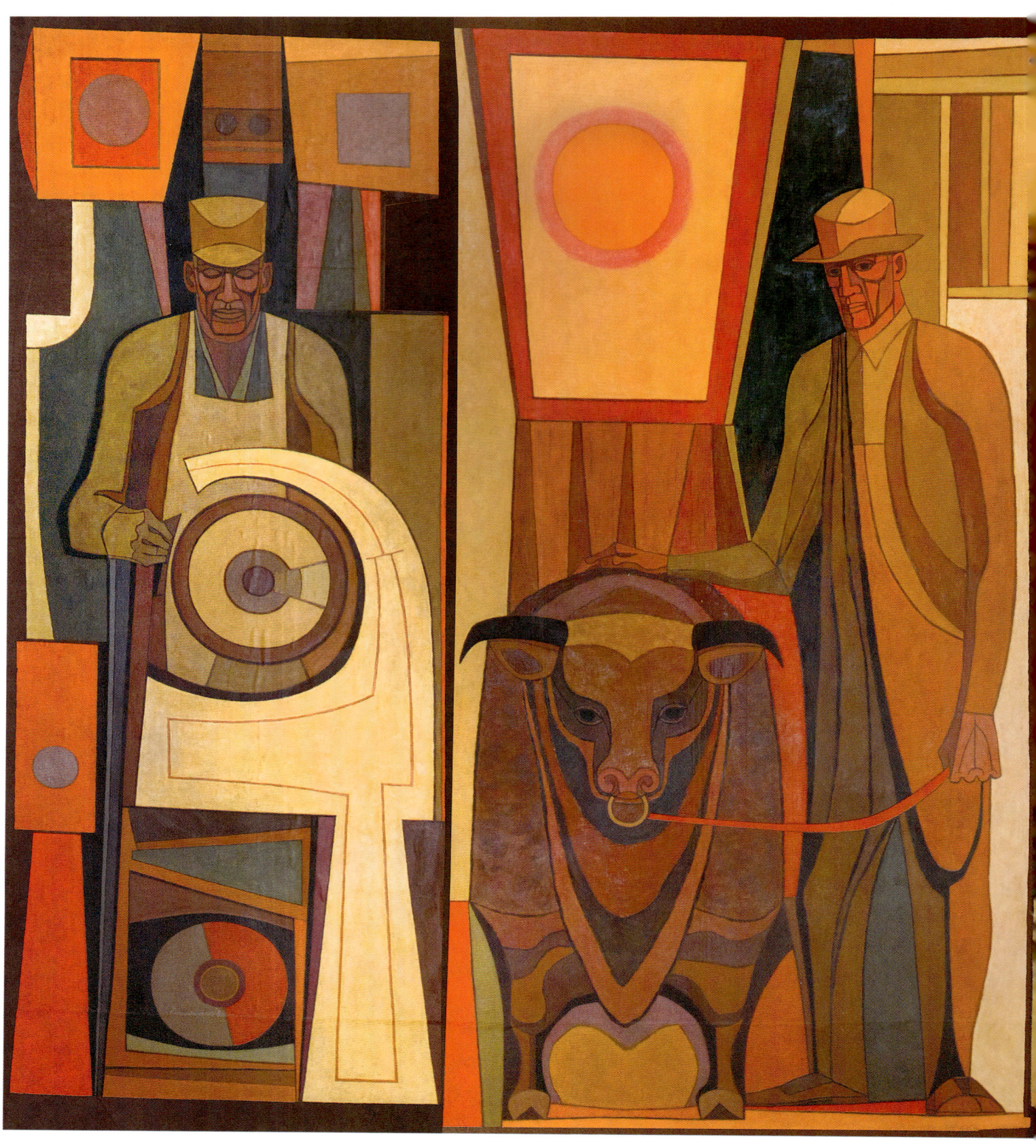

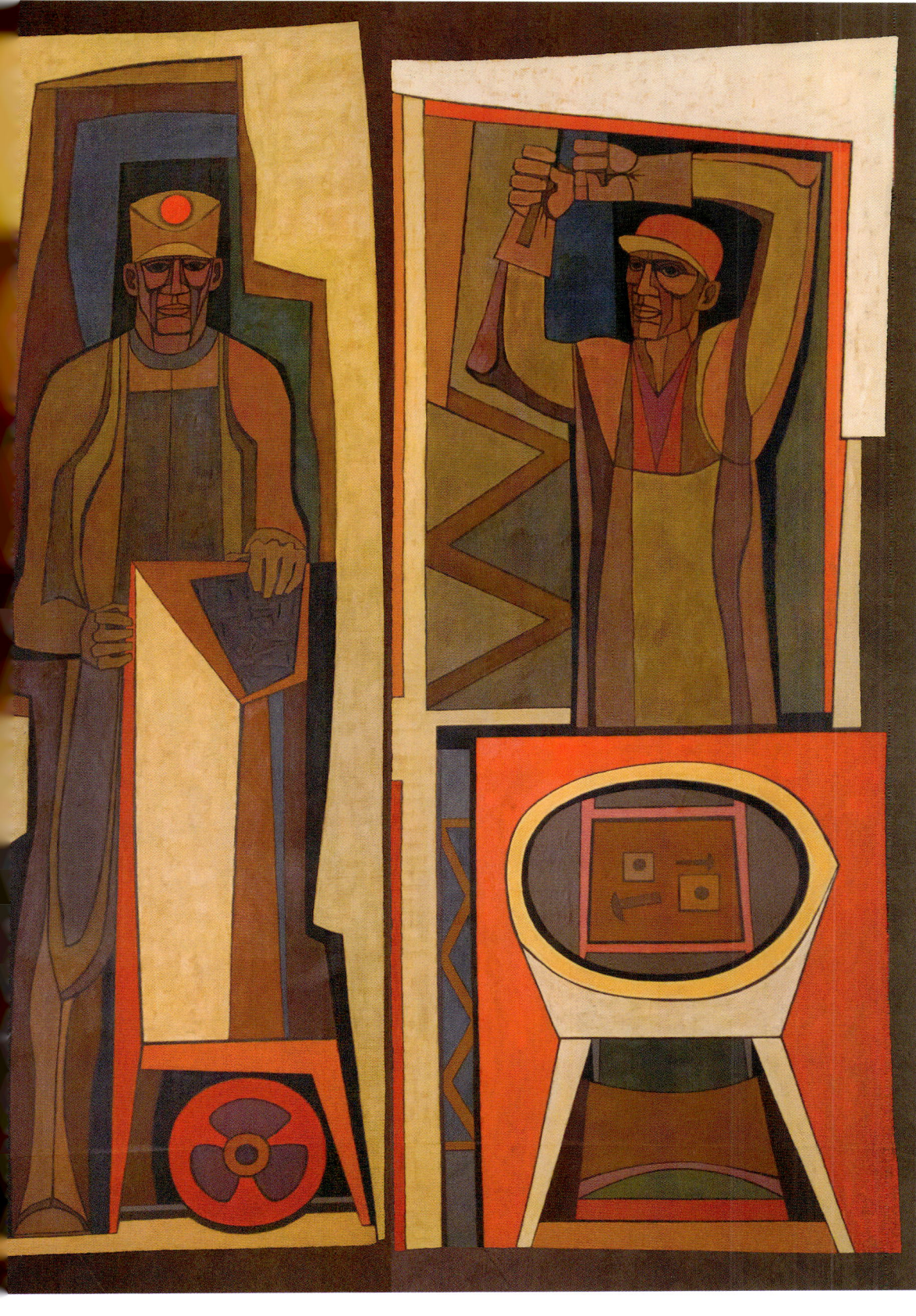

Kenneth Evett
Labors of the Hand, 1956
15 x 24 feet
Oil on canvas

All three of the "Labors" murals create together a portrayal of what people can achieve when utilizing the virtues and gifts bestowed upon them. Evett intended them to highlight the spirit of Nebraskans.

Labors of the Hand highlights the hard-working and industrious nature of Nebraskans.

Kenneth Evett
Labors of the Heart, 1956
15 x 24 feet
Oil on canvas

This mural depicts individuals taking part in artistic and creative endeavors. Two play music while one dances. Another draws and the last person crafts.

In a 1996 article, Evett said of his work and process, "Motifs extracted from nature's chaos are elements of energetic force . . . [and] the visual give and take between them generates geometric patterns of diagonal, horizontal, and vertical tensions that require resolution."

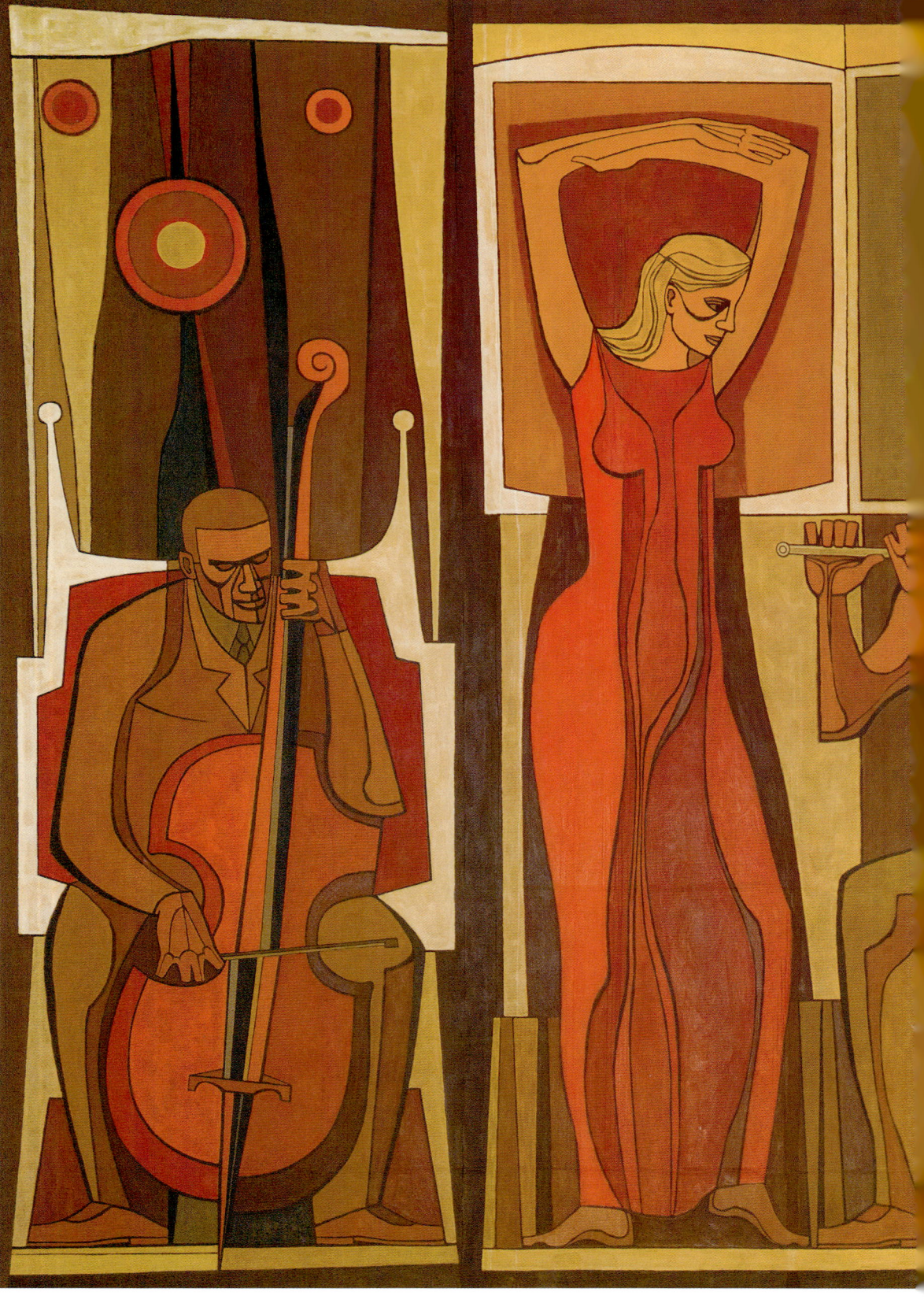

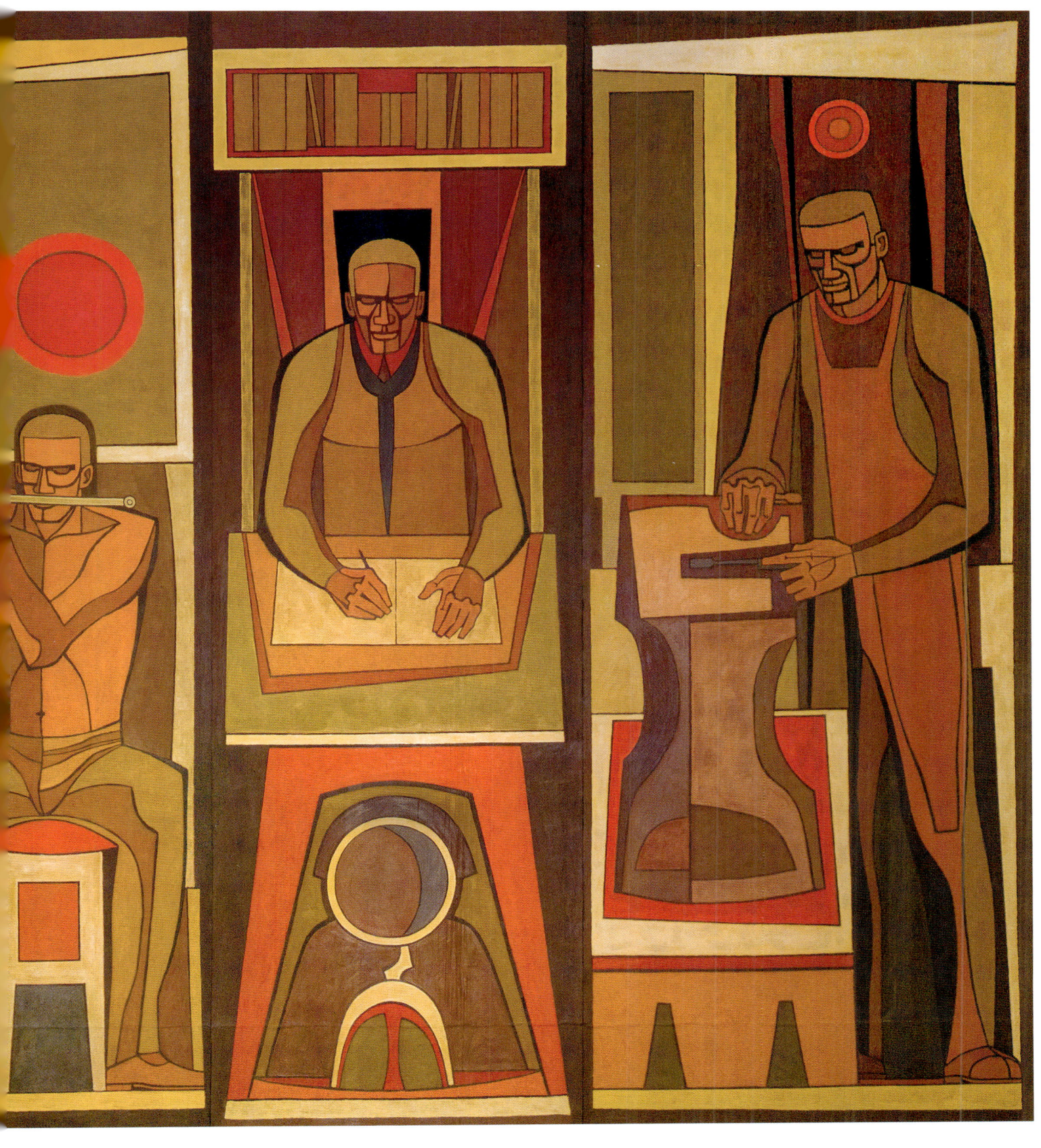

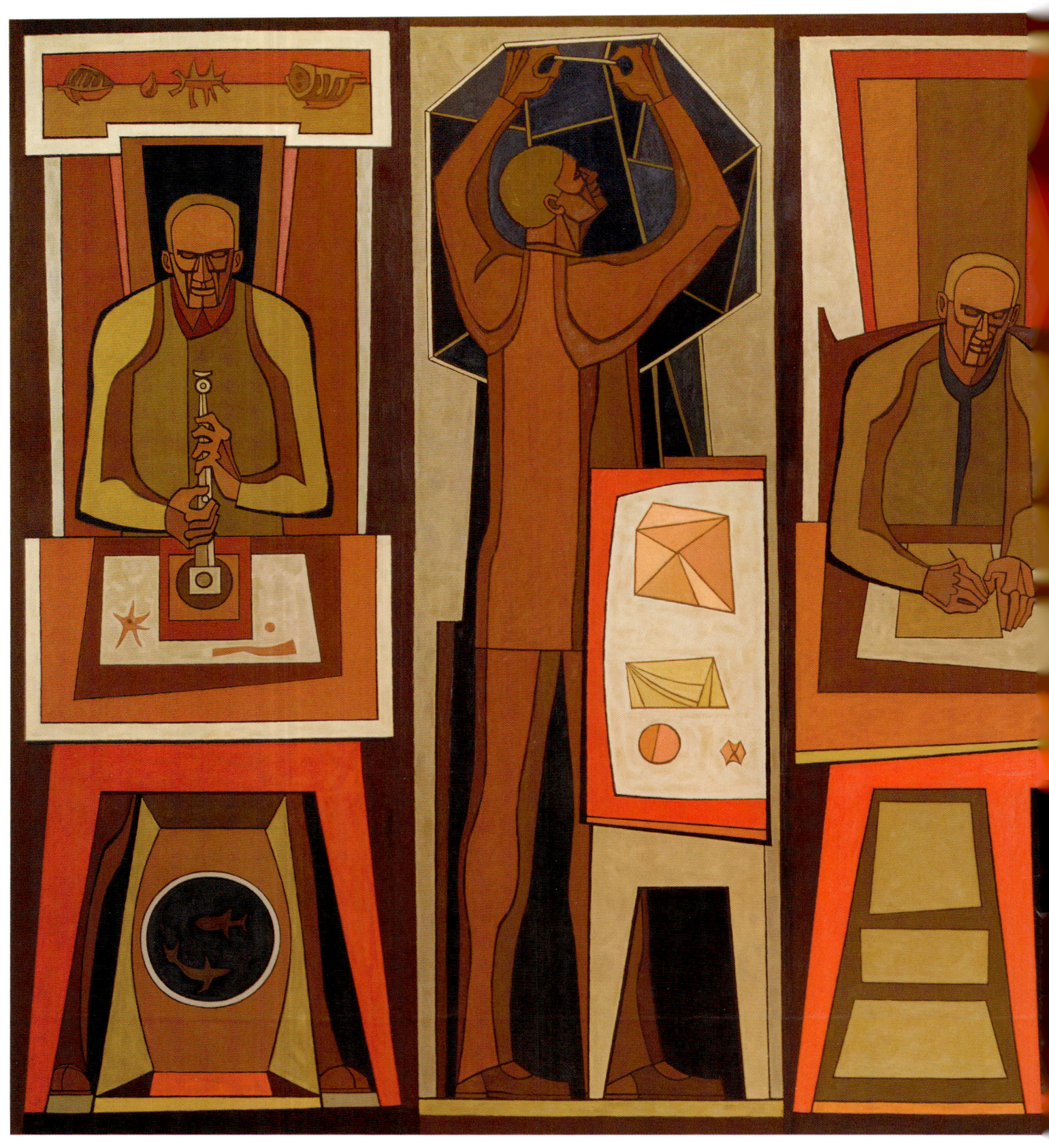

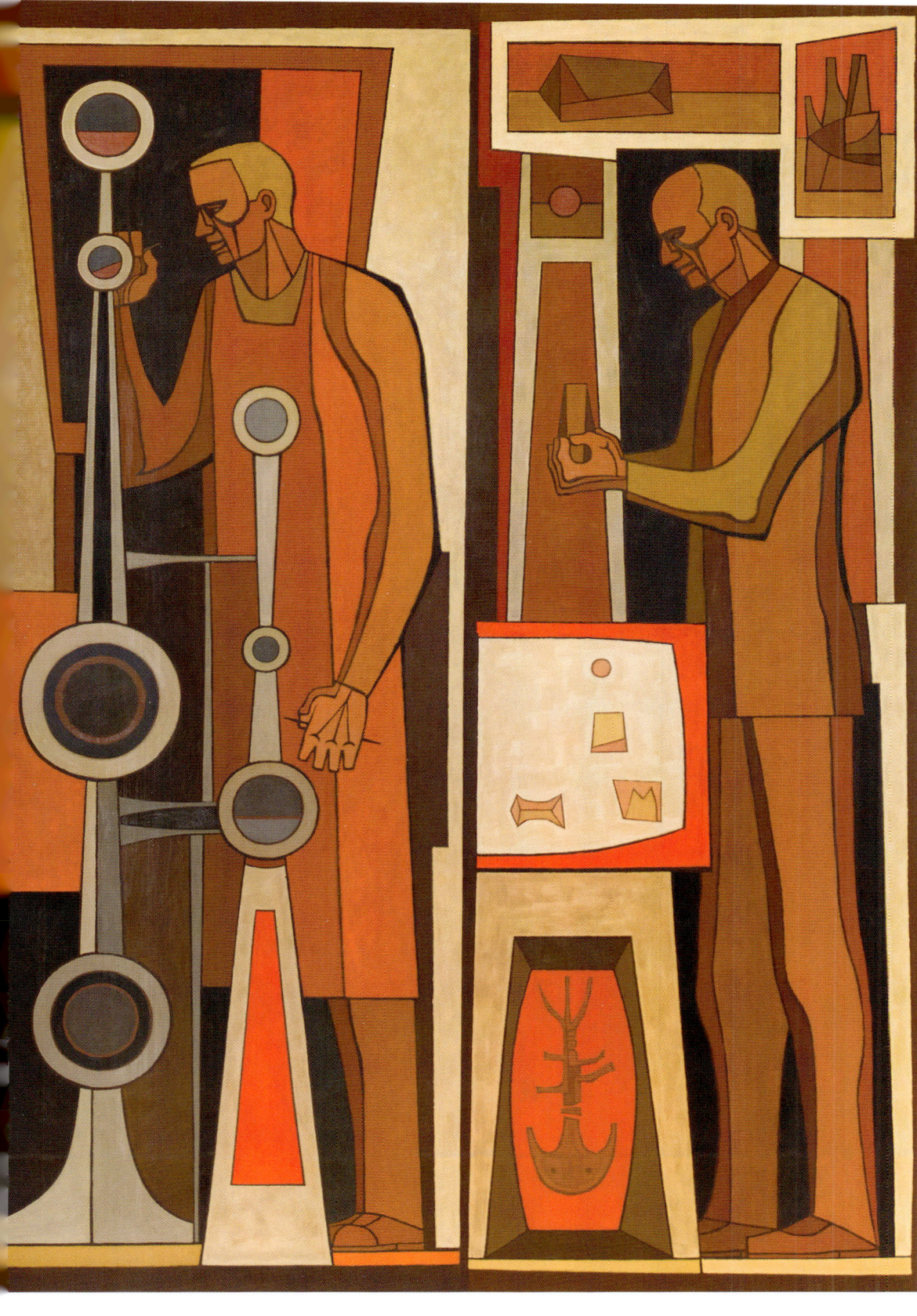

Kenneth Evett
Labors of the Head, 1956
15 x 24 feet
Oil on canvas

Labors of the Head illustrates scholarly and analytical endeavors, including individuals utilizing biology, geometry, writing, engineering, and chemistry.

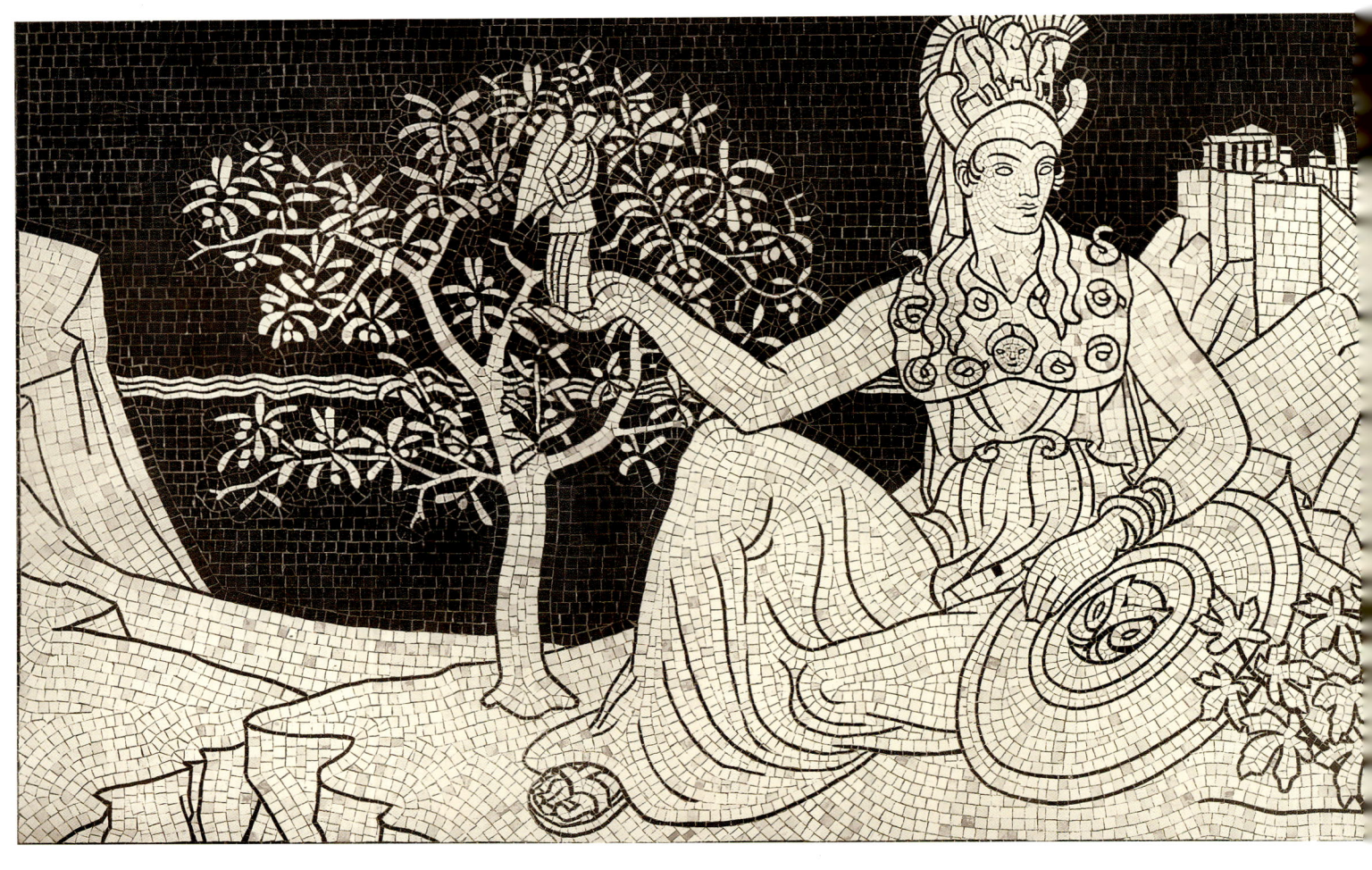

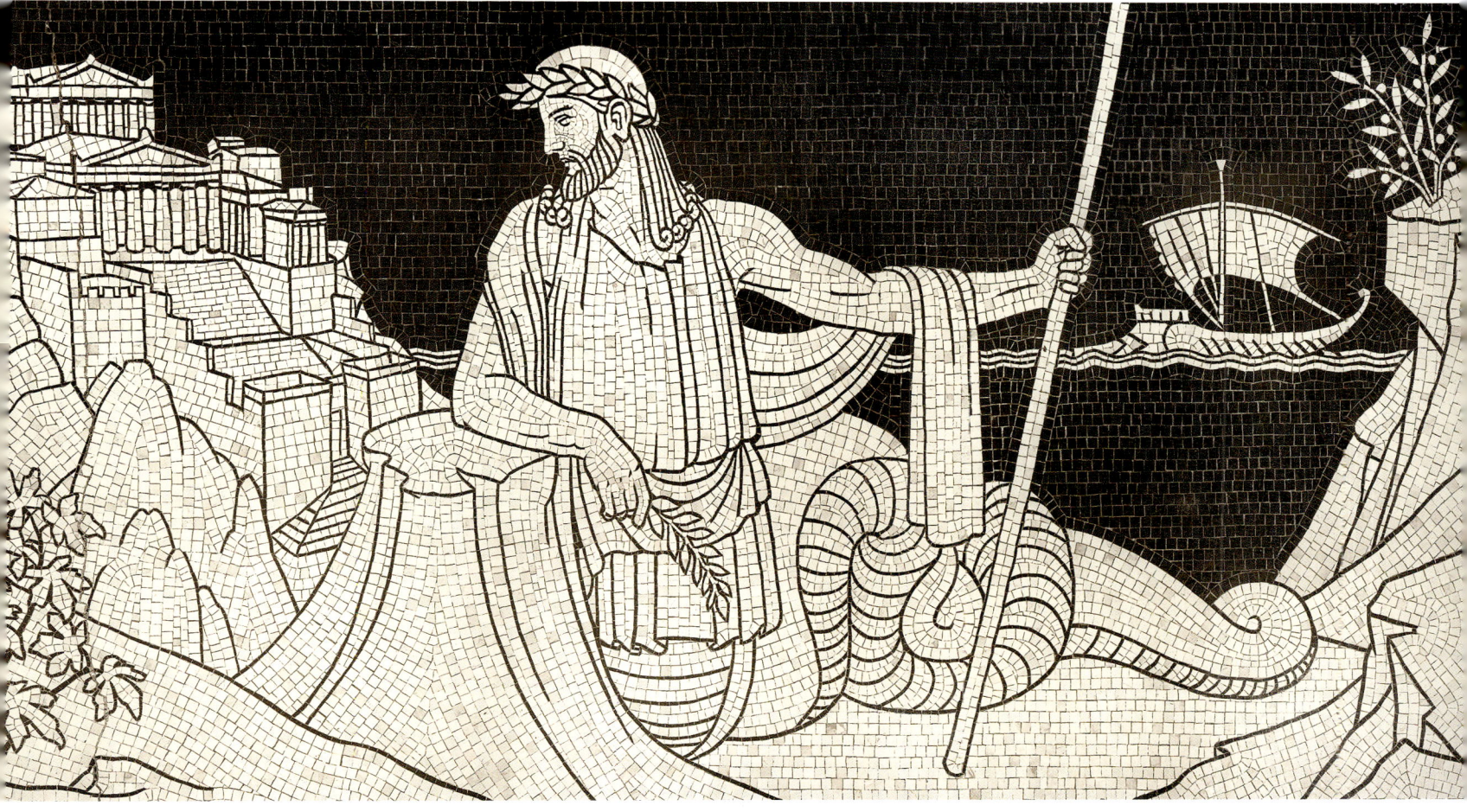

Hildreth Meière
*Acropolis of Greece, c.*1930
approx. 4.5 x 17 feet
Marble mosaic set in inlaid marble

While the murals of the rotunda portray modern citizens employing
the virtues in their works, the floors focus on the ancients. *The
Acropolis of Greece* signifies the contributions the Greeks made
to modern democracies. The goddess of war and wisdom Athena
rests in front of the Acropolis holding in her hand Nike, the goddess
of Victory. Across from her, Erechtheus, with a laurel wreath and
his serpent body, sits overseeing Athens. This earthborn son of
gods legendarily served as one of the first kings of Athens.

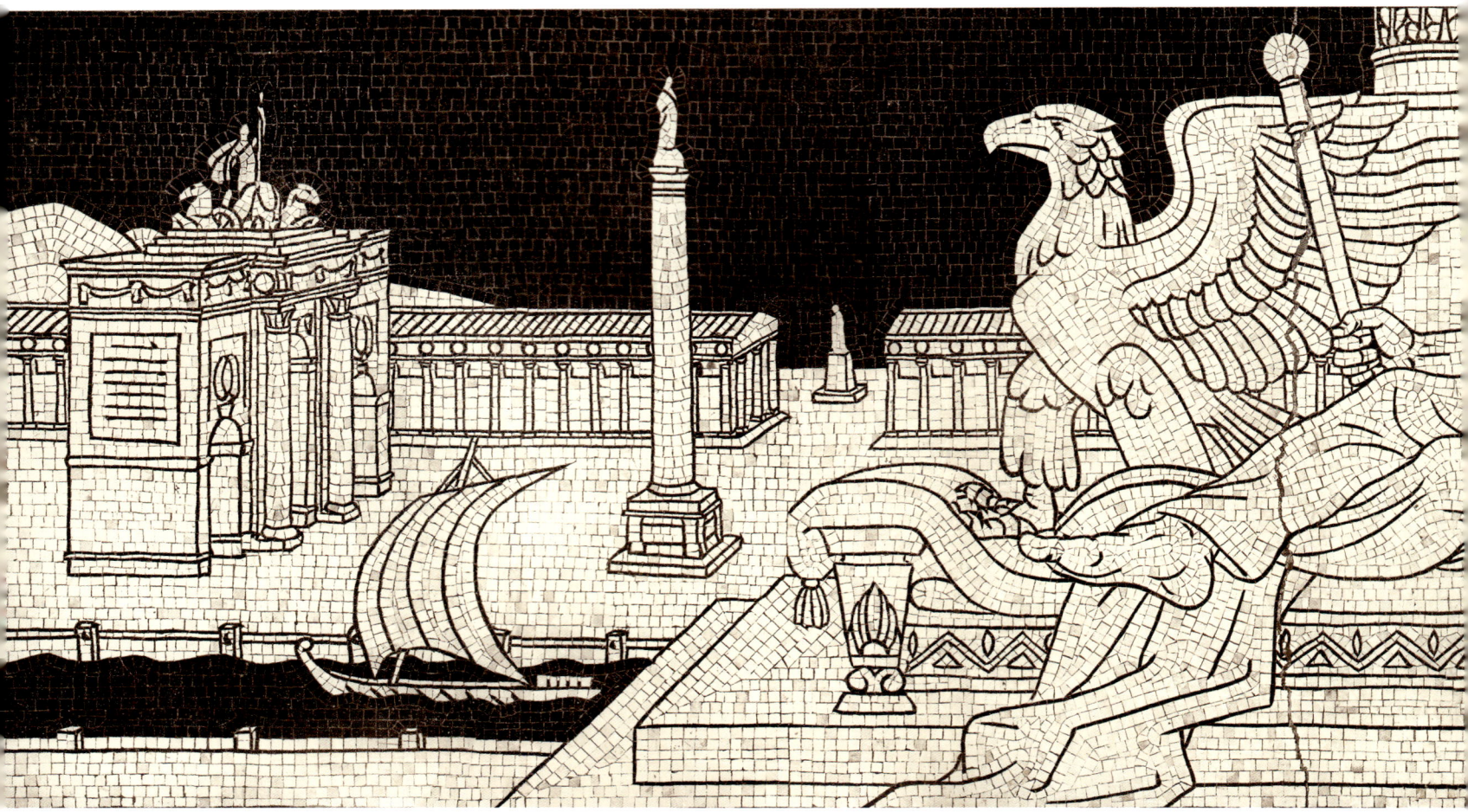

Hildreth Meière
Capitol Hill of Rome, c.1930
approx. 4.5 x 17 feet
Marble mosaic set in inlaid marble

This mosaic is located in front of the Warner Chamber and
represents the foundation of modern democracies that sprung
from the Romans. The Roman god Jupiter lounges in front of Roman
monuments, architecture, and ships. His trademark eagle—Jupiter's
sacred animal—symbolizes strength, courage, and prudence.

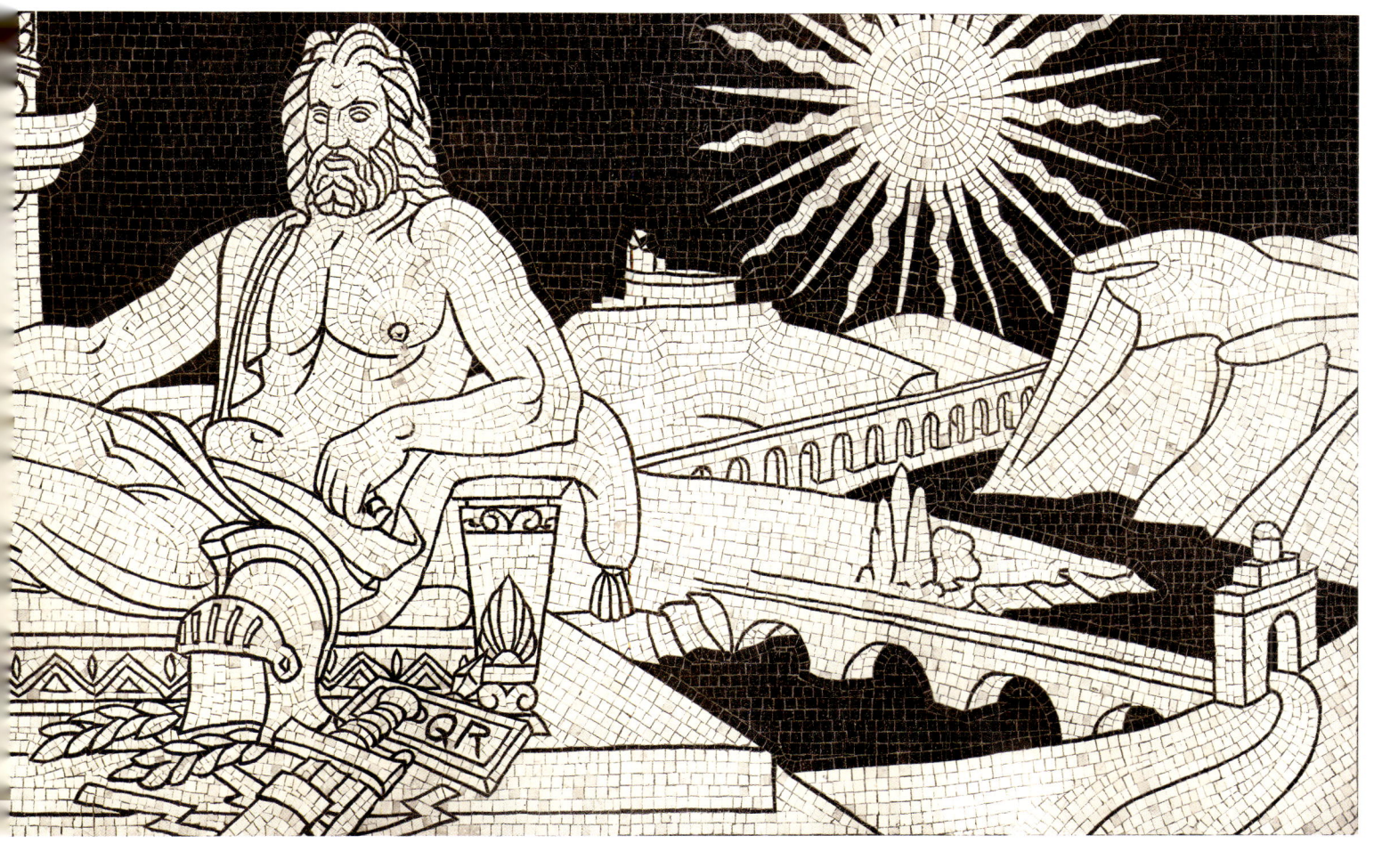

Edward F. Caldwell & Co.
Chandelier, c.1930
approx. 6 x 6 x 6 feet

The twelve-sided, 3500-pound
chandelier in the rotunda
depicts each of the zodiac signs
with intricate detail. Suns are
depicted above and below
the zodiacs with decorative
corn elements throughout.

Wrapping the walls around the
chandelier, bronzed inscriptions
encircle the rotunda, pronouncing
the words of Aristotle and Plato.

From Aristotle's *Politics*:

"He who would duly enquire
about the best form of the state
ought first to determine which
is the most eligible life."

"Men should not think it slavery to
live according to the rule of the
constitution for it is their salvation."

"Laws and constitutions spring
from the moral dispositions of
the members of the state."

From Plato's *Dialogues*:

"Law and order deliver the soul."

"A community like an
individual has work to do."

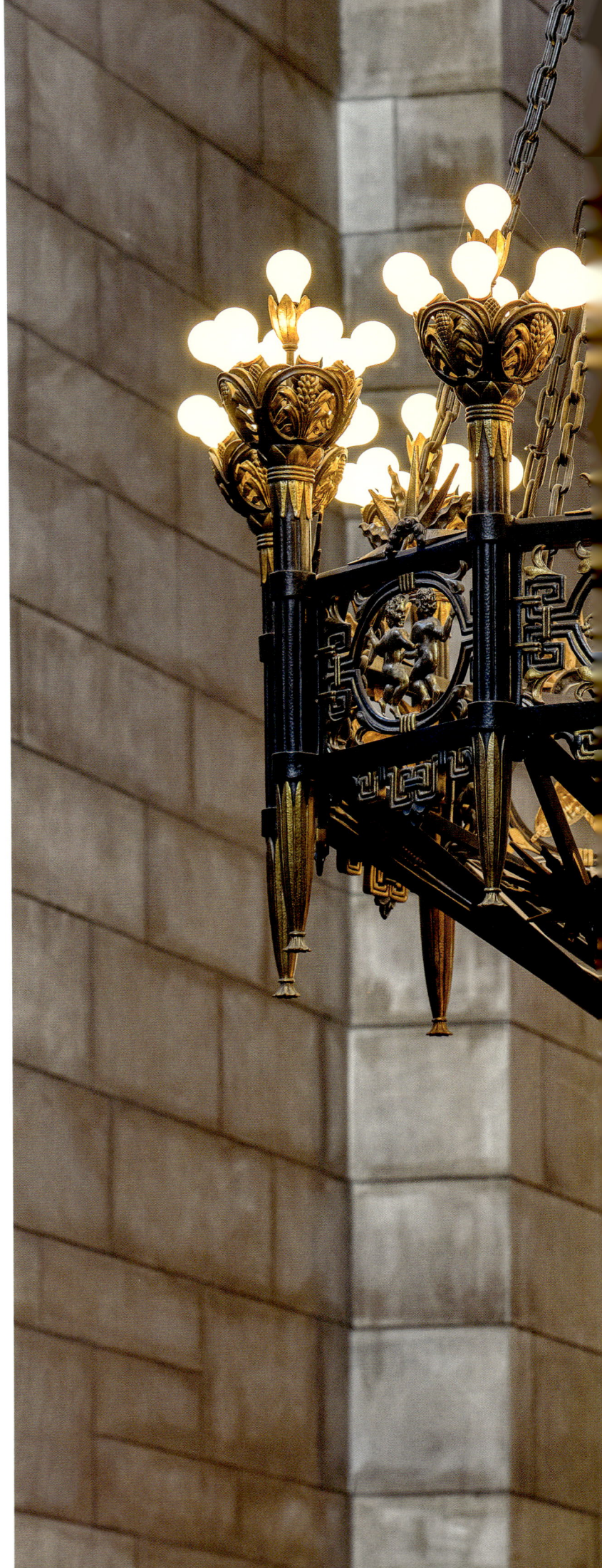

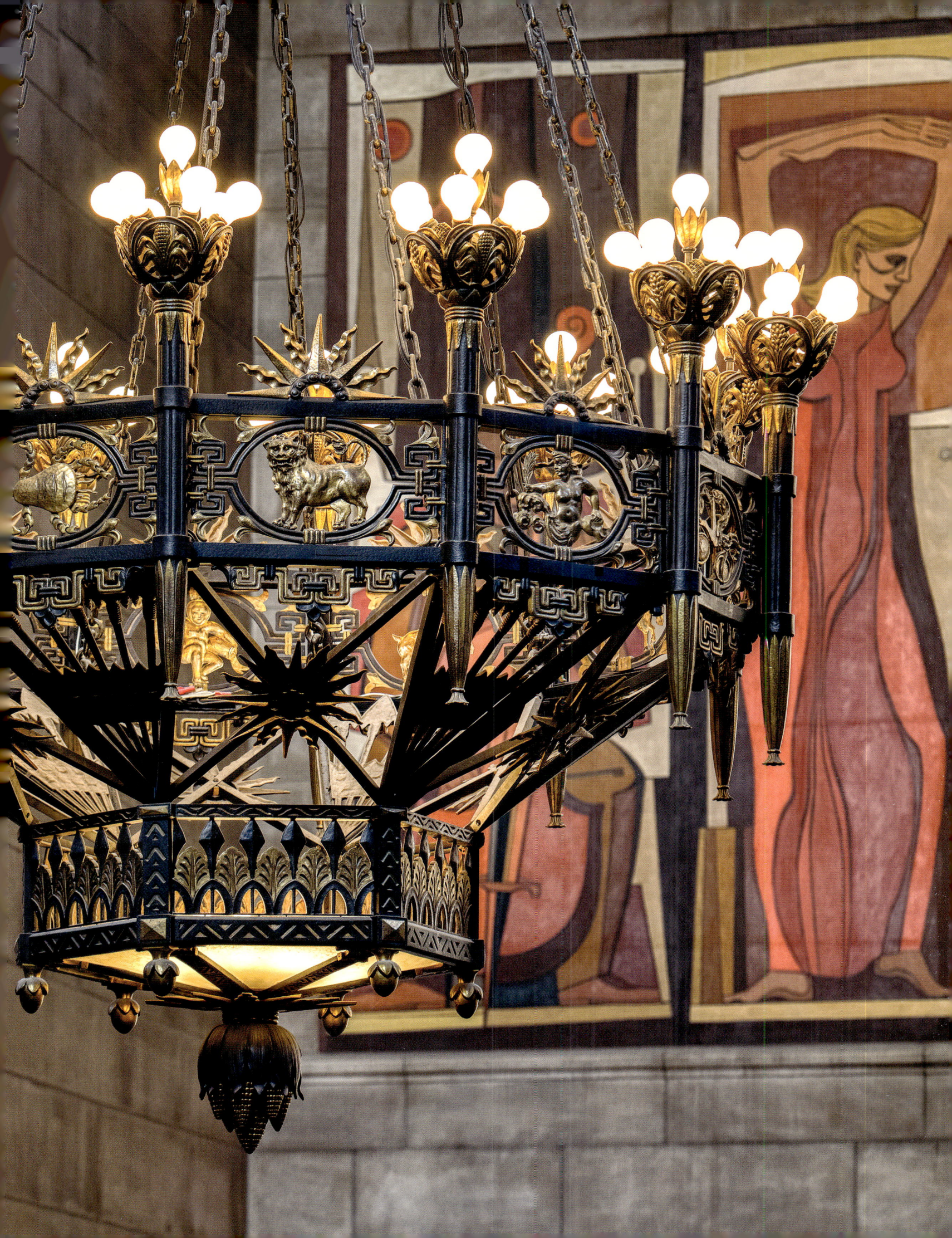

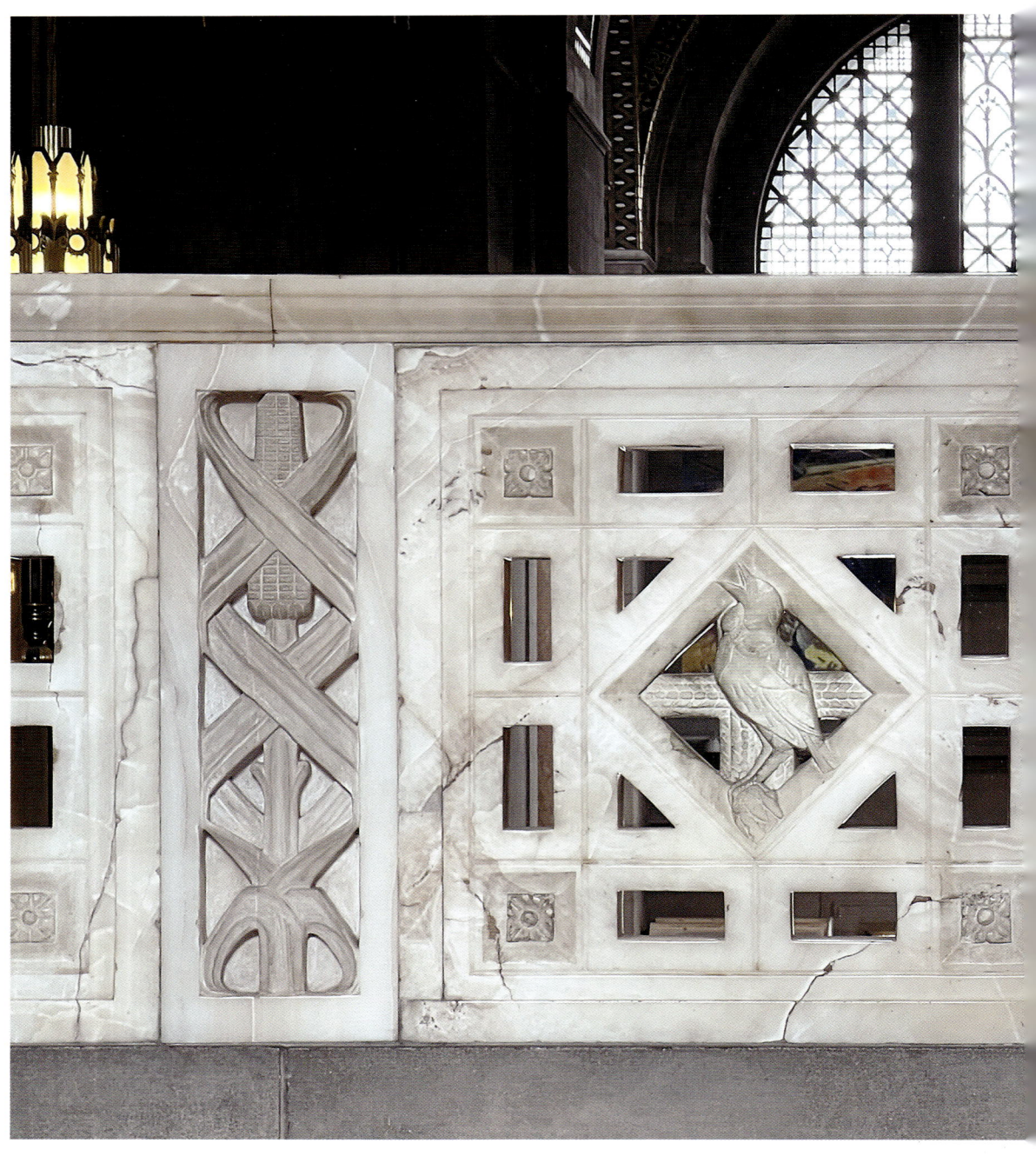

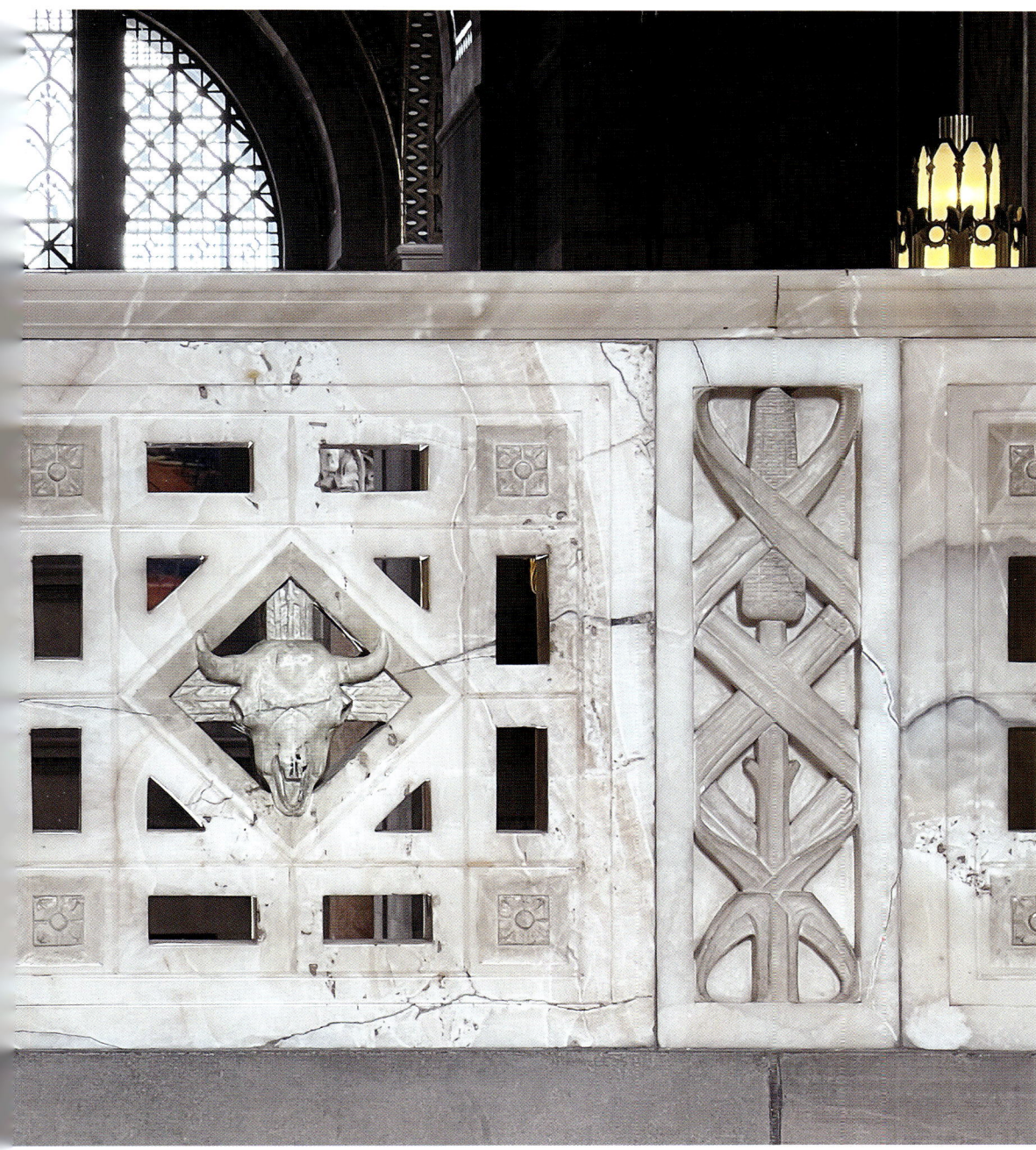

Lee Lawrie
Balcony Railings, c.1930
Carved onyx

The railings in the walkways of the rotunda are hand-carved onyx
featuring a bison skull and western meadowlark, the state bird.
Between them grow carved stalks of corn, a major crop of the state.

NATIVE AMERICAN CULTURE
AND LIFE, VIEWED IN ITS
INTIMATE RELATION TO
THE SOIL AS THE PATTERN
OF ELEMENTAL ACTIVITIES
OF ANY HUMAN SOCIETY.

WARNER CHAMBER

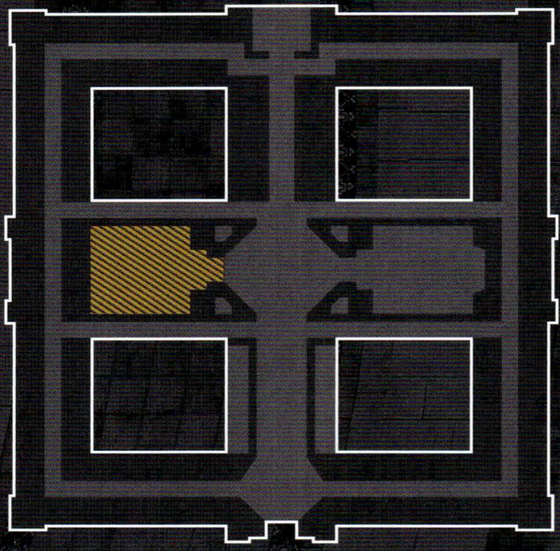

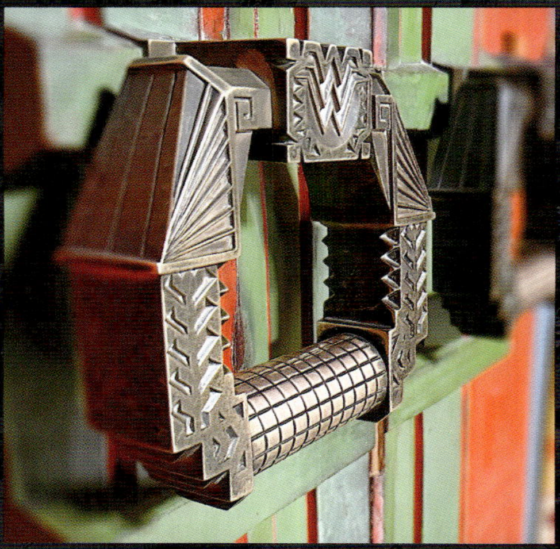

HARTLEY ALEXANDER

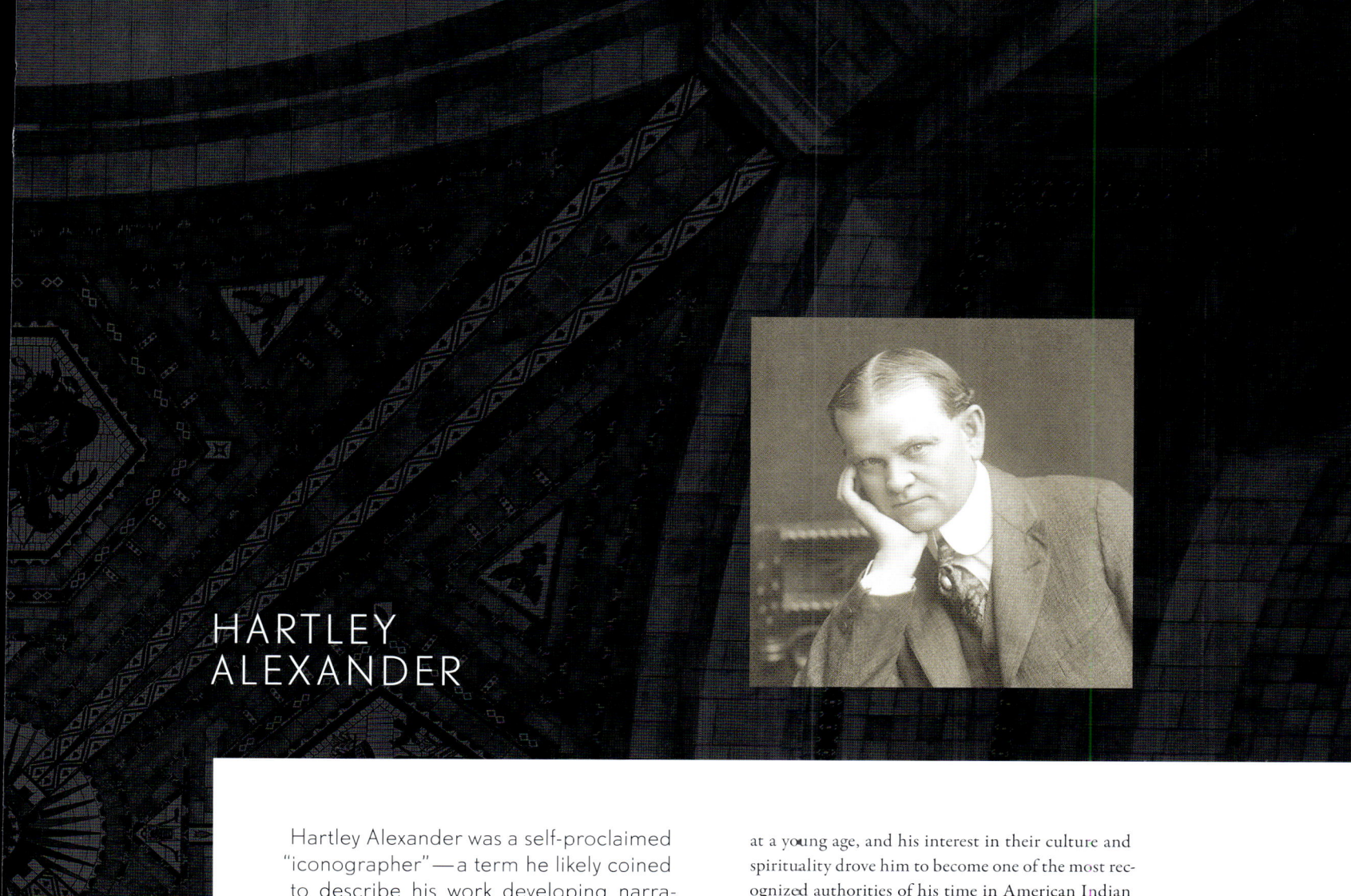

Hartley Alexander was a self-proclaimed "iconographer"—a term he likely coined to describe his work developing narratives and themes for public buildings across the United States.

In 1922, Bertram Goodhue contacted Alexander, a native of Syracuse, Nebraska, and asked if he would be willing to prepare a set of inscriptions for the Capitol. Alexander was well qualified for the work. A writer, poet, and scholar, he taught at the University of Nebraska as a professor of philosophy and served as the department's dean. Alexander also studied and wrote prolifically about Native American culture, democracy, and political thought.

Gradually, Goodhue was calling upon him to craft a complete thematic narrative for the Nebraska Capitol. Using a basic plan from Goodhue, Alexander created a theme for the art and symbolism that tapped into Native American culture and philosophy and contained stories of creation, democracy, and settlement in Nebraska. His theme created a clear and cohesive foundation for the artwork throughout the building.

Alexander held a deep admiration for Native American culture. Growing up as a pioneer on the Nebraska prairie exposed him to Native Americans at a young age, and his interest in their culture and spirituality drove him to become one of the most recognized authorities of his time in American Indian mythology and symbolism. Throughout his life, he educated and advocated for understanding and respect for Native Americans, views not commonly held by white Americans in his time.

Alexander proved keenly aware of the significance Native American culture played on life in Nebraska and wanted to highlight it throughout the Capitol. This vision fit perfectly with those of Goodhue and Hildreth Meière. Together, the trio incorporated Native American symbology throughout the building.

His work on the Capitol led to projects across the nation. In Nebraska, Alexander contributed to the design of Joslyn Art Museum in Omaha and the University of Nebraska's Memorial Stadium. He also worked on the Justice Department Building in Washington DC, Rockefeller Center in New York City, and another collaboration with Goodhue on the Los Angeles Public Library.

In 1928, Alexander established the philosophy program at Scripps College in Claremont, California. He remained there until his death in 1939.

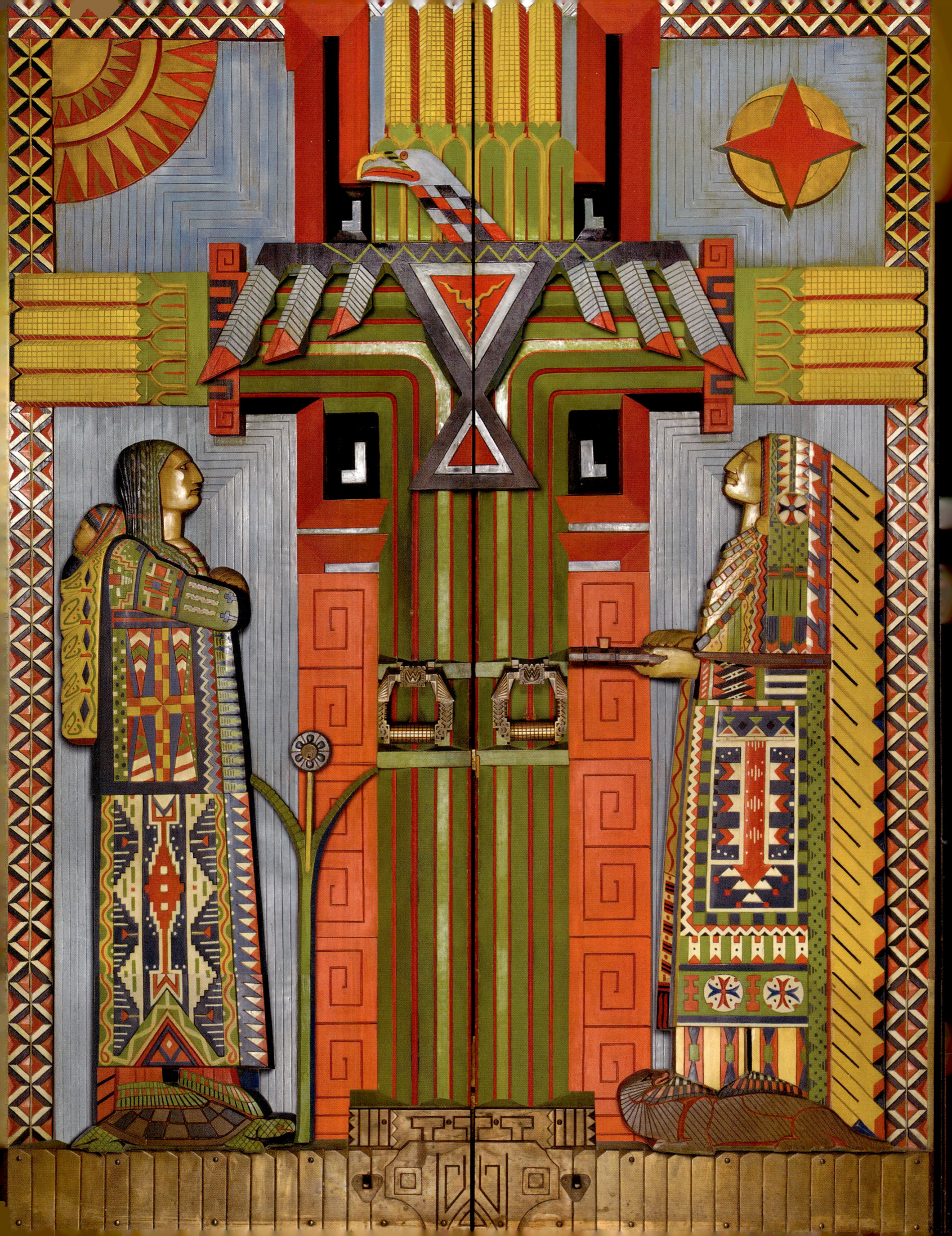

Lee Lawrie, designer
Keats Lorenz, sculptor
Warner Chamber Doors, 1929
99 x 77 inches
Carved and painted black mahogany doors

Two separate wings comprise the legislative chambers and coordinate together thematically to highlight the people who brought their cultures to the plains. The Warner Chamber to the east highlights the life and culture of the Native Americans, using their patterns and themes throughout the room. The Norris Chamber to the west shows the settlement of the plains by other groups, including the Spanish, French, and Anglo-Americans.

Centered on the beautiful doors of the Warner Chamber sits the Tree of Life with its branches of corn, the main agricultural crop and an important food source for the First People. This tree is based on the Lakota (Sioux) tribal symbology. A thunderbird hovers above, representing rain and life, as well as strength, power, and resilience. A woman with a baby stands on a turtle, a Native American symbol of fertility. She faces a man in a traditional headdress, holding a peace pipe and standing on an otter, a symbol of medicine.

Keats Lorenz hand-carved these black mahogany doors over a six-month period. Each door weighs over 750 pounds and its ringed door-pull weighs over 11 pounds.

Hildreth Meière
Lakota Sun Dance, 1932
approx. 15 x 20 feet
Woven tapestry

This wool tapestry sits prominently and grandly above the speaker's niche of the Warner Chamber. It depicts ten 19th-century Sioux dancers performing a ritualistic sun dance, one of the most important ceremonies practiced by the Lakota.

Guided by Alexander's theme, Meière fully expressed her creativity throughout the Capitol where she was allowed to work with a variety of materials and modes. She used her skills as a trained muralist to create stunning marble mosaics throughout the building. And she also designed this striking tapestry and painted the leather and wood doors for the Norris Chamber.

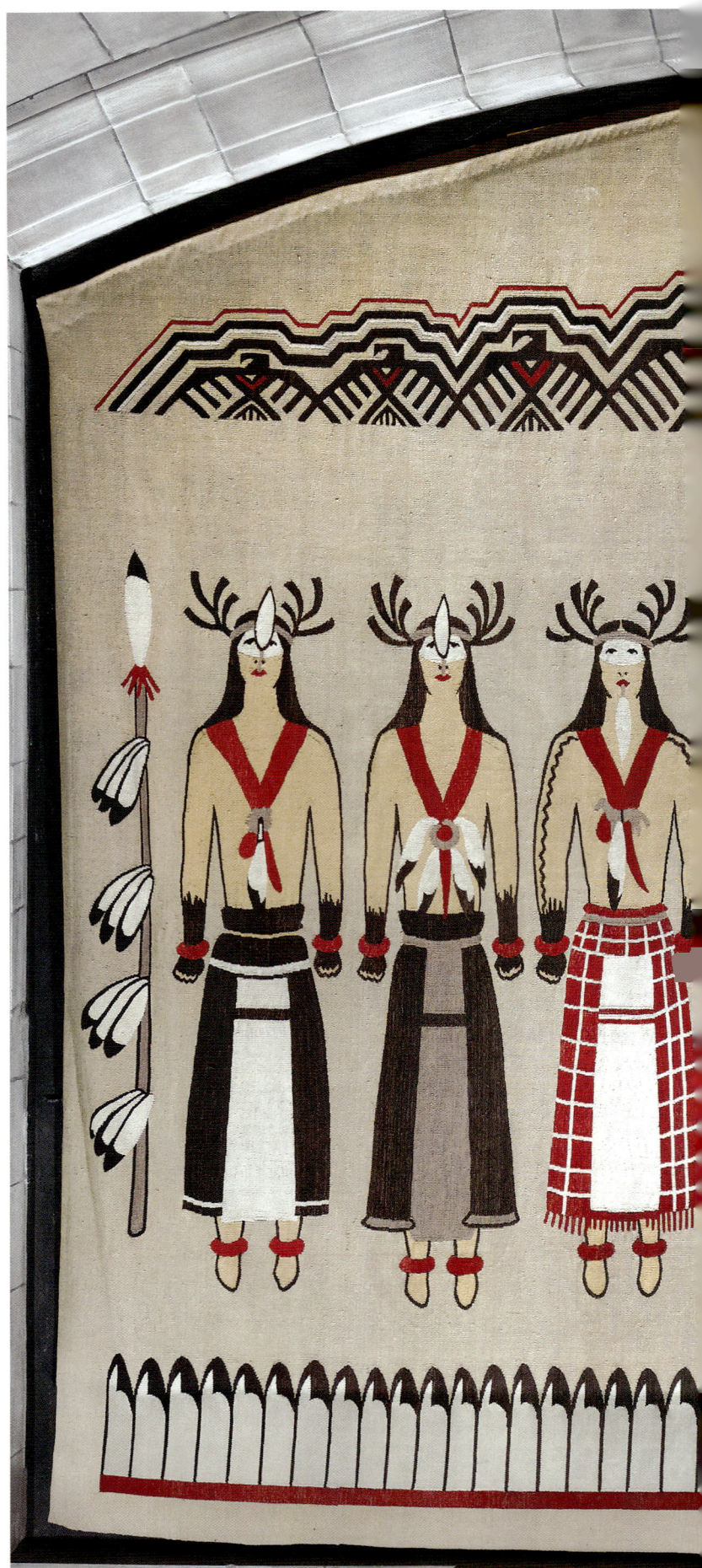

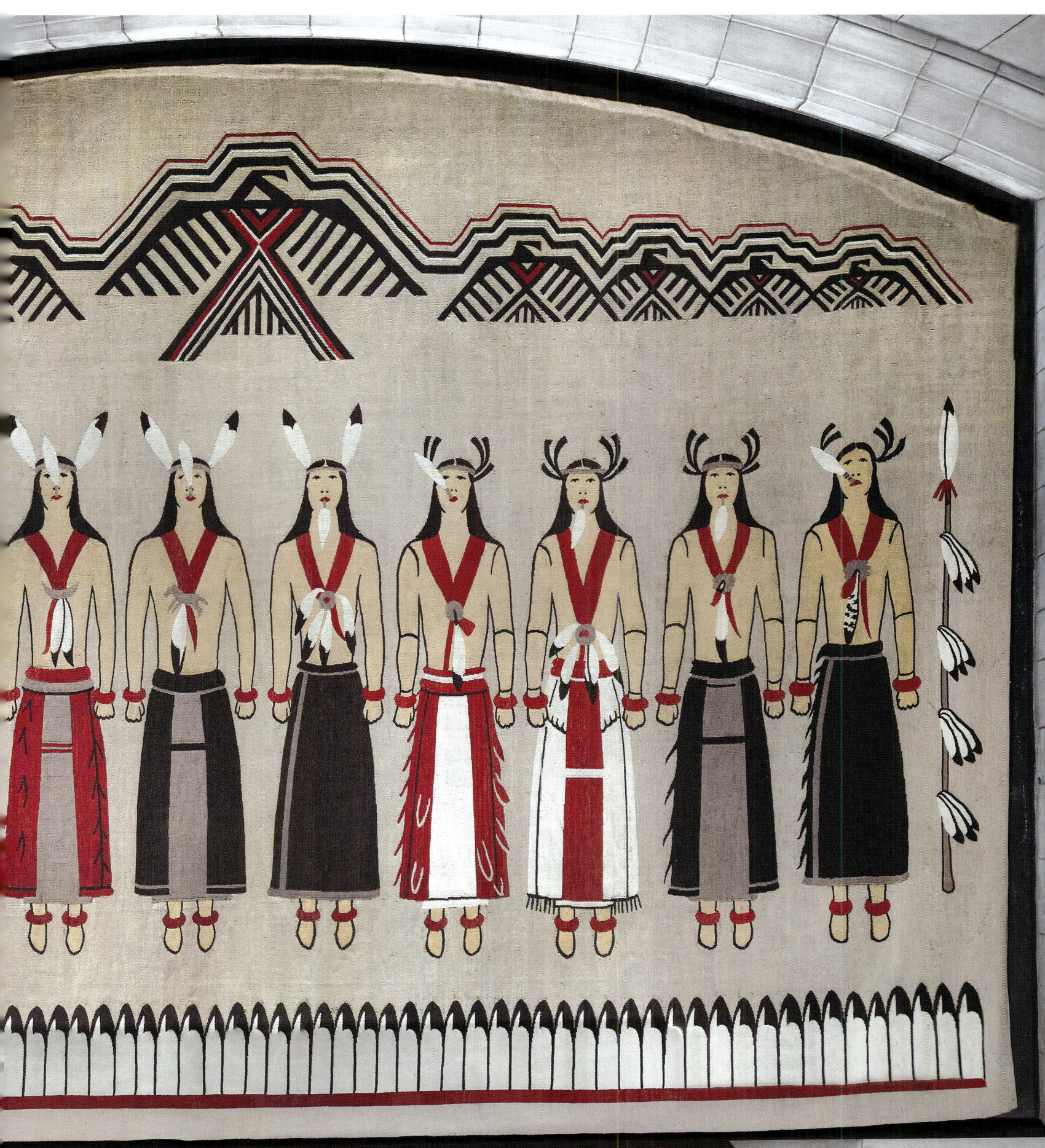

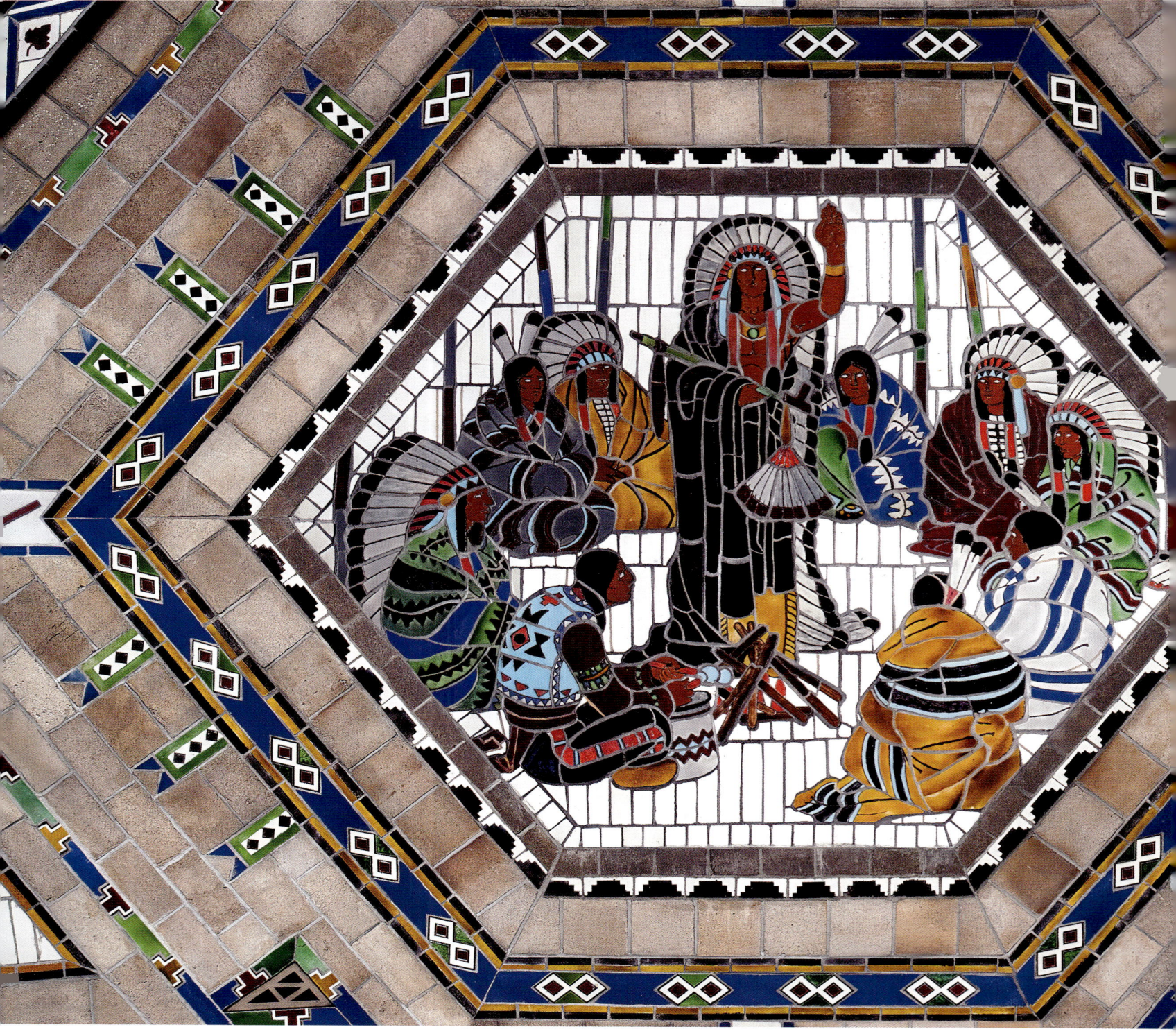

Hildreth Meière
Peace Council, 1927
approx. 8 x 12 feet
Glazed ceramic tile

In the form of a dome, the ceiling is quartered, and a different mosaic fills each section.
In the center at the crown of the dome rests the *Sun Disk*. The general pattern of the
geometric setting draws from Plains Indian ornamentation, while the mosaic panels
themselves depict important aspects of Native American life and culture.

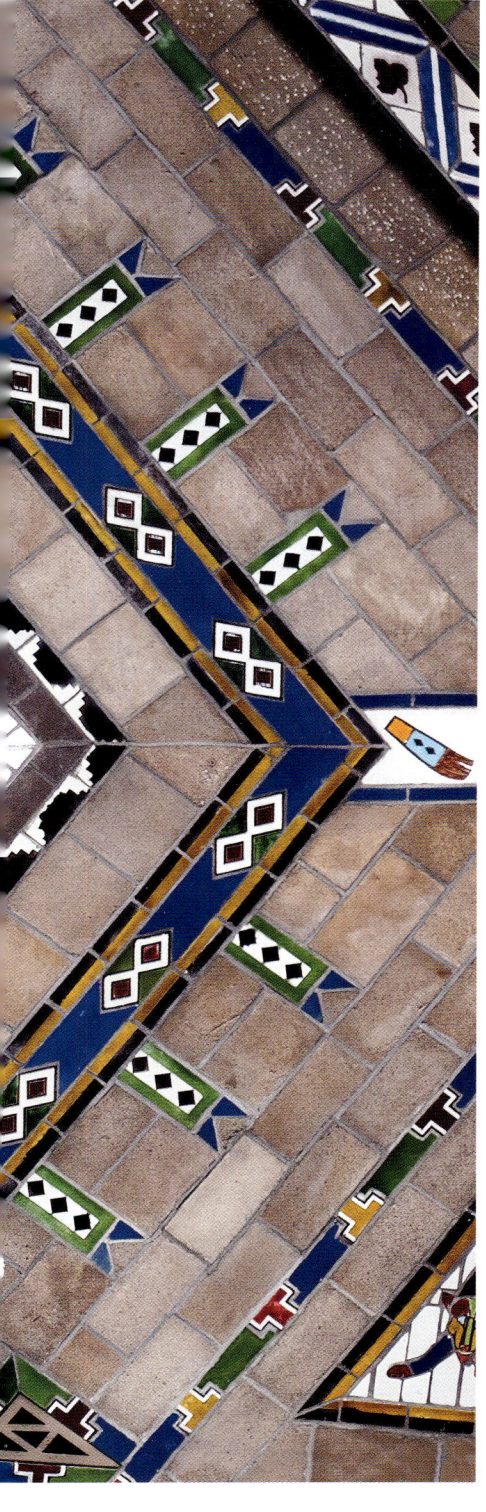

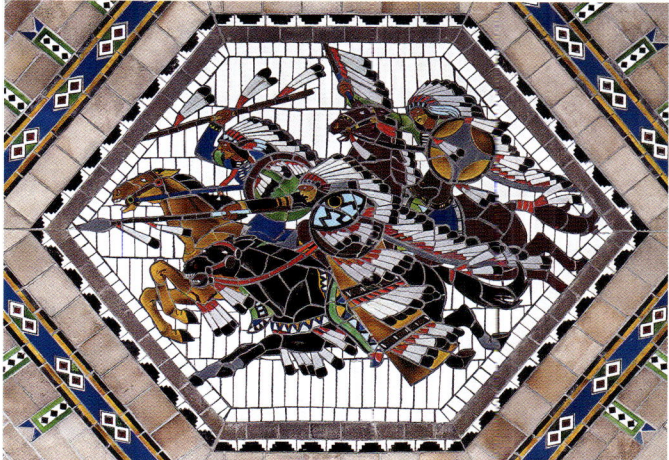

Hildreth Meière
War Party, 1927
approx. 8 x 12 feet
Glazed ceramic tile

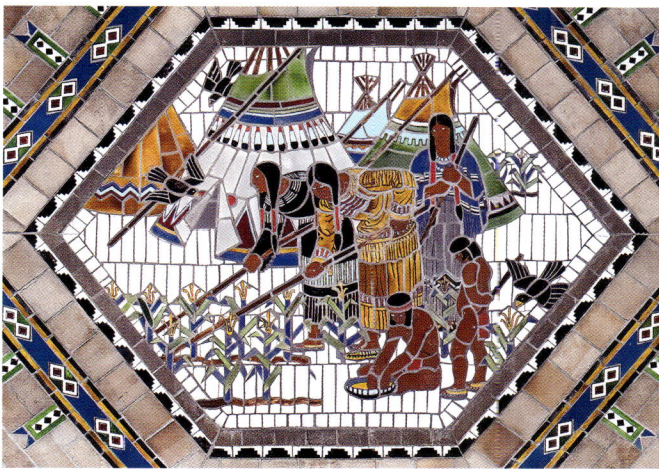

Hildreth Meière
Women Hoeing Corn, 1927
approx. 8 x 12 feet
Glazed ceramic tile

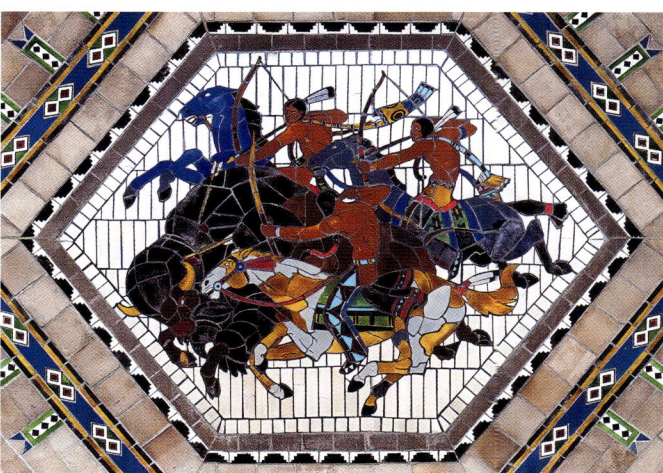

Hildreth Meière
Buffalo Hunt, 1927
approx. 8 x 12 feet
Glazed ceramic tile

The multicolored mosaics and borders adorning the ceiling
are designed to look like Native American beadwork.
Together, they depict Native American life on the plains, as
imagined by Alexander and interpreted by Meière.

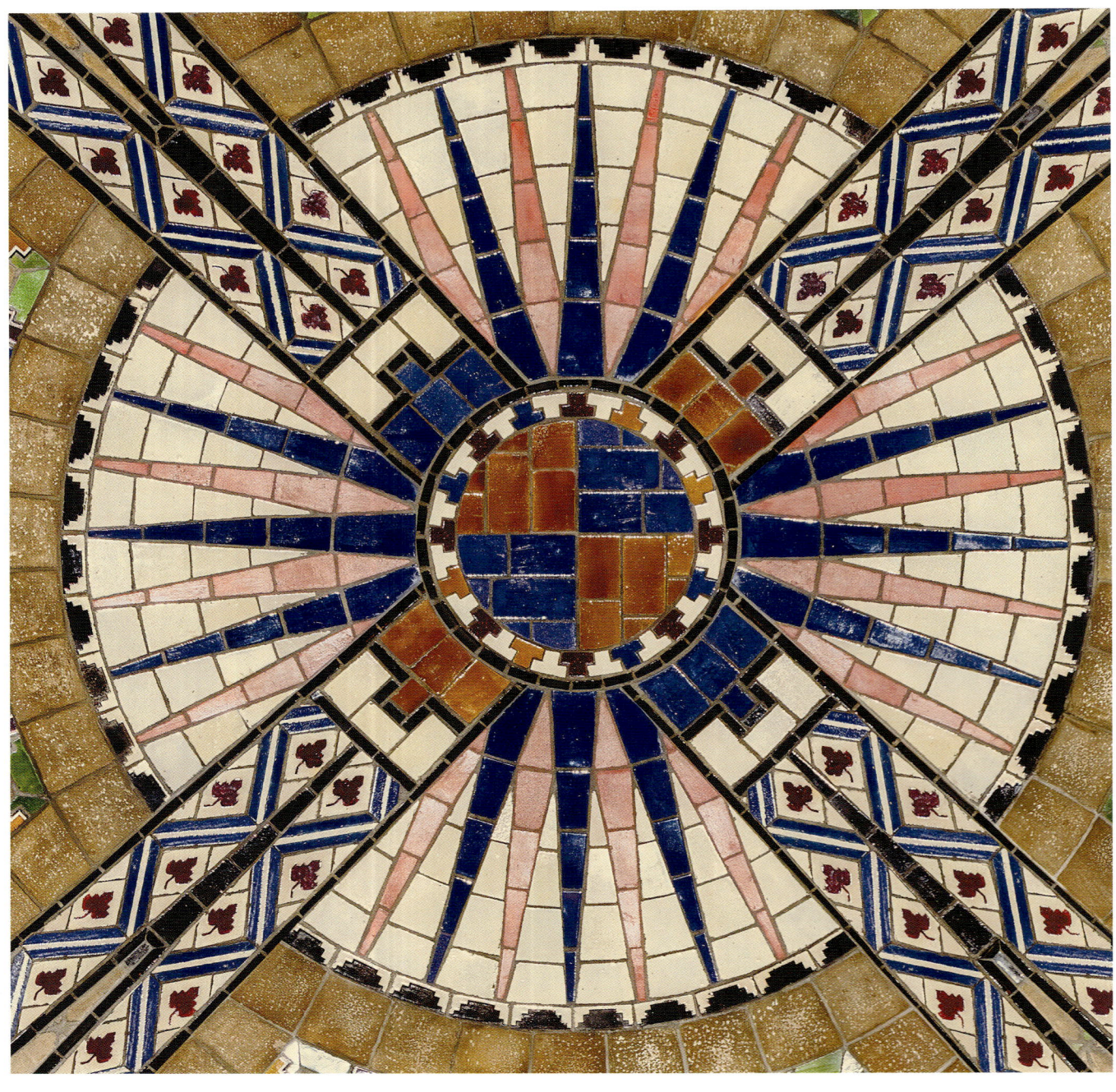

Hildreth Meière
Sun Disk, 1927
approx. 9.5 x 9.5 feet
Glazed ceramic tile

Regarding the mosaics in the Warner Chamber, Meière explained: "I think Dr. Alexander and I both feel a special affection for the Indian ceiling of the Senate Chamber. Being an authority, as he is, on Indian art and life, he was particularly anxious that this commemoration of the first inhabitants of the state should be adequately handled. He lent me many photographs of Indian beadwork, blankets, etc., as well as examples of their art. I based my style as nearly as I honestly could, on theirs, and as far as we know, this ceiling is the first important attempt to portray Indian subjects as the Indians themselves would do. . . . The colors, the ornament, the very shapes of the panels themselves in this ceiling are Indian, and the flavor of the whole is undoubtedly authentic. For this reason, I think it is the best thing that I have done."

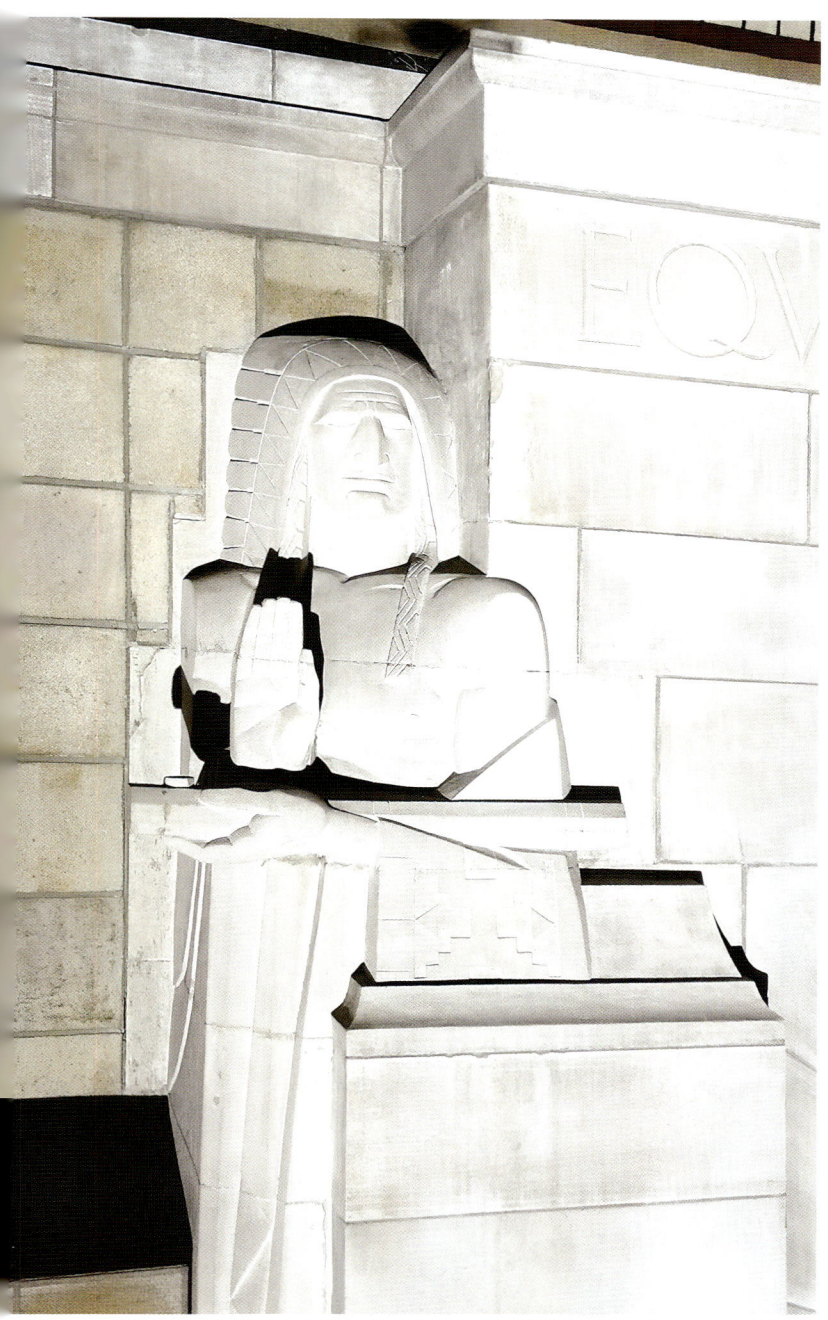

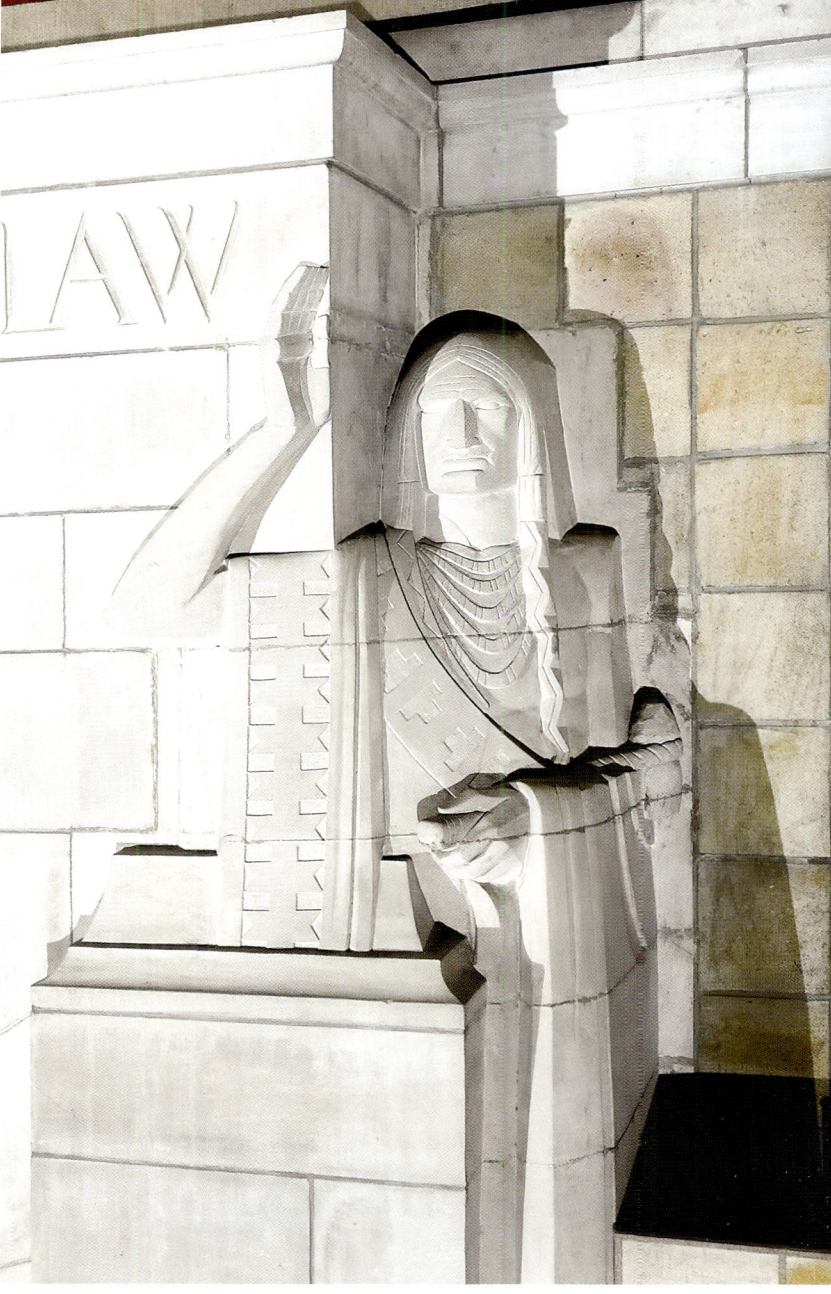

Lee Lawrie
The Counselor, c.1927
Indiana limestone sculpture

Lee Lawrie
The Guide, c.1927
Indiana limestone sculpture

This sculpture and its companion, *The Counselor*, together represent the wisdom of word and action necessary for creating laws. Between them is engraved, "Equality Before the Law," Nebraska's state motto

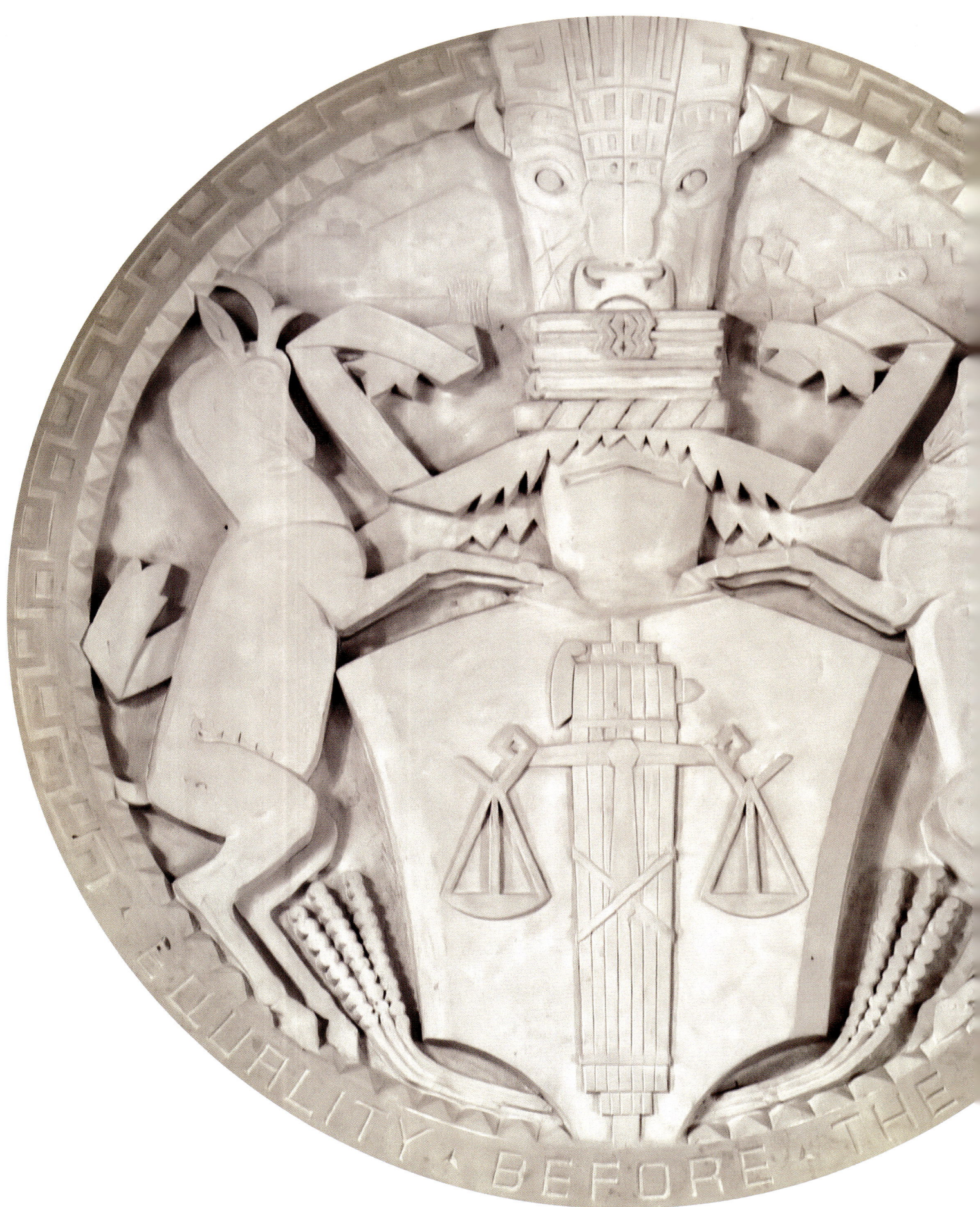

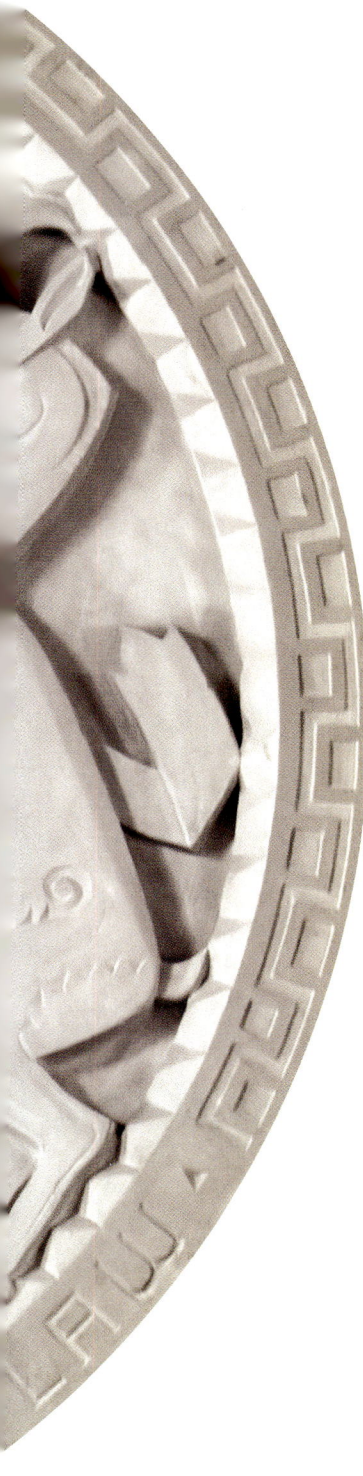

Lee Lawrie
Nebraska State Seal, c.1927
approx. 3 x 3 feet
Indiana limestone sculpture

Goodhue and Lawrie created three variations of a coat of arms
seal that they hoped would be adopted by the legislature. These
were carved in multiple locations throughout the Capitol
including on the building facade, in the Supreme Court, and in
the Warner Chamber. However, the bicameral legislature chose
the existing state seal, and this design was never adopted.

EUROPEAN SETTLEMENT,
REPRESENTED BY THE
SUCCESSIVE APPEARANCE OF
THE SPANISH, FRENCH, AND
ANGLO-AMERICANS UPON
THE SOIL OF NEBRASKA.

NORRIS CHAMBER

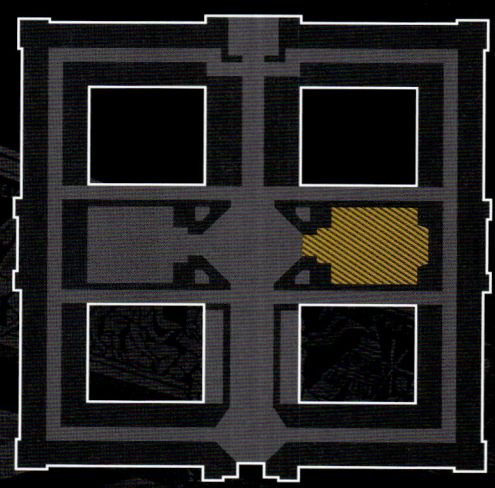

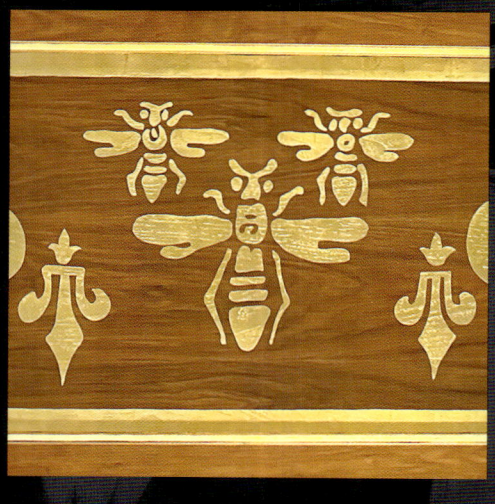

NEBRASKA'S UNICAMERAL

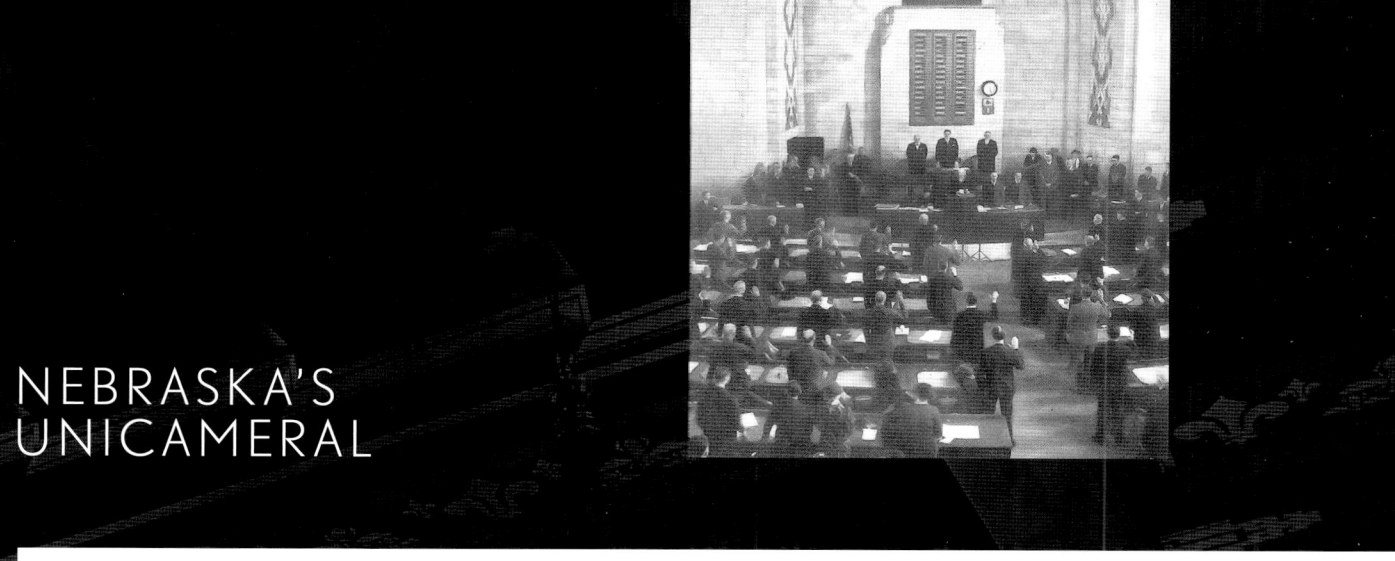

In 1935, Nebraska chose to take an unparalleled route for its government, something that sets it apart from every other state in the United States. That year, Nebraskans voted to change their legislature into a unicameral.

All other states in the United States have bicameral legislatures, much like the U.S. Congress, meaning the legislature is comprised of two separate and independent bodies — typically a Senate and a House of Representatives. Nebraska is the only state with one legislative body.

Up until 1935, Nebraska also had a bicameral legislature. But U.S. Senator George Norris believed a unicameral would be more fair, transparent, efficient, and less expensive. So he took the argument to the people. He drove across the state, wearing out two sets of tires, campaigning for a state constitutional amendment to make a non-partisan one-house legislature.

At the time and to this day, a major concern with a one-house legislature focuses on the lack of checks and balances. However, Norris argued that a streamlined system would simplify procedures and allow the press to provide greater public awareness.

He also believed the governor's veto power and Supreme Court's judicial authority provided appropriate checks. Most important to him, the people of Nebraska served as the ultimate check and balance through the right to vote and petition.

Ultimately, the effort was put to a vote of the people. Given Norris's passion and effort as well as the effects of the Depression, Nebraskans passed the measure in 1934. The newly formed unicameral met in the larger Norris Chamber of the Capitol. The Warner Chamber sits mostly unused since and is generally not open to the public, despite containing a breadth of beautiful artwork and fixtures.

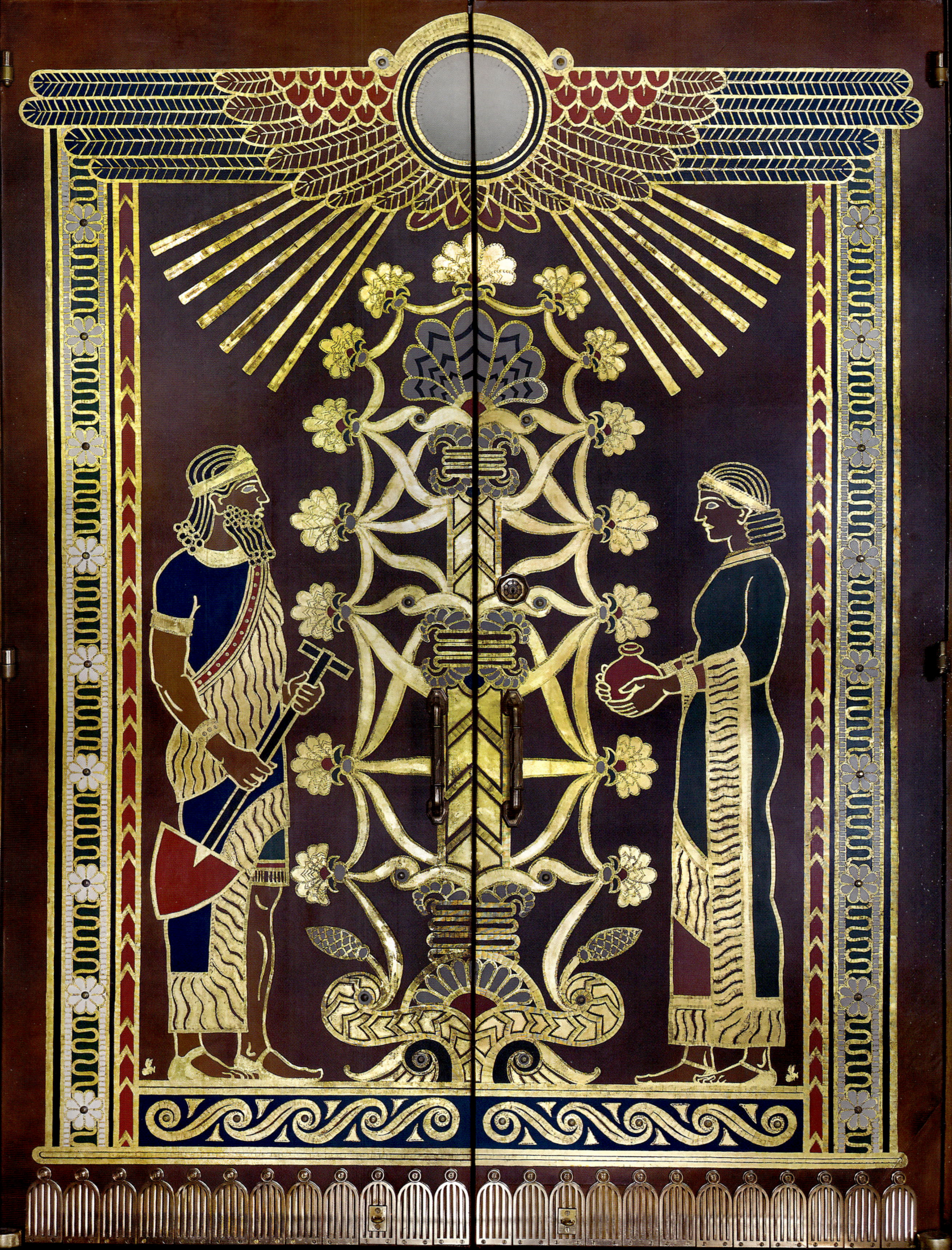

Hildreth Meière
Norris Chamber Doors, 1932
99 x 77 inches
Painted leather wrapped on wood

Opposite the Tree of Life doors of the Warner Chamber sits
another variation of a tree of life on the doors of the Norris
Chamber. Featuring Middle Eastern iconography, these hand-
tooled and warmly decorated leather doors seem to come
from an enormous, old medieval book. An Assyrian man and
woman plant a tree of life under a winged sun disk, symbolizing
the roots of agriculture in the ancient Middle Eastern region.

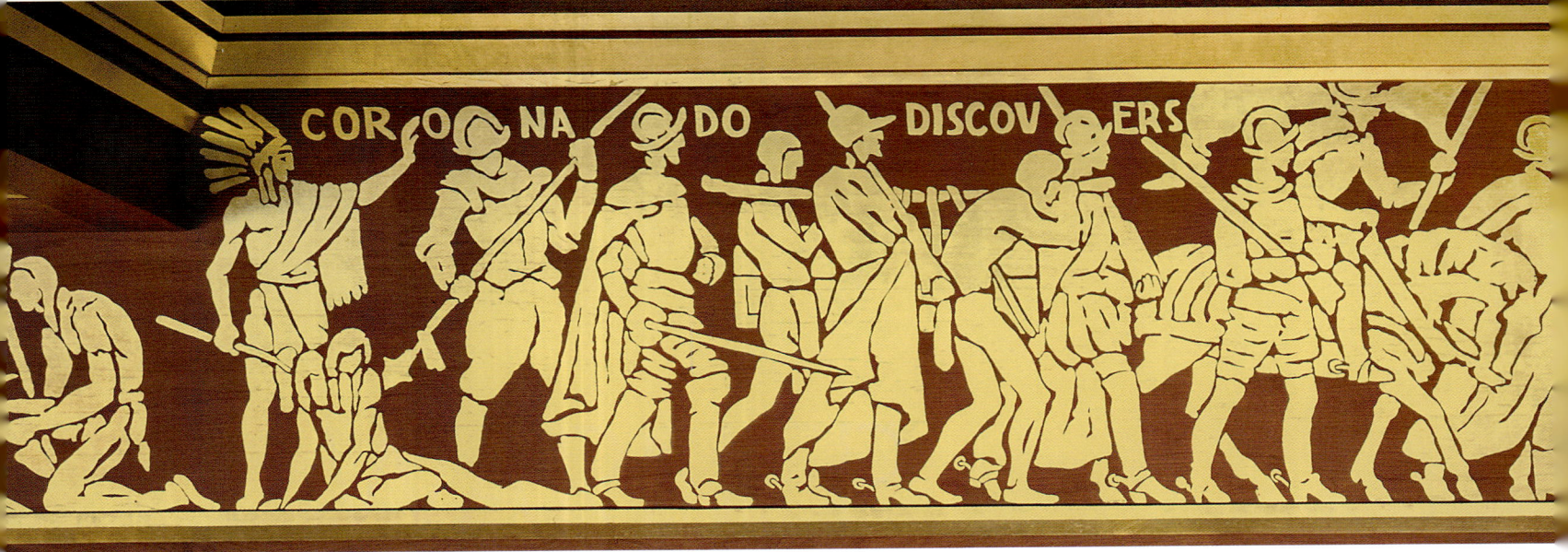

Hildreth Meière
Expedition of Coronado, c.1930
approx. 4 x 20 feet
Gold leaf on walnut

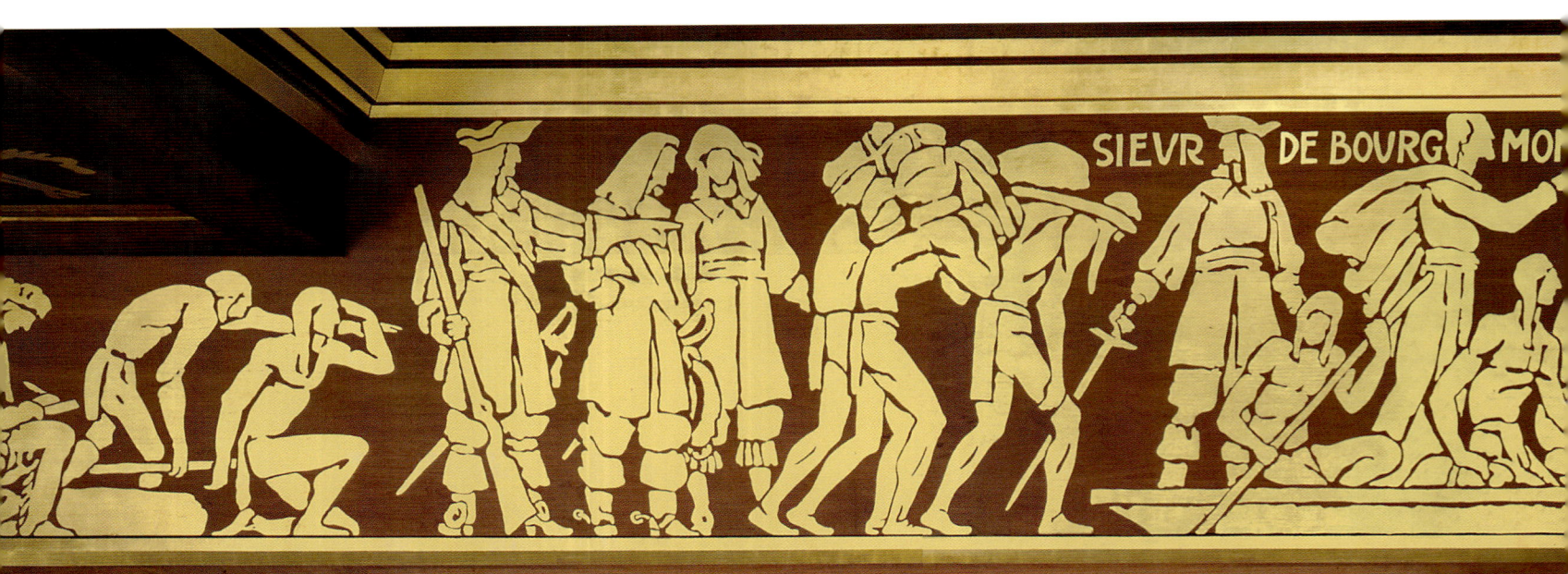

Hildreth Meière
Exploration of the Missouri by De Bourgmond, c.1930
approx. 4 x 20 feet
Gold leaf on walnut

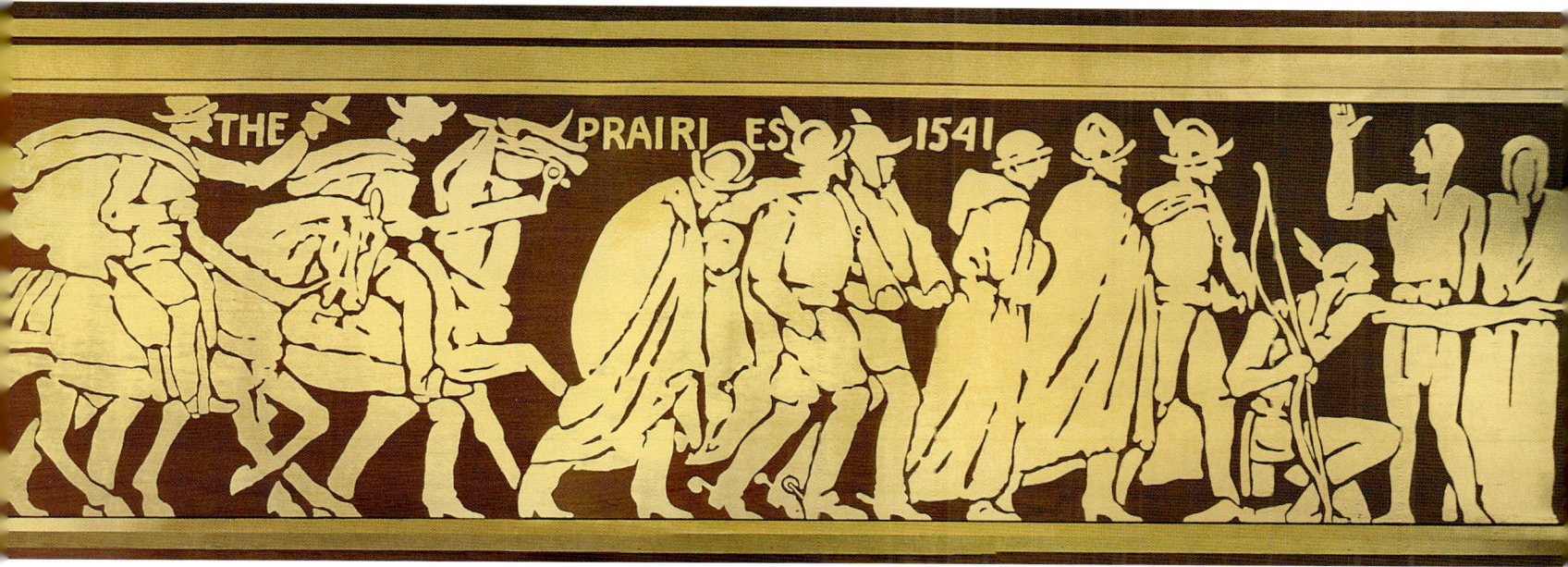

Six friezes lay out the various sovereignties that successively moved onto the plains, laying claim and settling Nebraska. Each is gilded in gold onto walnut ceiling beams.

Expedition of Coronado depicts the Spanish explorer Francisco Coronado's northern movement from Mexico in the 1540s. He was long considered to be the first European explorer to reach the Platte River of Nebraska, but now historians question whether he made it to Nebraska at all.

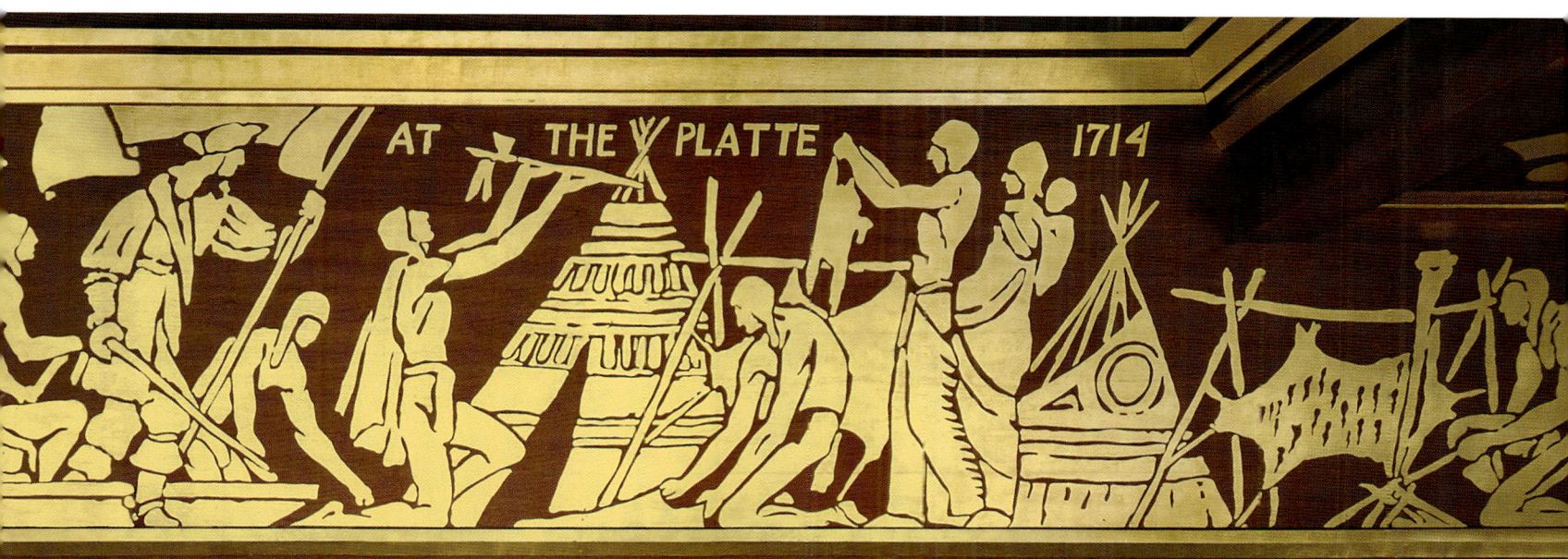

Etienne Véniard de Bourgmont, a French explorer, reached the mouth of the Platte River in 1714. Tasked by private investors to explore and map the territory, he established treaties with Native Americans and found sites for trading posts.

Bourgmont first used "Nebraskiér," meaning "flat water" in Otoe, in print to describe the river. Later other French explorers changed the name to Platte, the French word for "flat."

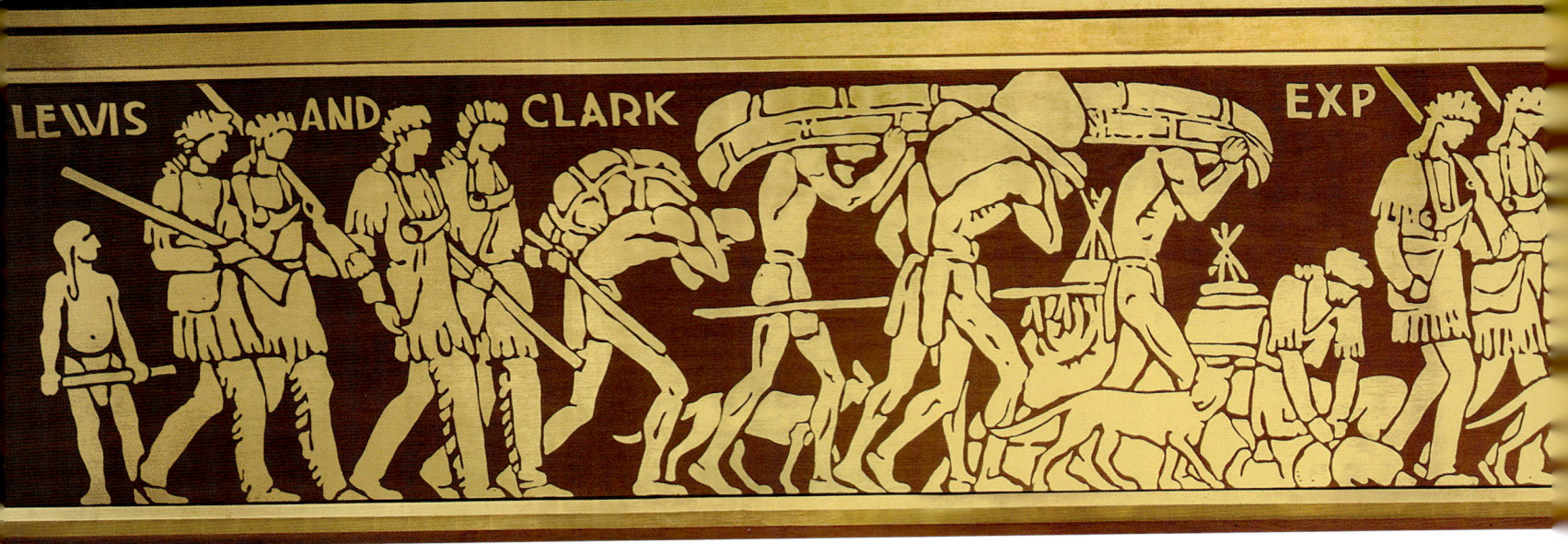

Hildreth Meière
Lewis and Clark Expedition, c.1930
approx. 4 x 20 feet
Gold leaf on walnut

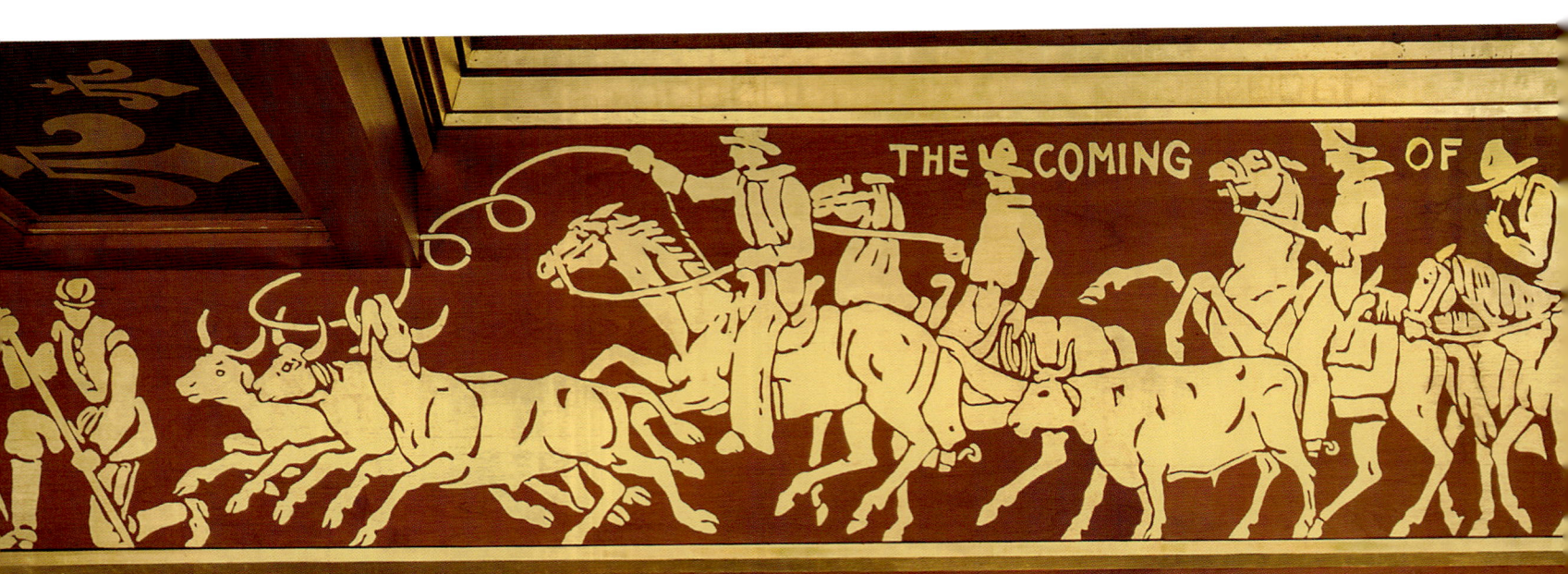

Hildreth Meière
The Coming of the Cattlemen, c.1930
approx. 4 x 20 feet
Gold leaf on walnut

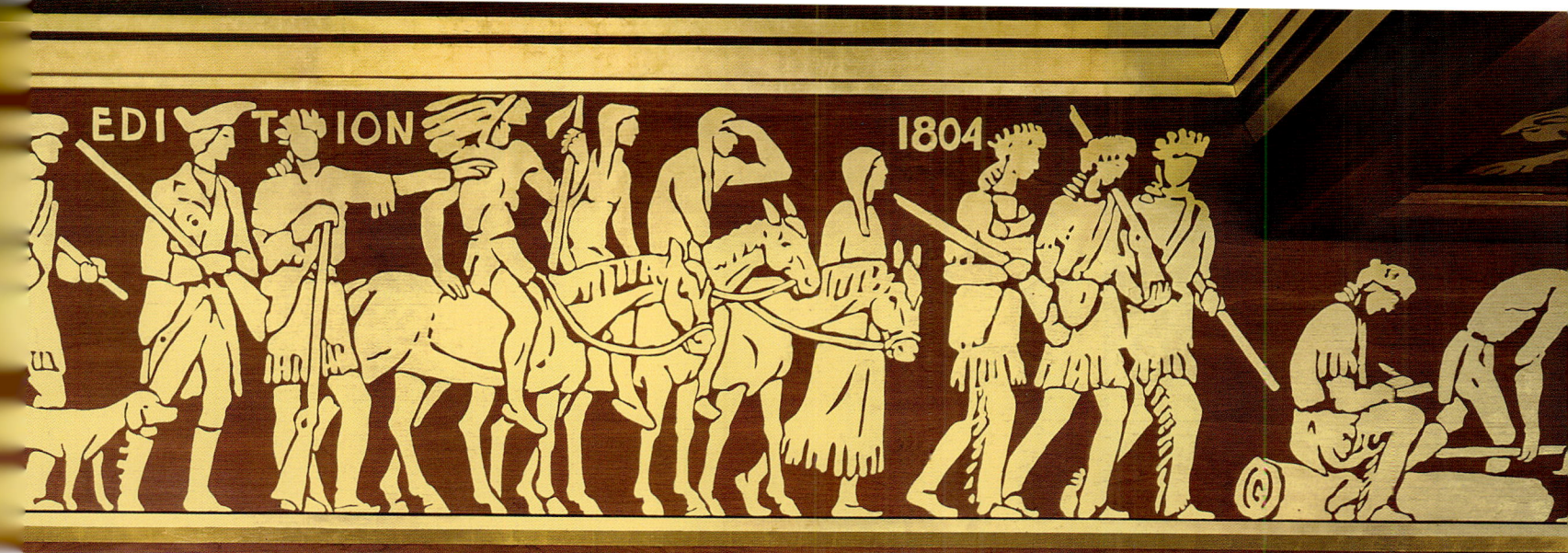

Meriwether Lewis and William Clark led their famous expedition through Nebraska following the Louisiana Purchase. Called the Corps of Discovery, the group landed in modern-day Nebraska in July of 1804. President Thomas Jefferson, hoping to find the mythic Northwest Passage, tasked them with mapping the land and studying the Native American tribes along their way to the western coast of the nation.

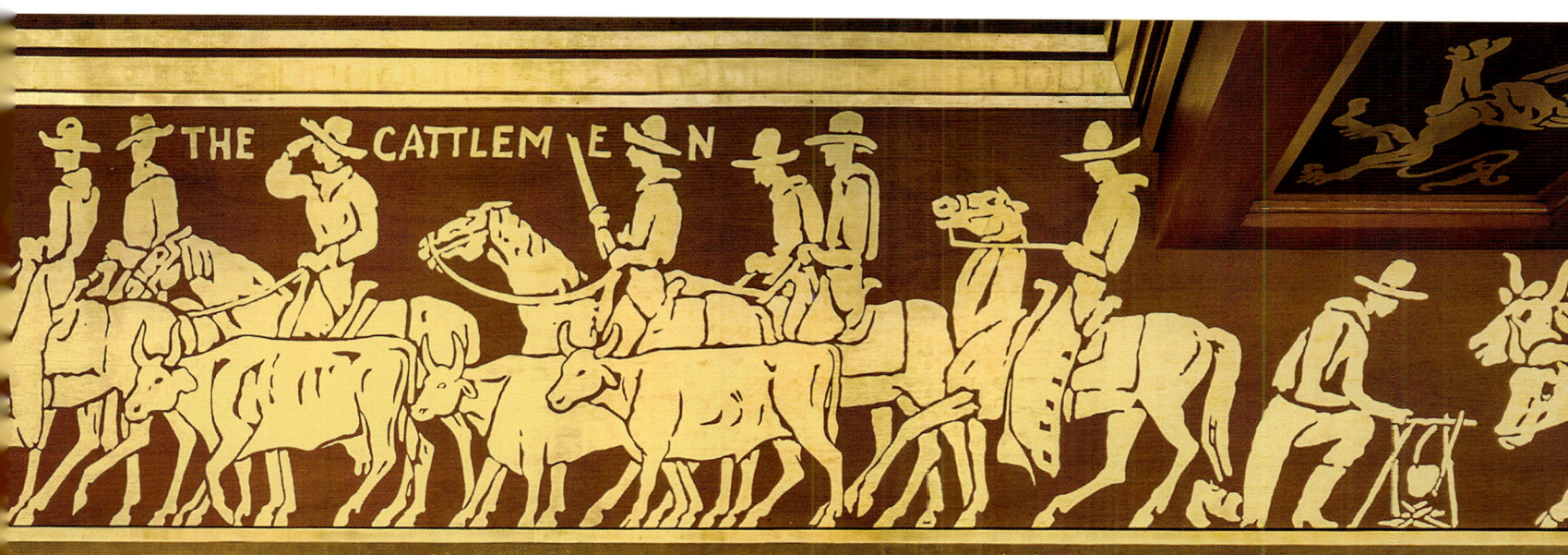

Drawn by the promise of open ranges, cattlemen settled in the state before the U.S. government opened up the land for a mass influx of homesteaders.

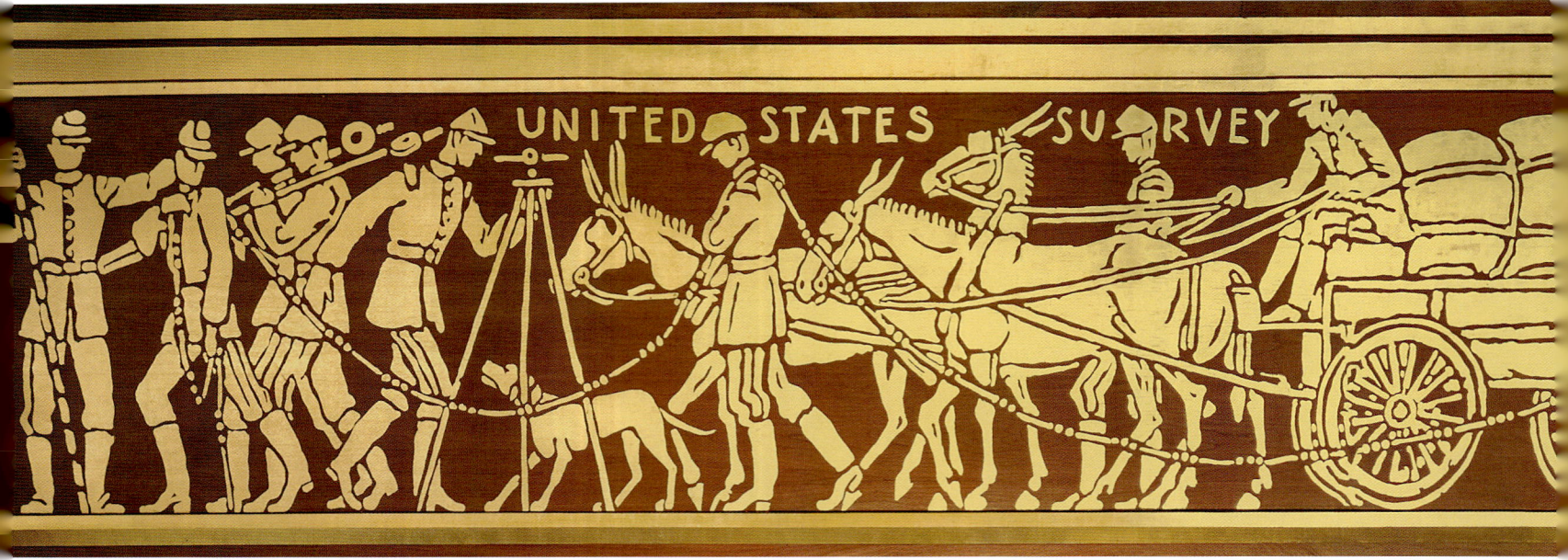

Hildreth Meière
United States Survey, c.1930
approx. 4 x 20 feet
Gold leaf on walnut

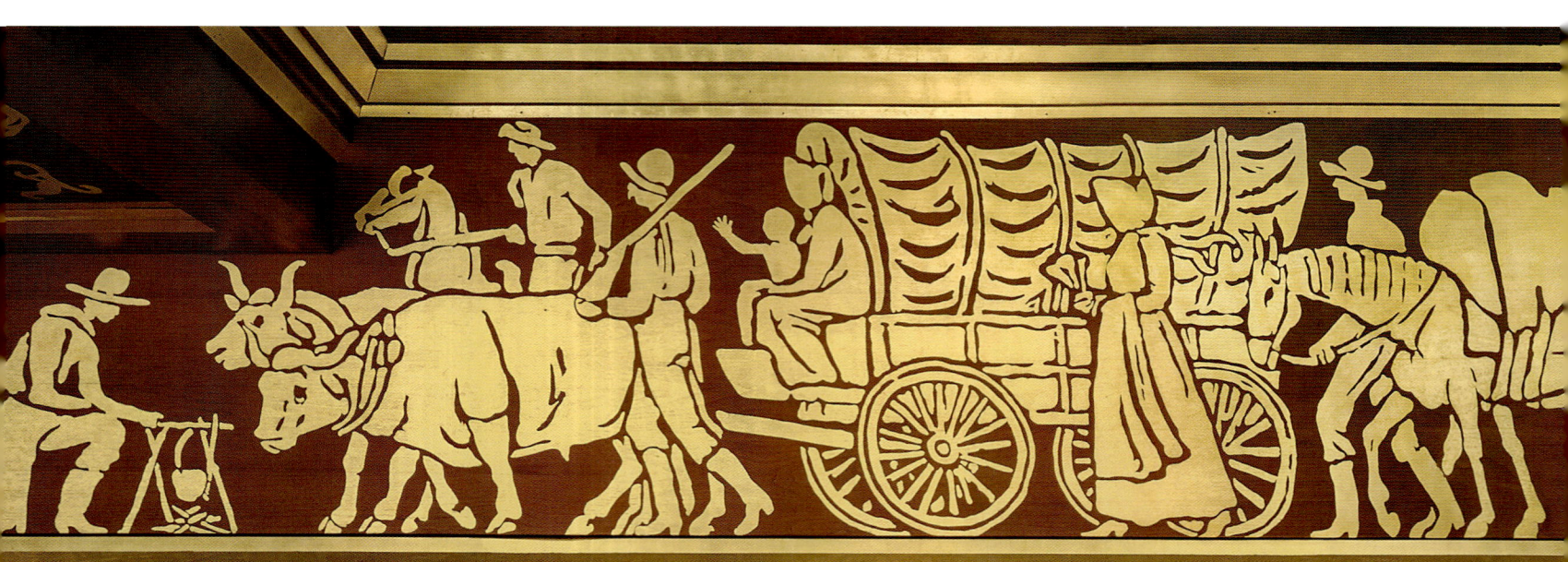

Hildreth Meière
The Homesteaders, c.1930
approx. 4 x 20 feet
Gold leaf on walnut

CREATIVE GENIUS

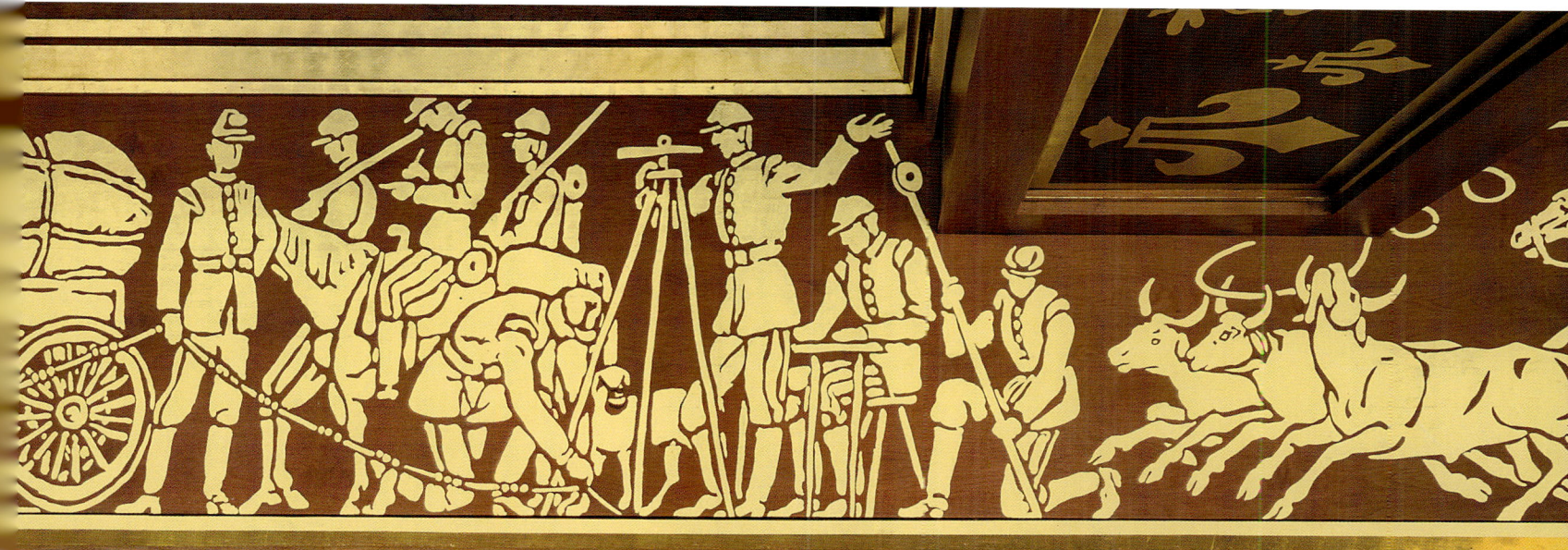

In 1867, the U.S. Congress authorized the first exploration and geological survey of the West. Set to study the area along the 40th parallel route of the transcontinental railroad, the Army Corp of Engineers surveyed the geology and natural resources of the new state of Nebraska and the surrounding territory.

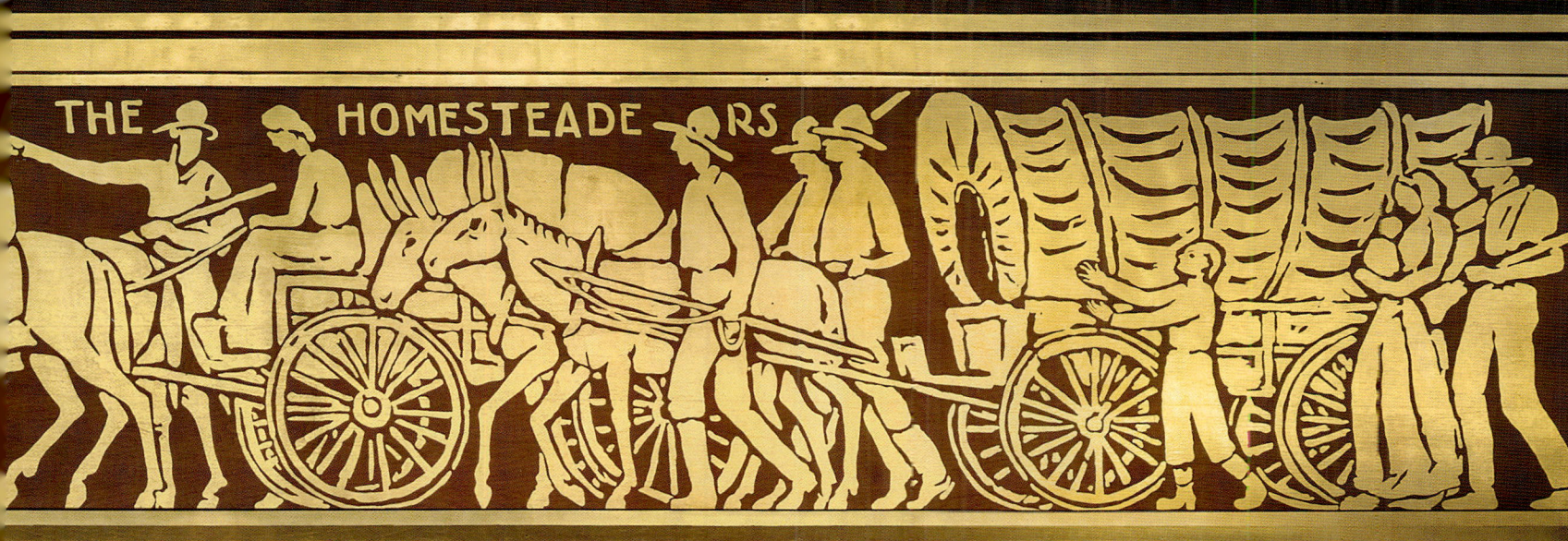

The Homestead Act of 1862 accelerated an already marked movement across the western territory of the United States. With a promise of 160 acres of land, homesteaders began settling in Nebraska at the end of the Civil War, starting at the Missouri River. The movement was slow and steady, taking over three decades to fan out to the central, western, and northwestern portions of the state.

GOVERNOR'S SUITE

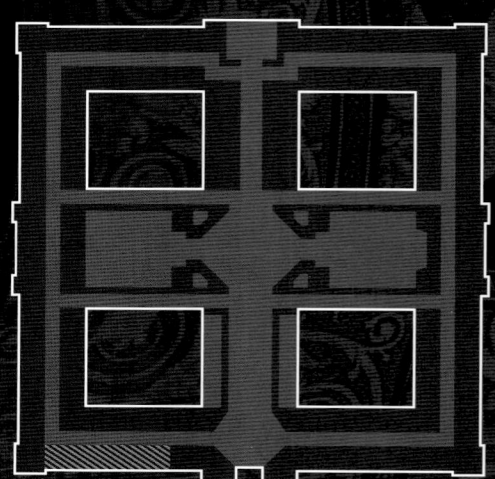

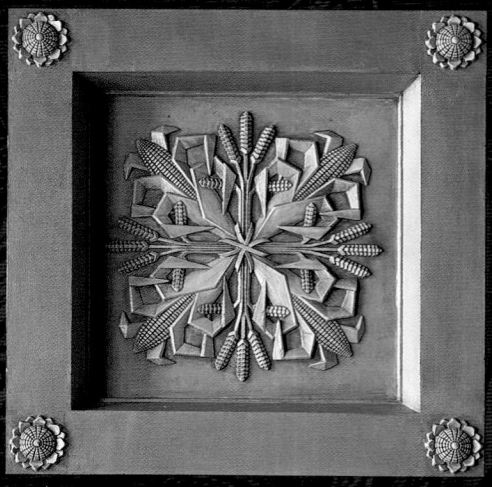

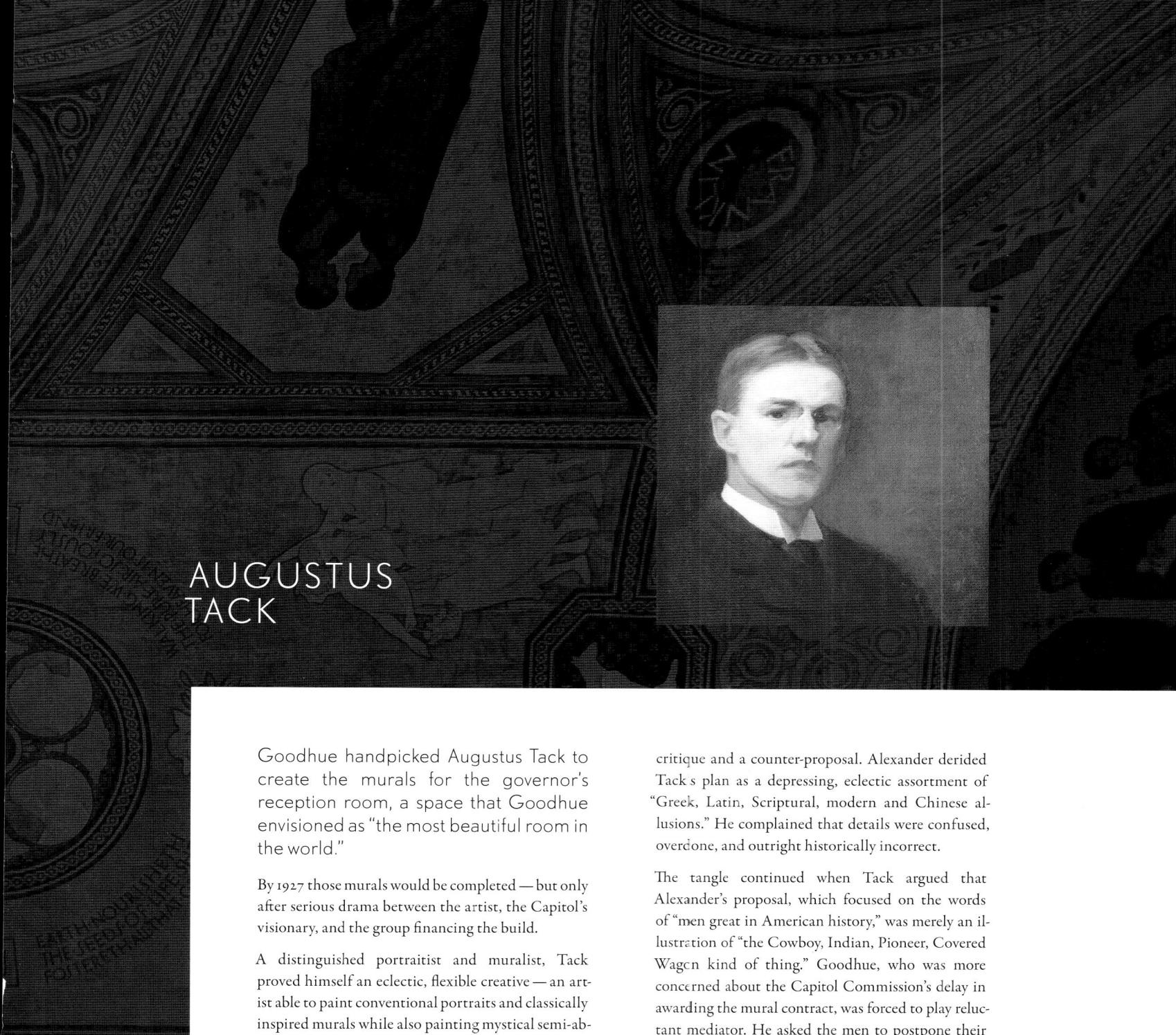

AUGUSTUS TACK

Goodhue handpicked Augustus Tack to create the murals for the governor's reception room, a space that Goodhue envisioned as "the most beautiful room in the world."

By 1927 those murals would be completed — but only after serious drama between the artist, the Capitol's visionary, and the group financing the build.

A distinguished portraitist and muralist, Tack proved himself an eclectic, flexible creative — an artist able to paint conventional portraits and classically inspired murals while also painting mystical semi-abstract landscapes centered around spiritual themes. His work often merged photography, Oriental mysticism, and an interest in the Old Masters.

In his original concept proposed for the Capitol murals, Tack relied on more impressionistic methods and themes than those in other areas of the building. He incorporated his appreciation for the metaphysical and Asian mysticism to explore the human experience. He quickly found that his ideas did not always resonate with others.

After Goodhue sent Tack's concept to Alexander, the man who created the symbolism and story of the Capitol, Alexander sent back a harsh, specific critique and a counter-proposal. Alexander derided Tack's plan as a depressing, eclectic assortment of "Greek, Latin, Scriptural, modern and Chinese allusions." He complained that details were confused, overdone, and outright historically incorrect.

The tangle continued when Tack argued that Alexander's proposal, which focused on the words of "men great in American history," was merely an illustration of "the Cowboy, Indian, Pioneer, Covered Wagon kind of thing." Goodhue, who was more concerned about the Capitol Commission's delay in awarding the mural contract, was forced to play reluctant mediator. He asked the men to postpone their fight until he could convince the Capitol Commission to pay for the mural. Unfortunately, Goodhue died unexpectedly, and the argument was never negotiated. Instead, Tack was hired by the Capitol Commission to complete the work. He wholly ignored Alexander's input. Alexander in turn specifically excluded the governor's rooms from his acknowledgment when he discussed his symbology of the Capitol, claiming no responsibility for the art or message.

Tack became well regarded as an early modern artist who merged his traditional painting with Impressionist training — creating a style all his own. The famed artist died in New York City in 1949.

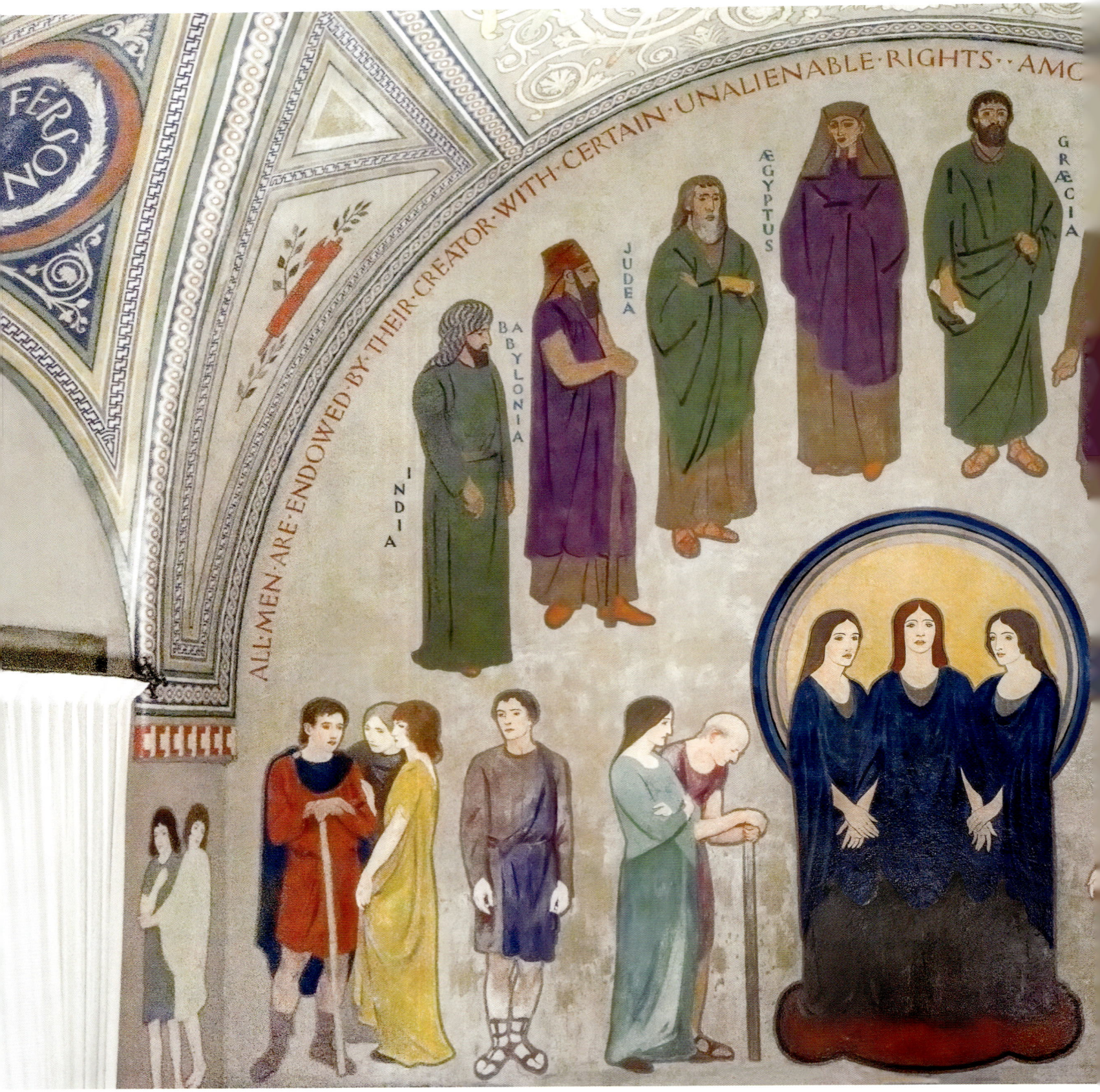

Augustus Tack
Conditions of Life: Youth and Old Age, 1927
Oil on canvas

Augustus Tack
Understanding, Justice, and Mercy, 1927
Oil on canvas

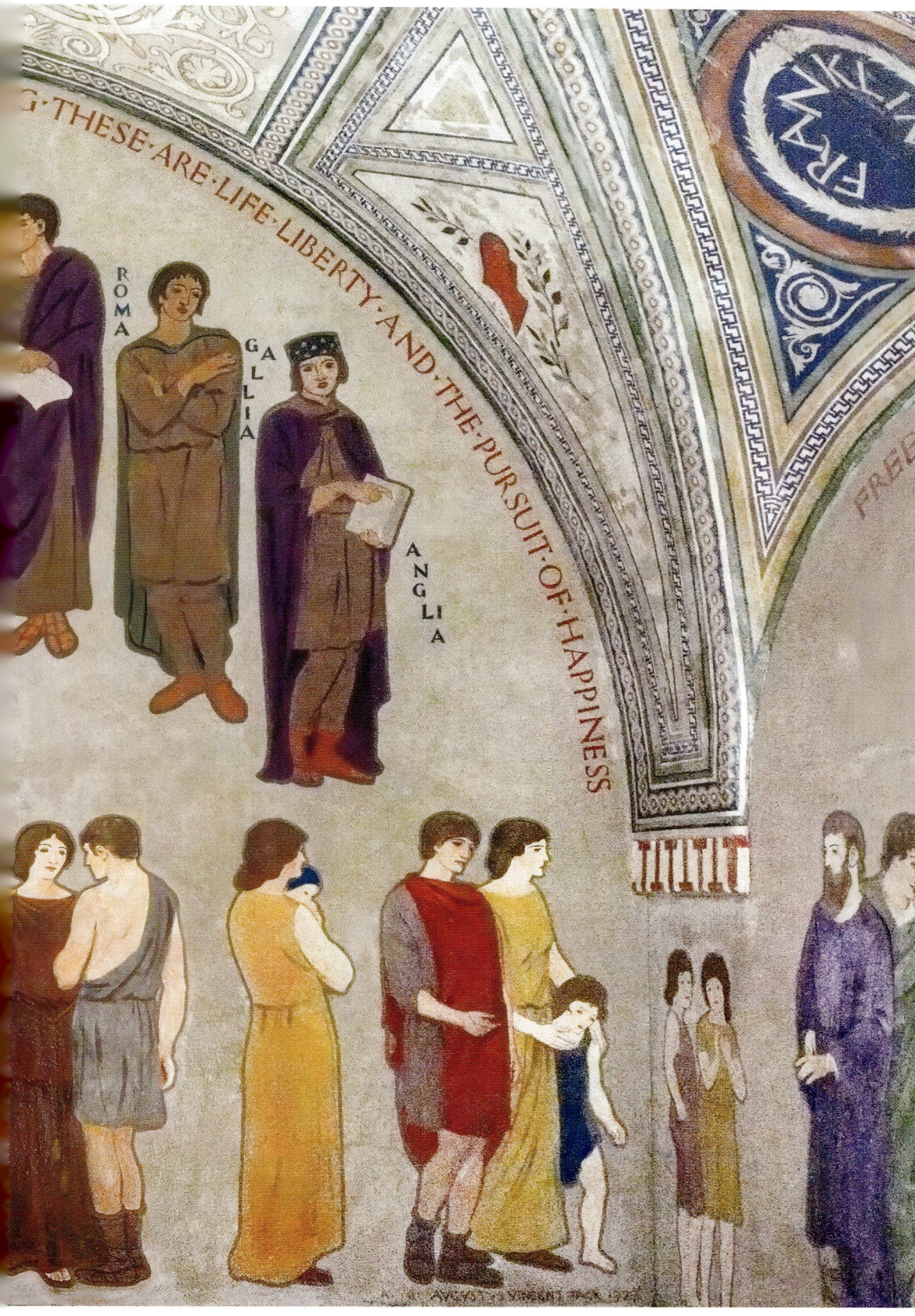

G·THESE·ARE·LIFE·LIBERTY·AND·THE·PURSUIT·OF·HAPPINESS

ROMA

GALLIA

ANGLIA

FREE

Augustus Tack
Wisdom of Past Governments, 1927
Oil on canvas

Tack chose a different medium and style from the rest of the Capitol artwork. In the governor's suite, he utilized oil on canvas for murals that simulated frescos. Painted in an Italian Renaissance style, the subjects in the rooms resemble idealized citizens of a timeless period. Tack said that his pieces were like figures decorating "the surface of the wall much in the way the Greeks employed the figure to decorate the surface of a vase."

During the 1927 ceremony to showcase the entire suite's completion, reaction was mixed. They have been described as having a medieval feeling, archaic and flat. However, though they do not match the style of the other art of the Capitol, they do fit the overall theme of the role of government and society.

Throughout the reception room, Tack represented the eternal and steady nature of democratic rights and responsibilities. His overall theme for the paintings was "Ideal Government and Ideal Life." A variety of the citizenry on multiple walls represent the responsibilities of the state, including freedoms of speech, religion, and the right of suffrage.

Augustus Tack
Conditions of Life: Young Lovers, Motherhood, and Family, 1927
Oil on canvas

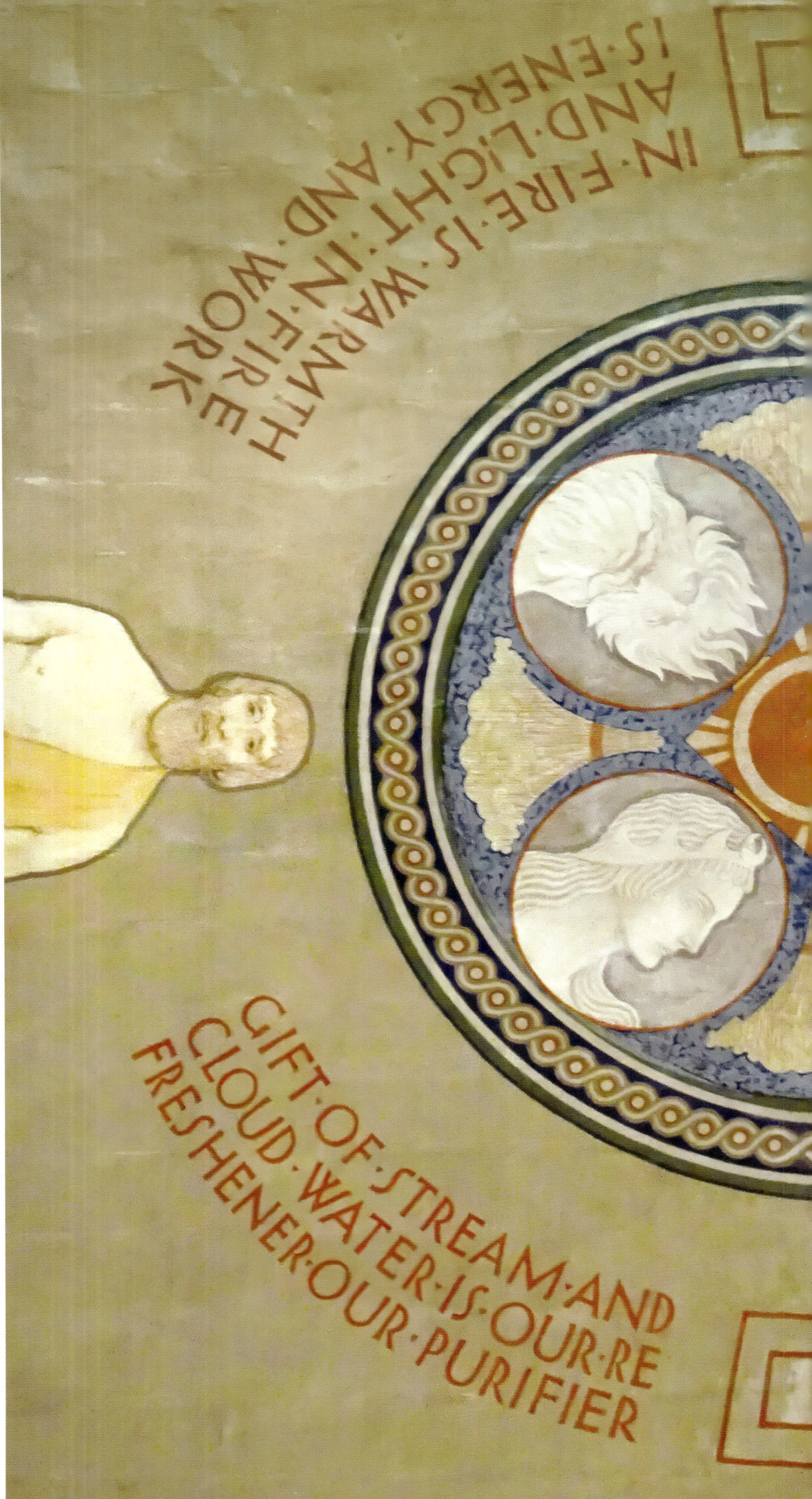

Augustus Tack
Earth, Air, Fire, Water, 1927
Oil on canvas

In the center of the dome, the four elements encircle the sun. Surrounding them stand representations of agriculture and industry, the occupations of life.

IN·FIRE·IS·WARMTH·IN·FIRE·IS·ENERGY·AND·LIGHT·AND·IN·FIRE·WORK

GIFT·OF·STREAM·AND·CLOUD·WATER·IS·OUR·RE FRESHENER·OUR·PURIFIER

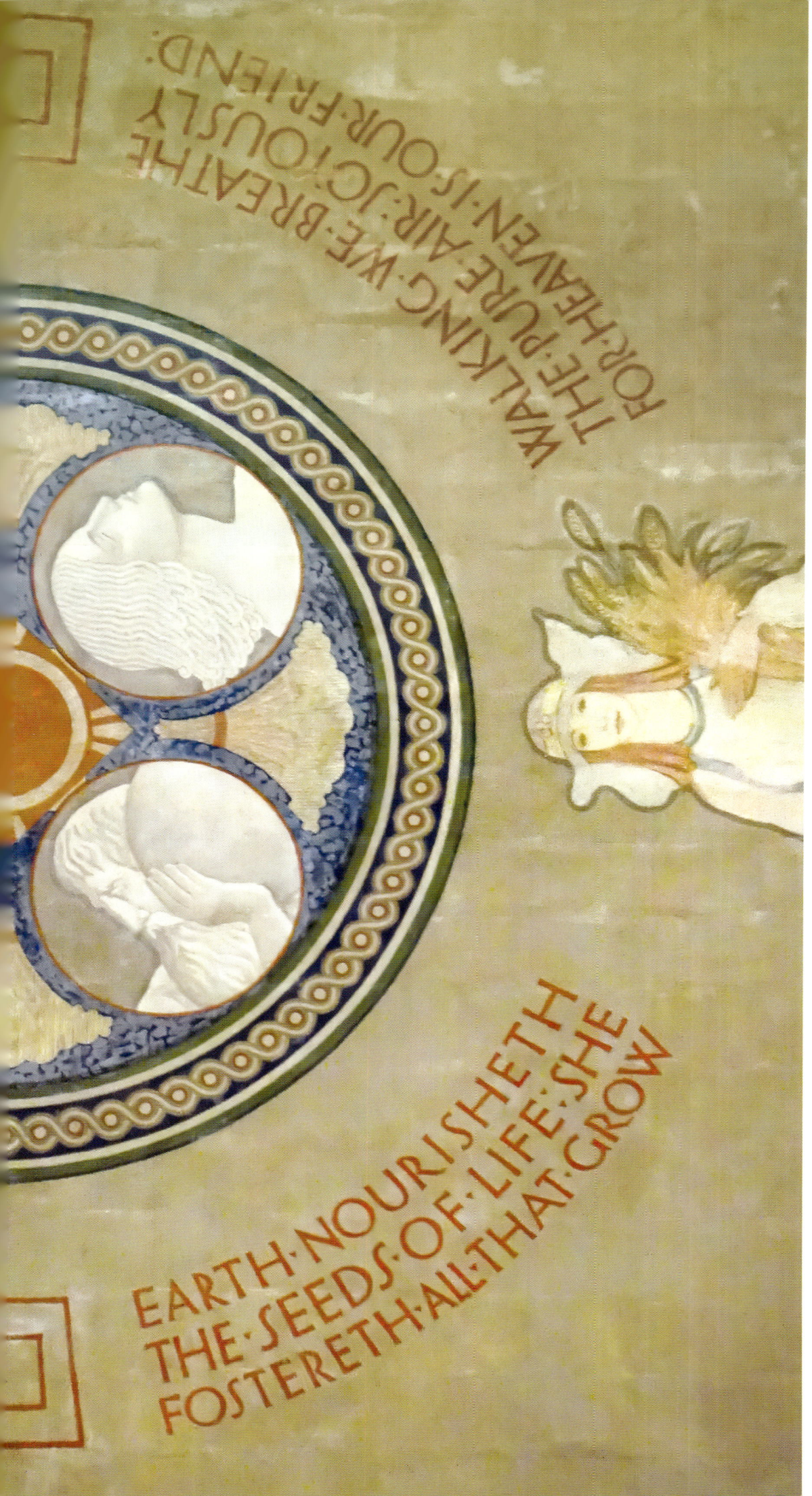

WALKING·WE·BREATHE
THE·PURE·AIR·JOYOUSLY
FOR·HEAVEN·IS·OUR·FRIEND·

EARTH·NOURISHETH
THE·SEEDS·OF·LIFE·SHE
FOSTERETH·ALL·THAT·GROW

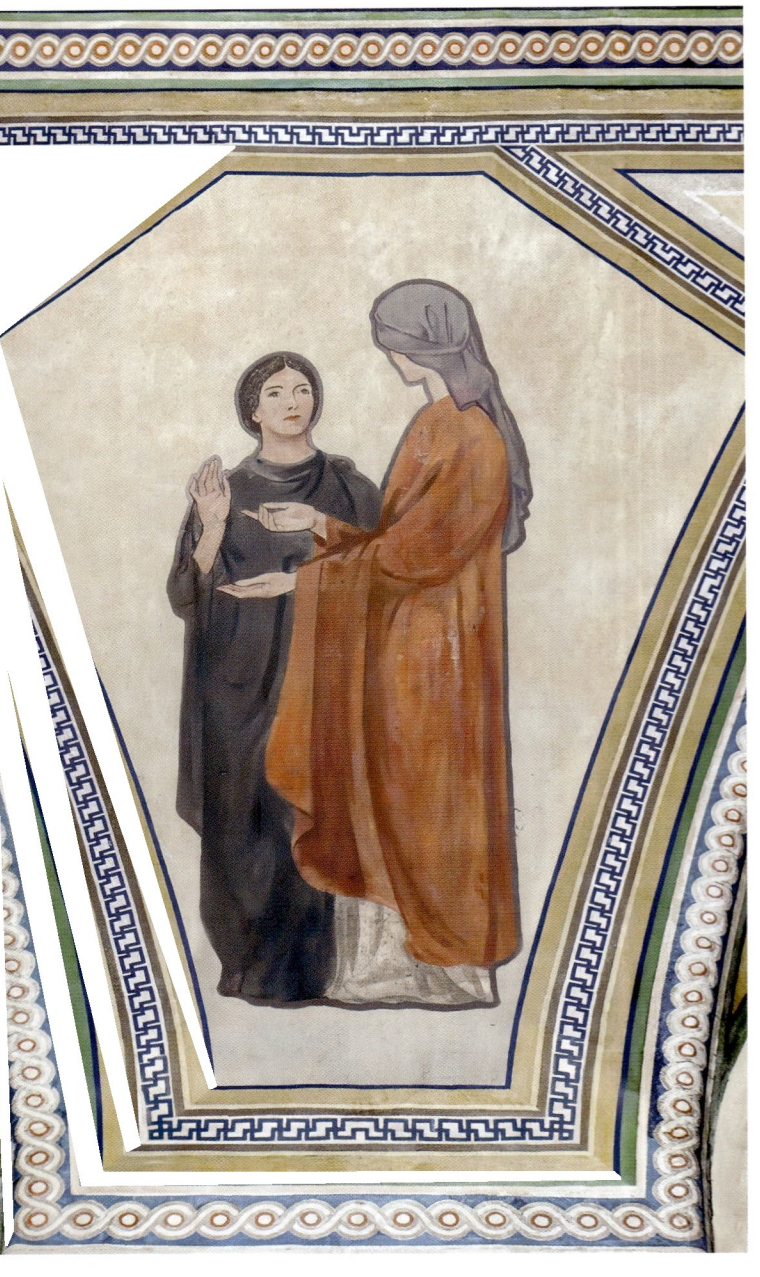

Augustus Tack
Honesty, 1927
Oil on canvas

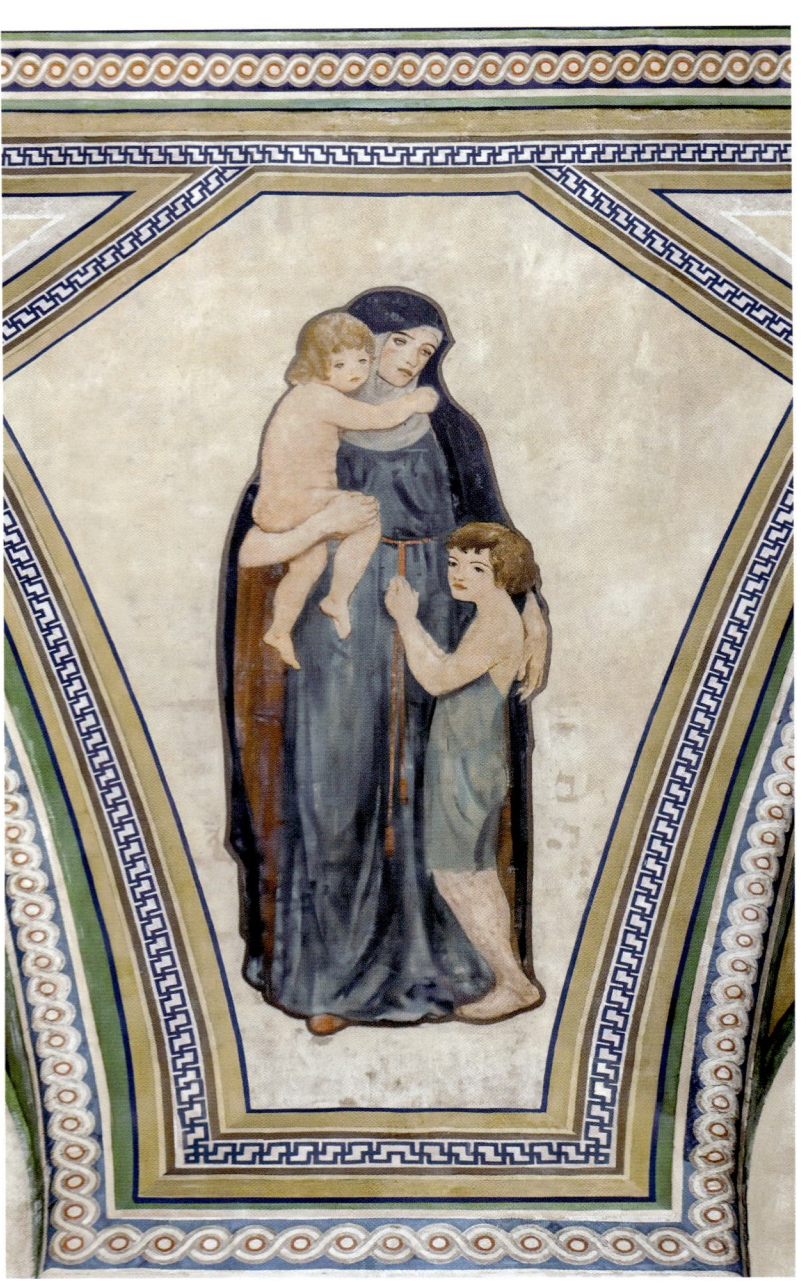

Augustus Tack
Charity, 1927
Oil on canvas

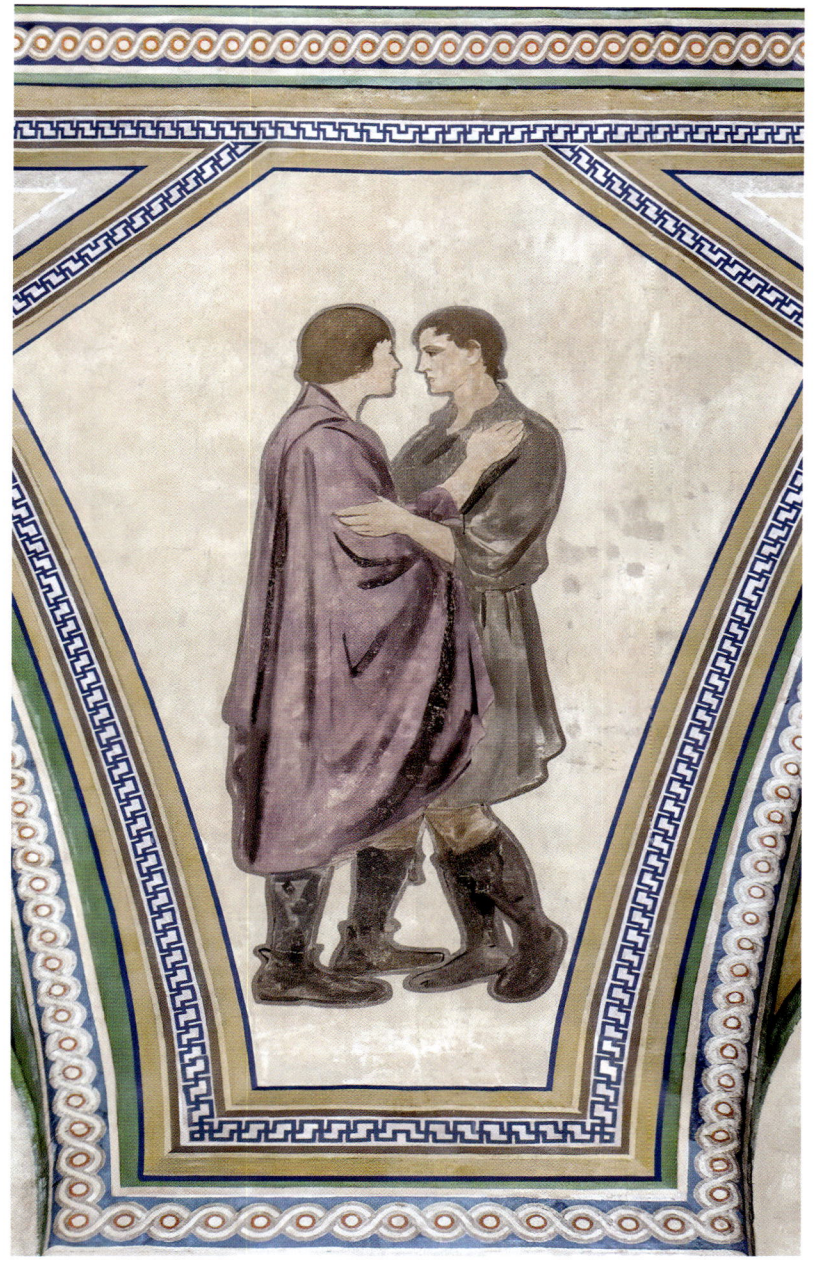

Augustus Tack
Friendship, 1927
Oil on canvas

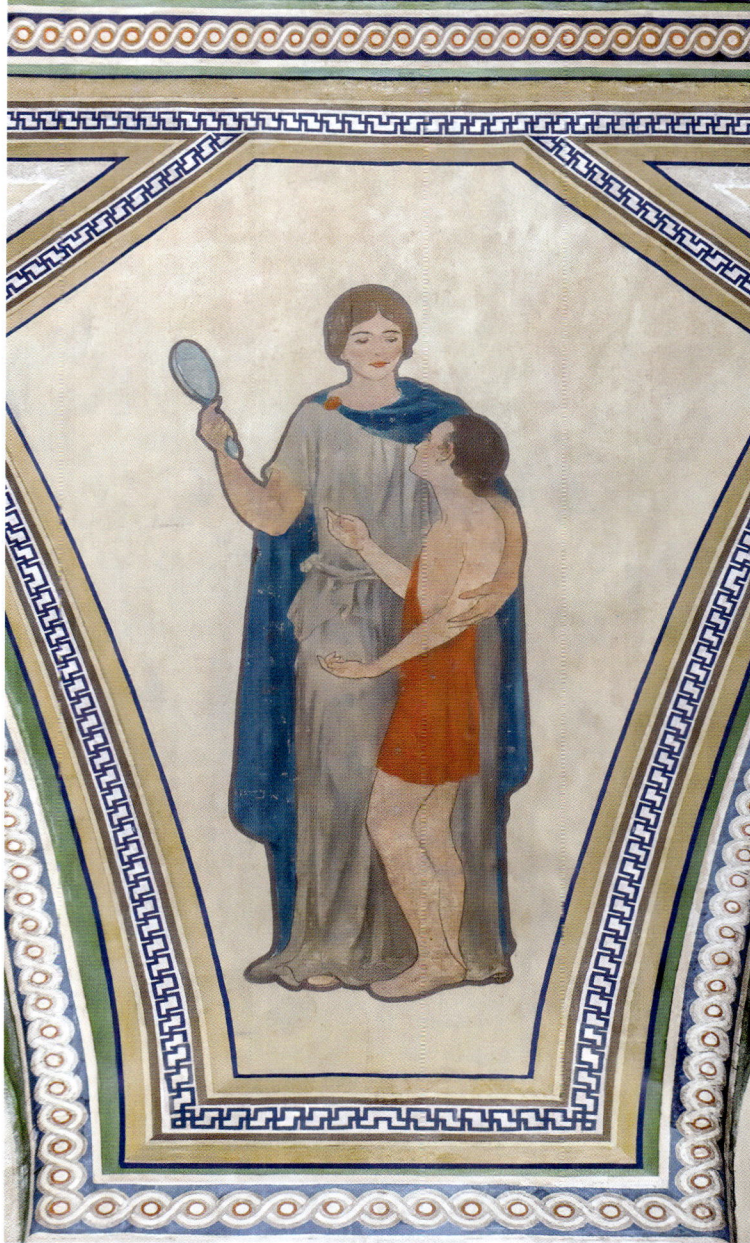

Augustus Tack
Hospitality, 1927
Oil on canvas

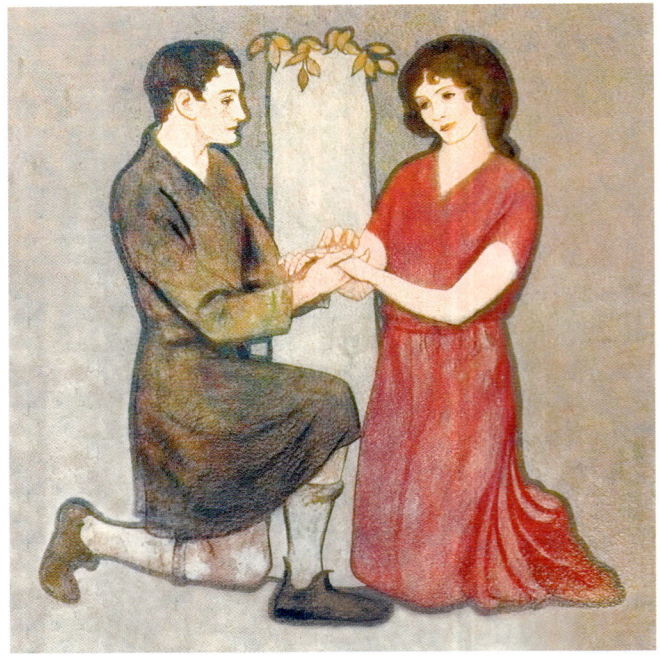

Augustus Tack
Marriage, 1927
Oil on canvas

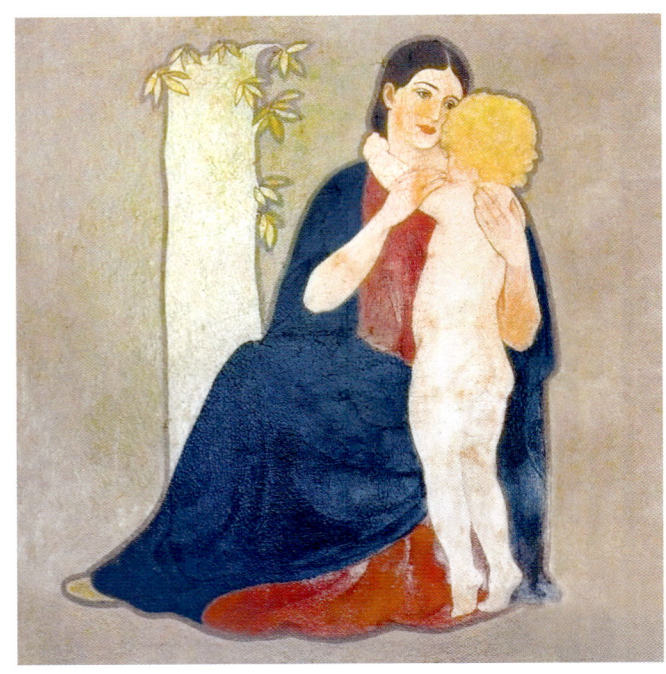

Augustus Tack
Motherhood, 1927
Oil on canvas

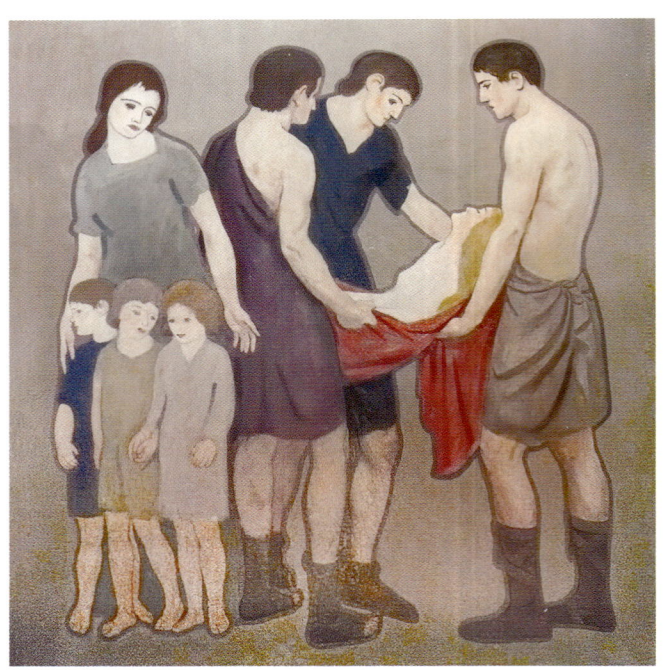

Augustus Tack
State as the Protector of the Sick, 1927
Oil on canvas

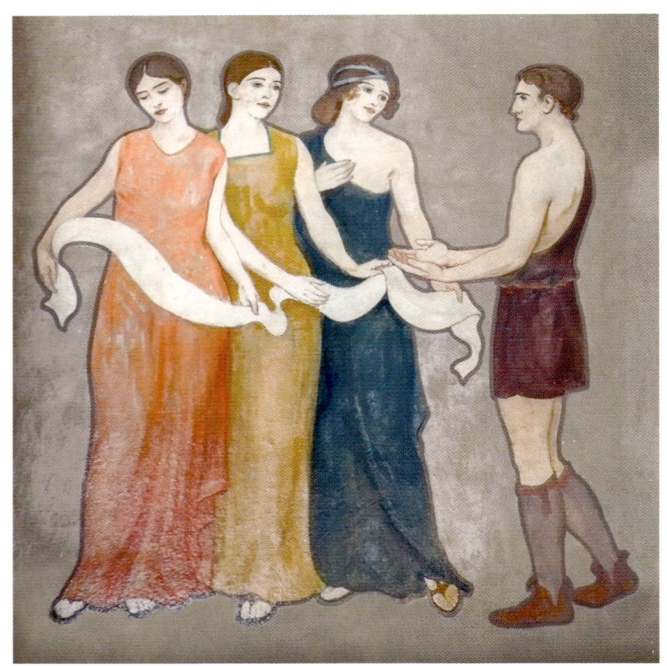

Augustus Tack
State as the Provider of Learning, 1927
Oil on canvas

Augustus Tack
Fortune, 1927
Oil on canvas

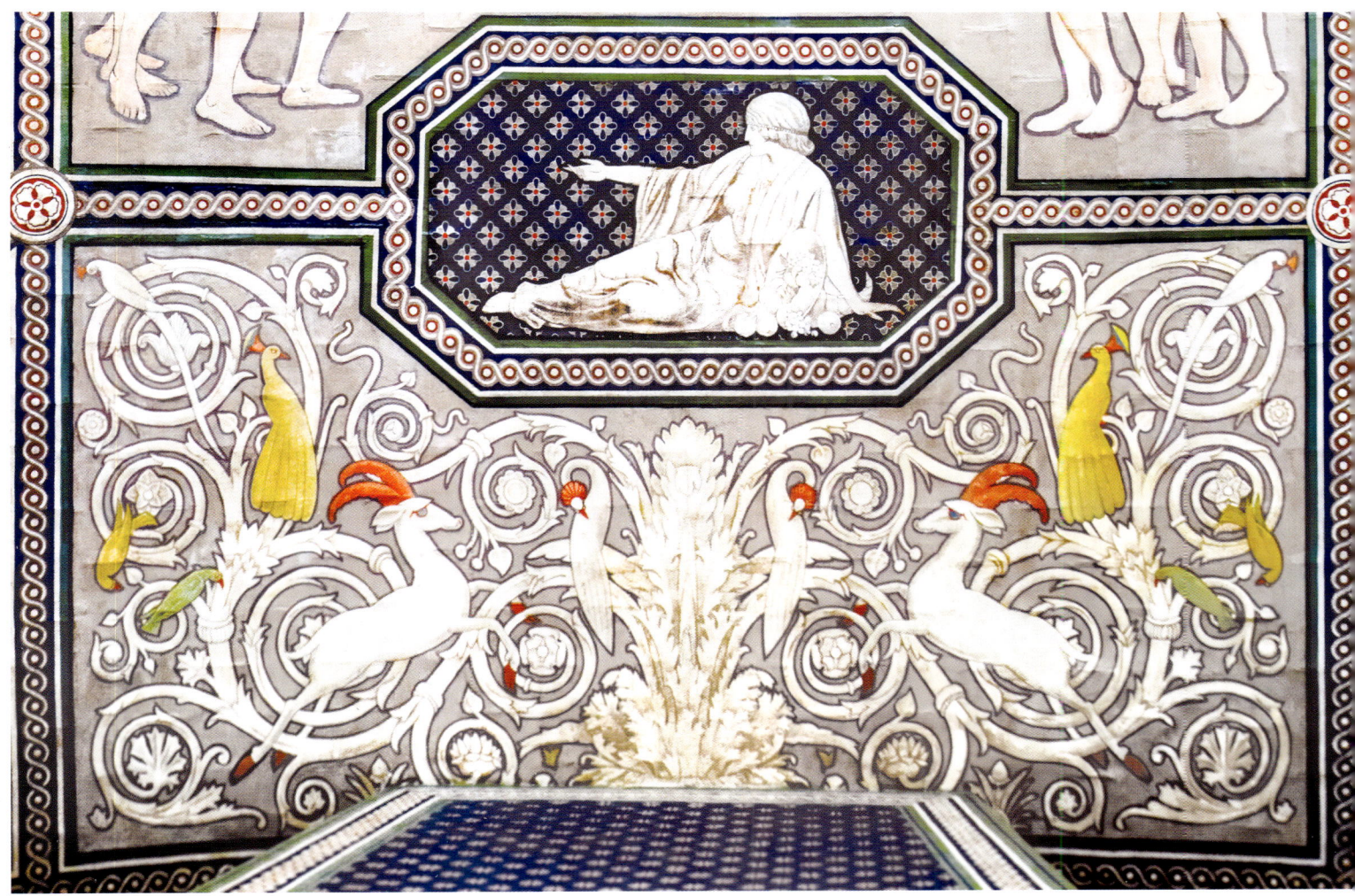

Augustus Tack
Tree of Life, 1927
Oil on canvas

The Tree of Life springs from the center, its branches supporting
the flora and fauna surrounding it. Fortune lounges above.

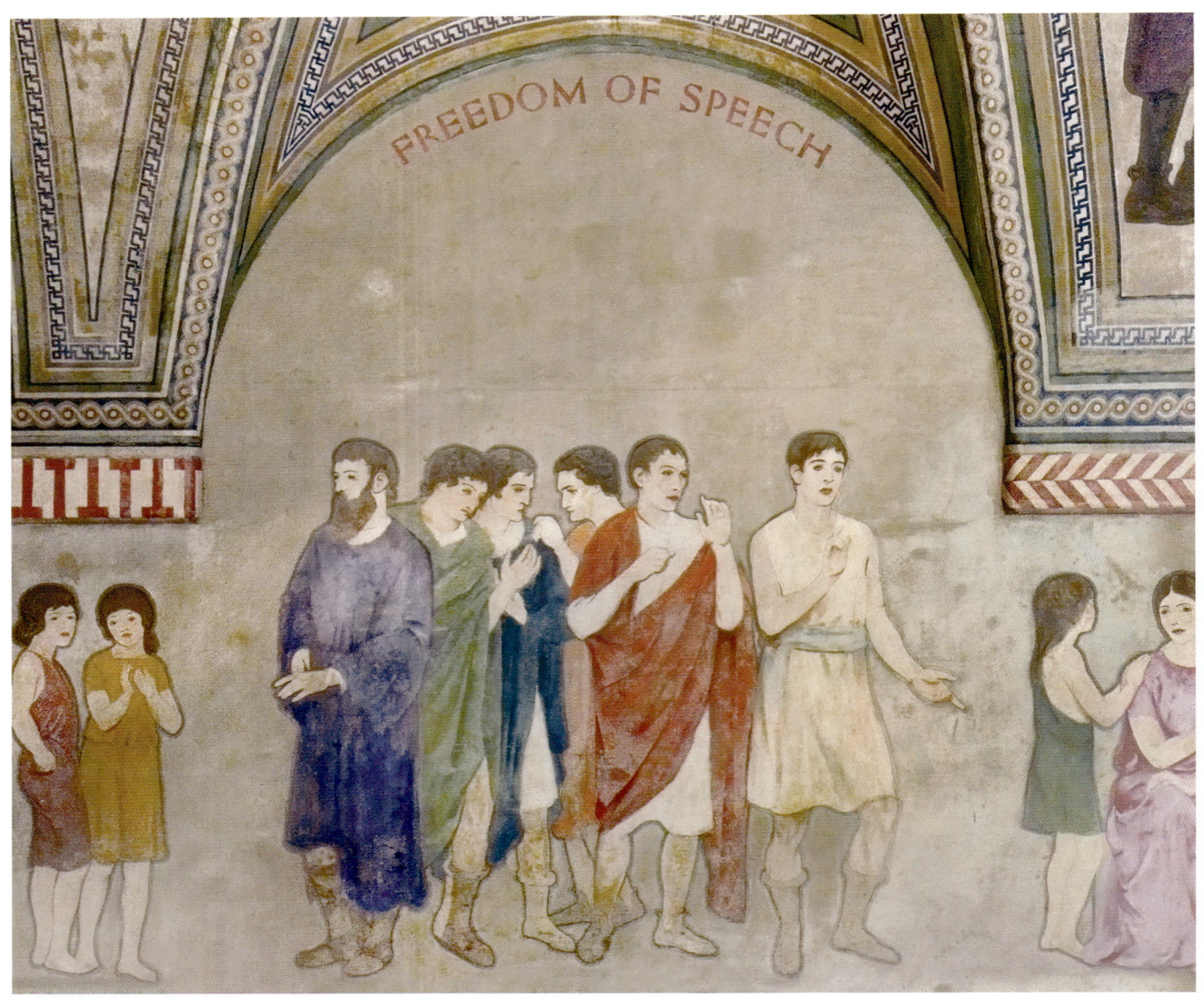

Augustus Tack
Liberty of Speech, 1927
Oil on canvas

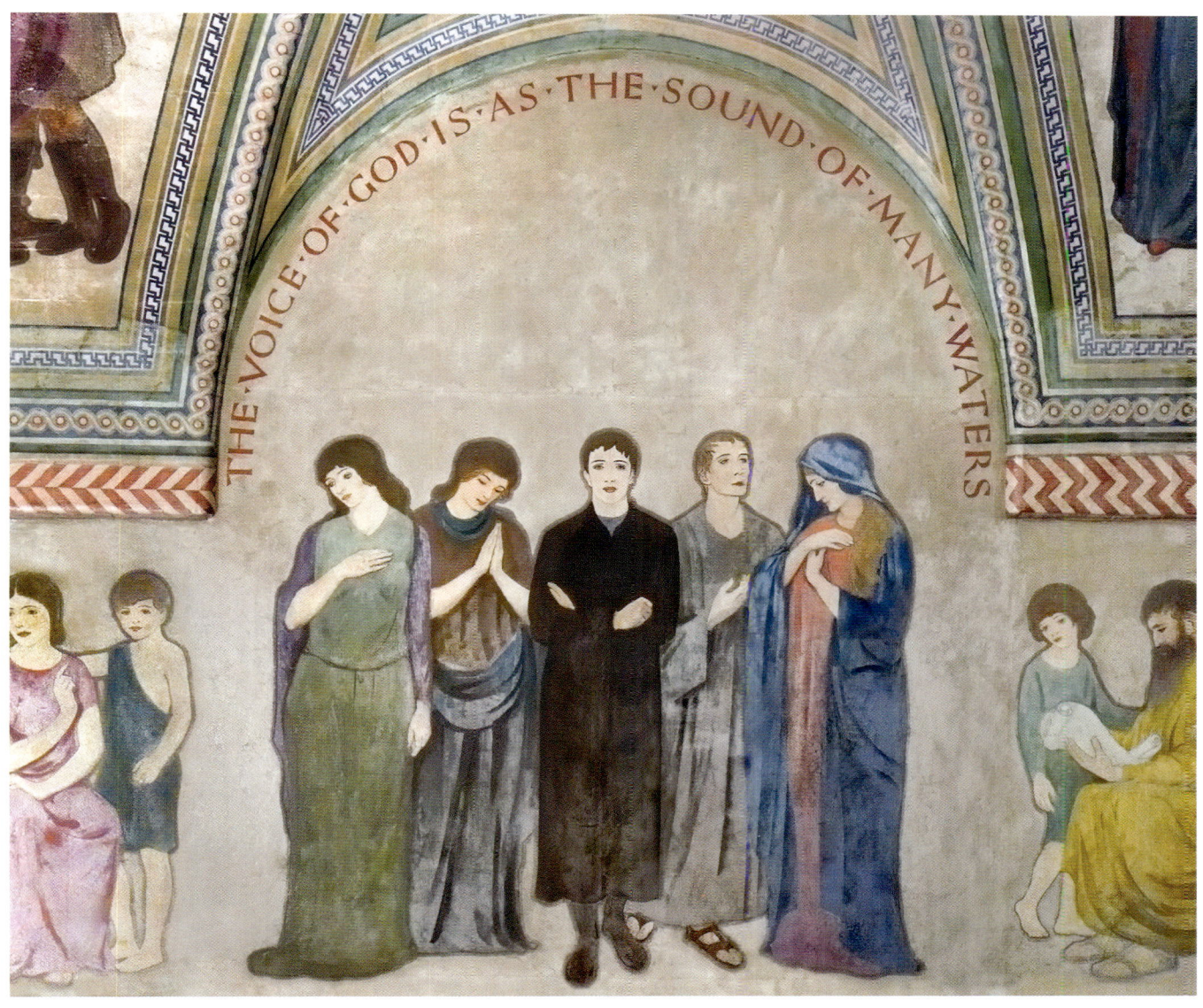

Augustus Tack
Liberty of Divine Worship, 1927
Oil on canvas

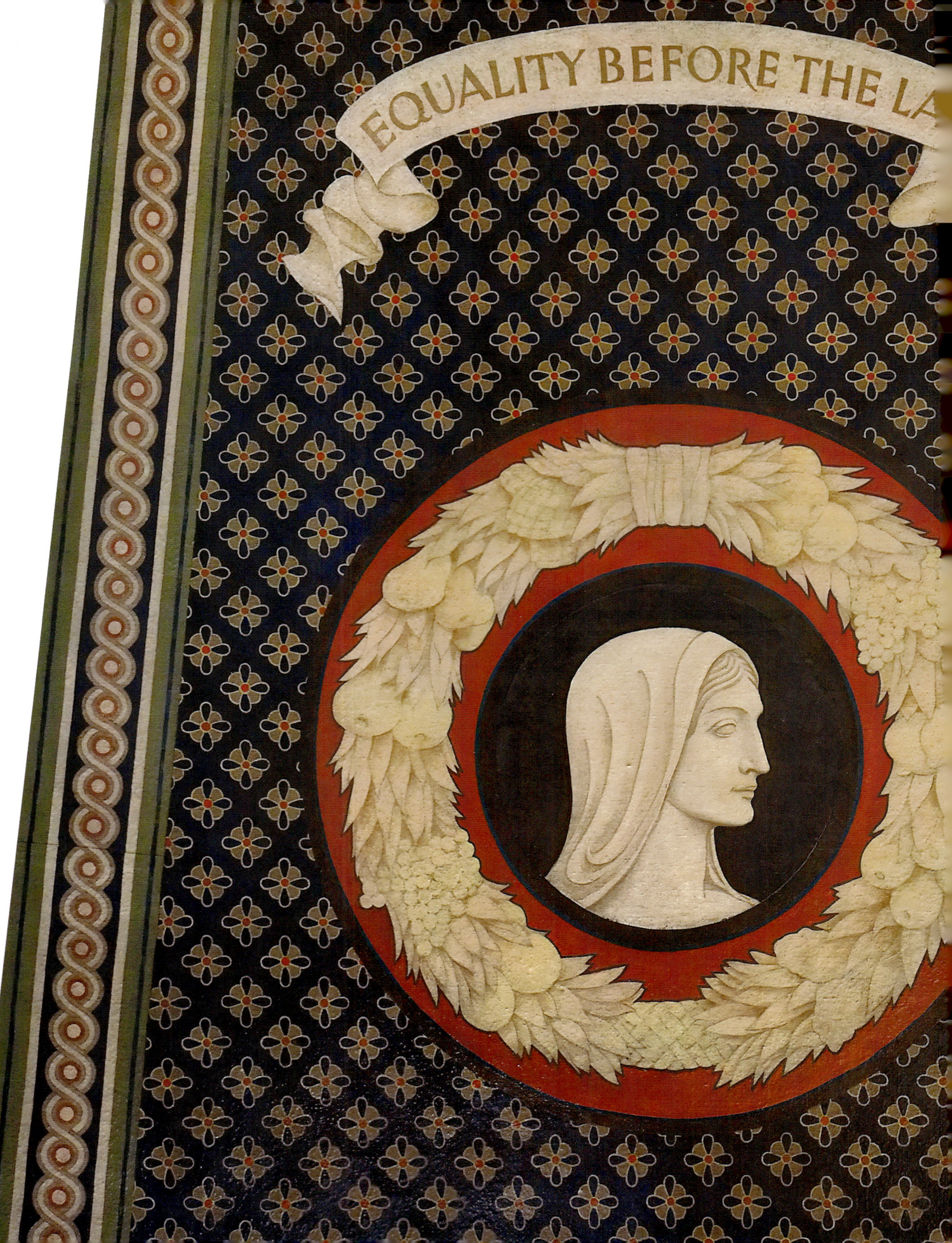

EQUALITY BEFORE THE LA

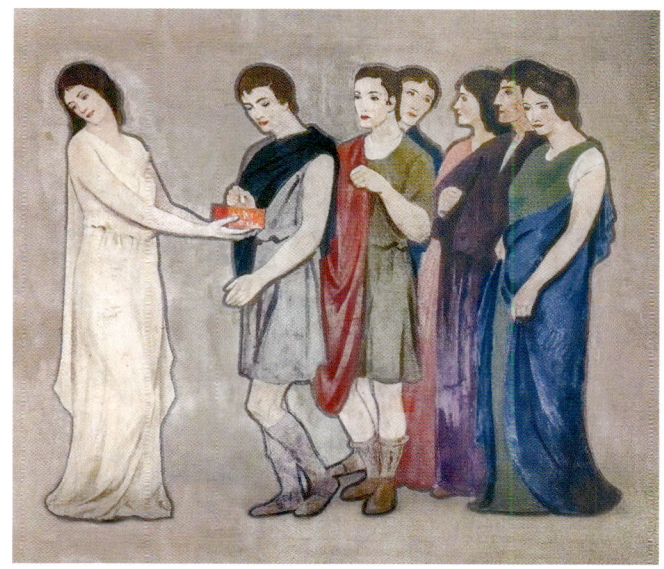

Augustus Tack
Rights of Suffrage, 1927
Oil on canvas

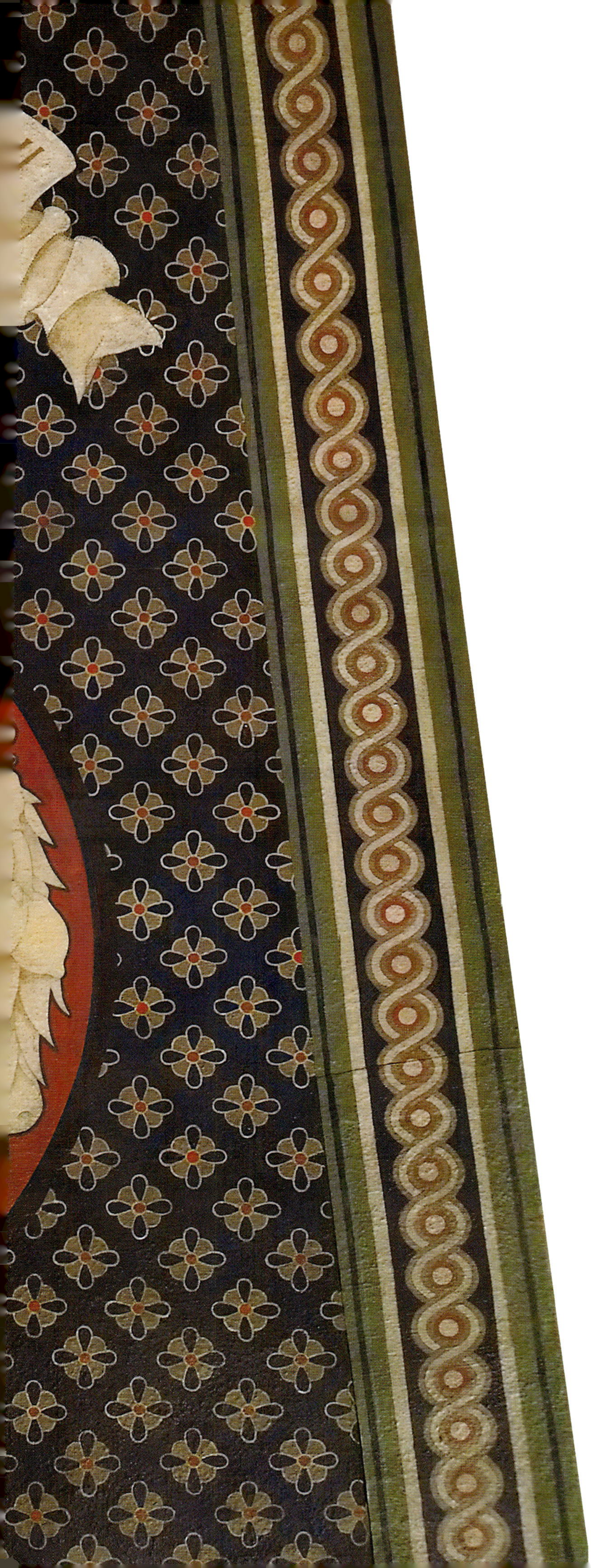

Augustus Tack
The State, 1927
Oil on canvas

By the time he met Goodhue,
Tack painted commissioned
murals in multiple churches
and state institutions
throughout North America.
He was also a well-known
portraitist whose notable
subjects included Helen
Keller, Nebraska's General
John J. Pershing, and two
future presidents, General
Dwight D. Eisenhower
and Harry S. Truman.

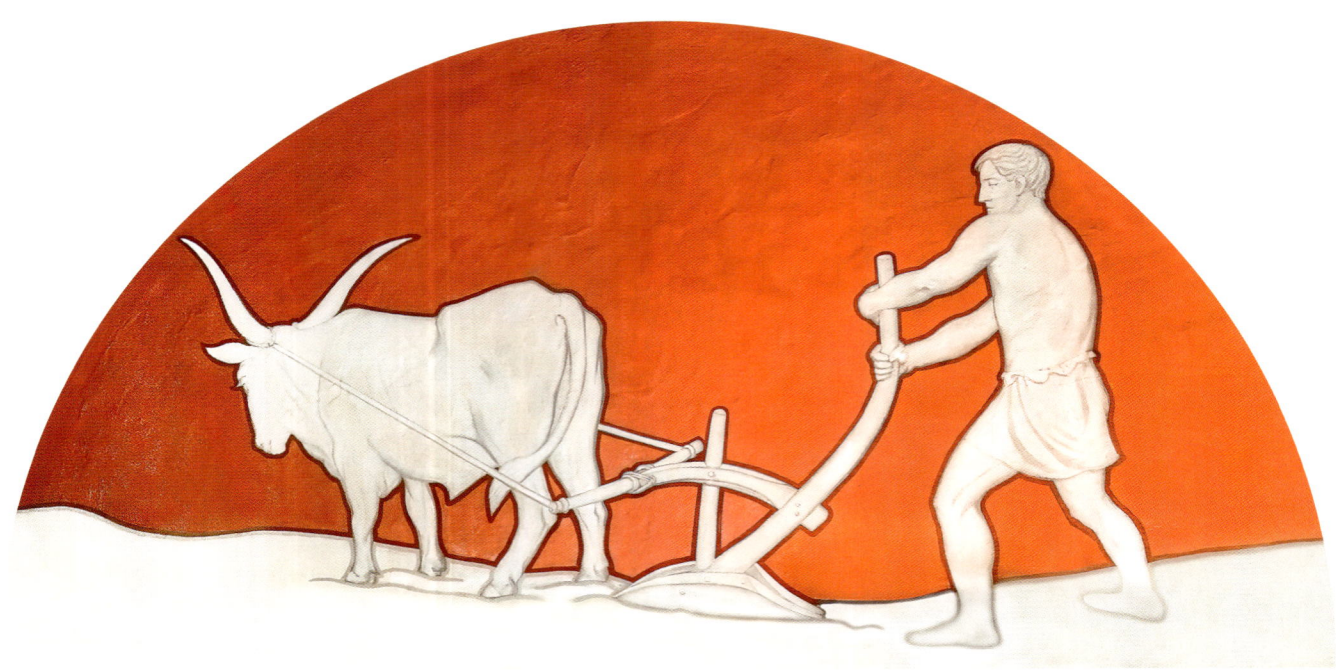

Augustus Tack
Spring Tilling, 1927
Oil on canvas

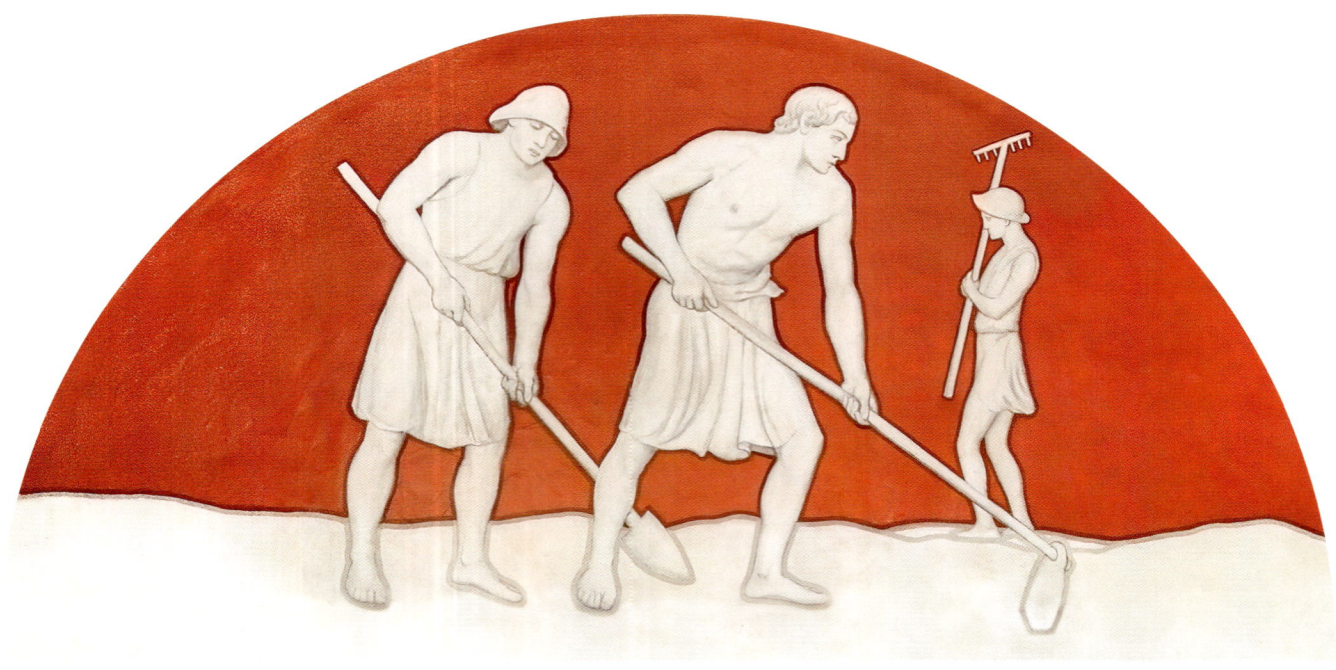

Augustus Tack
Summer Cultivation, 1927
Oil on canvas

Within the Governor's private office, the theme focuses on the
seasons within the context of Nebraska's agricultural heritage.

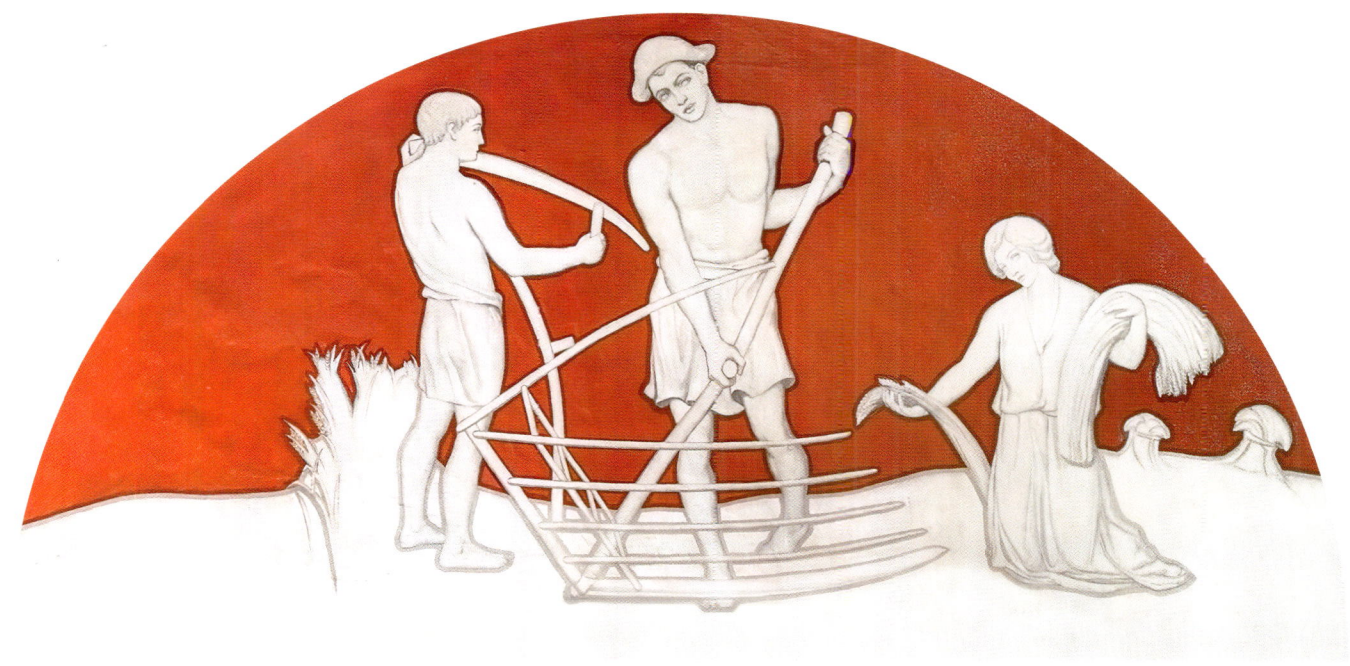

Augustus Tack
Fall Harvest, 1927
Oil on canvas

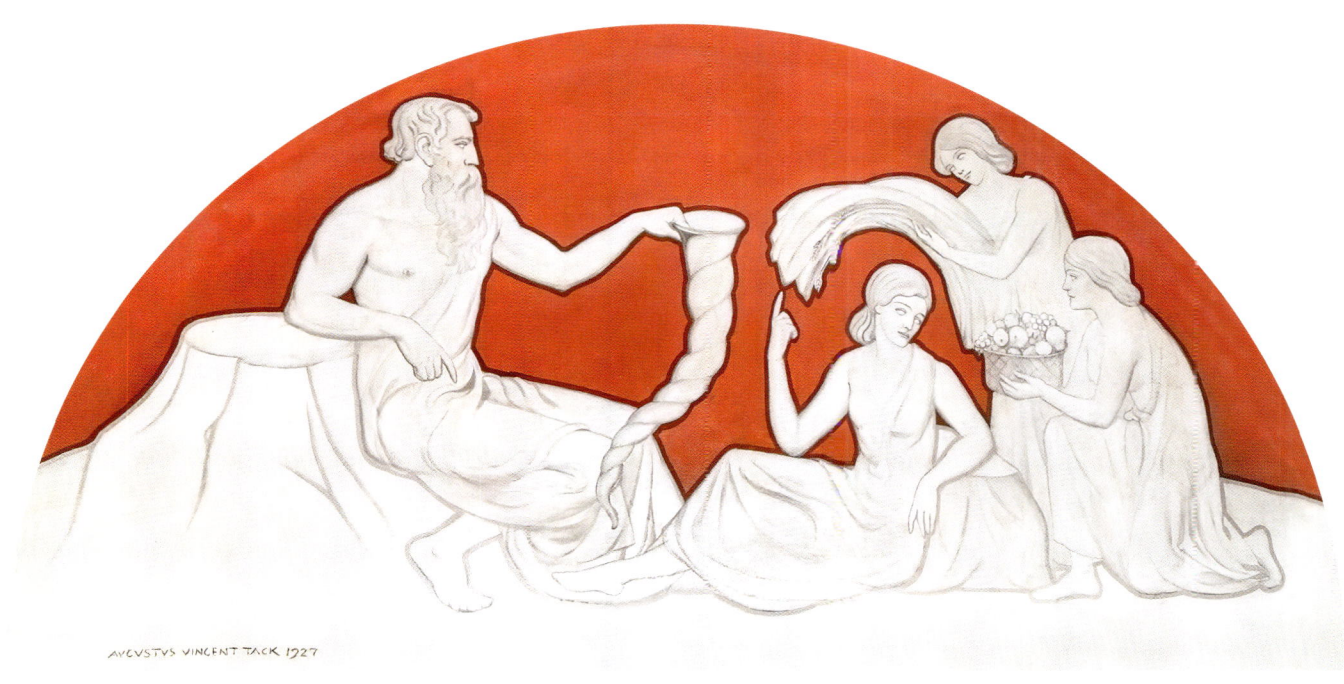

AVGVSTVS VINCENT TACK 1927

Augustus Tack
Winter of Content, 1927
Oil on canvas

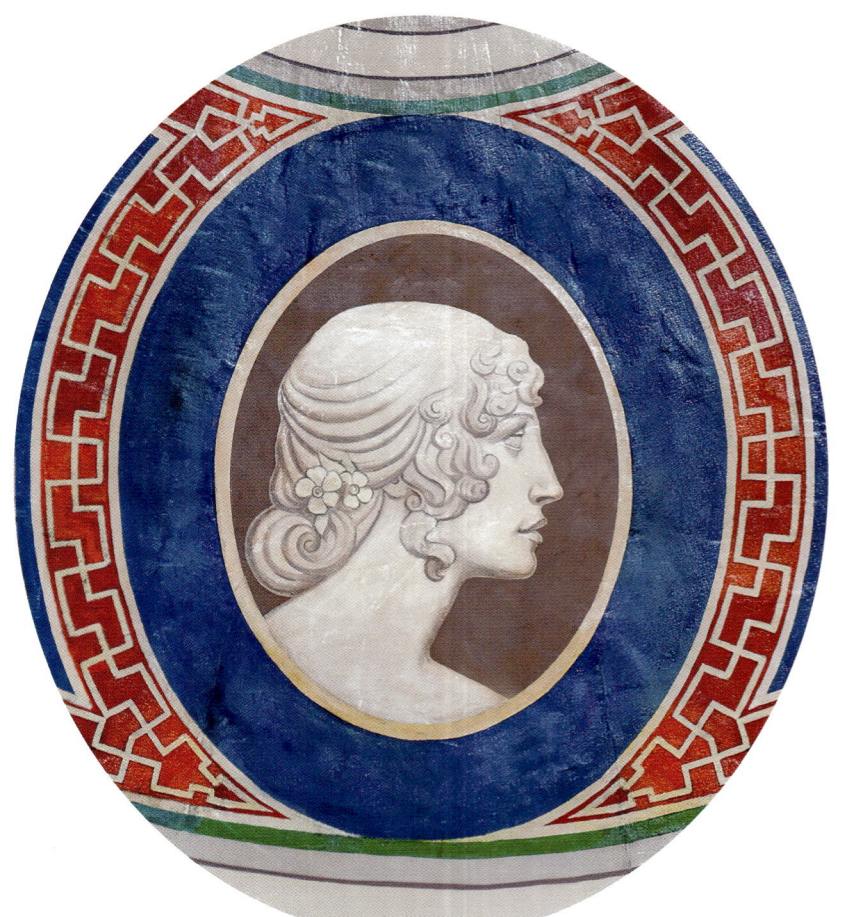

Augustus Tack
Spring, 1927
Oil on canvas

Augustus Tack
Summer, 1927
Oil on canvas

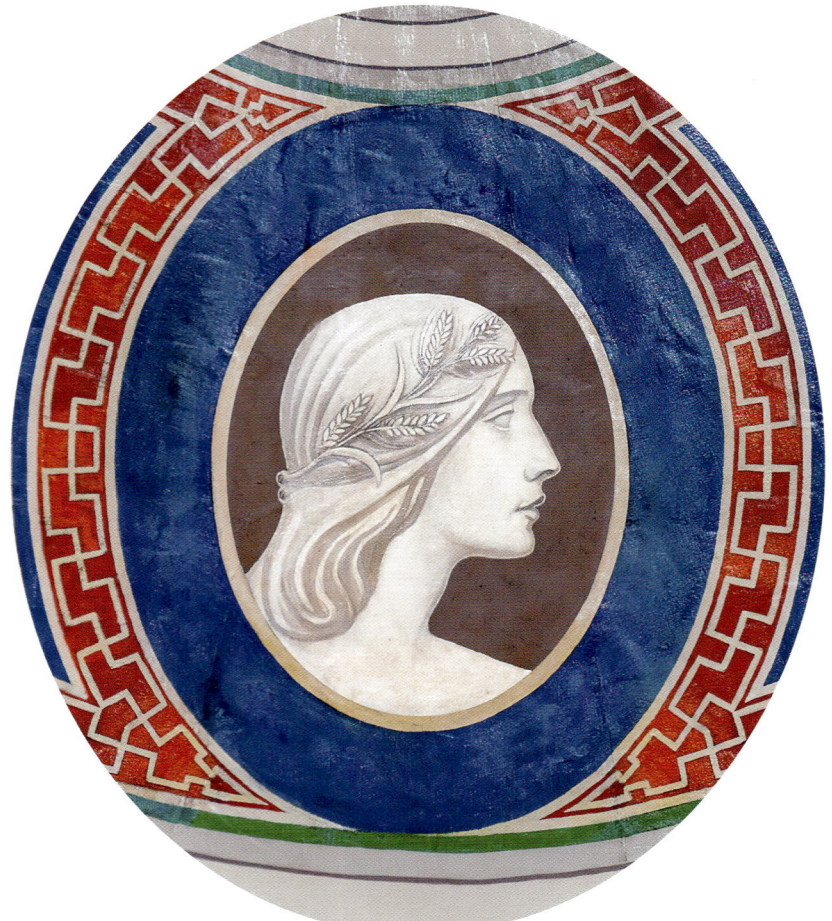

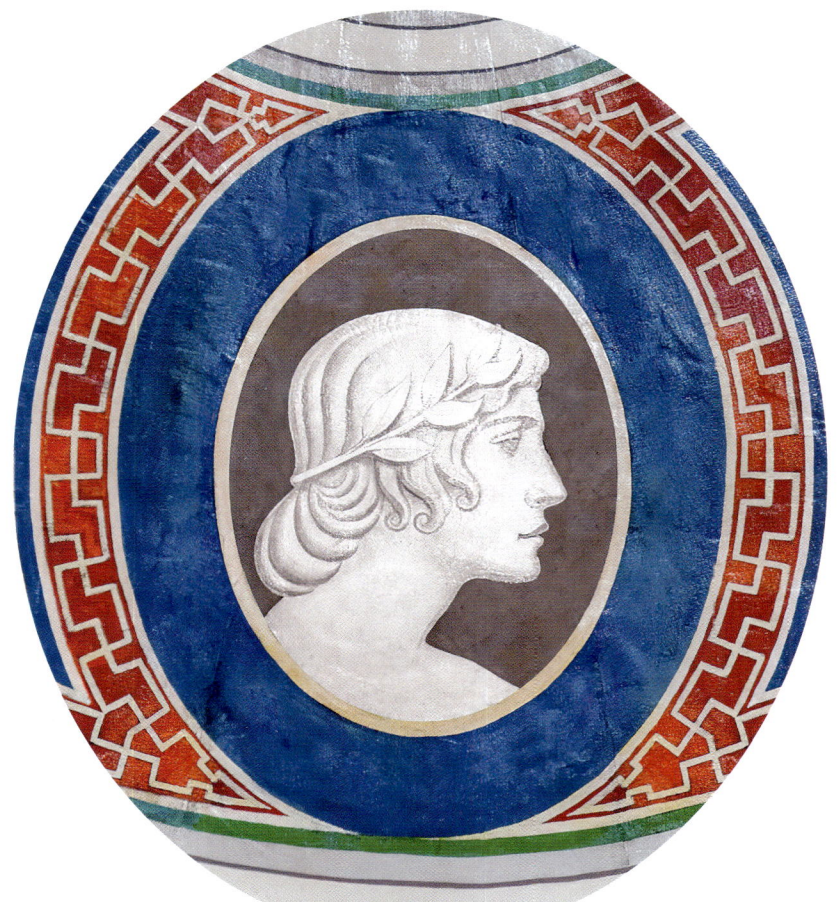

Augustus Tack
Fall, 1927
Oil on canvas

Augustus Tack
Winter, 1927
Oil on canvas

The surrounding figures on the ceiling depict
the four seasons of agriculture. In the center, the
four seasons themselves are shown as women.

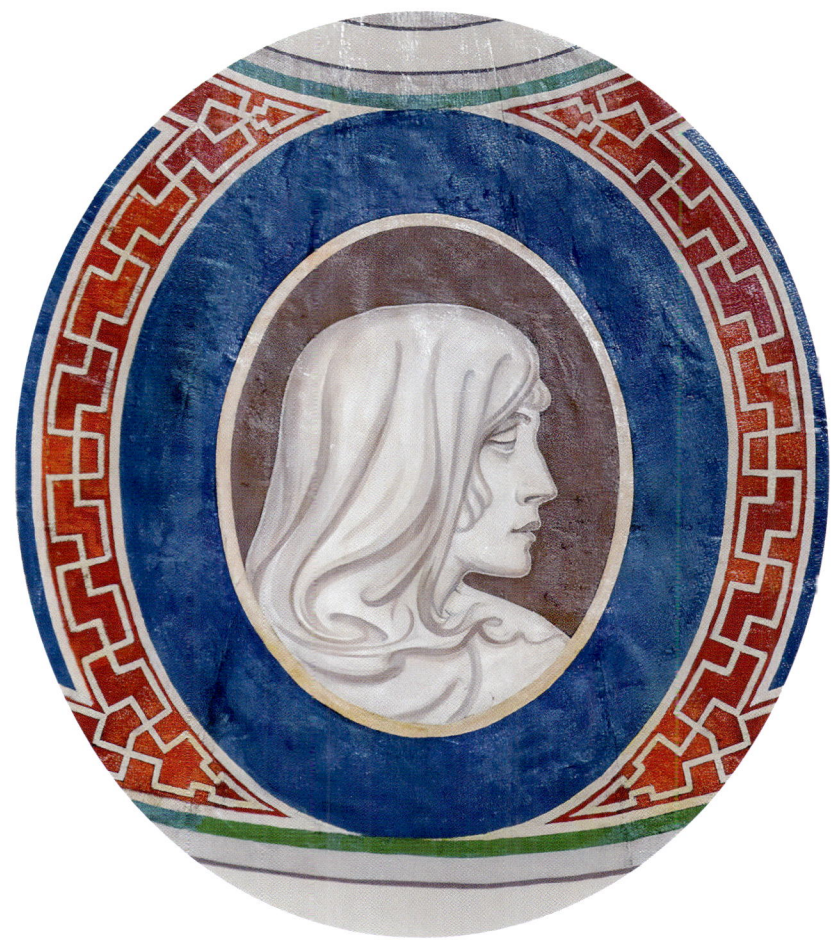

LAW LIBRARY & COURTS

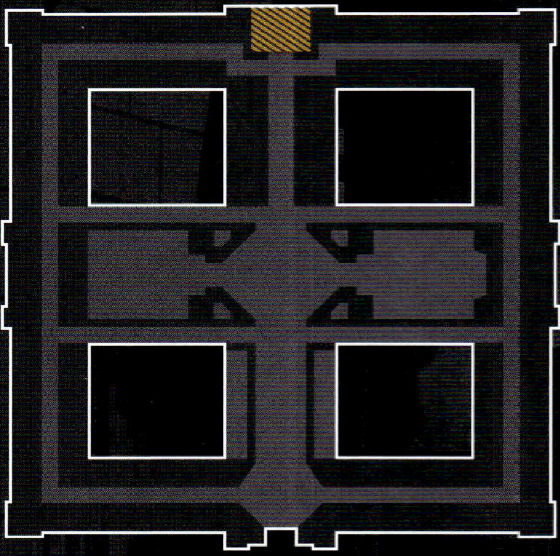

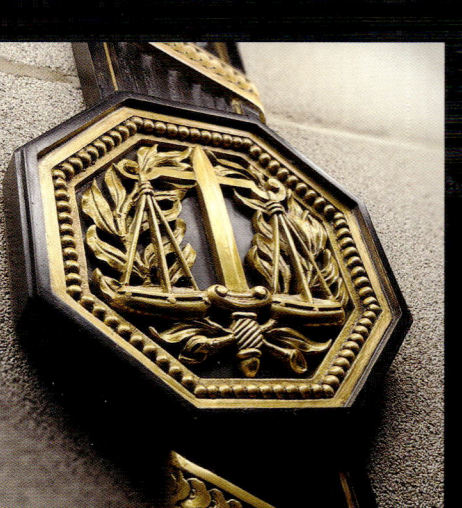

ELIZABETH DOLAN

In the vibrant history of female artists in Nebraska, Elizabeth Dolan's work is arguably the most prominent to this day.

In the Lincoln area alone her work is displayed in the Nebraska Capitol, Morrill Hall, the Sheldon Art Gallery, the Lux, the Masonic Temple, and the University of Nebraska Union.

Dolan's family moved from Iowa to Lincoln when she was an infant. She studied Fine Arts at the University of Nebraska in 1891 for one year and then spent time in 1894 studying with another important Nebraska female artist, Sarah Hayden. There's a considerable gap in her history until she registered at the Art Institute of Chicago in 1912, where she graduated two years later.

After Chicago, she spent three years in New York at the Art Students League, where she received the opportunity to attend the Académie Julian in Paris, which led to a scholarship to attend the Conservatoire Americain Fontainebleau south of Paris. At the school, she studied under a master of fresco painting Francis Garguit and quickly became a recognized talent in her own right. A tremendously private person, she would not allow anyone to watch her as she worked. She graduated from Fontainebleau in 1925 and contributed two permanent frescos to the school walls.

In 1926 she was on a trip back home to Nebraska when she learned about plans for the University of Nebraska's new natural history museum. She reached out to E. H. Barbour, the museum's director, with the idea of painting frescos in the interior and was awarded the commission with the title "decorator."

That work drew national attention and was featured in the *American Magazine of Art*. Dolan later said "Barbour gave me my first big chance." She was 51 years old when those pieces were painted.

In 1930 she volunteered to do the *Spirit of the Prairie* fresco for the Law Library in the Capitol. She charged the state only $110 for supplies and $200 for two months of living. To this day, it is considered her most well-known work.

She also received some larger commissions, including a piece called *The Age of Man* in the American Museum of Natural History in New York. Dolan spent the rest of her years working and living out of a small studio in downtown Lincoln. She died at the age of 73 in 1948.

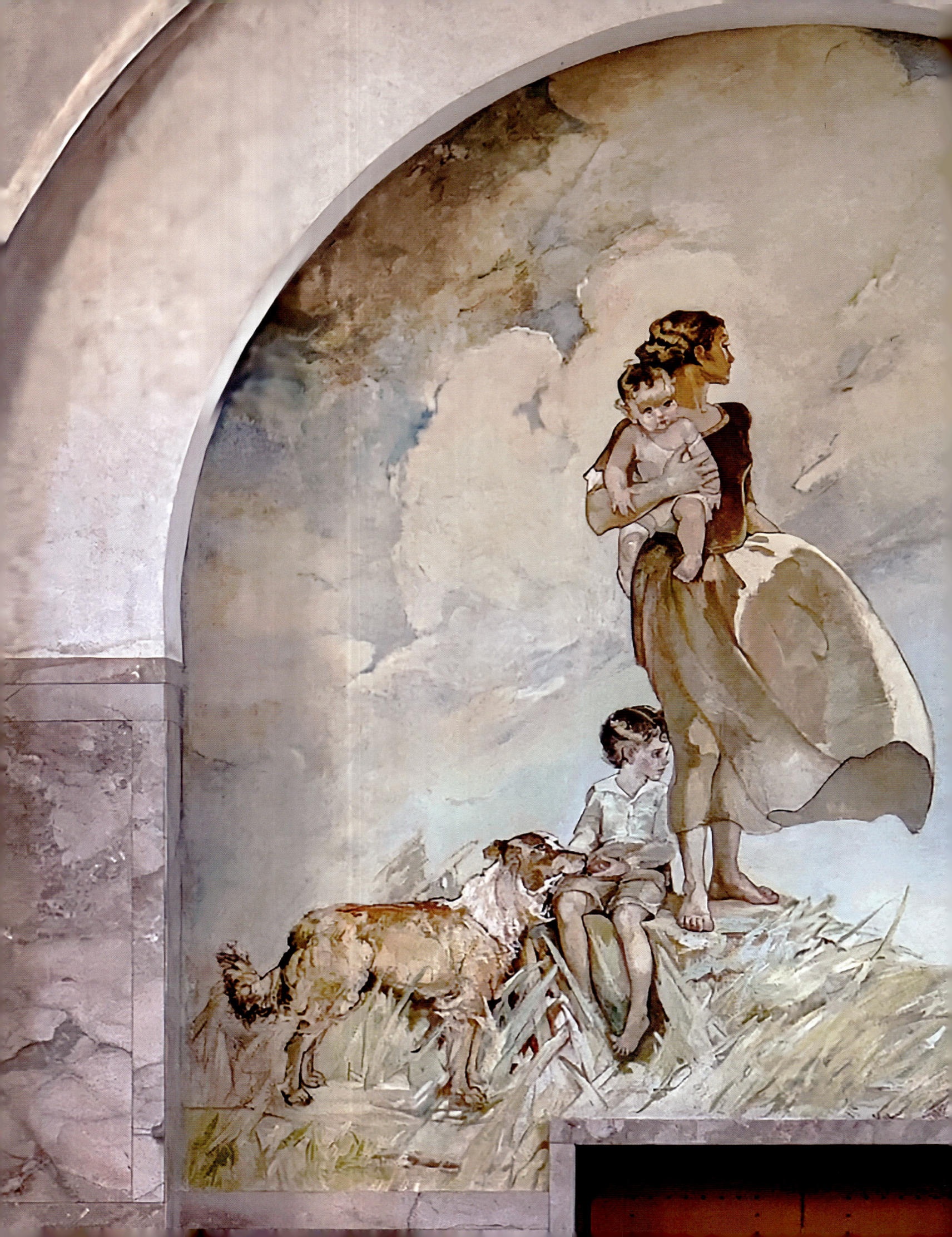

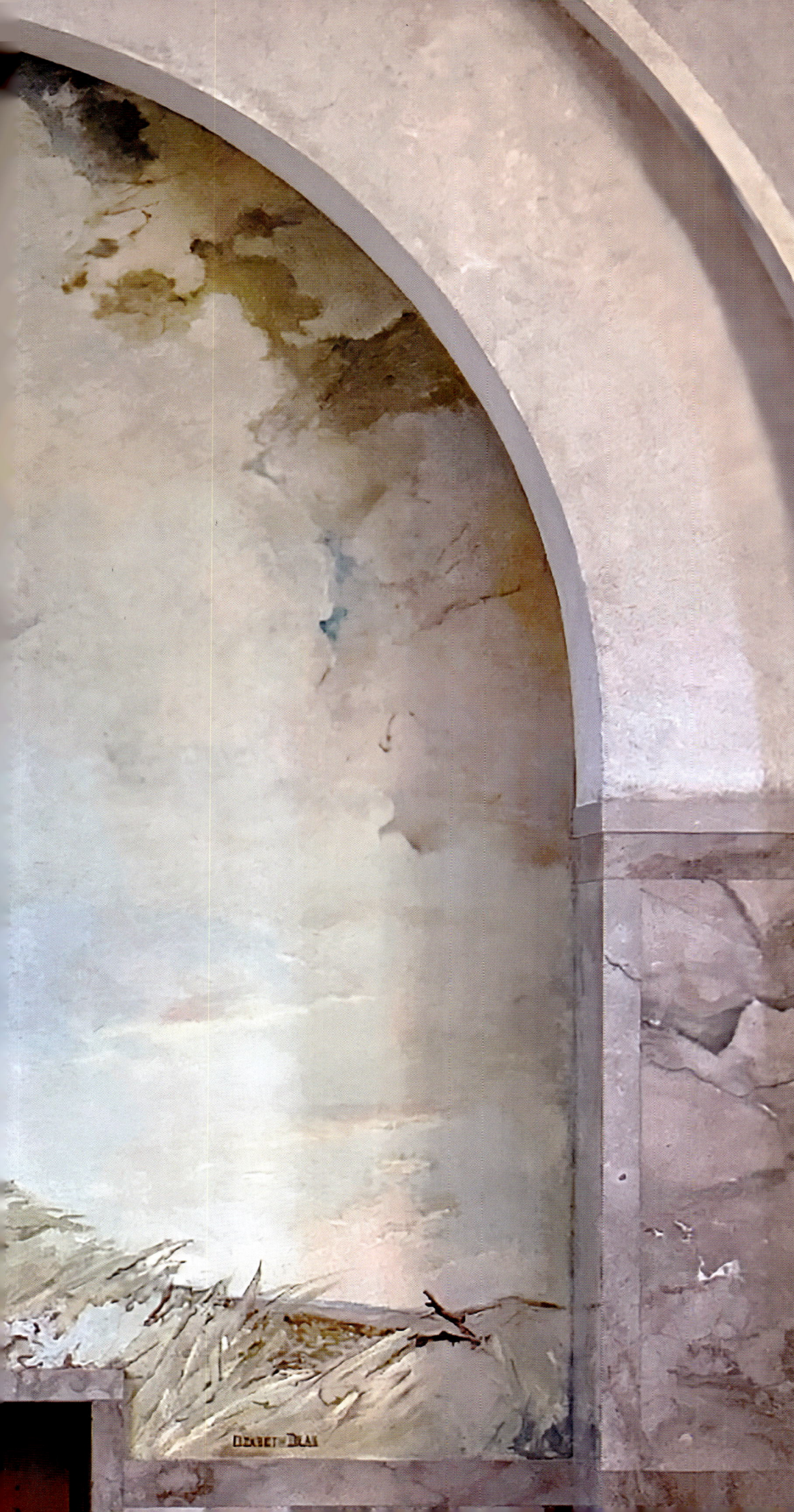

Elizabeth Dolan
Spirit of the Prairie, 1930
approx. 18 x 16 feet
Oil on canvas

The pioneer woman looks
over her shoulder to the east,
remembering the life she
left, while firmly standing in
her new home with her young
family. *Spirit of the Prairie*
sits above the entrance door
to the east and receives no
direct sunlight. Therefore it
is well-preserved to this day.

Lee Lawrie
Nebraska State Seal, c.1930
approx. 4 x 2.5 feet
Painted limestone sculpture

Goodhue and Lawrie created
three variations of a coat of
arms seal and placed them
throughout the Capitol. They
hoped the design would be
adopted by the legislature,
which never happened. This
seal found in the Supreme
Court is opulently painted,
making it especially striking.

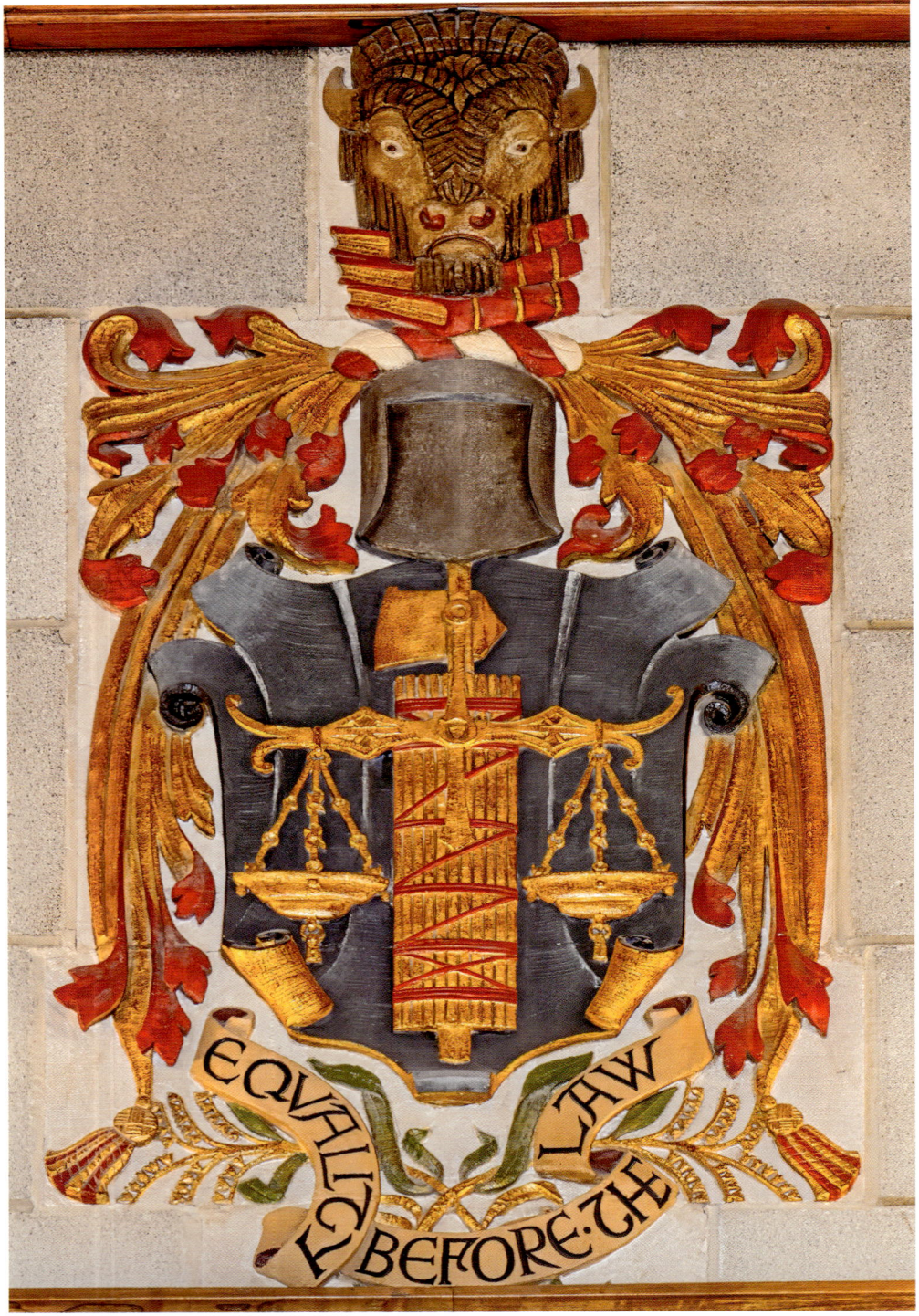

Lorentz Kleiser
Louisiana Purchase Tapestry: River Traffic, c.1930
approx. 9 x 6 feet
Woven tapestry

Three handmade tapestries adorn the walls of the Supreme Court chambers.
They depict the early exploration and settlement of the Louisiana Territory.

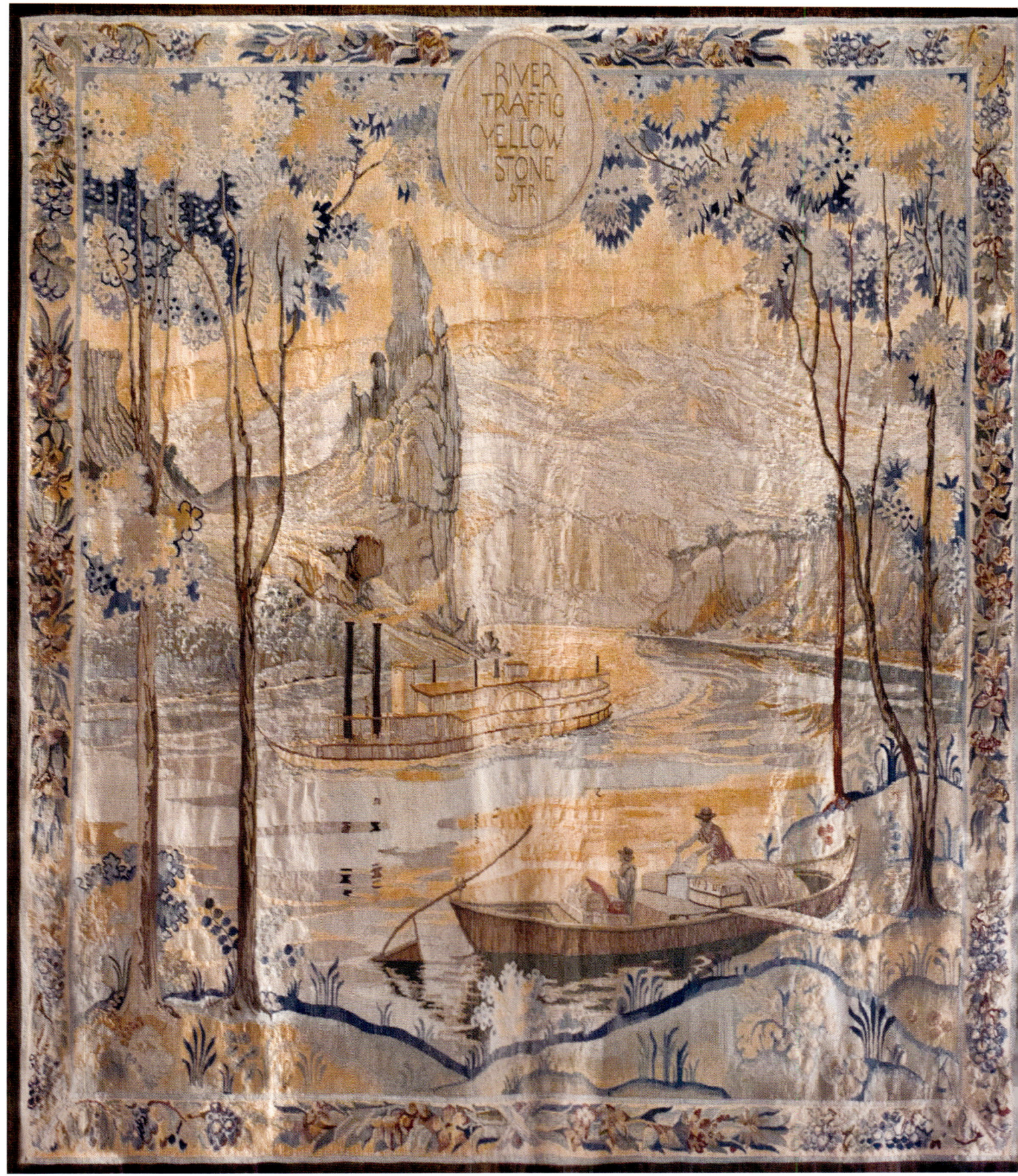

Lorentz Kleiser
Louisiana Purchase Tapestry:
Agriculture, c.1930
approx. 12 x 6 feet
Woven tapestry

The top oval refers to Manuel
Lisa, an explorer, prominent
fur trader, and merchant
important in the development
of Nebraska. When Lisa
heard of Lewis and Clark's
epic journey and the rumors
of riches to be found through
the beaver hide trade (an
extremely lucrative business
at the time), he headed west.
In 1814 he established Fort
Lisa north of current-day
Omaha as a trading post. He
gained alliances with local
tribes and even married
Mitane, the daughter of
Big Elk, the principal chief
of the Omaha tribe.

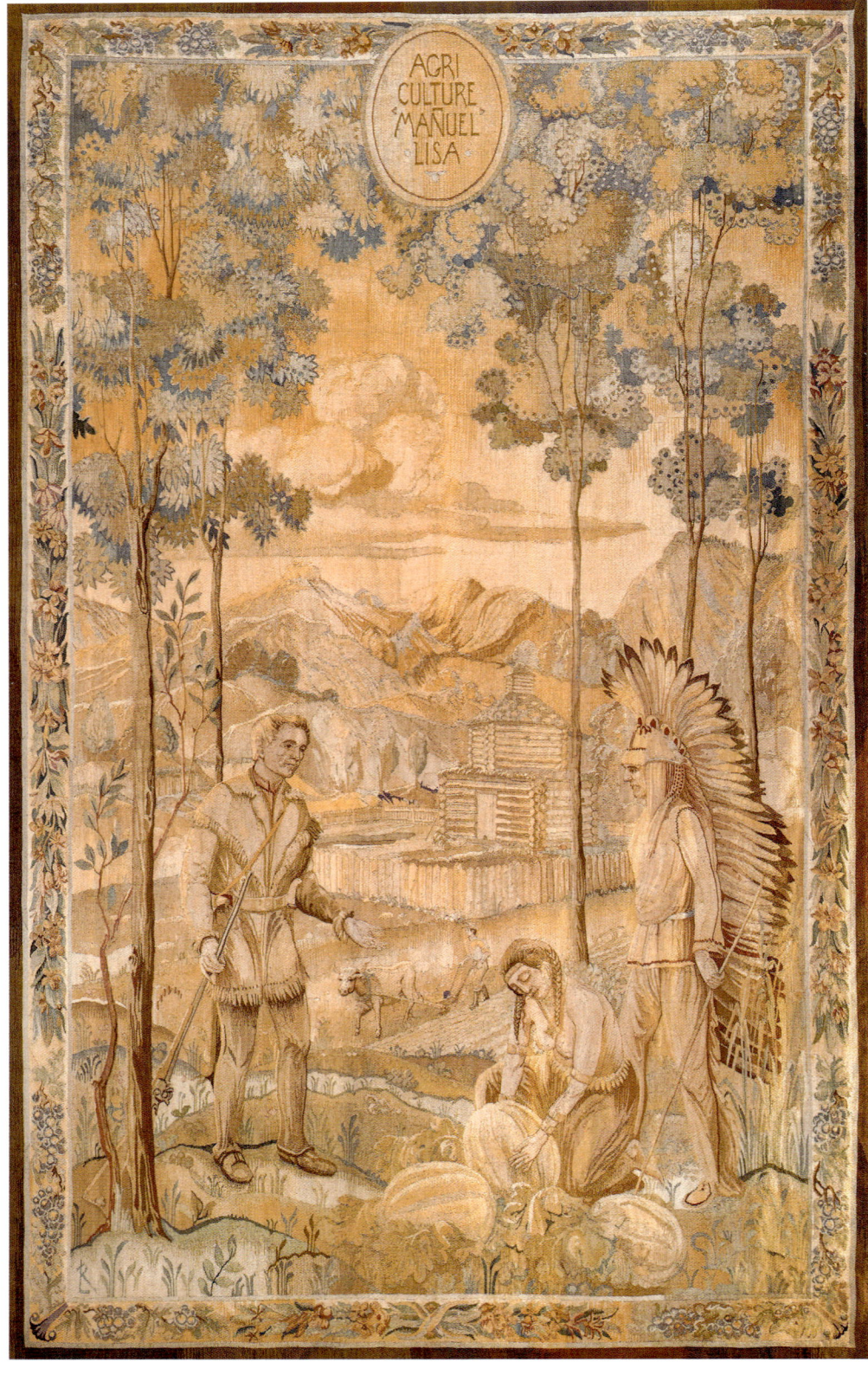

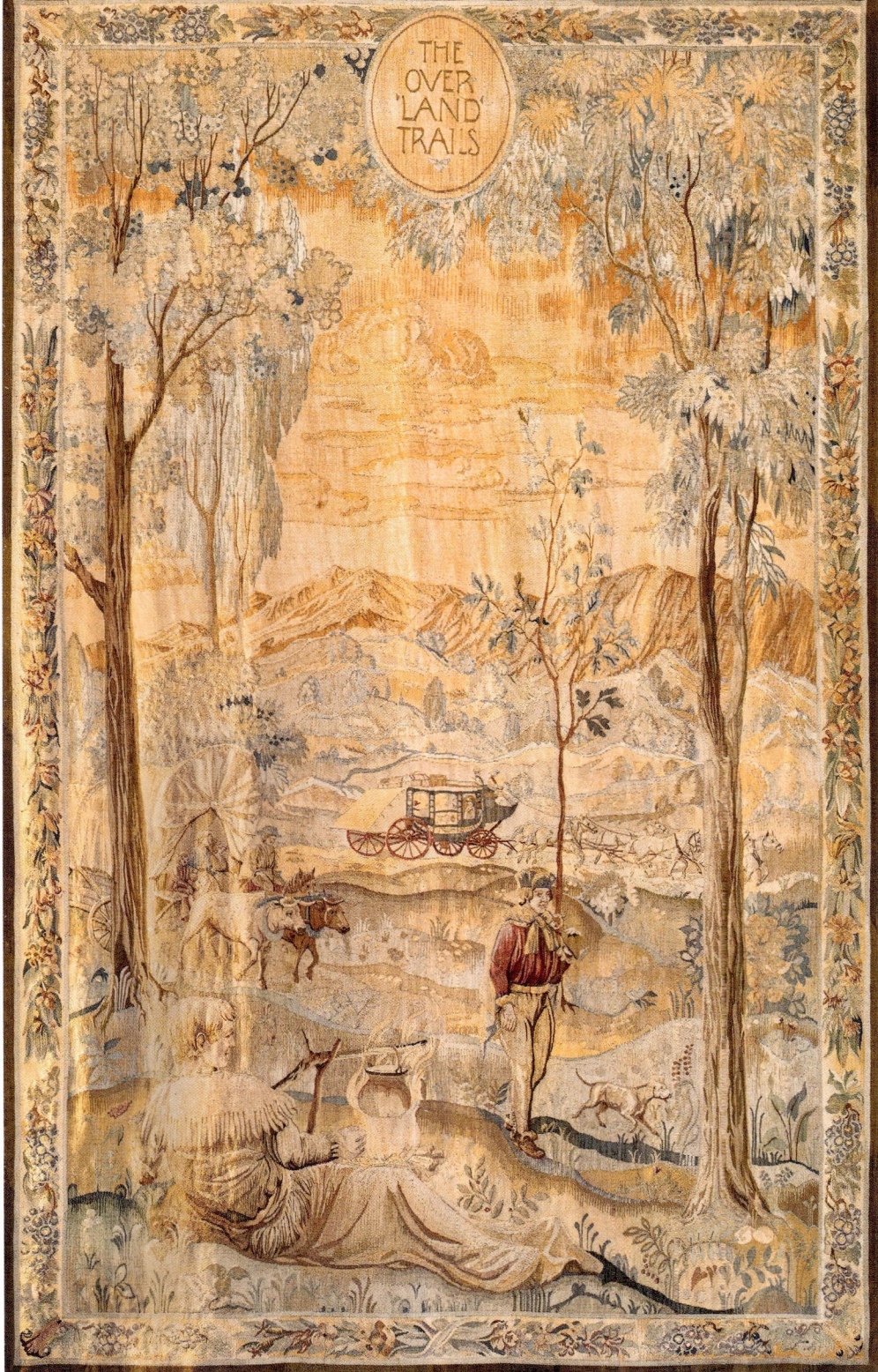

Lorentz Kleiser
Louisiana Purchase Tapestry:
Overland Trails, c.1930
approx. 12 x 6 feet
Woven tapestry

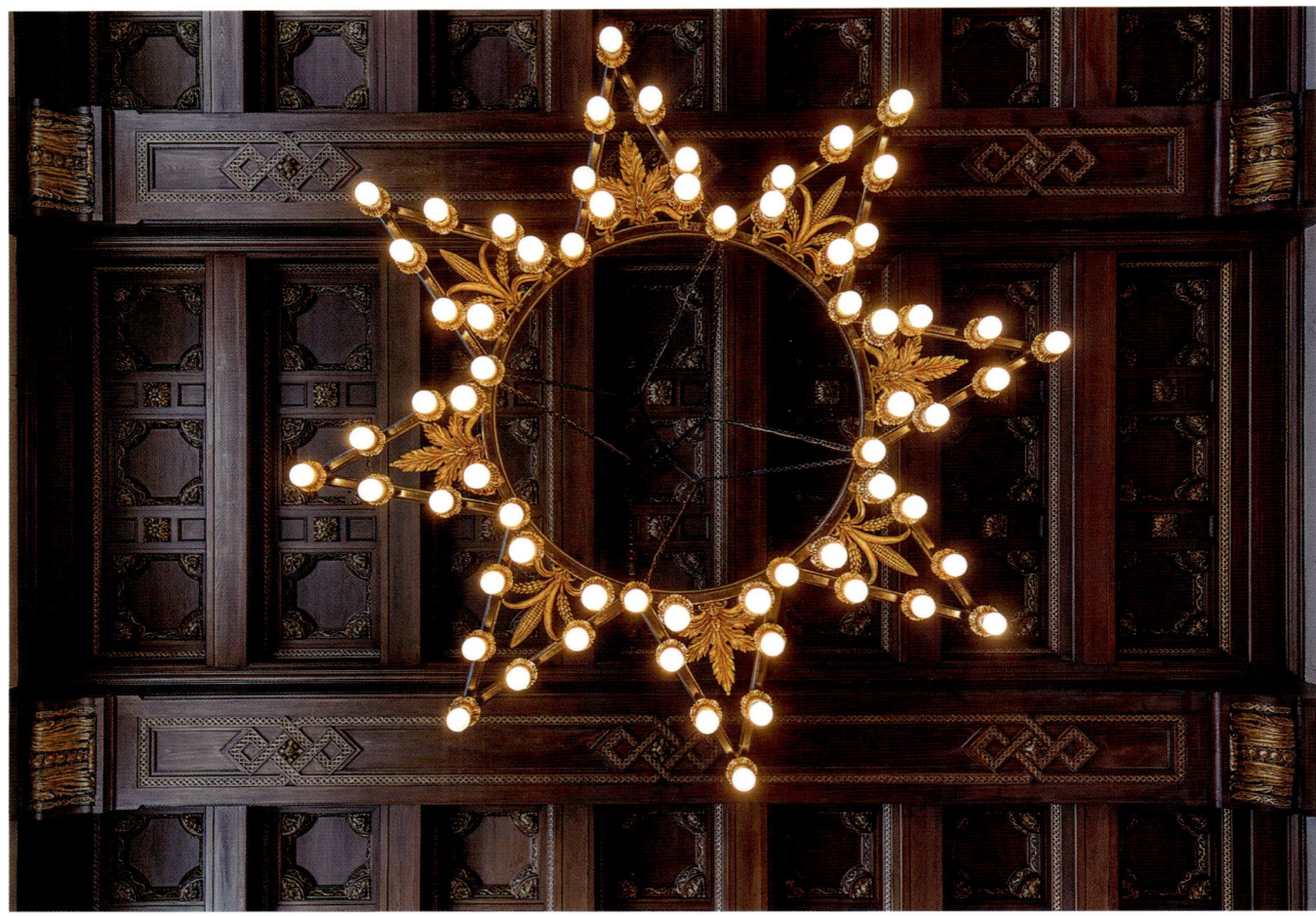

Edward F. Caldwell & Co.
Chandelier, c.1930

The chandelier in the Court of Appeals features Nebraska motifs
depicted in the other chandeliers, including corn and wheat.

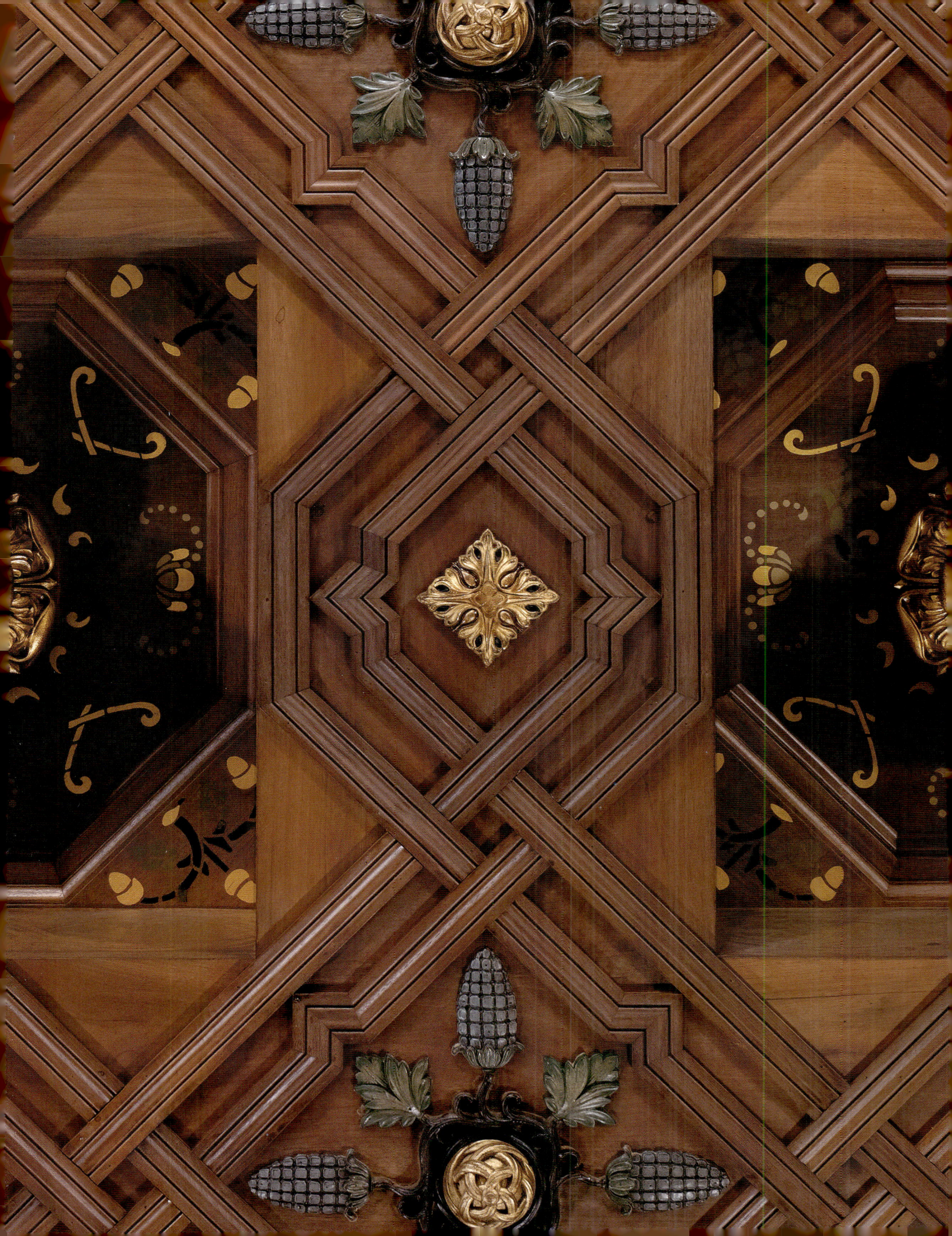

MEMORIAL CHAMBER

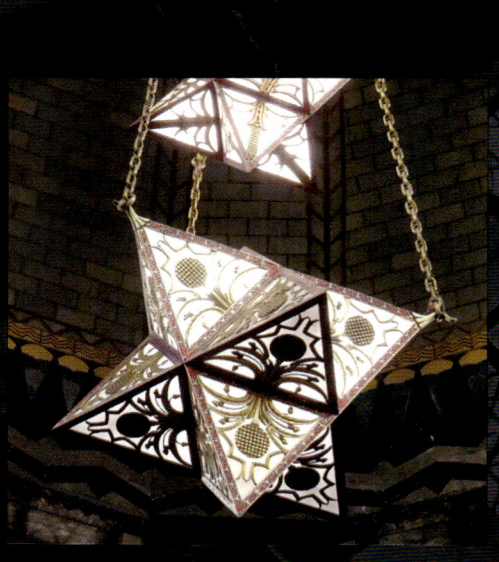

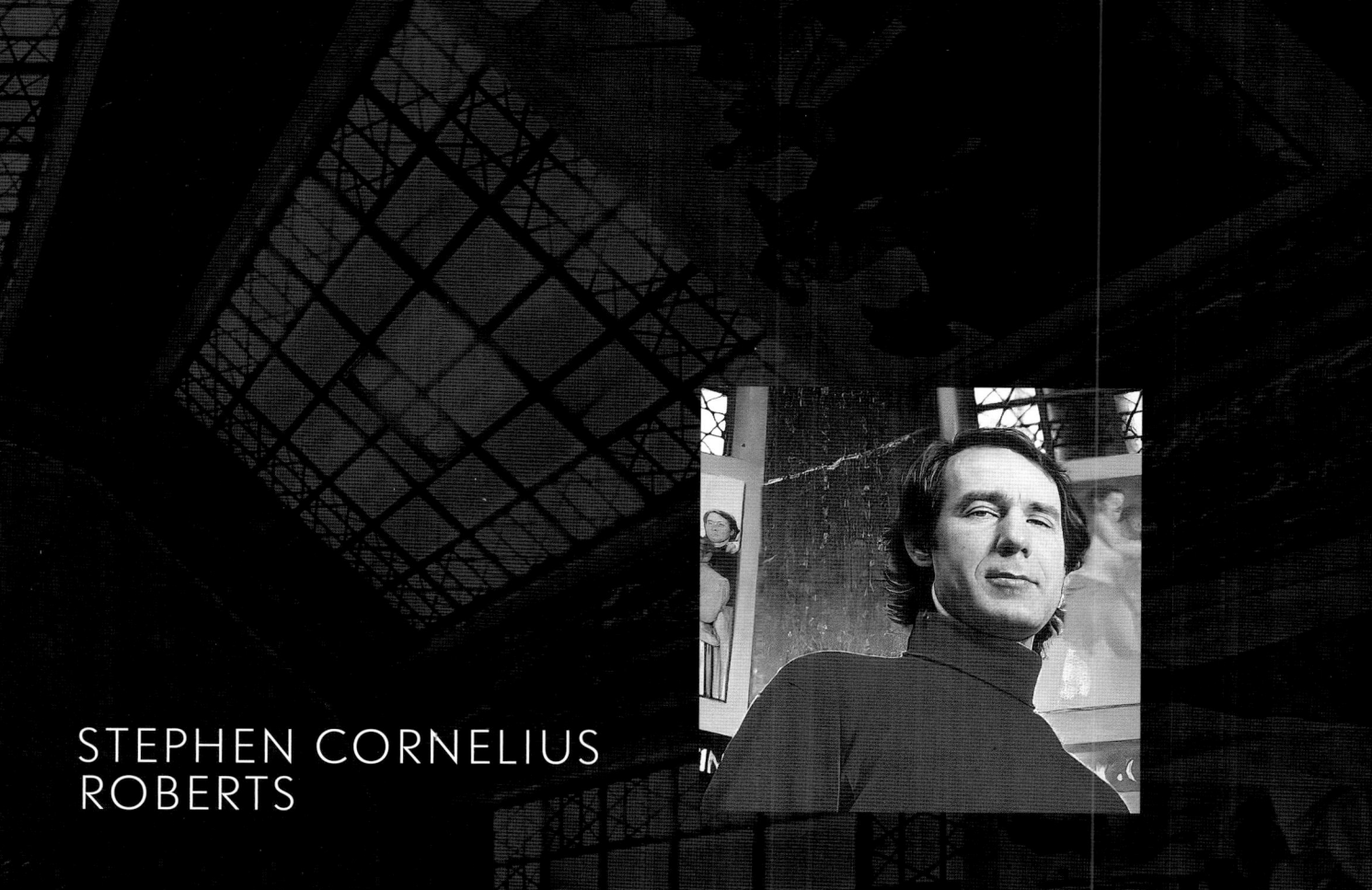

STEPHEN CORNELIUS ROBERTS

When Stephen Cornelius Roberts installed his eight murals in the Memorial Chamber of the Capitol, Hartley Alexander's full vision for the building was completed. The dedication occurred on Veteran's Day in November of 1996, exactly 74 years after the cornerstone of the Capitol was laid.

Born in Omaha in 1952, Roberts describes himself as a fifth-generation, die-hard Nebraskan. He graduated with a bachelor of fine arts degree in painting from the University of Nebraska at Omaha and started his career in New York City, showing his artwork in a small gallery.

In 1989 the Nebraska Legislature approved the creation of an art commission to lead the effort to complete the murals, and a national competition process was established. Roberts decided at the last minute to submit a proposal. He became one of three finalists, the only one from Nebraska. Roberts said, "I almost wasn't picked at all for the finalist selection. One guy said, 'Ah, throw him in. He's not going to win anyway.' I was incredibly lucky to be selected."

The commission developed a list of themes for the murals along with a long list of additional thoughts and concepts it wanted included. Rather than get lost in the clutter of ideas as one finalist did, Roberts chose a different route. "There was just so much stuff, so I zeroed in on one idea for each." He said, "I wanted something simpler, something you could read from a distance."

Roberts also incorporated Nebraska history and people into his pieces. Ultimately, Roberts attributes his selection to his clarity and Nebraska focus.

The entire process took Roberts five and a half years to complete. The final four months of the project were spent painting in the Memorial Chamber with the paintings on the walls. When groups of grade school students came through for tours, he enjoyed coming down from his scaffolding to talk to them.

Roberts views this project as the pinnacle of his career It's not just the longevity of the project, but what it means to him personally. "To be able to do this in your own state . . . it's just an unbelievable dream come true."

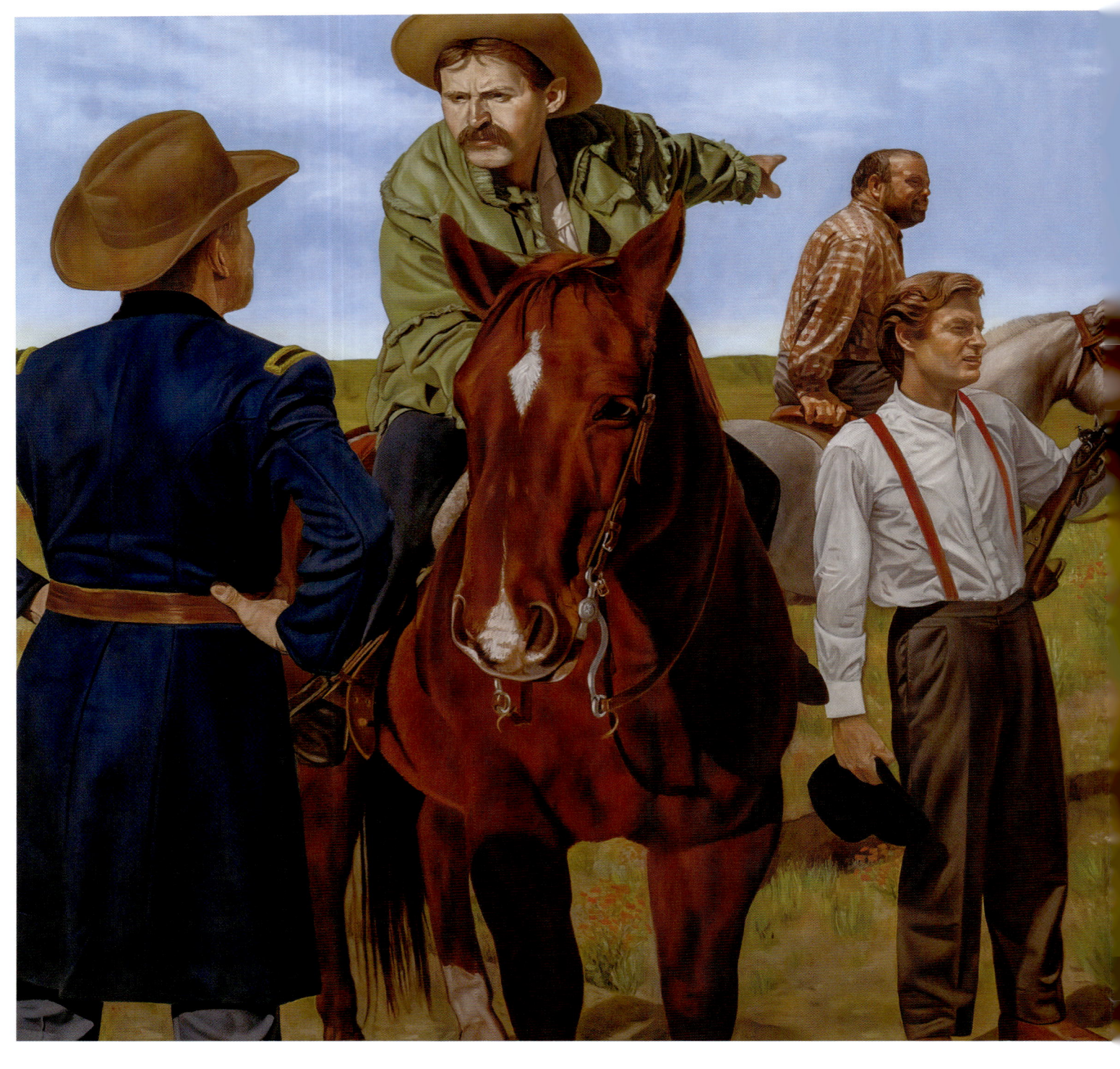

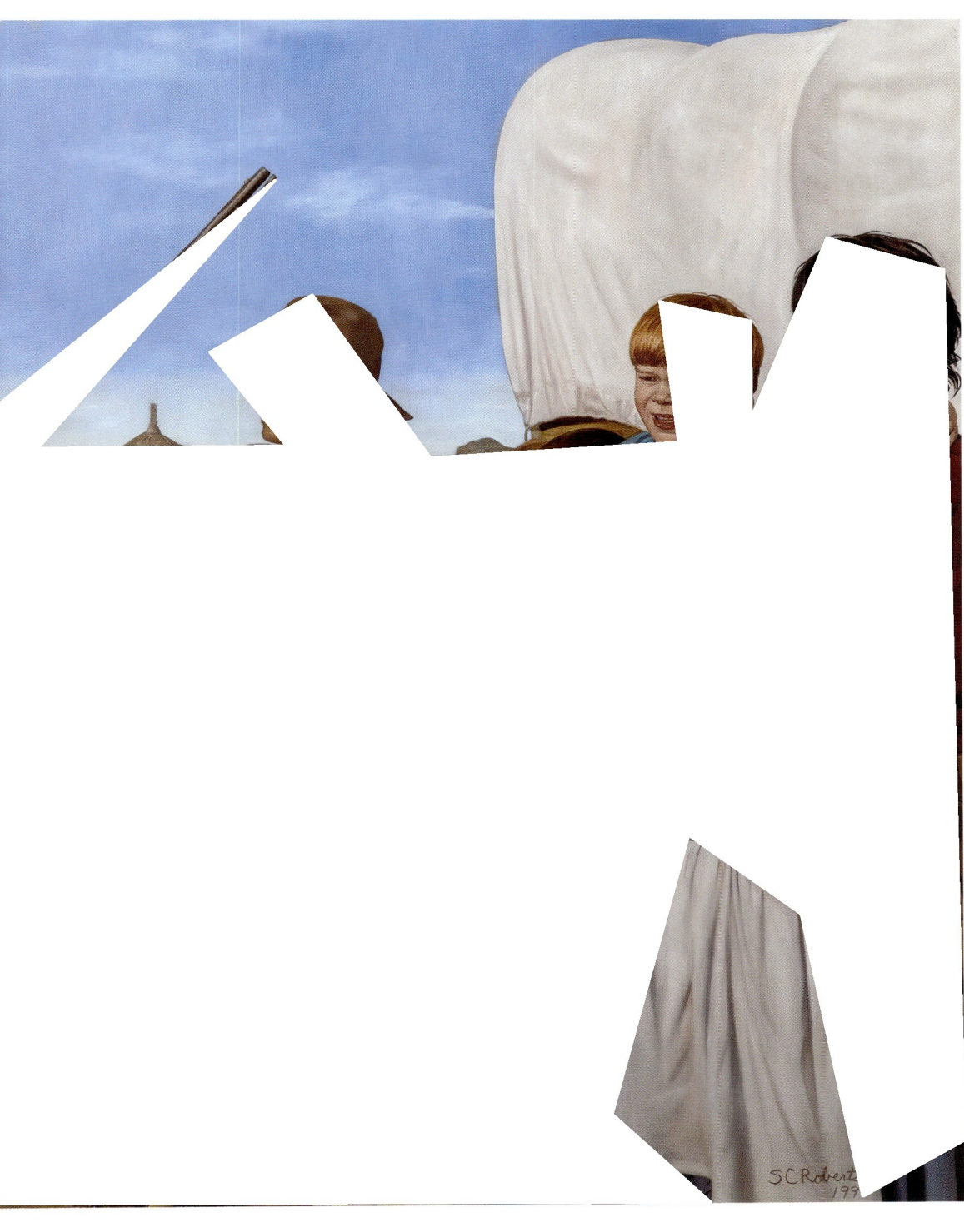

Stephen Cornelius Roberts
The Ideal of Self-Determination, 1996
6.75 x 12 feet
Oil on linen

All of Roberts's Memorial Chamber murals look almost photographic. He drew and painted from "billions and billions of photographs" of real Nebraskans he used as models. He photographed each person posed individually and then stitched them together to create a composition.

He then created a series of free-handed sketches and paintings until he completed the final product.

In *The Ideal of Self-Determination*, Roberts included himself, his wife, and his two children as subjects. He said, "As a descendent of pioneers, I chose to portray my family at the far right of this mural." Roberts in the red shirt stands with his family next to a covered wagon. His brother is in the middle with the gun.

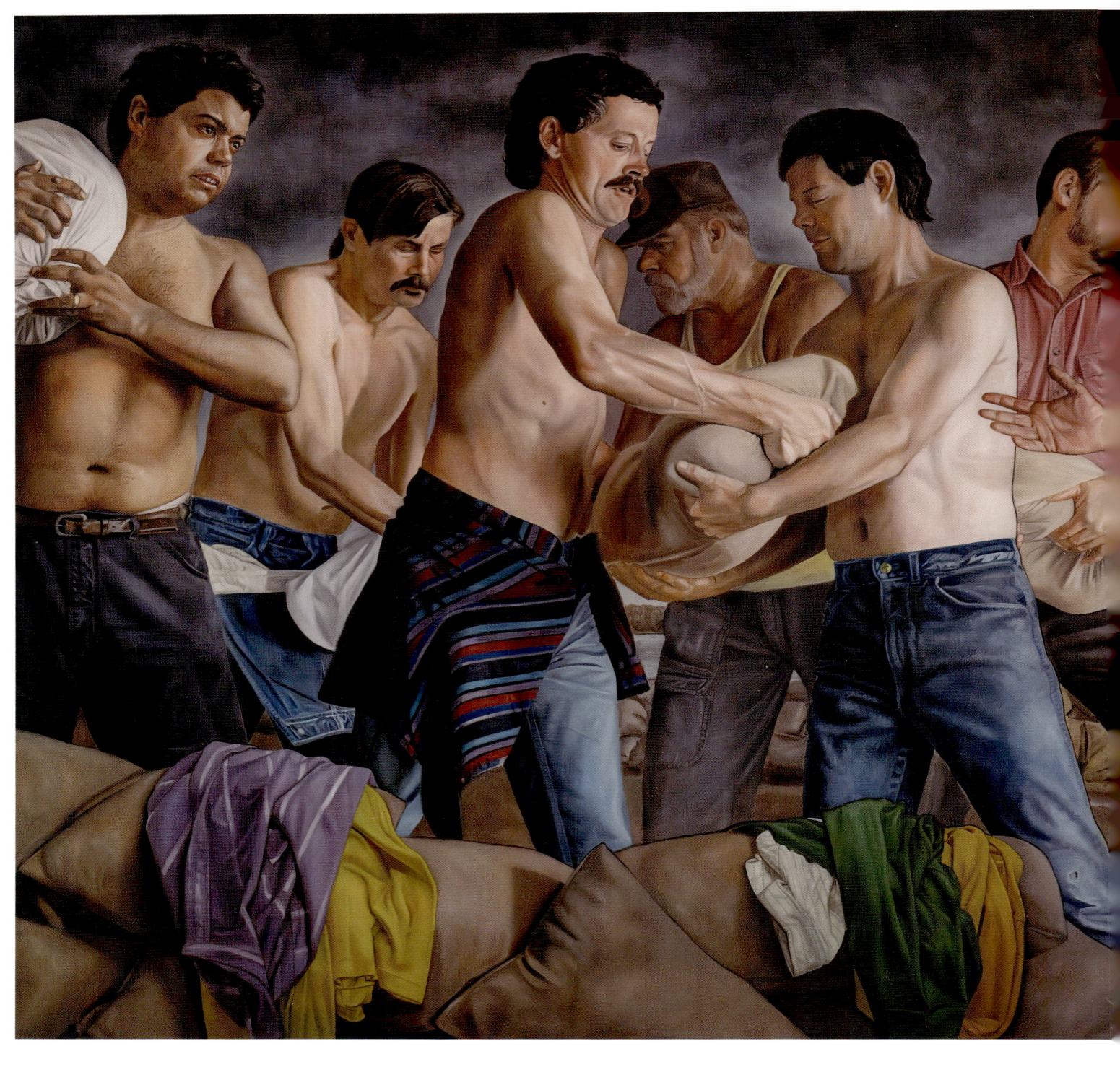

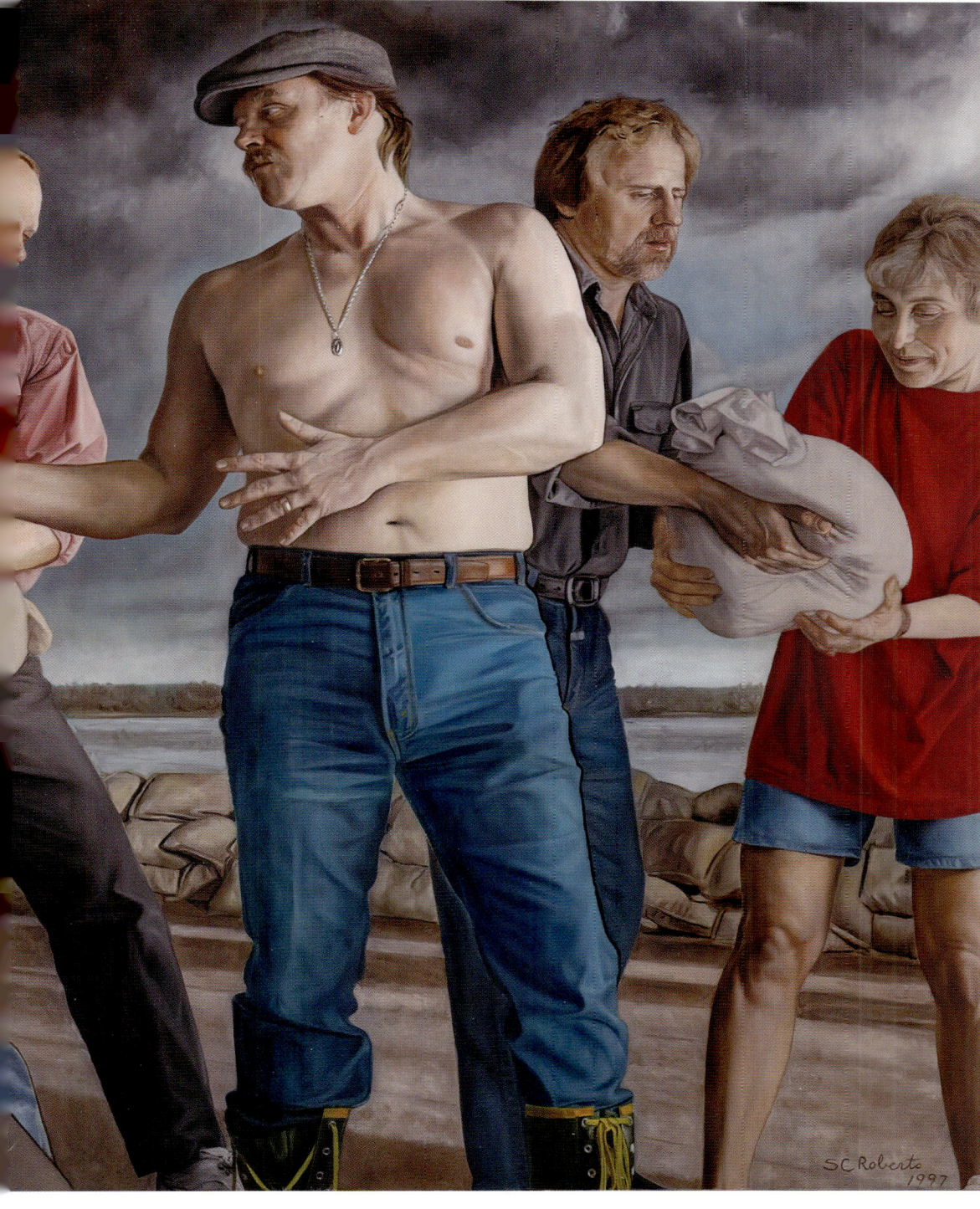

Stephen Cornelius Roberts
The Scourge of Famine, 1996
6.75 x 12 feet
Oil on linen

The people in this mural make
a wall of sandbags to protect
against a coming flood, a
metaphor for all challenges
faced by a community.

After Roberts exhibited the first
small drafts of the murals in the
Capitol rotunda, the response
was swift, with most in support
of his work. Criticism came
from a women's group who felt
the murals underrepresented
the contributions of
women. Already planning
on making revisions to the
final products, Roberts
considered the comments
and added more women.
The woman on the right was
one of those additions.

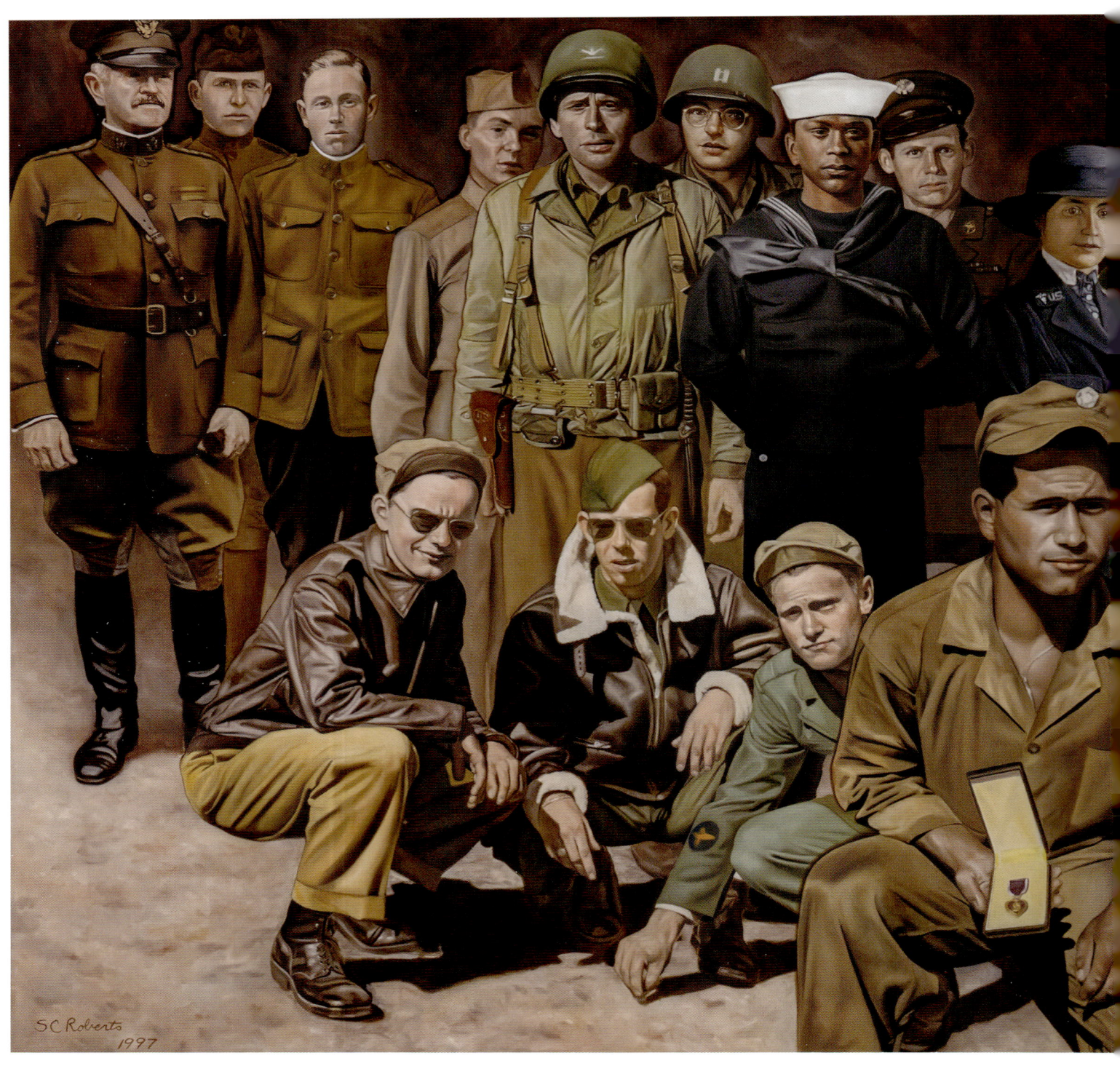

SC Roberts
1997

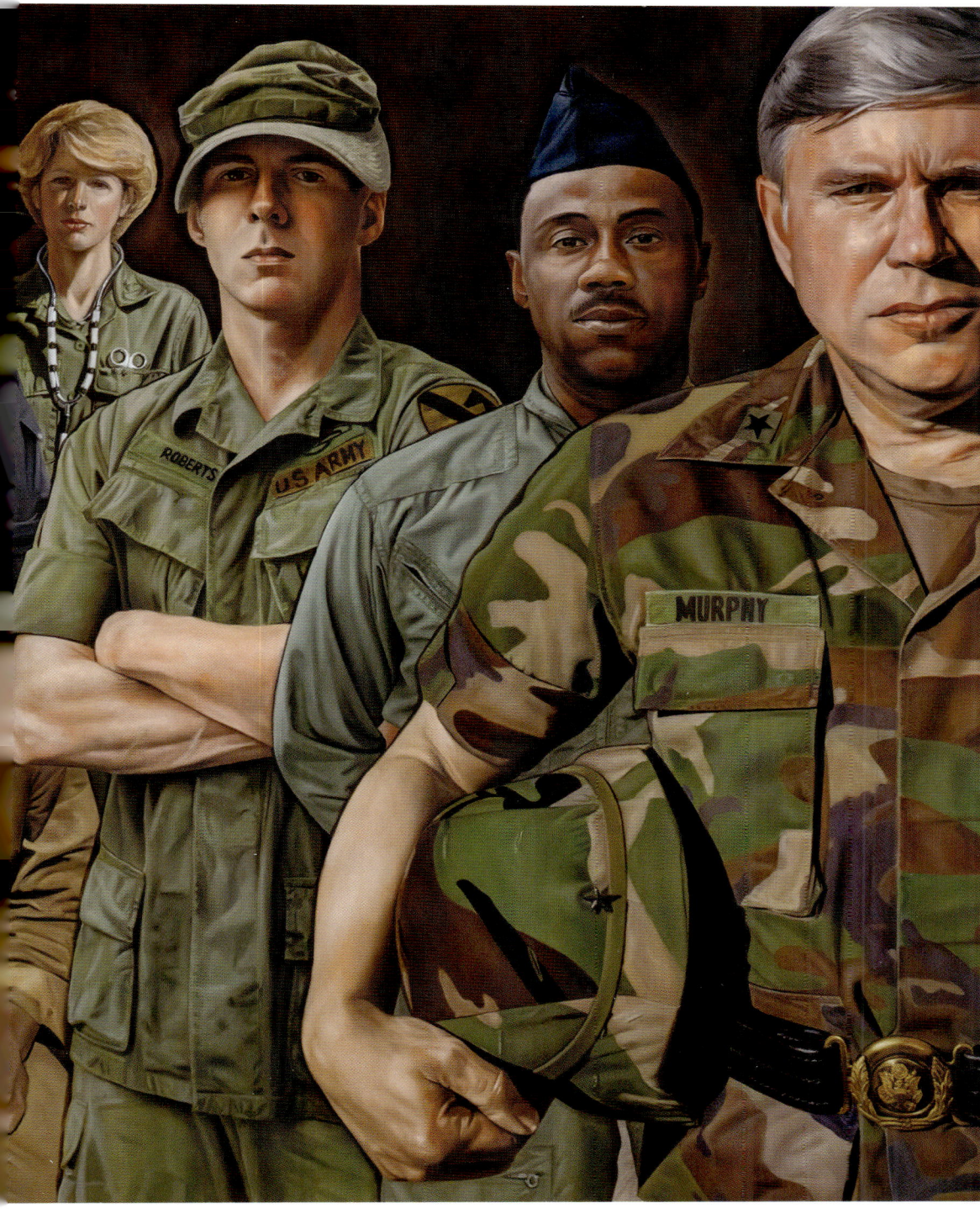

Stephen Cornelius Roberts
The Ideal of International Law, 1996
6.75 x 12 feet
Oil on linen

Roberts featured historic
military figures and members
of his own family in this mural.
They stand as a timeline,
starting with World War I
heroes on the left, followed
by soldiers from World
War II, the Korean War, the
Vietnam War, and ending
with soldiers from the 1990s.

General John J. Pershing
stands at the far left. Roberts's
grandfather who served in
WWI and WWII is placed
two away from Pershing. Also
included are Roberts's father
and brother. In the center,
Edward "Babe" Gomez holds
his holds his Medal of Honor,
earned for bravery and
valor during the Battle of the
Punchbowl in Korea in 1951.

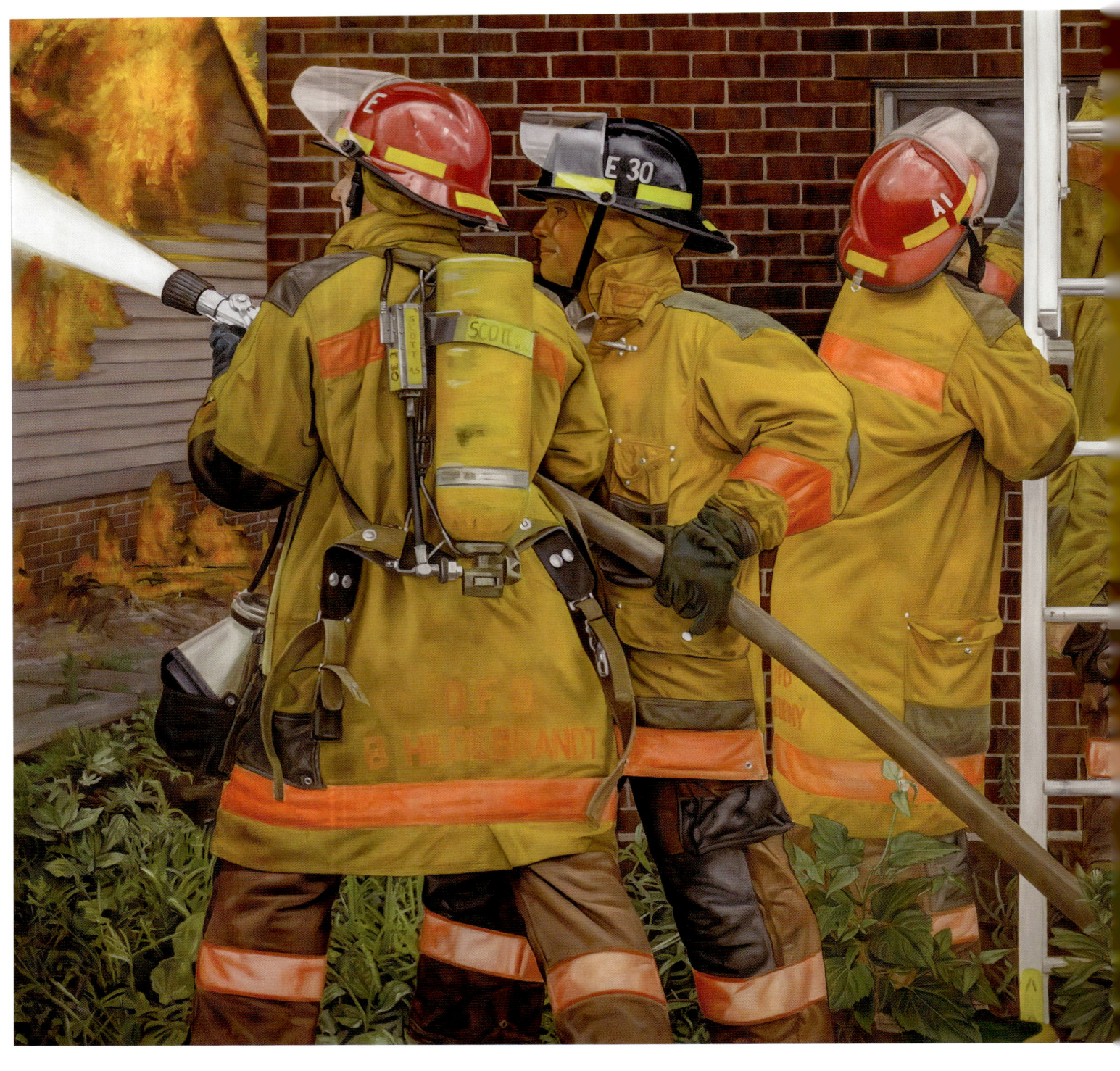

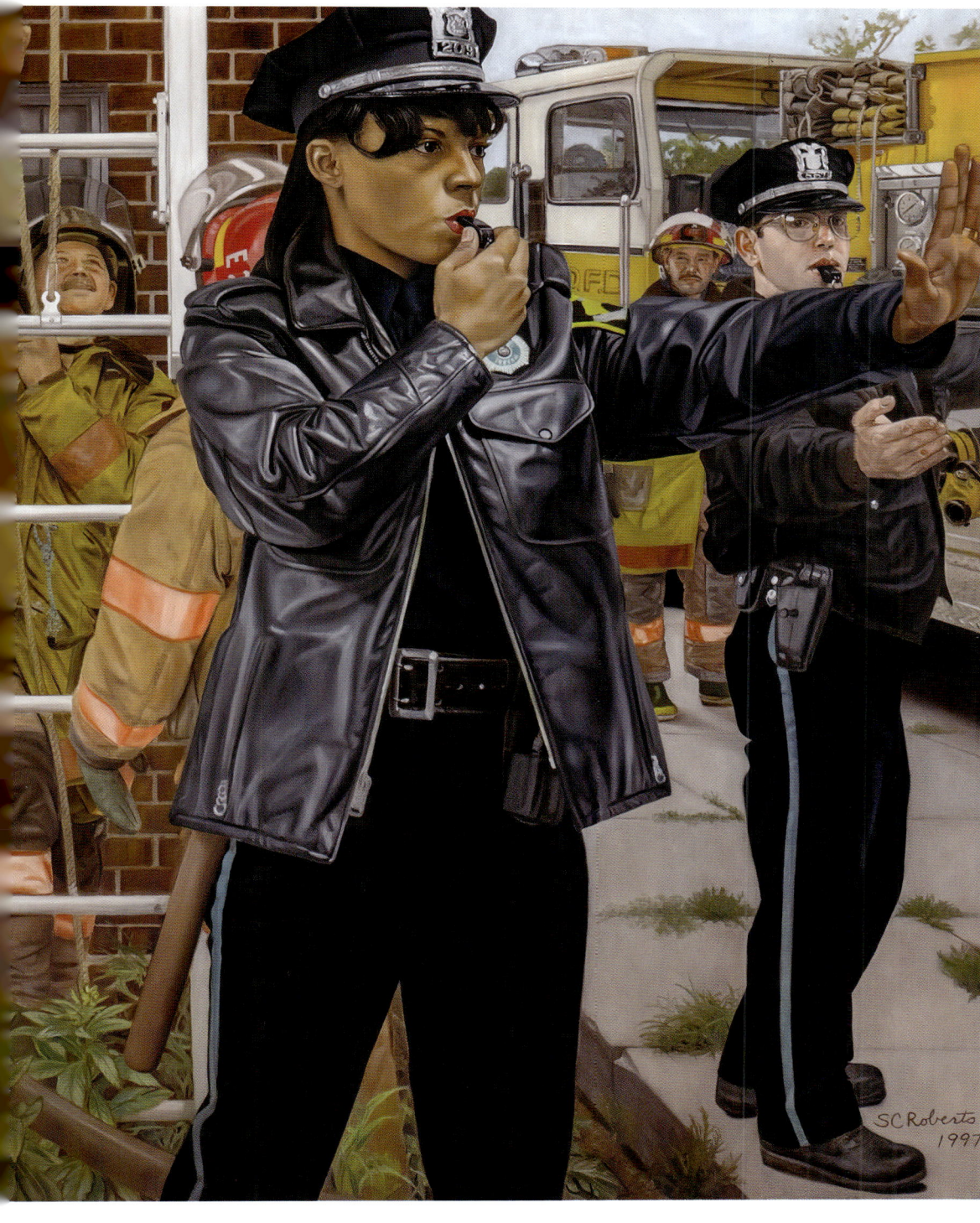

Stephen Cornelius Roberts
The Perils of Fire, 1996
6.75 x 12 feet
Oil on linen

Alexander originally planned the Memorial Chamber to honor those who gave their lives for the state and nation. He envisioned eight 7-foot by 12-foot murals that would serve as the focal point, with four representing military service and four depicting civilian service. Roberts's murals perfectly fulfilled that vision.

This mural, as in all of his pieces, contains real Nebraskans, a fact Roberts is very proud of. "There's the history of Nebraska in every individual that's up in those paintings. I didn't paint any imaginary people; those are all real people," Roberts said. "When you look at the painting that has the firefighters and police officers, those are real people. . . . It's about honoring those particular people too."

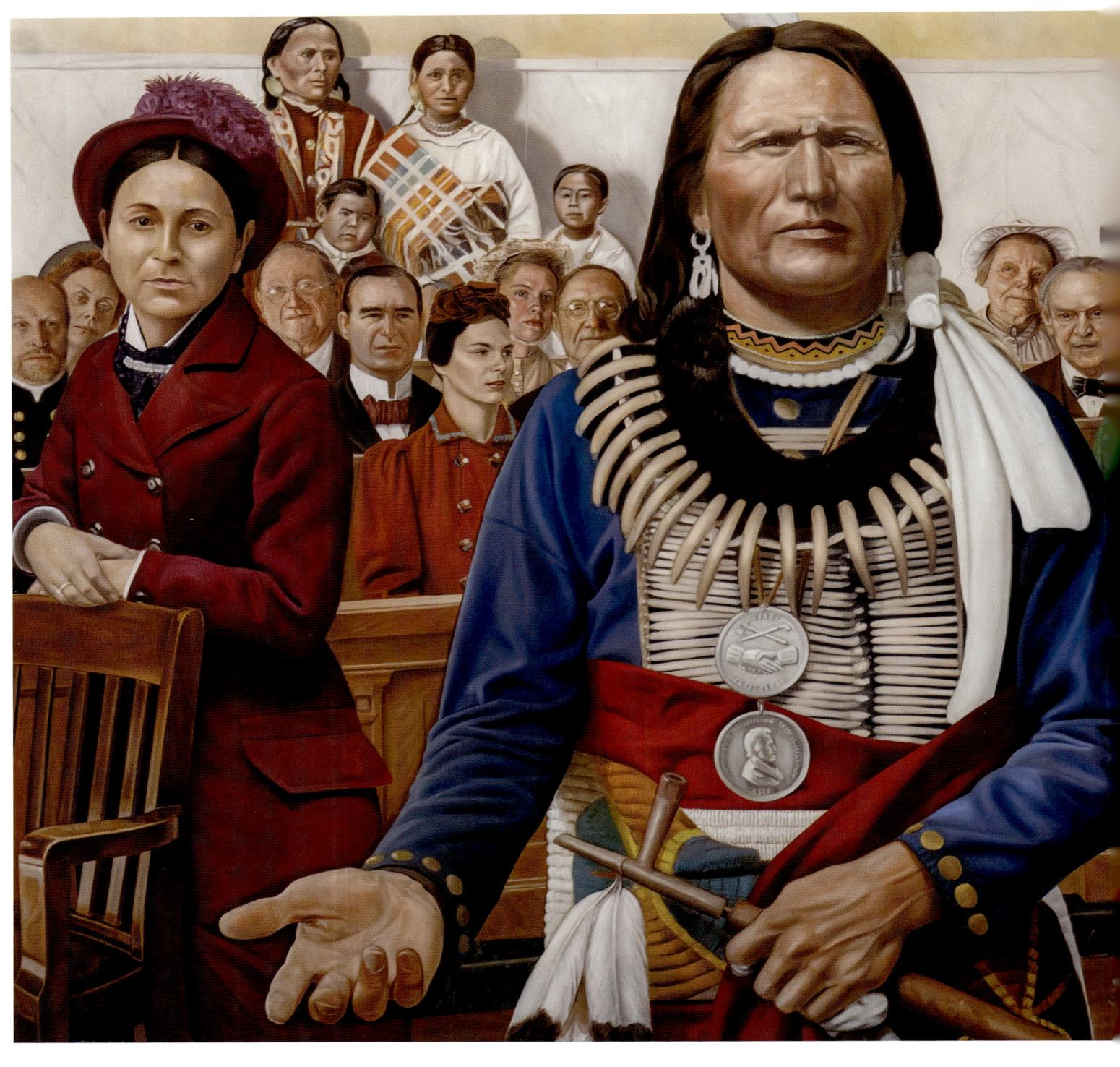

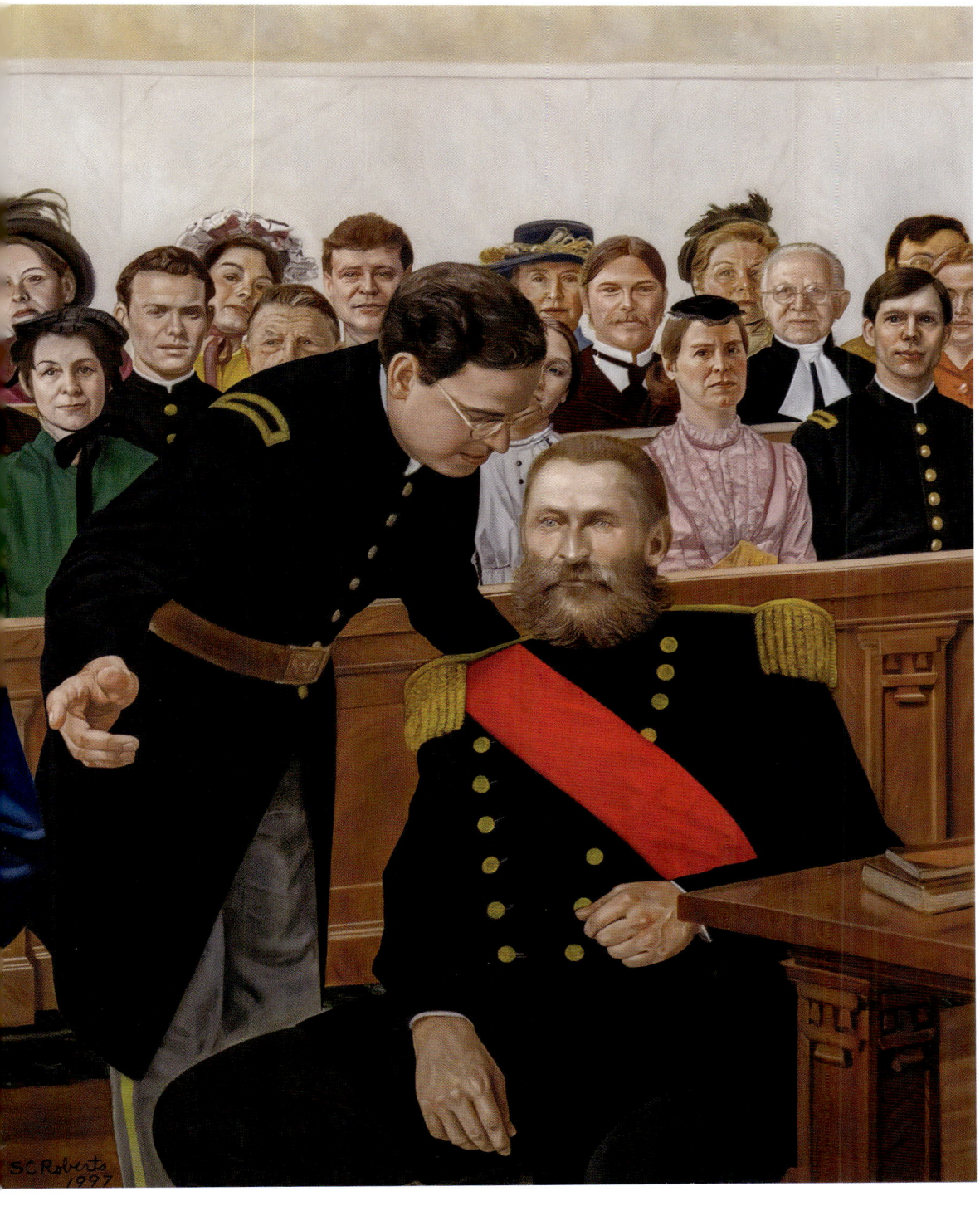

Stephen Cornelius Roberts
The Ideal of Freedom, 1996
6.75 x 12 feet
Oil on linen

During his remarkable 1879 trial, Chief Standing Bear of the Ponca tribe persuaded a federal judge to recognize Native Americans as persons who have the right to sue for their freedom.

In violation of prior treaties, the U.S. government banished the Ponca from their tribal lands in Nebraska and forcibly relocated them to Indian Territory (now in Oklahoma). One-third of the Ponca died within two years of the move.

In defiance of a federal order, Standing Bear and a small band of Ponca returned to their land in an effort to honor the dying wish of Standing Bear's 16-year-old son Bear Shield who wished to be buried in his homeland. Soon after returning, the group was imprisoned.

During Standing Bear's court case, the U.S. government argued that Native people were not protected under the constitution and therefore had no rights. Chief Standing Bear was allowed to give testimony and, in response, gave his famous impassioned "I Am a Man" speech, convincing the judge to grant his freedom and establishing that Native Americans were "persons" under the law. Standing Bear is today recognized as one of the nation's earliest civil rights heroes.

Roberts used the few available photos of Standing Bear and other important people of the trial to create the mural's figures. To the left stands Susette LaFlesche Tibbles, who interpreted for the chief, and seated on the right is General George Crook, who helped facilitate the trial and the chief's legal representation. In the back on the left stand members of Standing Bear's family.

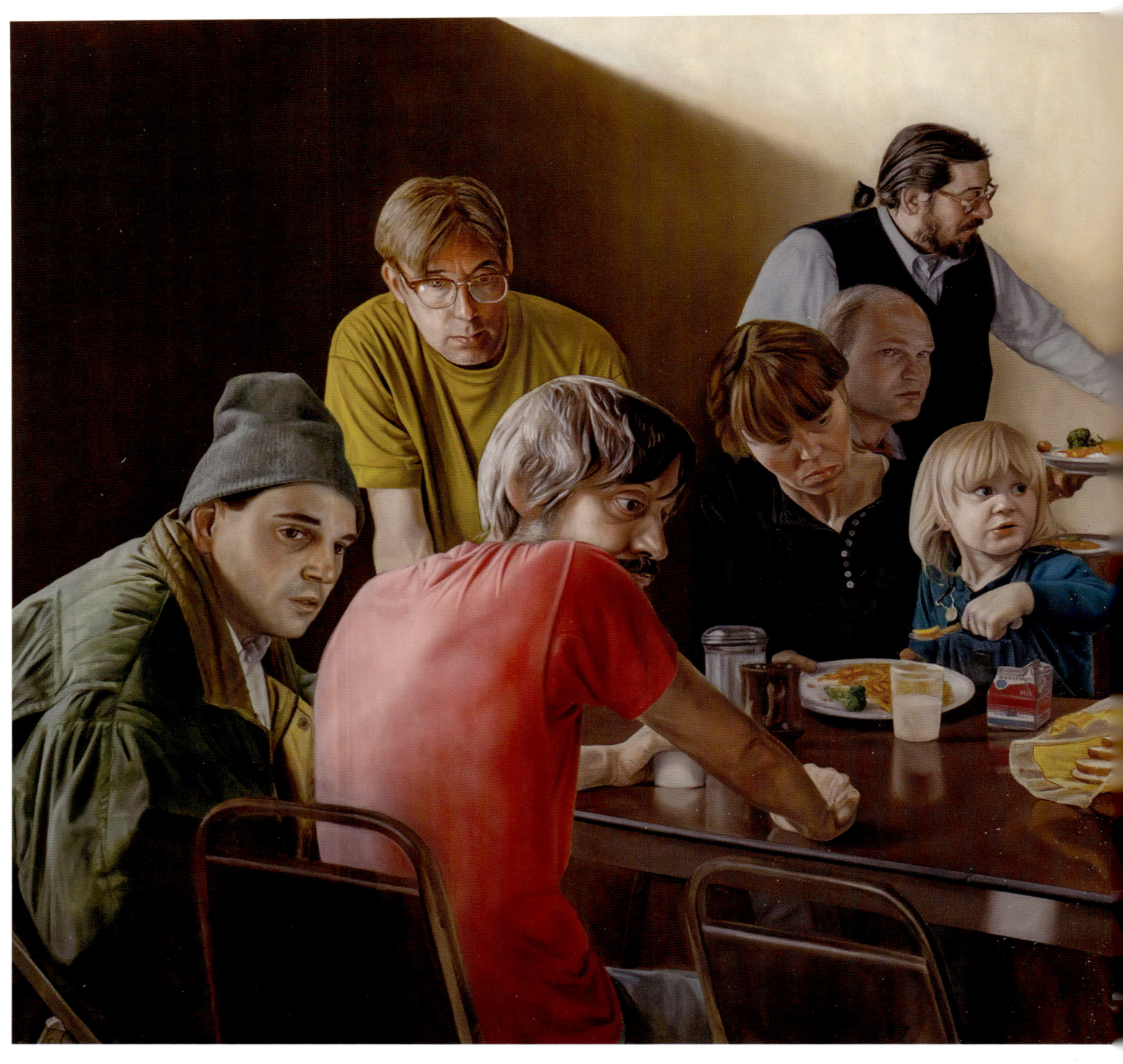

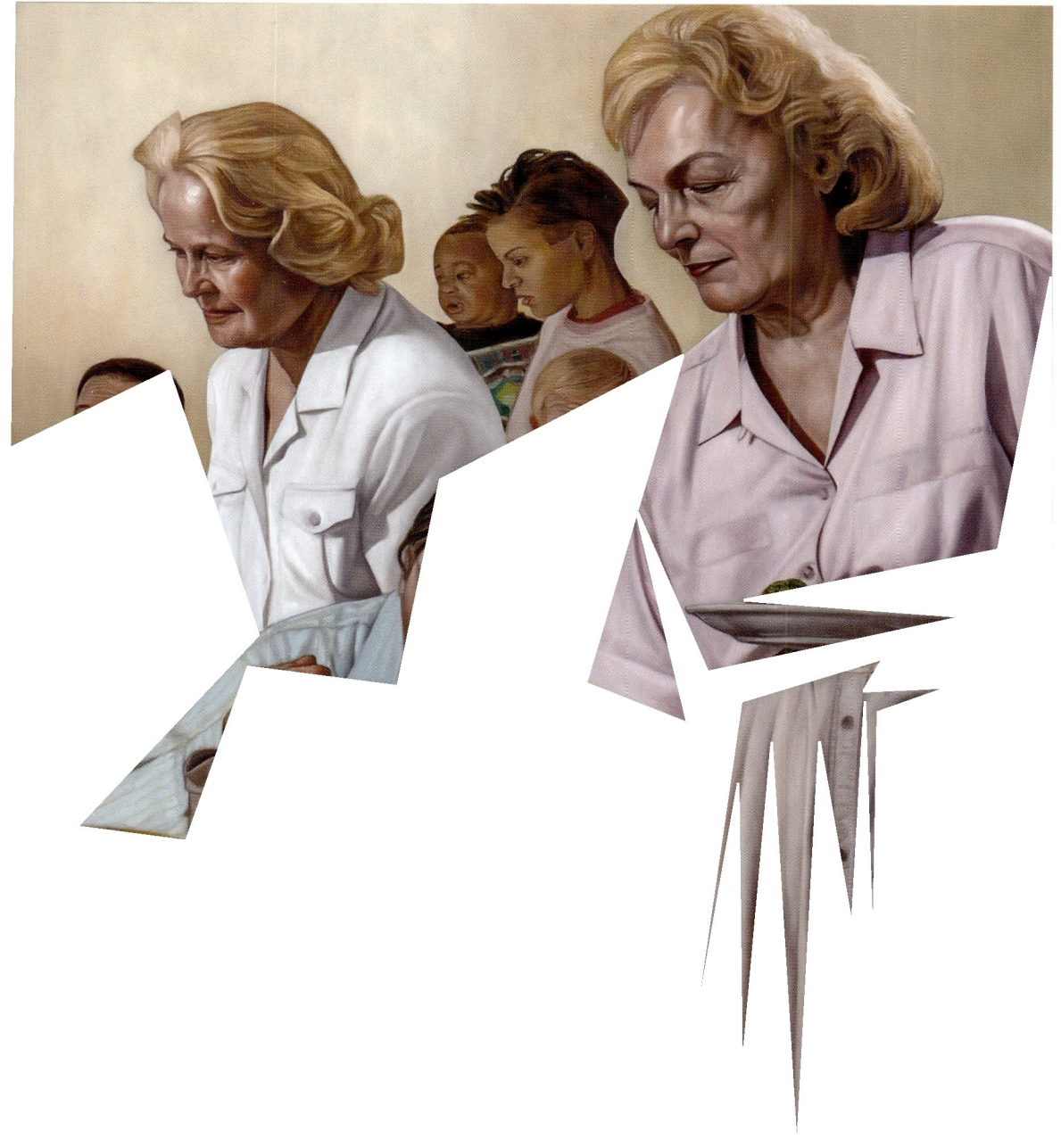

Stephen Cornelius Roberts
The Scourge of Poverty, 1996
6.75 x 12 feet
Oil on linen

Using friends and family members as models for his mural, Roberts celebrates those who care for those in need.

Roberts believes his incorporation of Nebraska history and people led to his selection as the painter for the Memorial Chamber murals. "The other artists [who submitted competition proposals] didn't have any connection to Nebraska. They didn't have any interest in representing the state. It was important to me to connect this all to Nebraska."

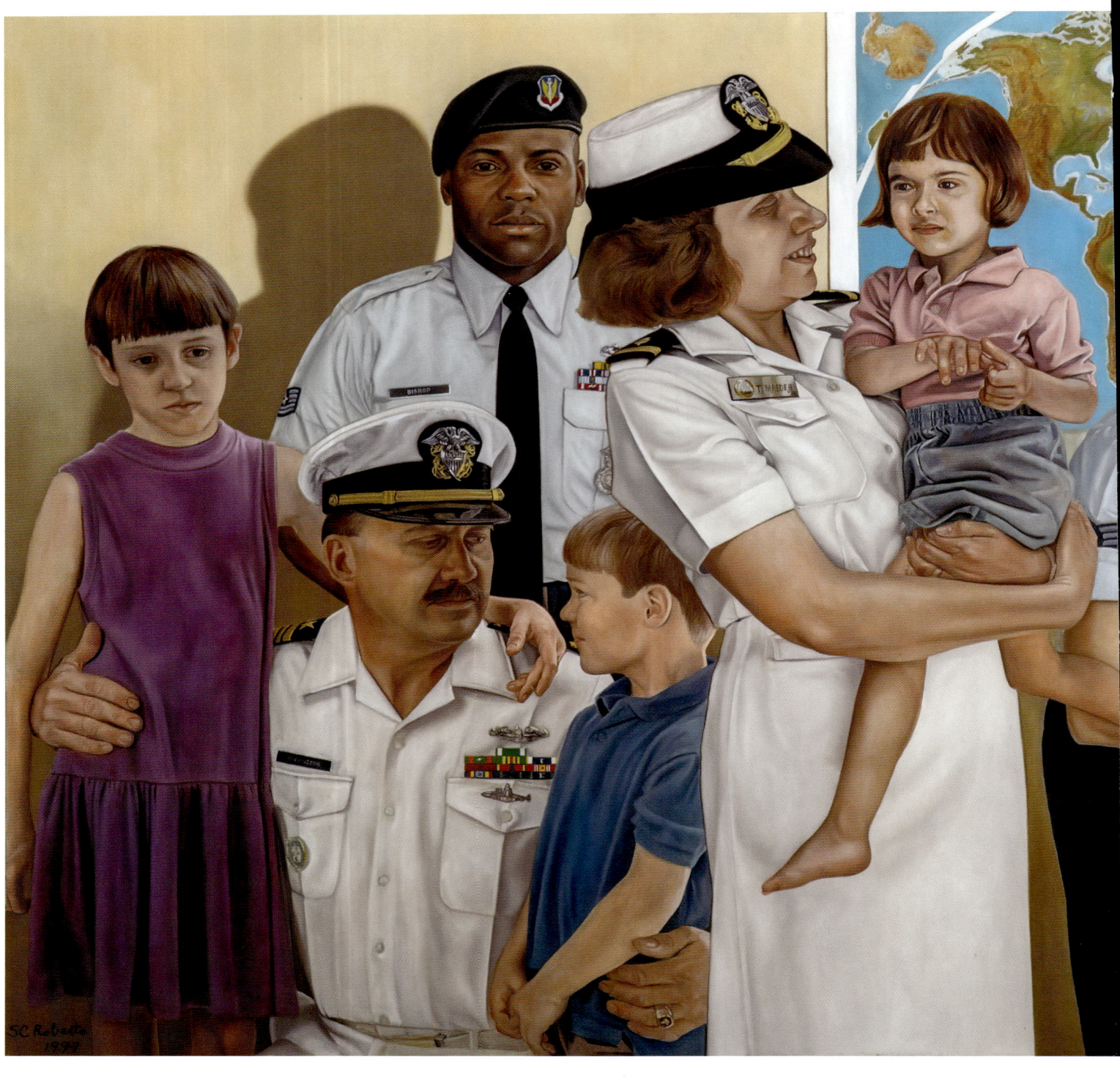

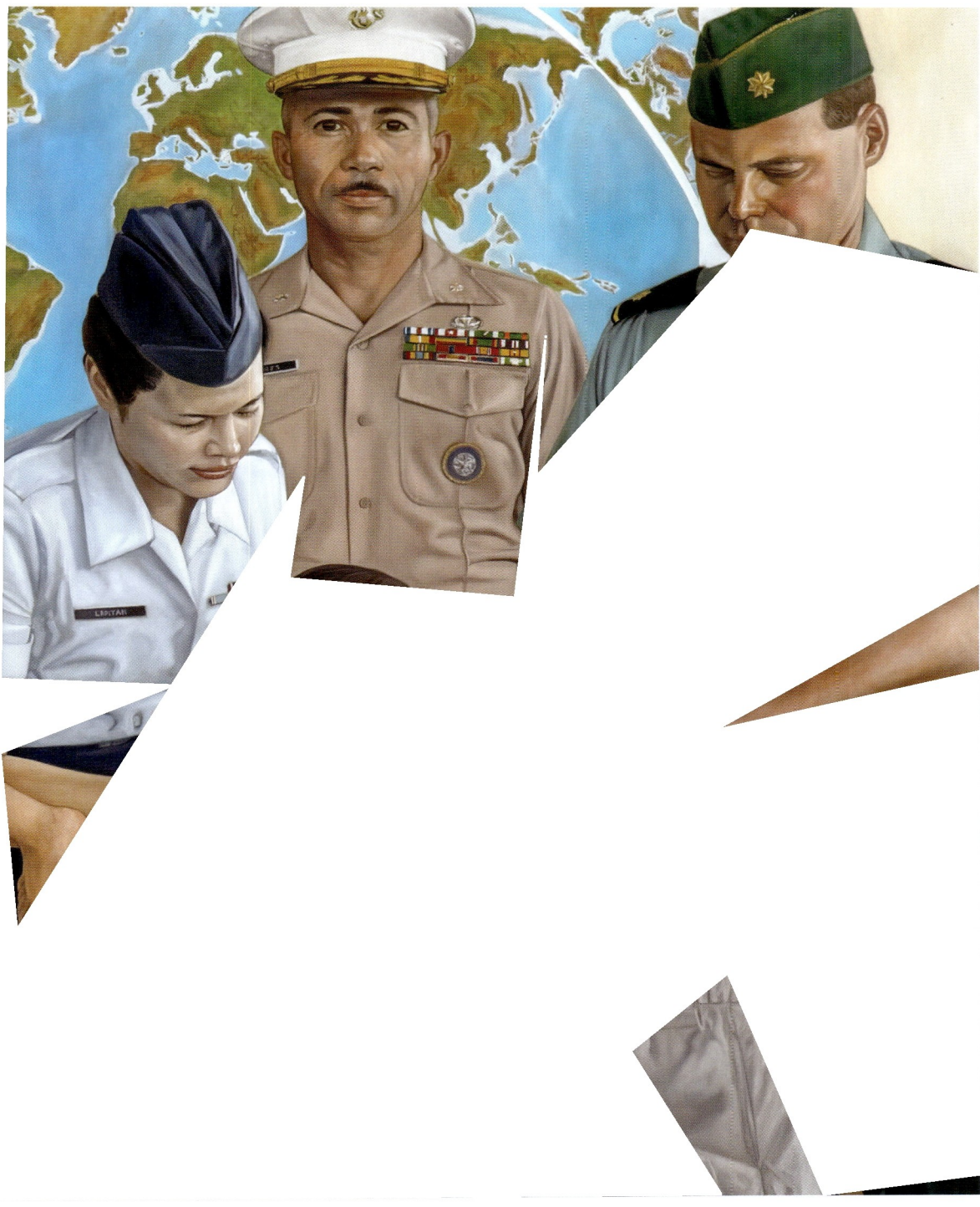

Stephen Cornelius Roberts
The Ideal of Universal Peace, 1996
6.75 x 12 feet
Oil on linen

Roberts said this mural was the most difficult for him to envision. In the end, he created a piece that honors those in the military acting as peacekeepers. He wanted to use children to portray the idea of peace. In the completed work, members of the military stand with their own children as they work to maintain freedom and justice.

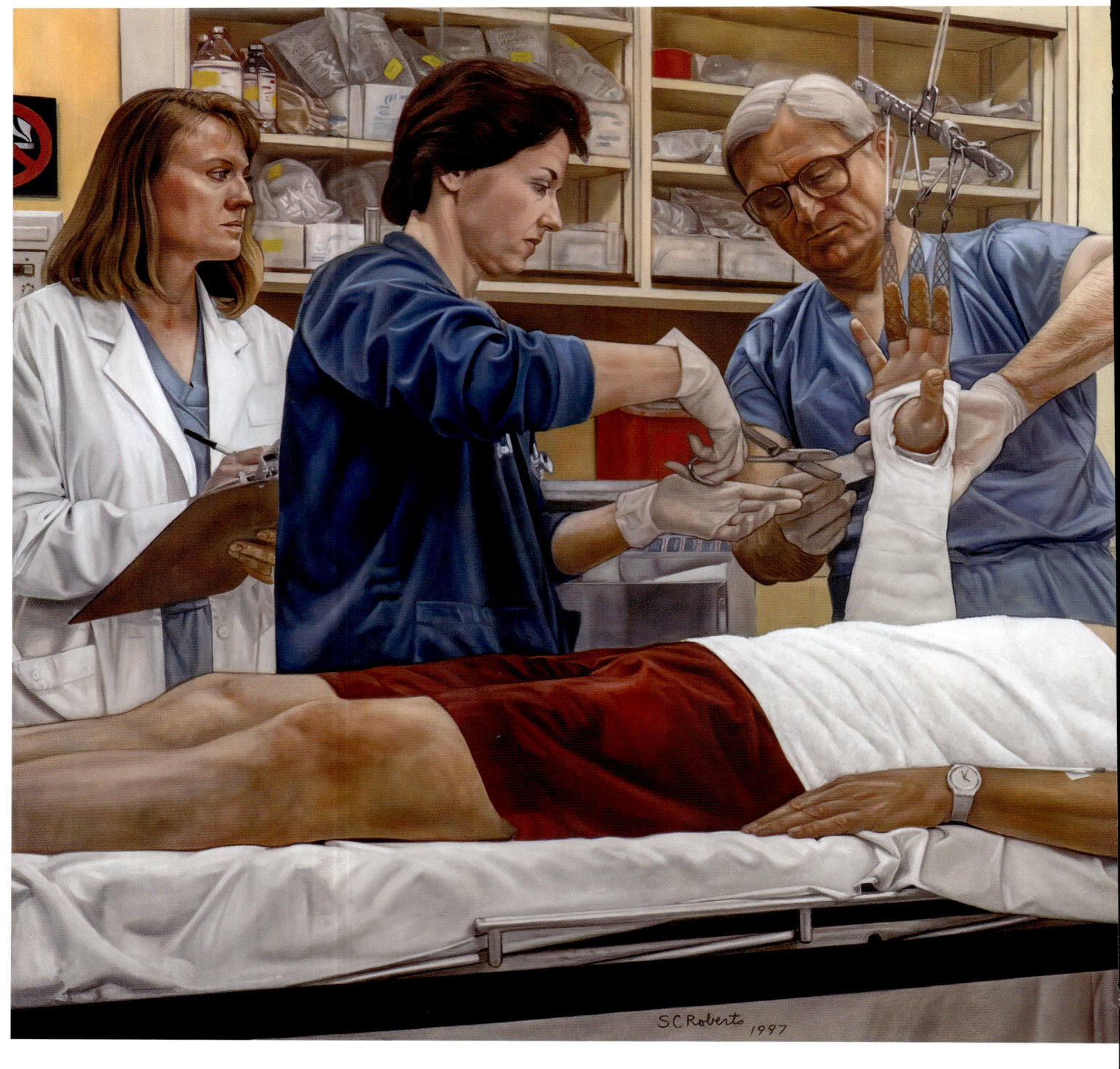

SC Roberts 1997

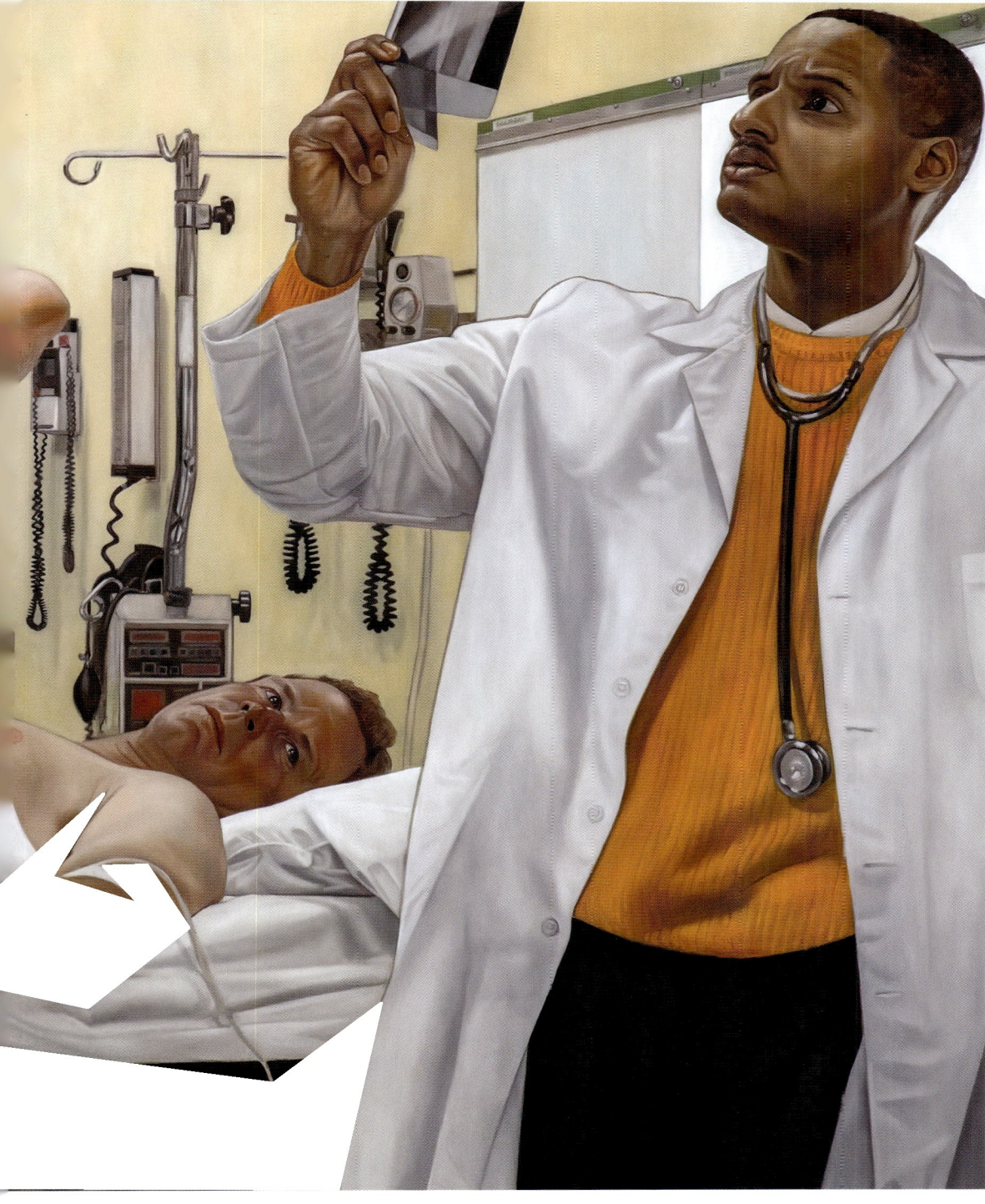

Stephen Cornelius Roberts
The Scourge of the Plague, 1996
6.75 x 12 feet
Oil on linen

Here, as in all of his murals, Roberts cast actual people in their jobs as his subjects. In *The Scourge of Plague*, real health care professionals are shown heroically providing care.

EXTERIOR

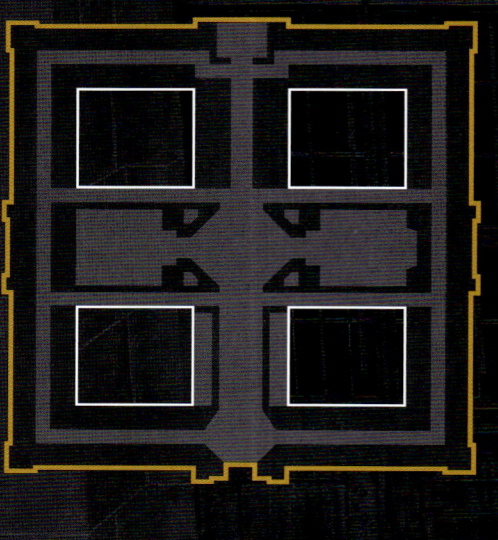

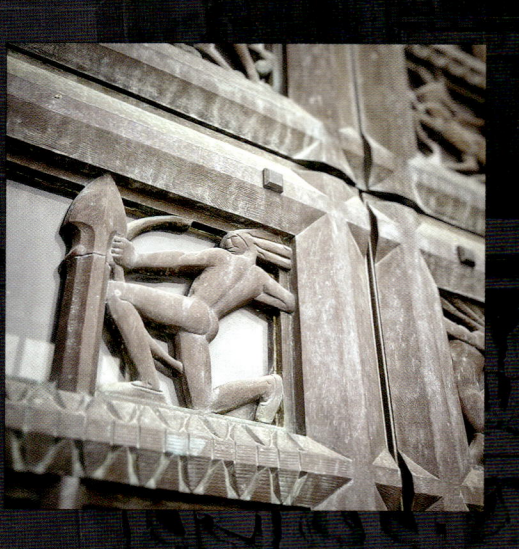

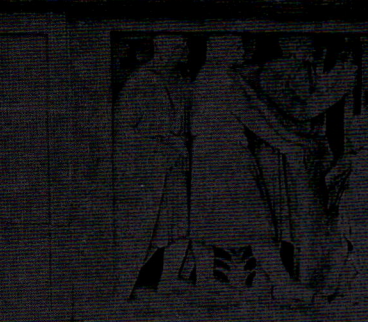

LEE LAWRIE

In 1895 an 18-year-old sculptor named Lee Lawrie so admired the design of a church that he sought out its architect, Bertram Goodhue. Their initial conversation sparked a 30-year collaboration. Together, Lawrie and Goodhue partnered on more than 100 buildings including the iconic Nebraska Capitol.

Born in 1877 in Germany, Lawrie moved at the age of four to the United States with his widowed mother. At age 14, he answered an ad placed by a neoclassical sculptor, and his own path as a sculptor began. He was hired and soon began watching and learning from the studio's artists. In the evenings after work, he taught himself to model clay and created his own pieces. Soon, he would begin taking on sculpture projects of his own.

Lawrie later became a professor at Yale College and Harvard University, where he taught sculpture. His style would eventually evolve to art deco.

But it was in Nebraska where Lawrie achieved a breakthrough that would become his specialty for the rest of his career and life — the use of sculpture in architecture. Working with Goodhue, he created an approach that made the sculpture blend with the building structure.

The Nebraska Capitol stands as the largest commissioned project of Lawrie's life and holds the largest and most complex collection of his work.

Lawrie's relationship with Goodhue proved powerful for both men. When Goodhue received a medal of merit from the American Institute of Architecture, he insisted that it be re-engraved to include Lawrie too. Lawrie sculpted Goodhue's memorial tomb with the images of many of Goodhue's most prominent buildings, with the Nebraska Capitol in the center.

After his work on the Capitol, Lawrie created some of the most well-known sculptures in the nation, including the art deco stone relief sculpture *Wisdom* on 30 Rockefeller Plaza and the huge bronze Atlas statue in Rockefeller Center. Another of his notable designs depicts President Franklin D. Roosevelt on the American dime.

Lawrie continued as an influential and iconic sculptor until his death in 1963. An energetic man in constant motion, he worked until eight days before his death at age 85.

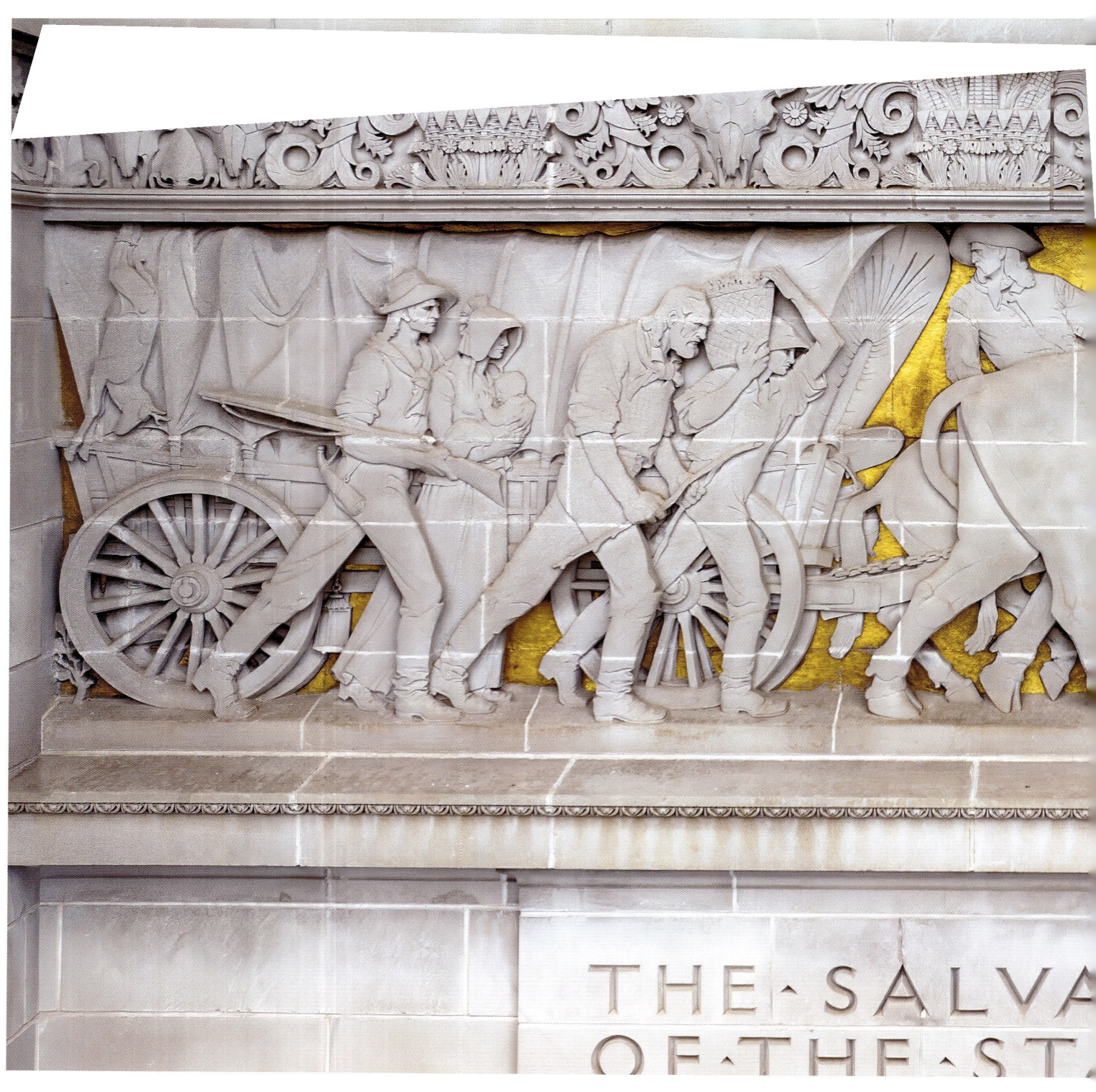

THE·SALVA
OF·THE·ST

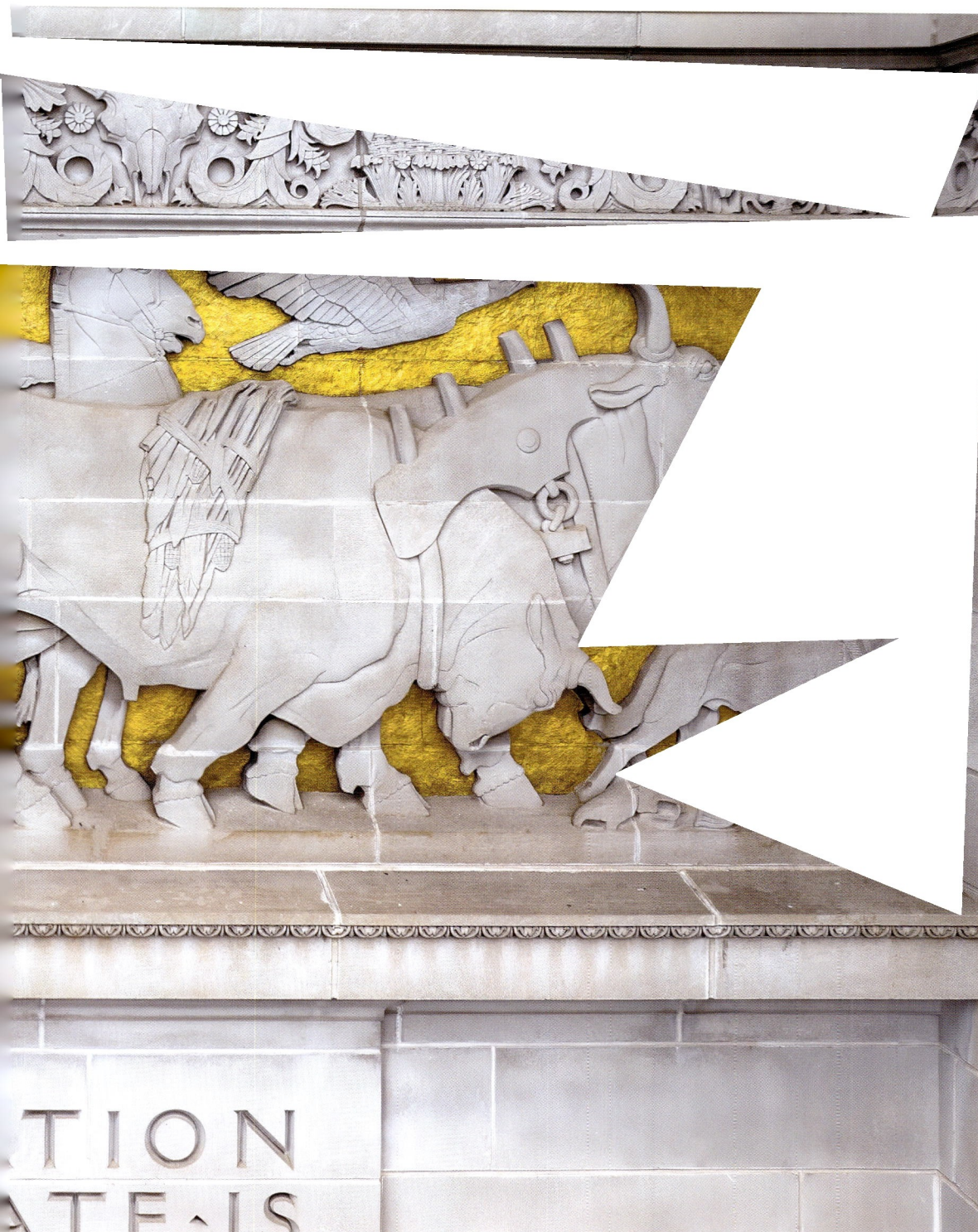

Lee Lawrie
Coming of the Pioneers, c.1932
approx. 7.5 x 24.5 feet
Indiana limestone sculpture

One look at the exterior of the Capitol makes clear that Goodhue, Alexander, and Lawrie wanted to provide a dramatic impression. The building's facade tells the epic story of, according to Alexander, "the Spirit of the Law as shown in its history." It strives to express Nebraska's place in the history of the world and to inspire all who visit.

In general, each side of the building provides its own focus and message. The north portal expresses the theme of "The Spirit of the Law."

Coming of the Pioneers, located prominently on the north portal, portrays the brave path undertaken by the pioneers who settled in Nebraska. Guided by Colonel "Buffalo Bill" Cody, the pioneer family travels the plains in a prairie schooner. The old man holds a water-finder's wand while the young man carries a basket of seeds. The Eagle of Destiny leads the way toward the rising sun. Below is etched "The Salvation of the State is Watchfulness in the Citizen."

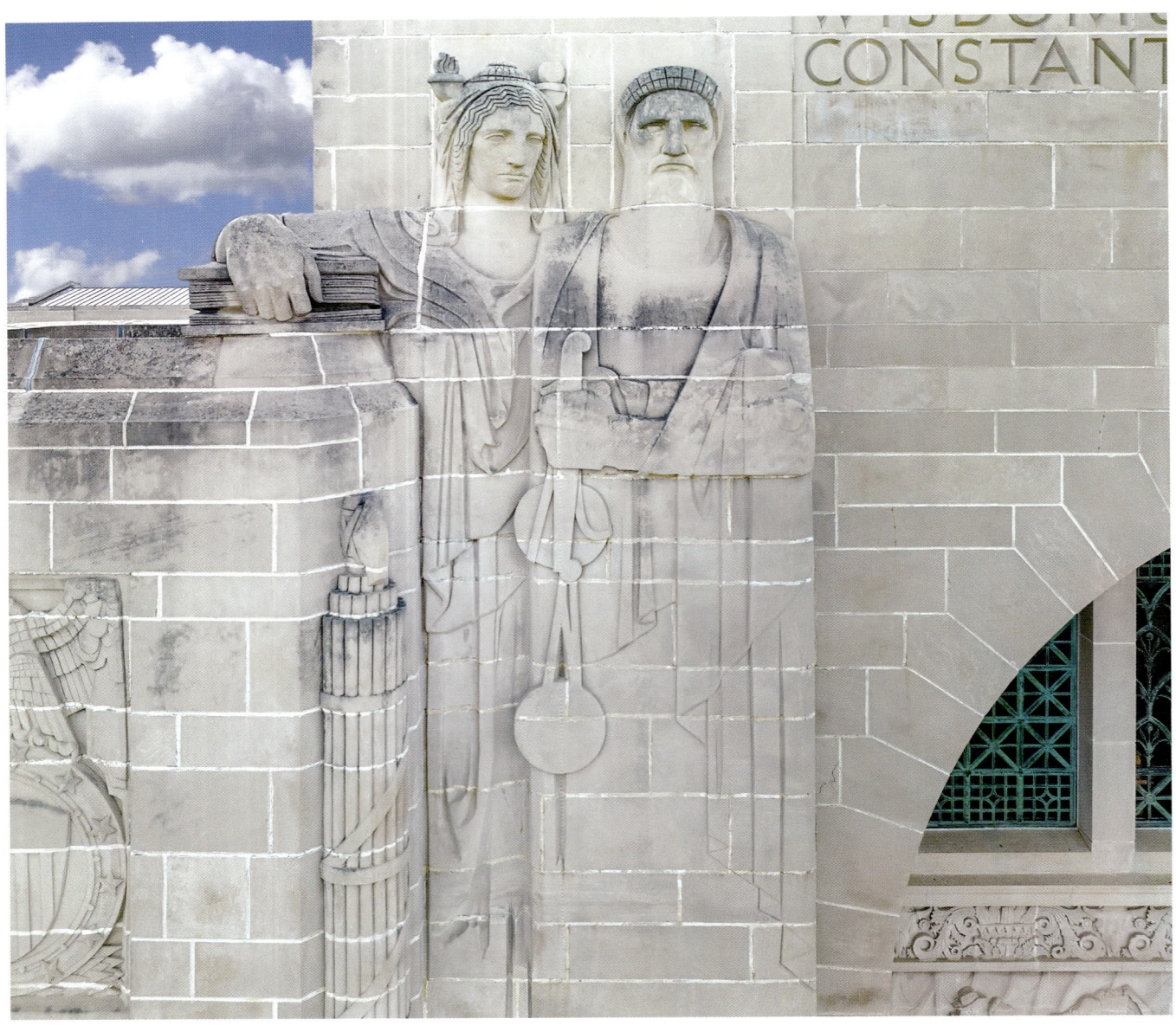

Lee Lawrie
Wisdom and Justice, c.1932
Indiana limestone sculpture

Above the north portal, *Wisdom and Justice* stand across
from *Power and Mercy*, with their role of "Constant
Guardians of the Law" etched between them.

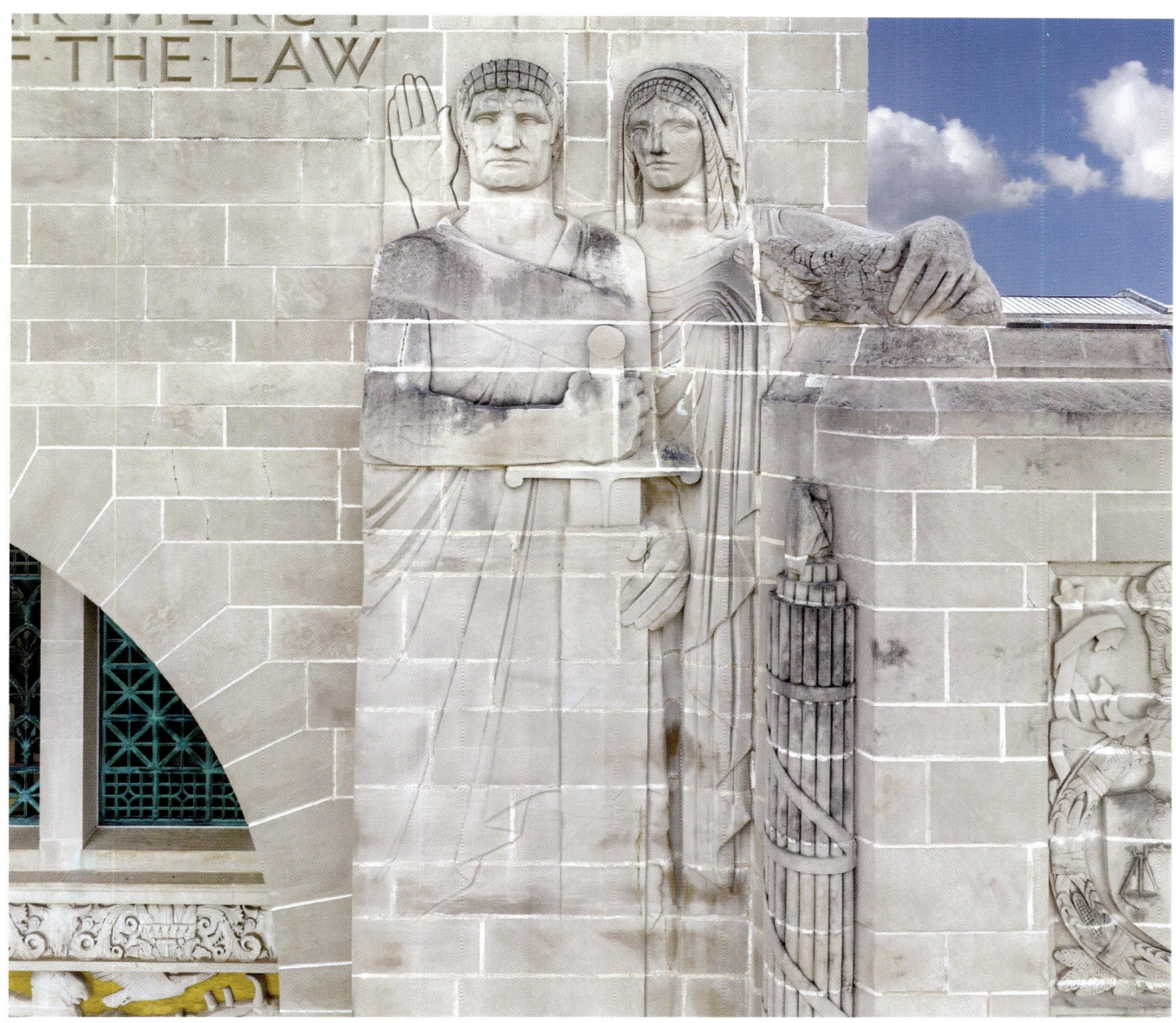

Lee Lawrie
Power and Mercy, c.1932
Indiana limestone sculpture

Lawrie carved figures to appear to be growing out of the building. At Goodhue's memorial service, Lawrie said, "In 1922 after a great many preliminary sketches for the work of the Nebraska Capitol, Mr. Goodhue and I arrived at a new kind of architectural sculpture that is essentially a part of the building rather than something ornate or applied. . . . Sculpture, here, is not sculpture, but a branch grafted on to the architectural trunk. Forms that portray animate life emerge from blocks of stone and terminate in historic expression."

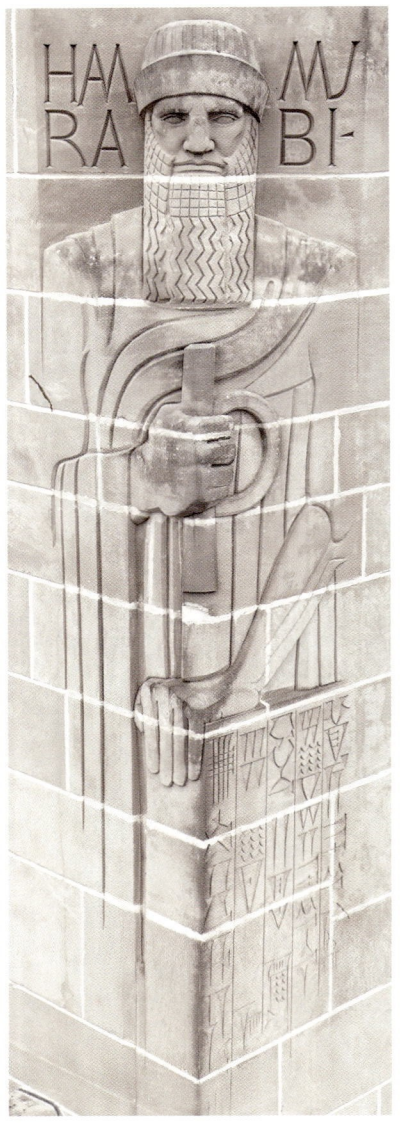

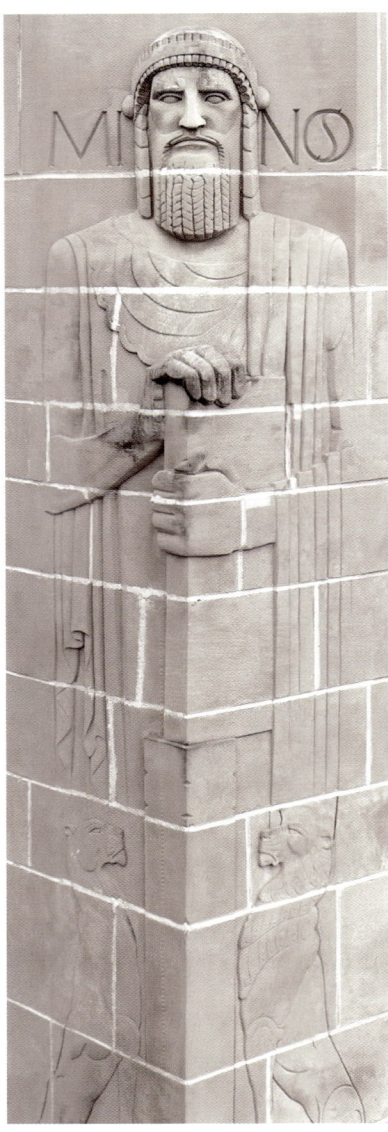

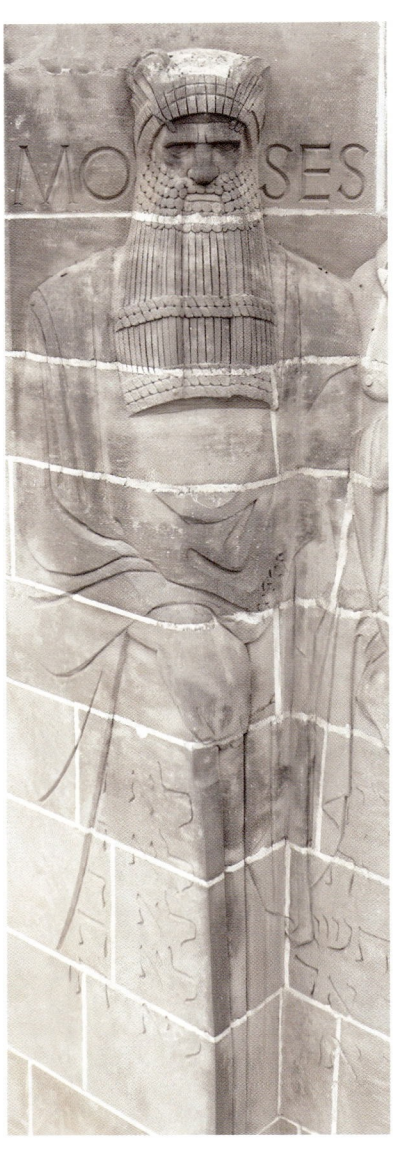

Lee Lawrie
Hammurabi, c.1932
approx. 16 x 4 feet
Indiana limestone sculpture

Lee Lawrie
Minos, c.1932
approx. 16 x 4 feet
Indiana limestone sculpture

Lee Lawrie
Moses, c.1932
approx. 16 x 4 feet
Indiana limestone sculpture

All sides of the Capitol are adorned with carvings of great leaders.

The south facade includes ten that Alexander called "Great Legislators of the Western World." They are set in front of the law chambers housing the Supreme Court and State Law Library. Alexander designed this side of the building to embody "Written Law."

Goodhue and Lawrie originally intended to place great explorers in this area, representing a kind of individual heroism. After Goodhue's death, Alexander changed this to the current figures, which he believed represented great explorers of the spirit.

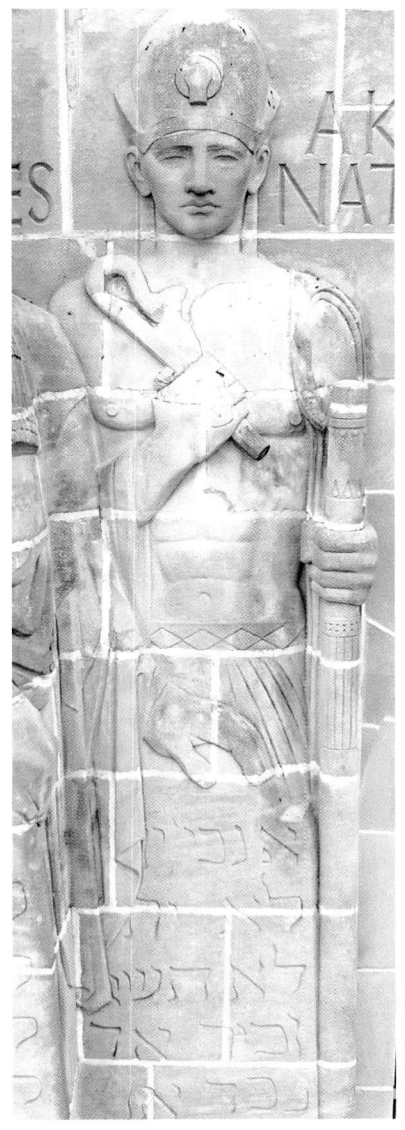

Lee Lawrie
Akhenaton, c.1932
approx. 16 x 4 feet
Indiana limestone sculpture

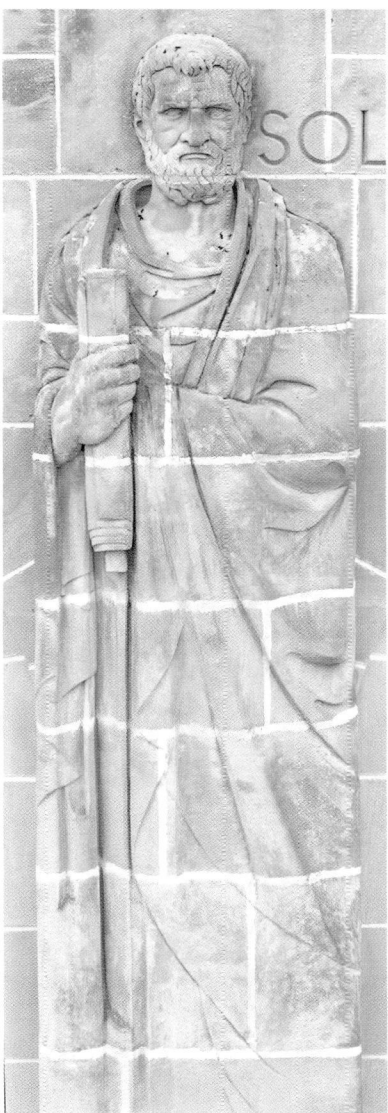

Lee Lawrie
Solon, c.1932
approx. 16 x 4 feet
Indiana limestone sculpture

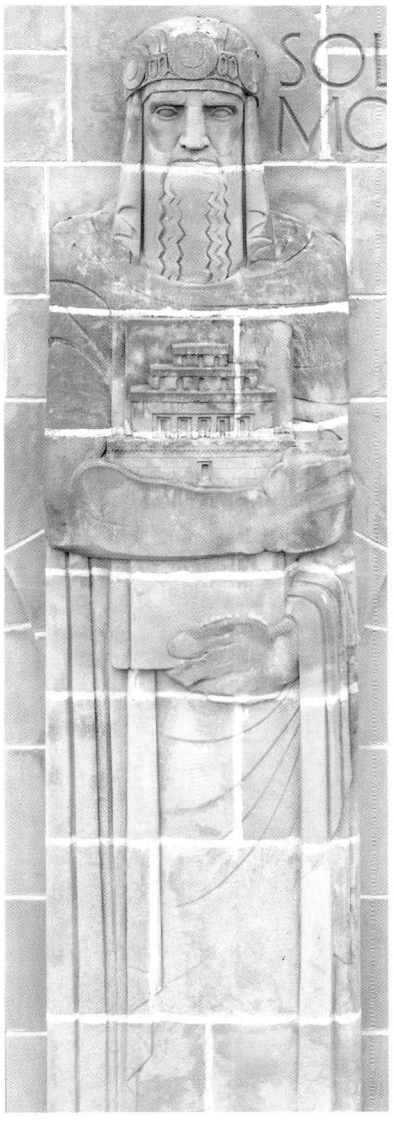

Lee Lawrie
Solomon, c.1932
approx. 16 x 4 feet
Indiana limestone sculpture

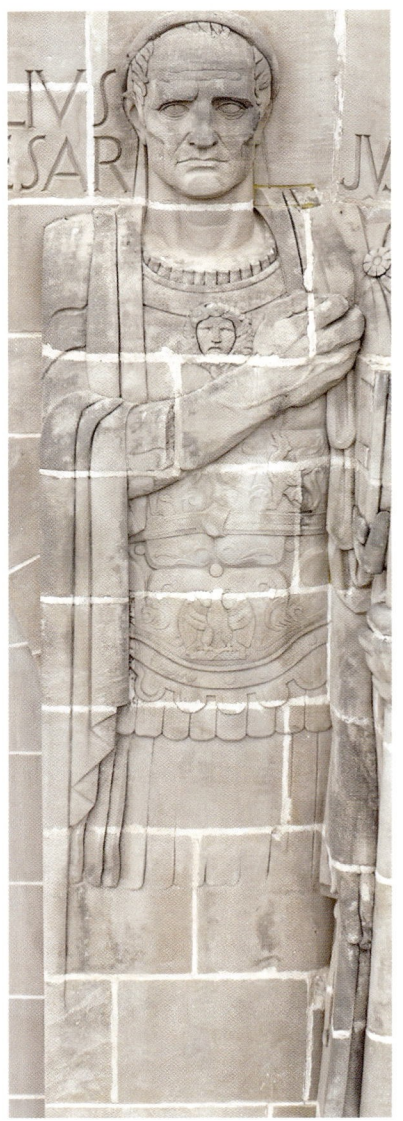

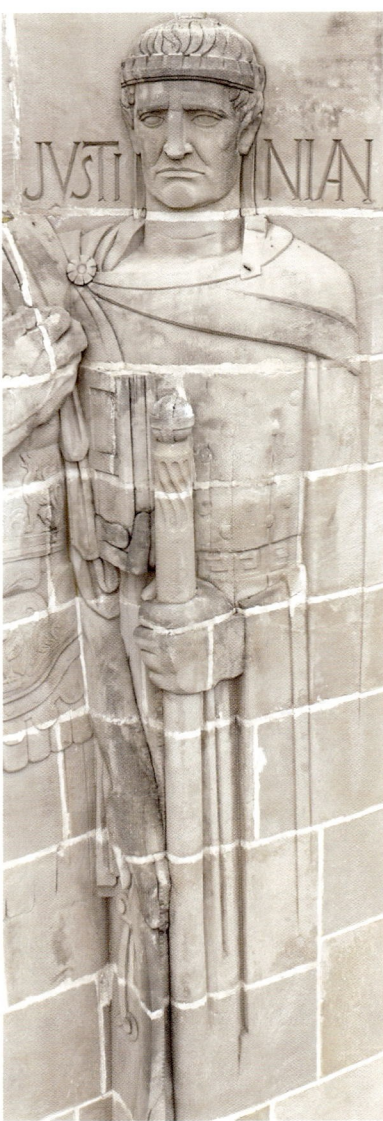

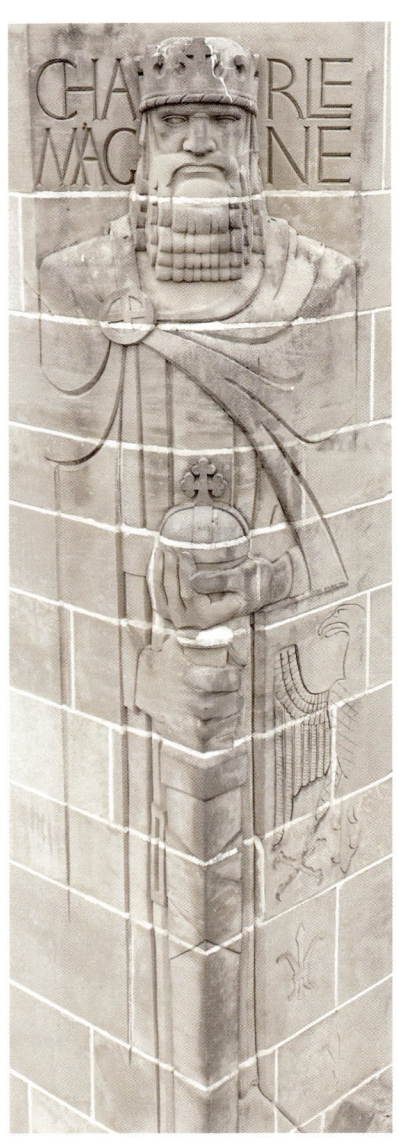

Lee Lawrie
Julius Caesar, c.1932
approx. 16 x 4 feet
Indiana limestone sculpture

Lee Lawrie
Justinian Caesar, c.1932
approx. 16 x 4 feet
Indiana limestone sculpture

Lee Lawrie
Charlemagne, c.1932
approx. 16 x 4 feet
Indiana limestone sculpture

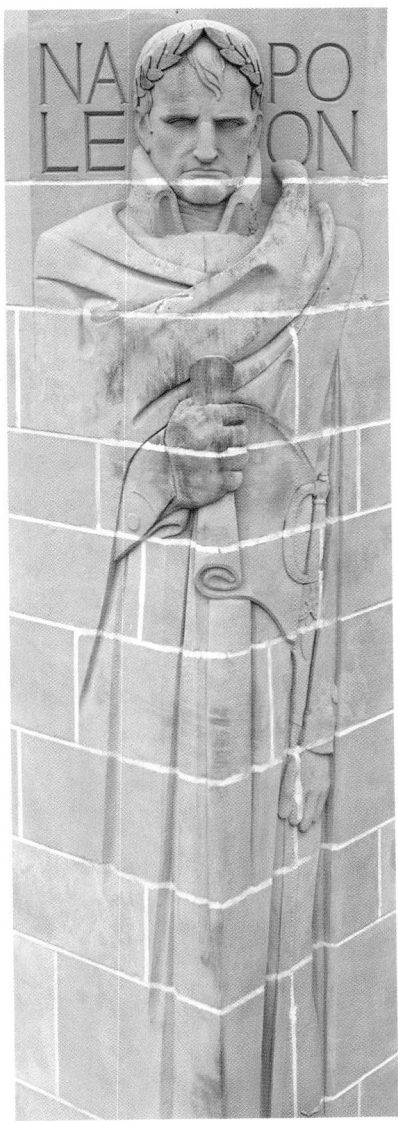

Lee Lawrie
Napoleon, c.1932
approx. 16 x 4 feet
Indiana limestone sculpture

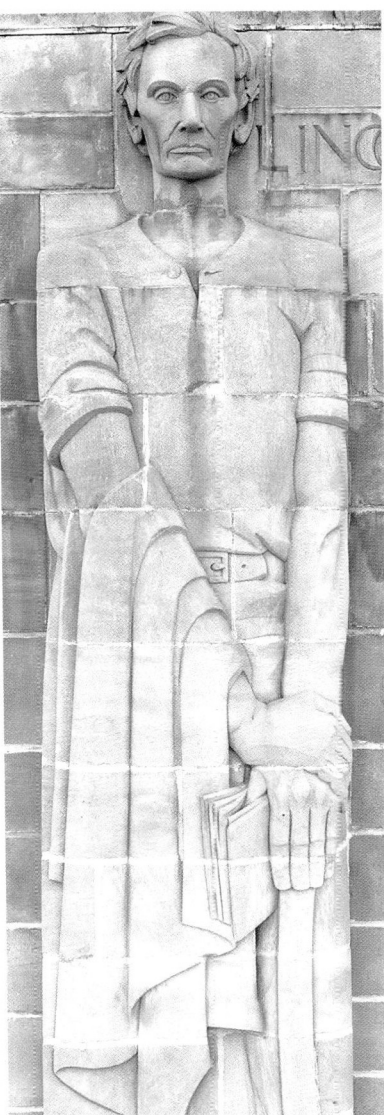

Lee Lawrie
Lincoln, c.1932
approx. 16 x 4 feet
Indiana limestone sculpture

Lincoln and Pentaour, an Egyptian
scribe, are set on the north facade
of the tower. For Alexander, these
figures represented the beginning
and end of the nature of human
thought on governance. Pentaour
believed leaders should be revered
and remembered, while Lincoln
embraced the belief that the people
represent a nation's humanity and
significance and should be honored.

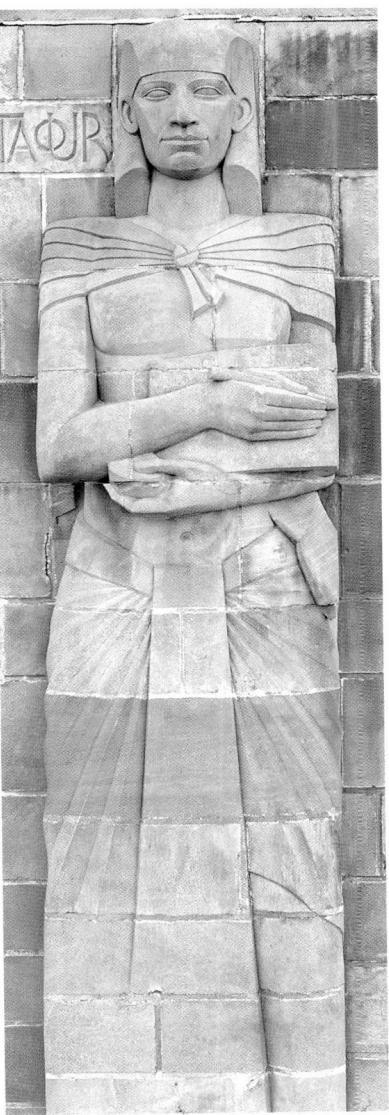

Lee Lawrie
Pentaour, c.1932
approx. 16 x 4 feet
Indiana limestone sculpture

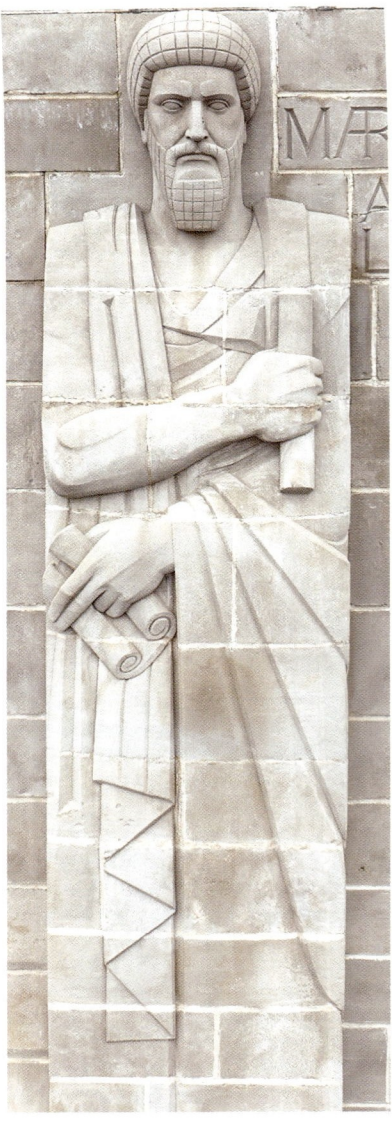

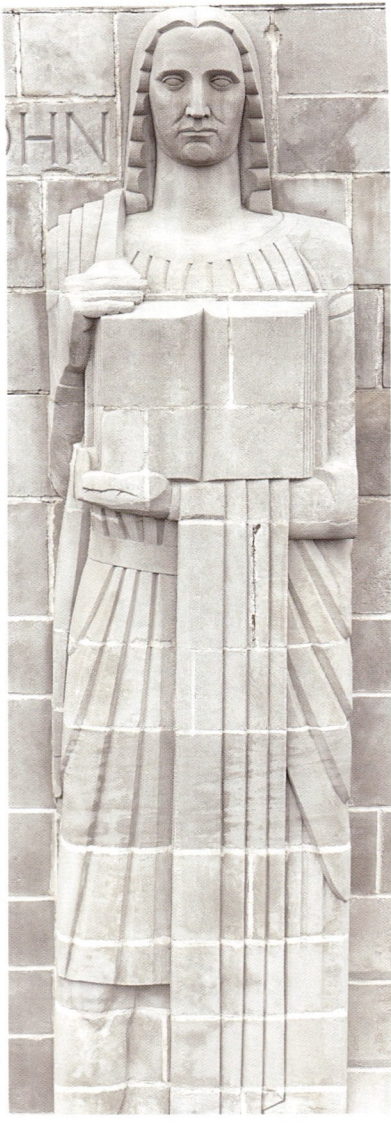

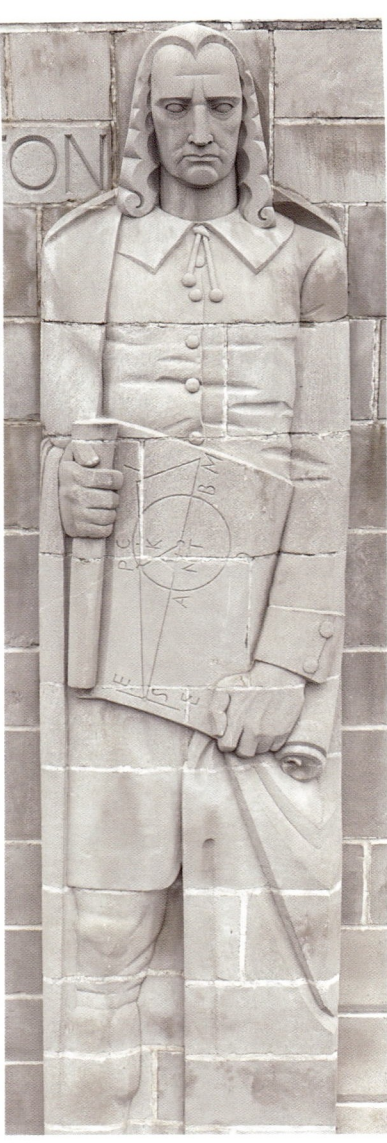

Lee Lawrie
Marcus Aurelius, c.1932
approx. 16 x 4 feet
Indiana limestone sculpture

Standing on the south facade of
the tower, Marcus Aurelius and
John the Apostle debate different
philosophies of decision-making,
from law based on reason in the stoic
tradition to laws based in faith.

These figures are set below
an inscription based upon
Aristotle: "Political society exists
for the sake of noble living."

Lee Lawrie
John the Apostle, c.1932
approx. 16 x 4 feet
Indiana limestone sculpture

Lee Lawrie
Newton, c.1932
approx. 16 x 4 feet
Indiana limestone sculpture

On the east side of the tower, Newton
stands with Louis IX to represent
different rules that guide man's life,
from the laws of nature to the rules
of fairness, chivalry, and morality.

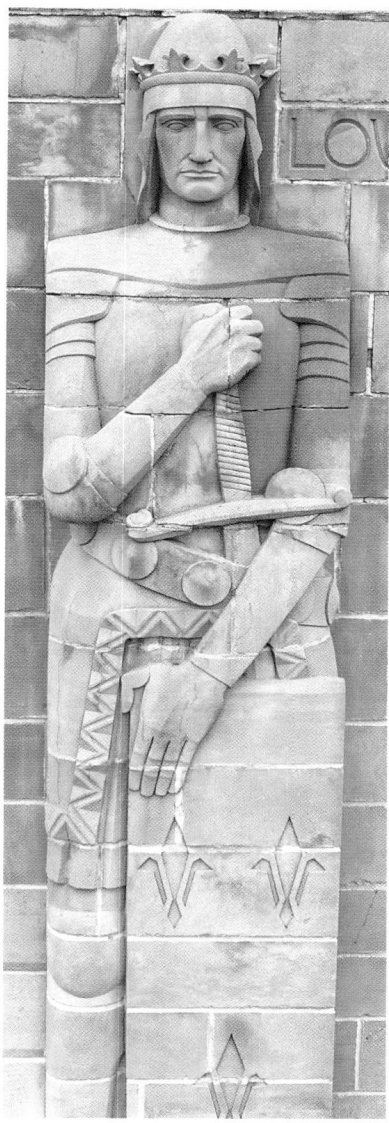

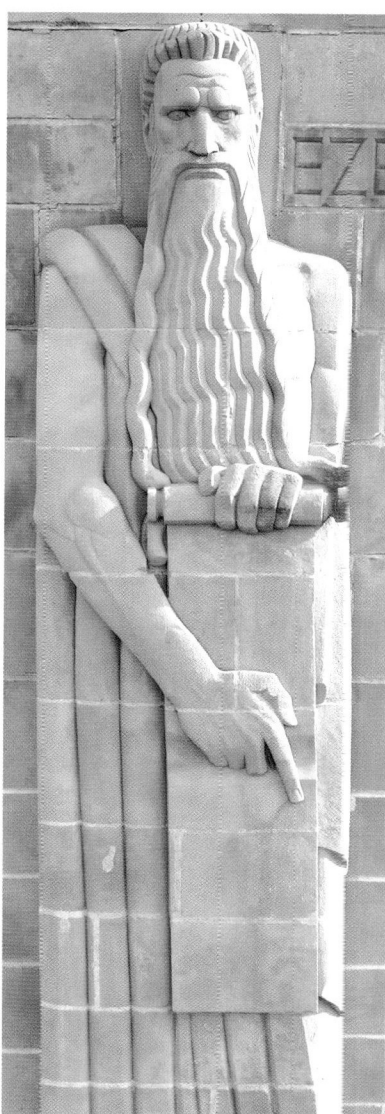

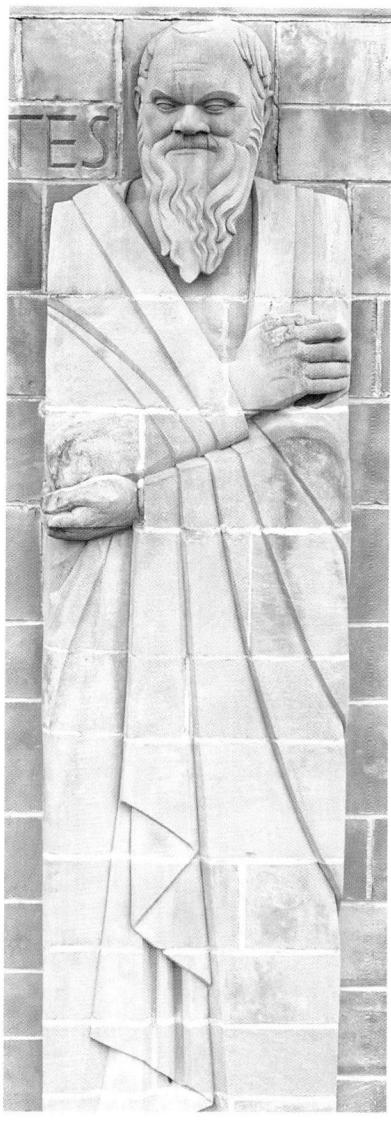

Lee Lawrie
Louis IX, c.1932
approx. 16 x 4 feet
Indiana limestone sculpture

Lee Lawrie
Ezekiel, c.1932
approx. 16 x 4 feet
Indiana limestone sculpture

Ezekiel stands with Socrates on
the west facade of the tower to
represent contrasting philosophical
traditions, from what Alexander
called "cosmic tradition" to
reason and empirical thought.

Lee Lawrie
Socrates, c.1932
approx. 16 x 4 feet
Indiana limestone sculpture

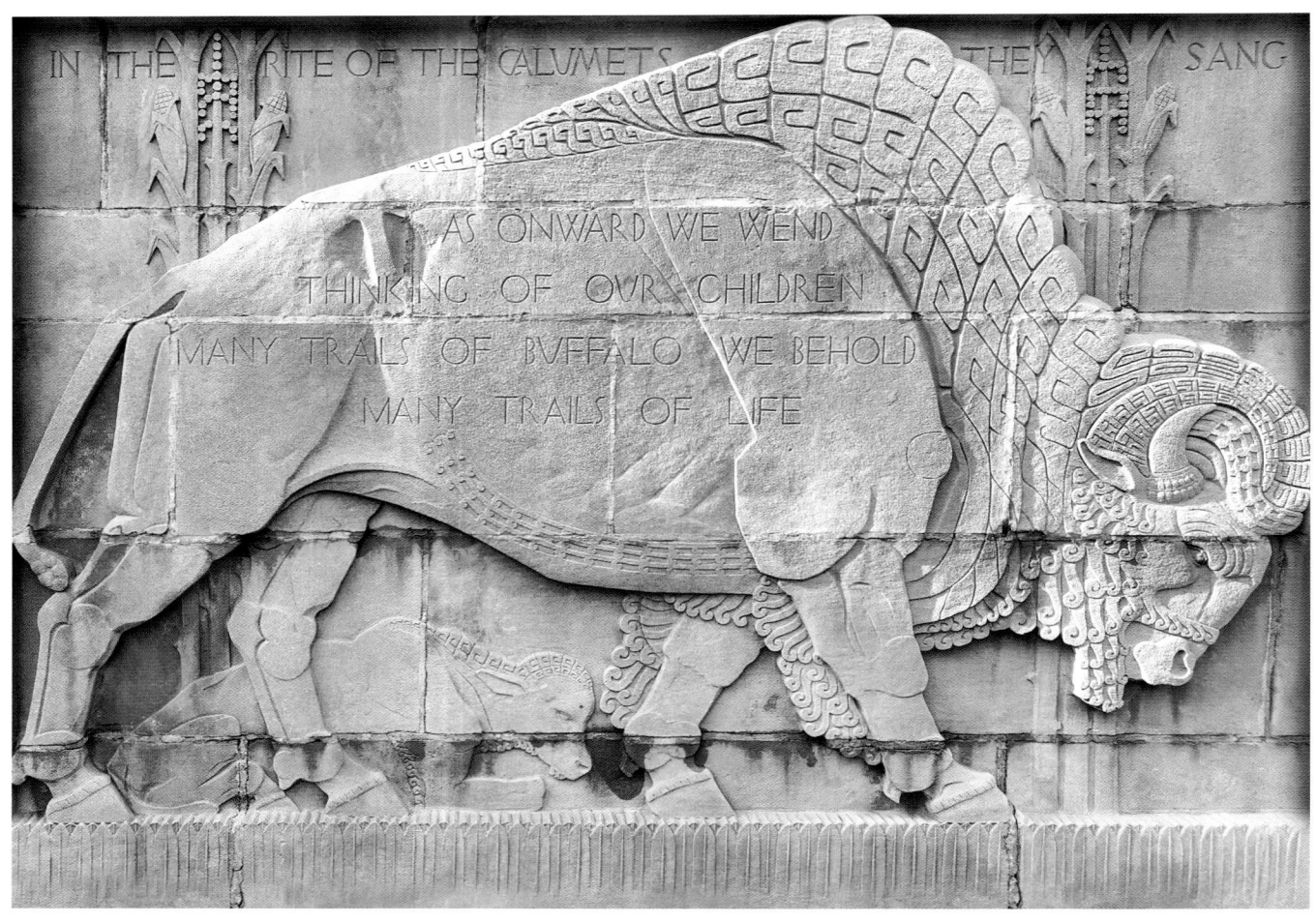

Inscribed on the sculpture:

IN THE RITE OF THE CALVMETS ... THE ... SANG
AS ONWARD WE WEND
THINKING OF OVR CHILDREN
MANY TRAILS OF BVFFALO WE BEHOLD
MANY TRAILS OF LIFE

Lee Lawrie
Female Buffalo, c.1932
approx. 8.5 x 11 feet
Indiana limestone sculpture

Originally conceived as winged buffalo by Goodhue, Alexander convinced him that wings were "false to all American lore" and substituted maize instead. Bison and corn provided fundamental food sources for the first farmers of Nebraska—the Plains Indians—and the settlers coming later. Inscribed on the cow and calf is a passage taken from the Pawnee ritual of Hako representing the gift of life through corn and children.

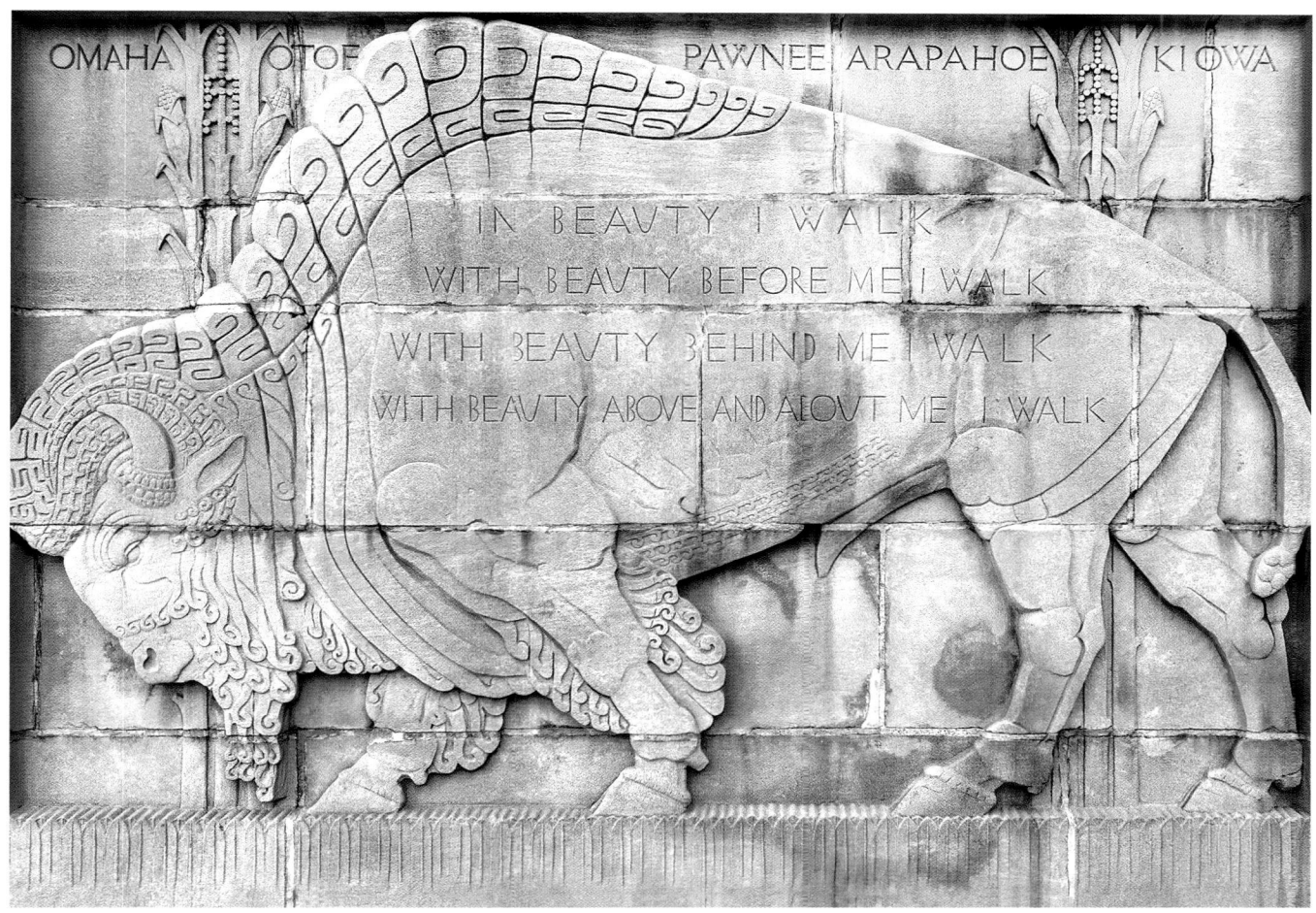

Lee Lawrie
Male Buffalo, c.1932
approx. 8.5 x 11 feet
Indiana limestone sculpture

The tribes that once hunted on Nebraska land—Omaha,
Otoe, Pawnee, Arapahoe, Kiowa, Sioux, Cheyenne,
Winnebago, Ponca, and Arikara—fill the panel backgrounds
behind both bison. On the bull itself is a passage from a
Navajo hymn sung to celebrate a refreshing shower.

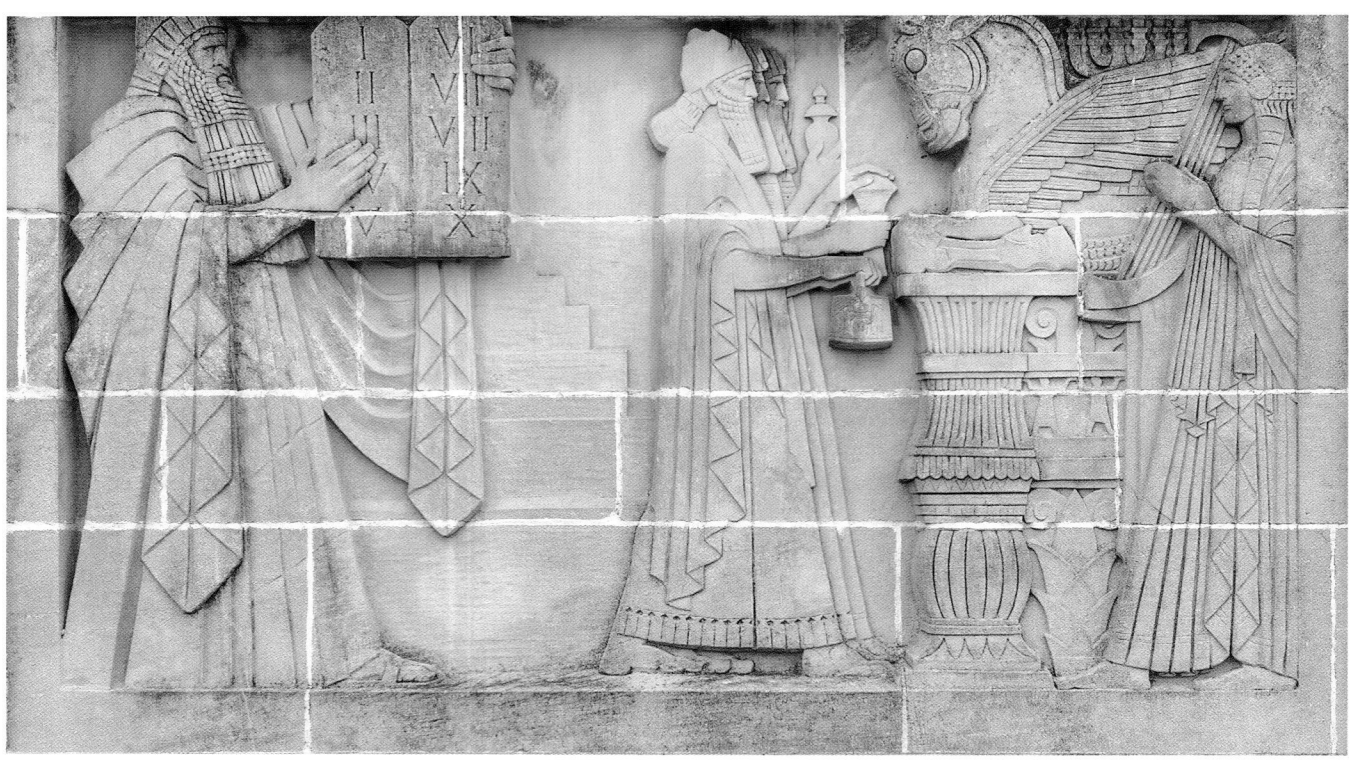

Lee Lawrie
Moses Brings the Law from Sinai, c.1932
approx. 6 x 10 feet
Indiana limestone sculpture

The terrace level encircling the building provides a
chronological history of law and society leading to U.S.
democracy, recounting some of the most significant moments
in the world. Alexander sought to show through each panel
the sequence of progress and the emergence of a good
society through conflict, negotiation, and reconciliation.

The east facade represents law in the ancient world, while
the west depicts law in the modern world. To the south,
the story turns to the written and constitutional law.

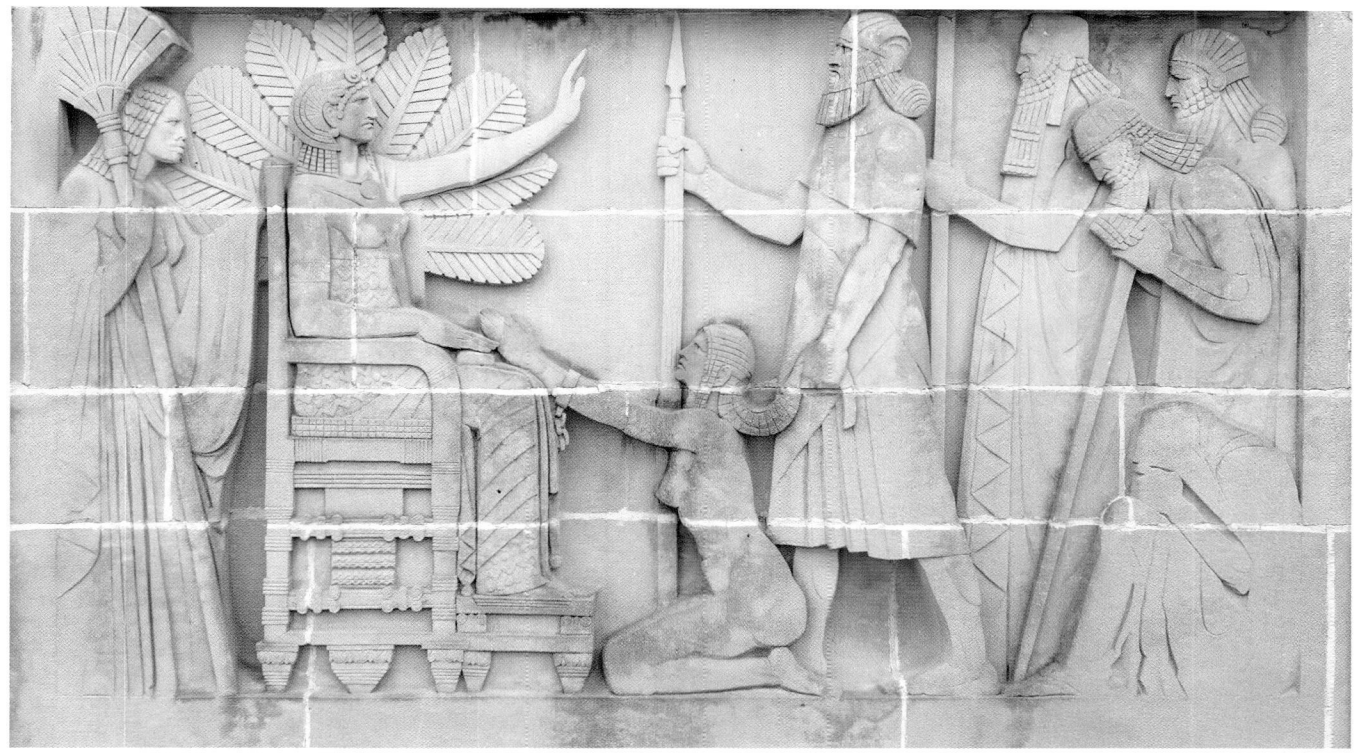

Lee Lawrie
Deborah Judging Israel, c.1932
approx. 6 x 10 feet
Indiana limestone sculpture

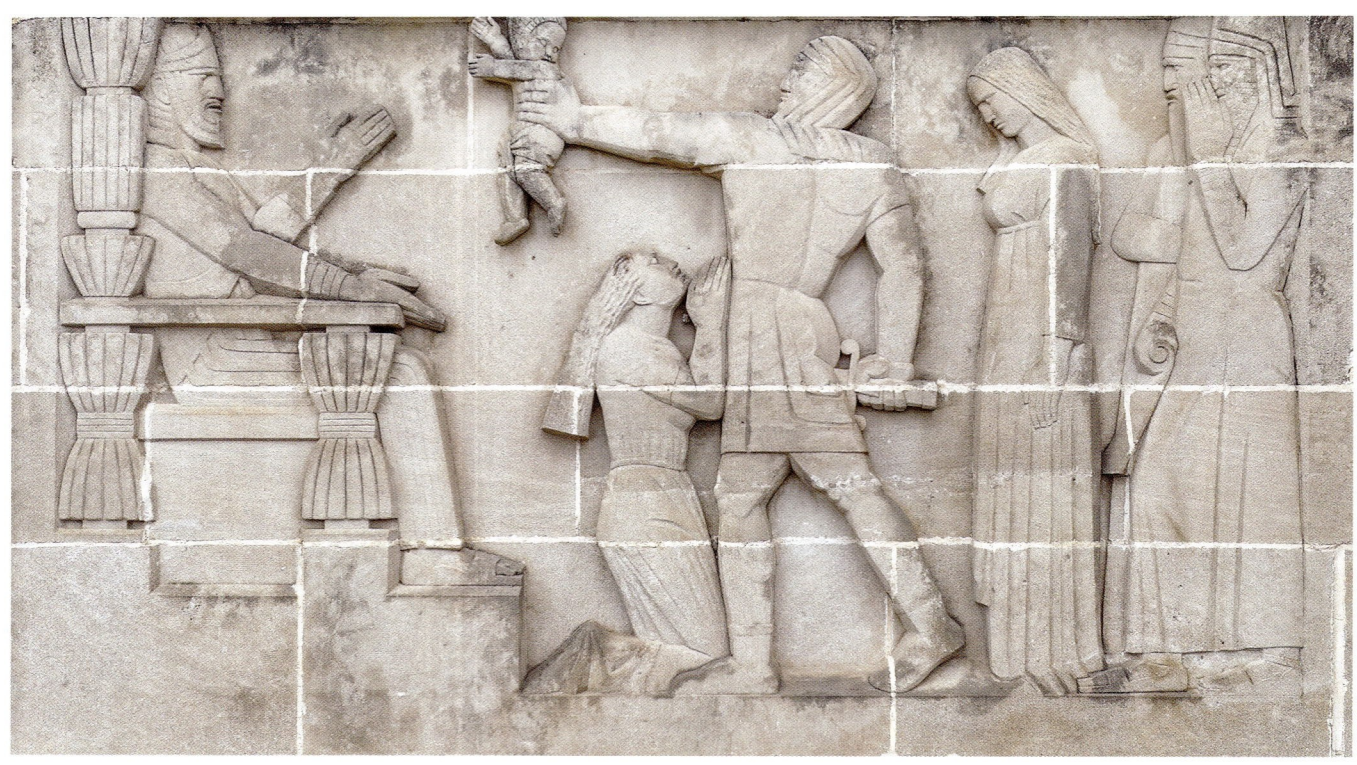

Lee Lawrie
The Judgement of Solomon, c.1932
approx. 6 x 10 feet
Indiana limestone sculpture

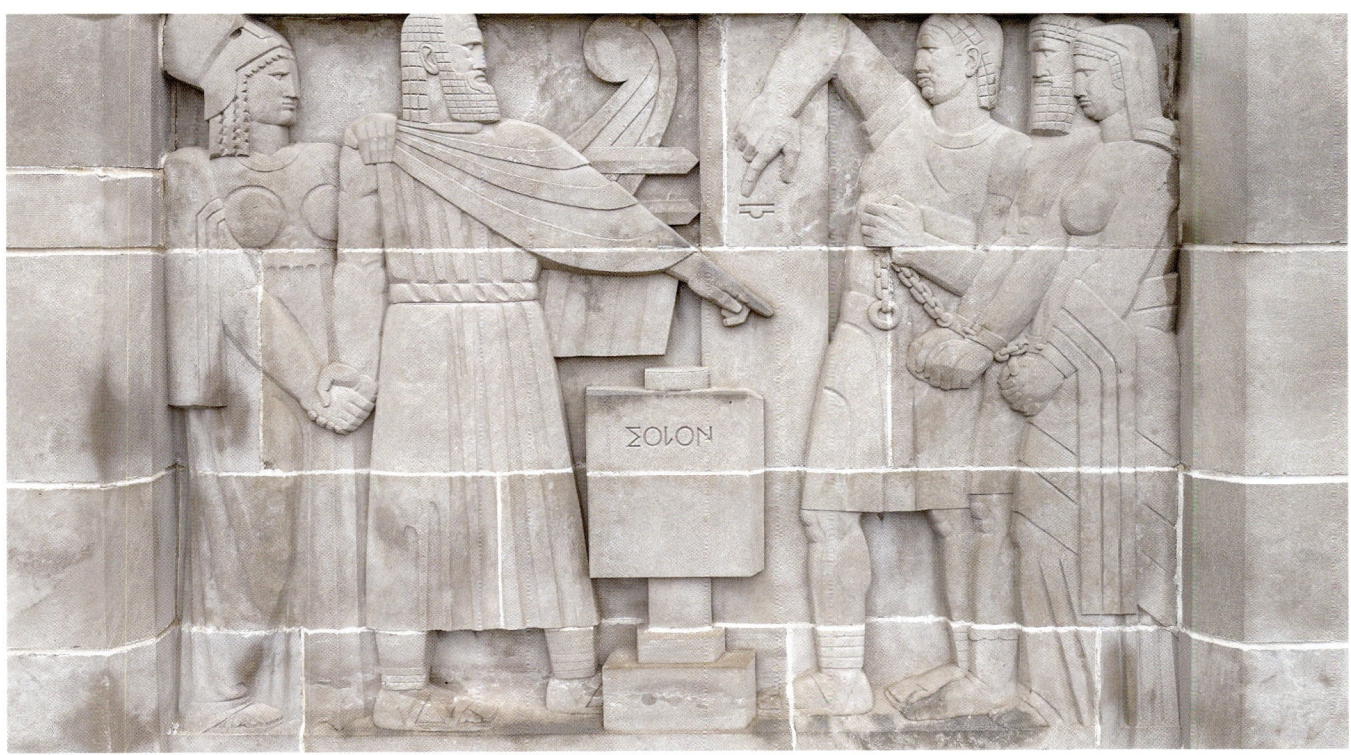

Lee Lawrie
Solon Gives a New Constitution to Athens, c.1932
approx. 6 x 10 feet
Indiana limestone sculpture

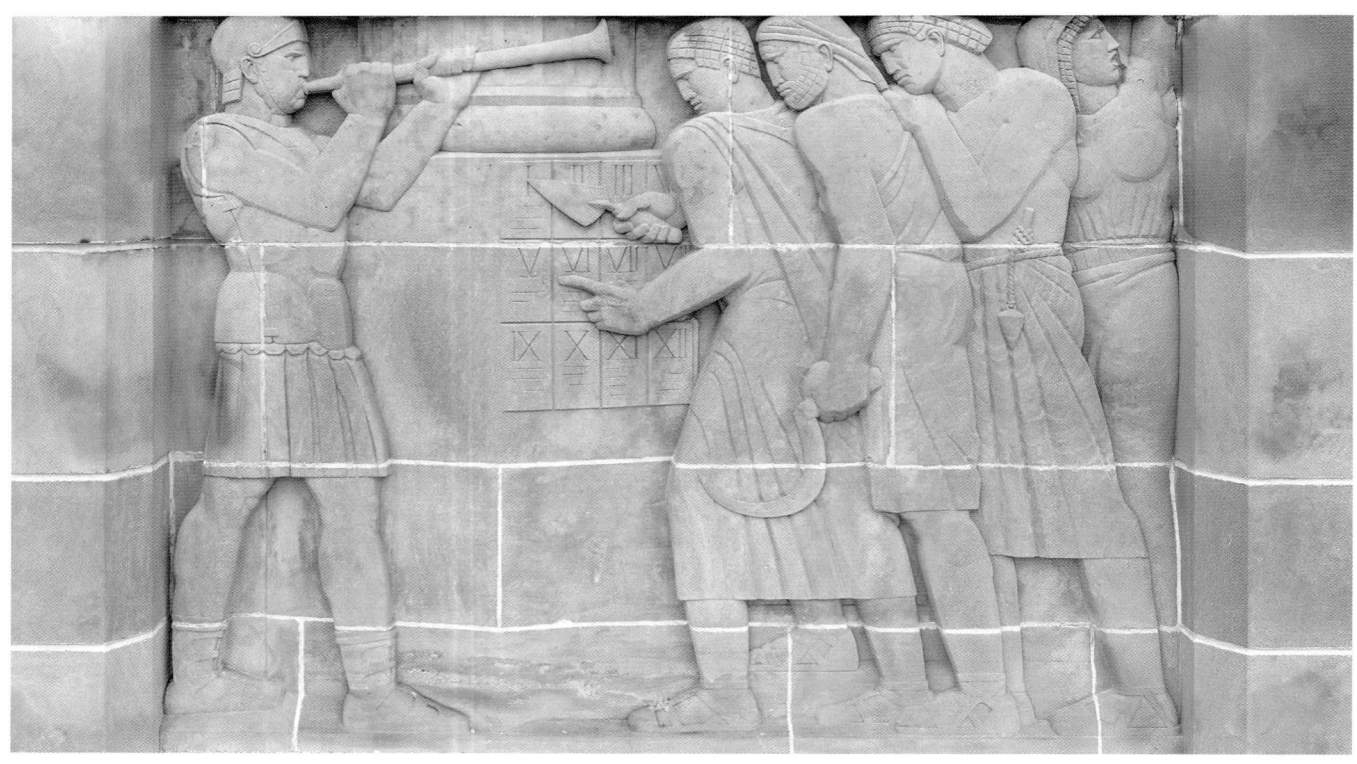

Lee Lawrie
The Publishing of the Twelve Tablets in Rome, c.1932
approx. 6 x 10 feet
Indiana limestone sculpture

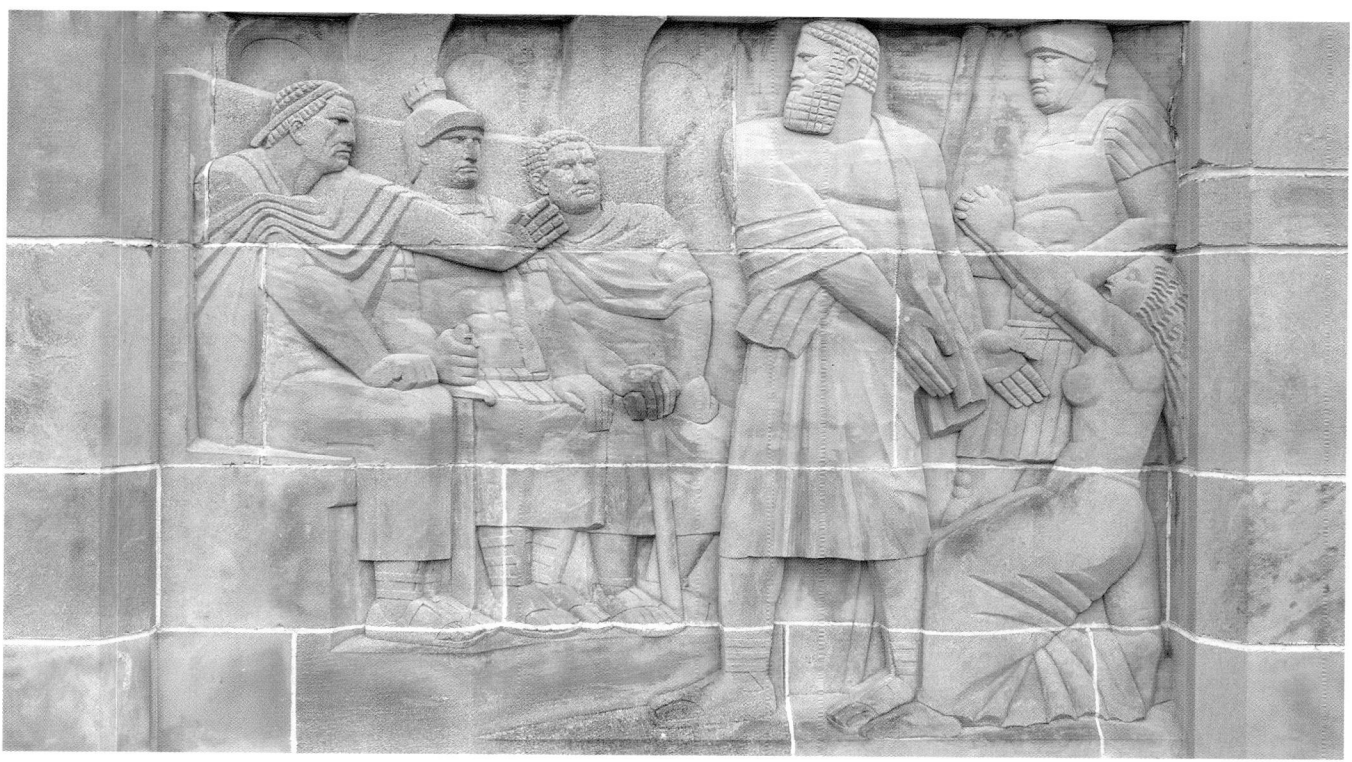

Lee Lawrie
The Establishment of the Tribunate of the People, c.1932
approx. 6 x 10 feet
Indiana limestone sculpture

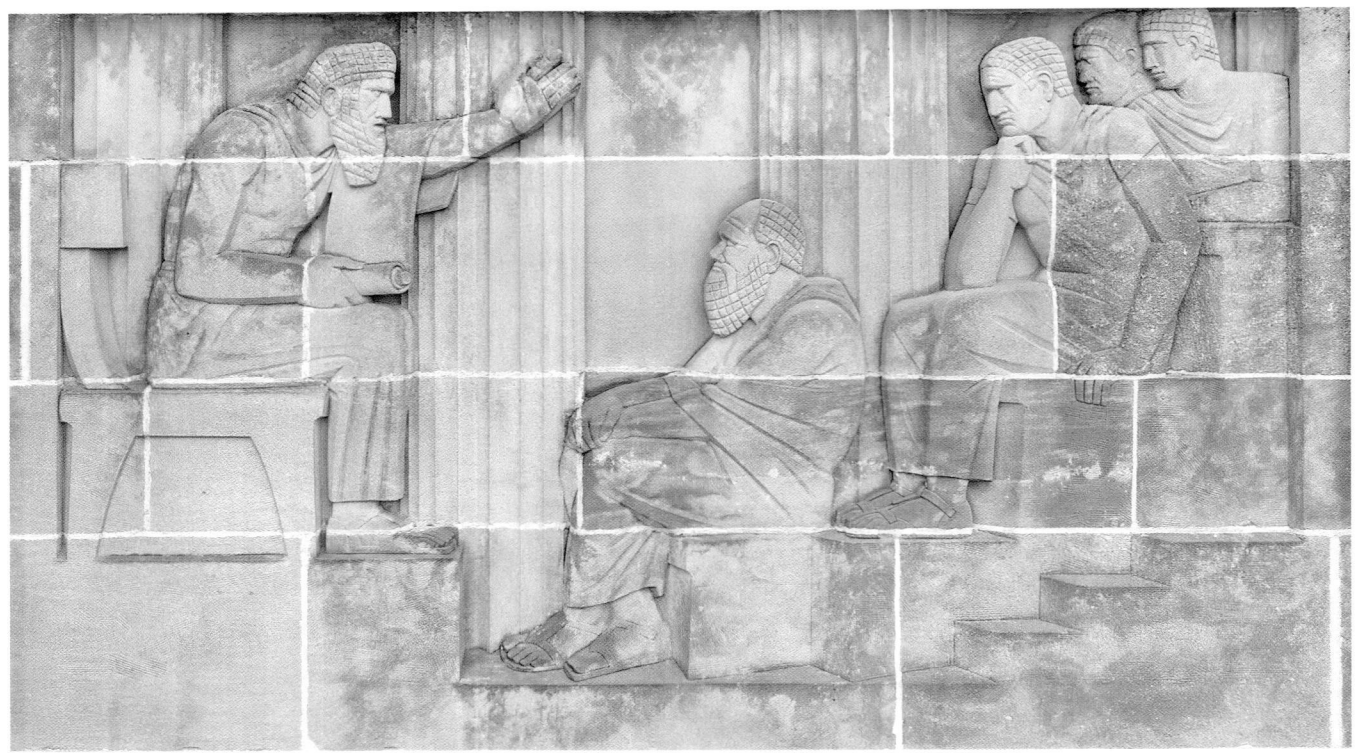

Lee Lawrie
Plato Writing His Dialogs, c.1932
approx. 6 x 10 feet
Indiana limestone sculpture

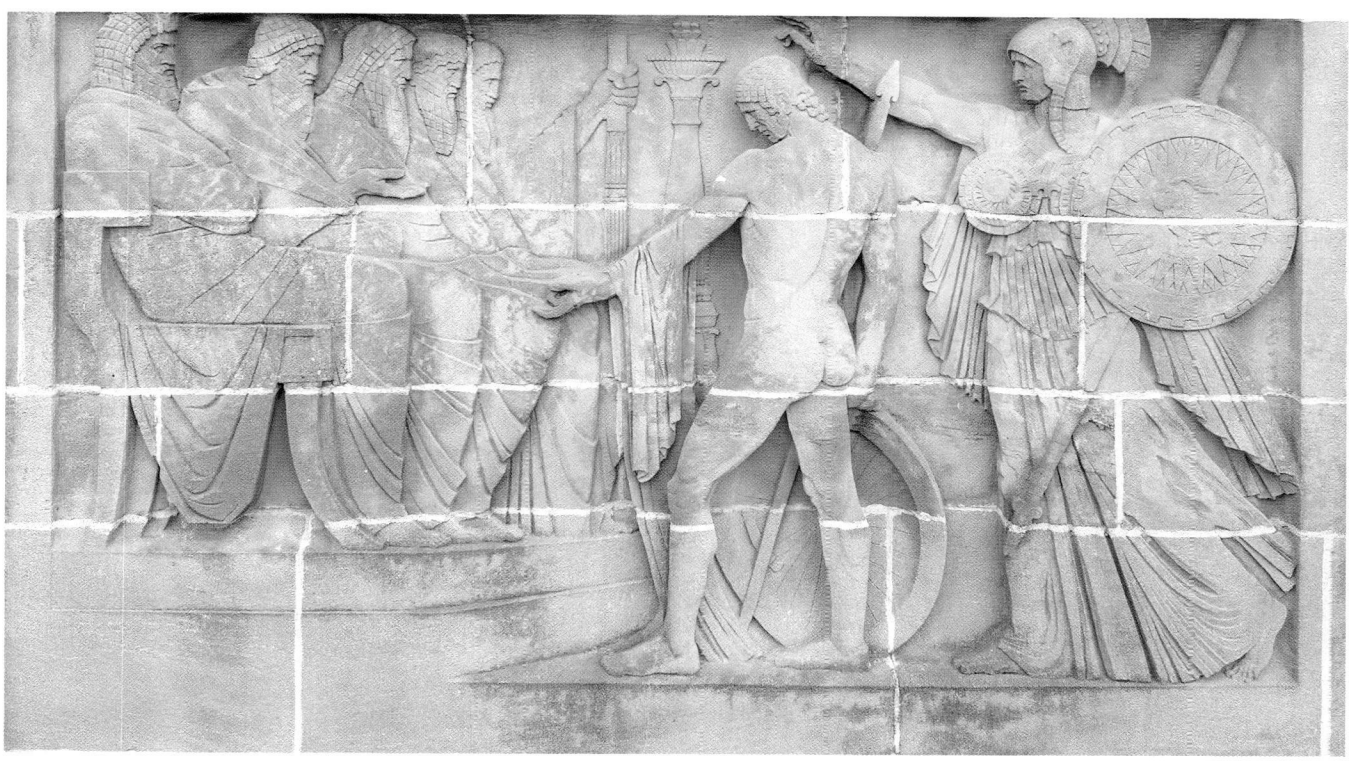

Lee Lawrie
Orestes Before the Areopagites, c.1932
approx. 6 x 10 feet
Indiana limestone sculpture

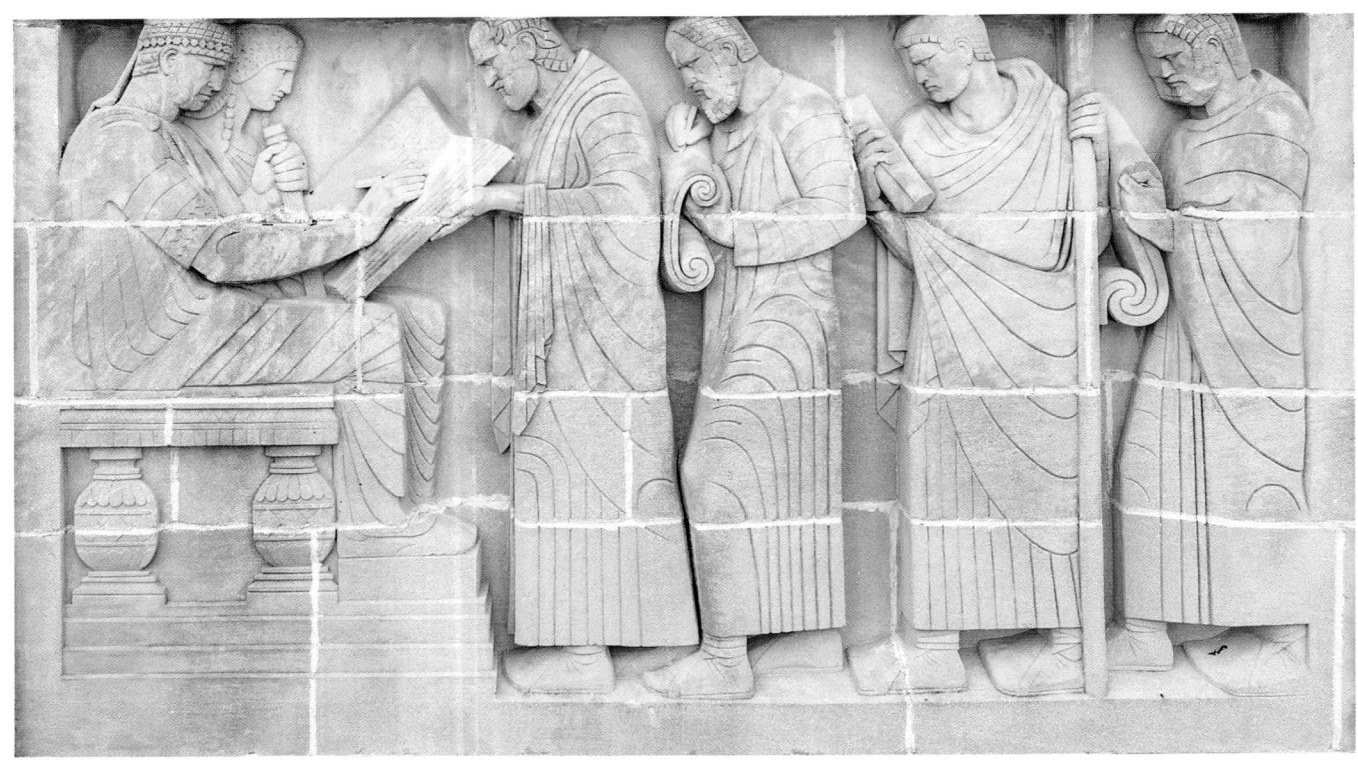

Lee Lawrie
Justinian Codifies Roman Law, c.1932
approx. 6 x 10 feet
Indiana limestone sculpture

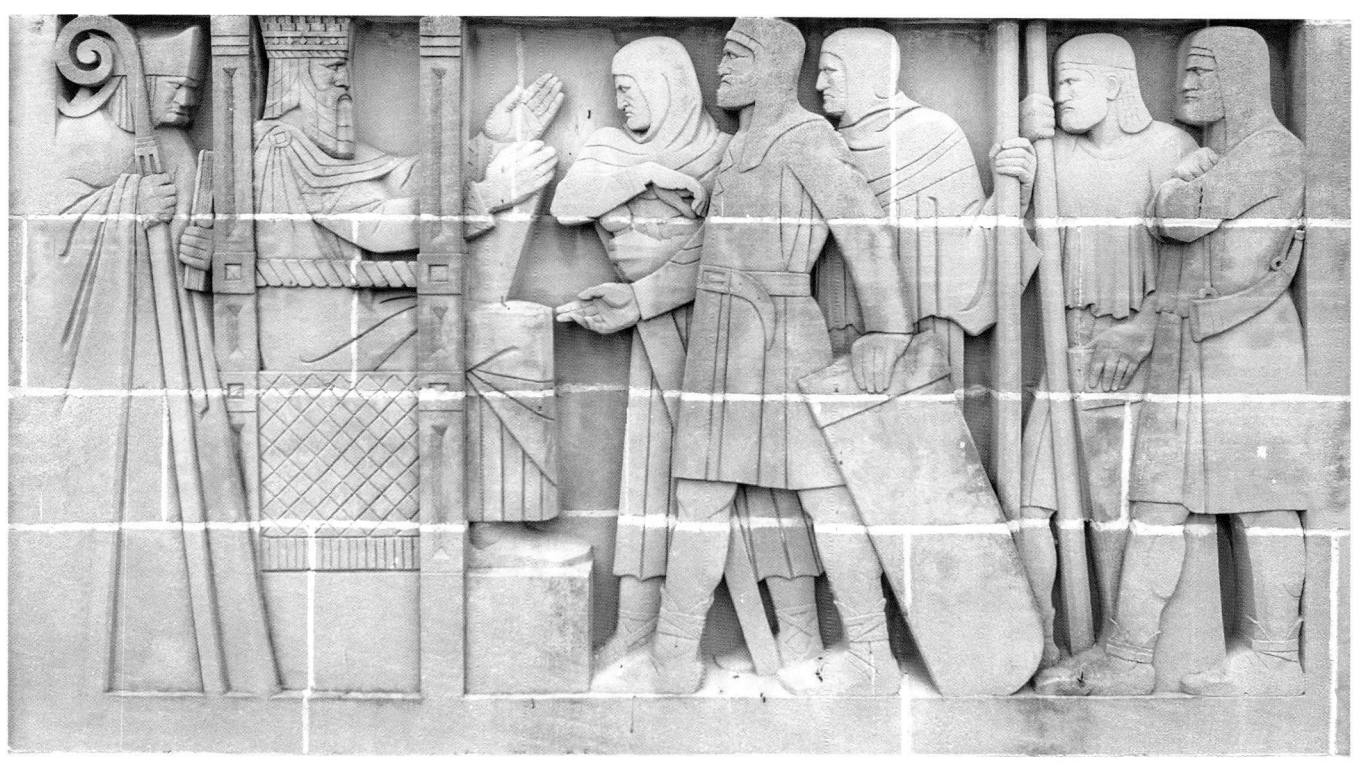

Lee Lawrie
Ethelbert Codifies Anglo-Saxon Law, c.1932
approx. 6 x 10 feet
Indiana limestone sculpture

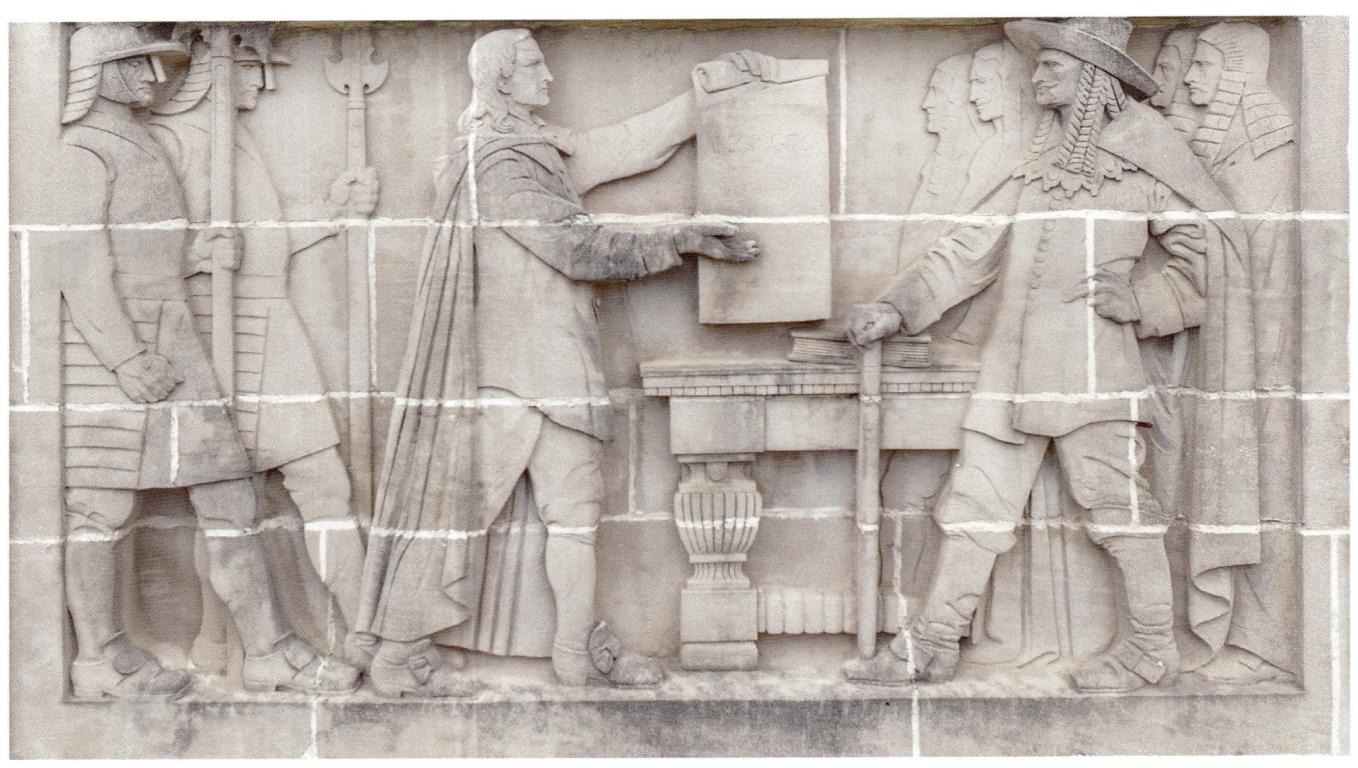

Lee Lawrie
Milton Defending Free Speech Before Cromwell, c.1932
approx. 6 x 10 feet
Indiana limestone sculpture

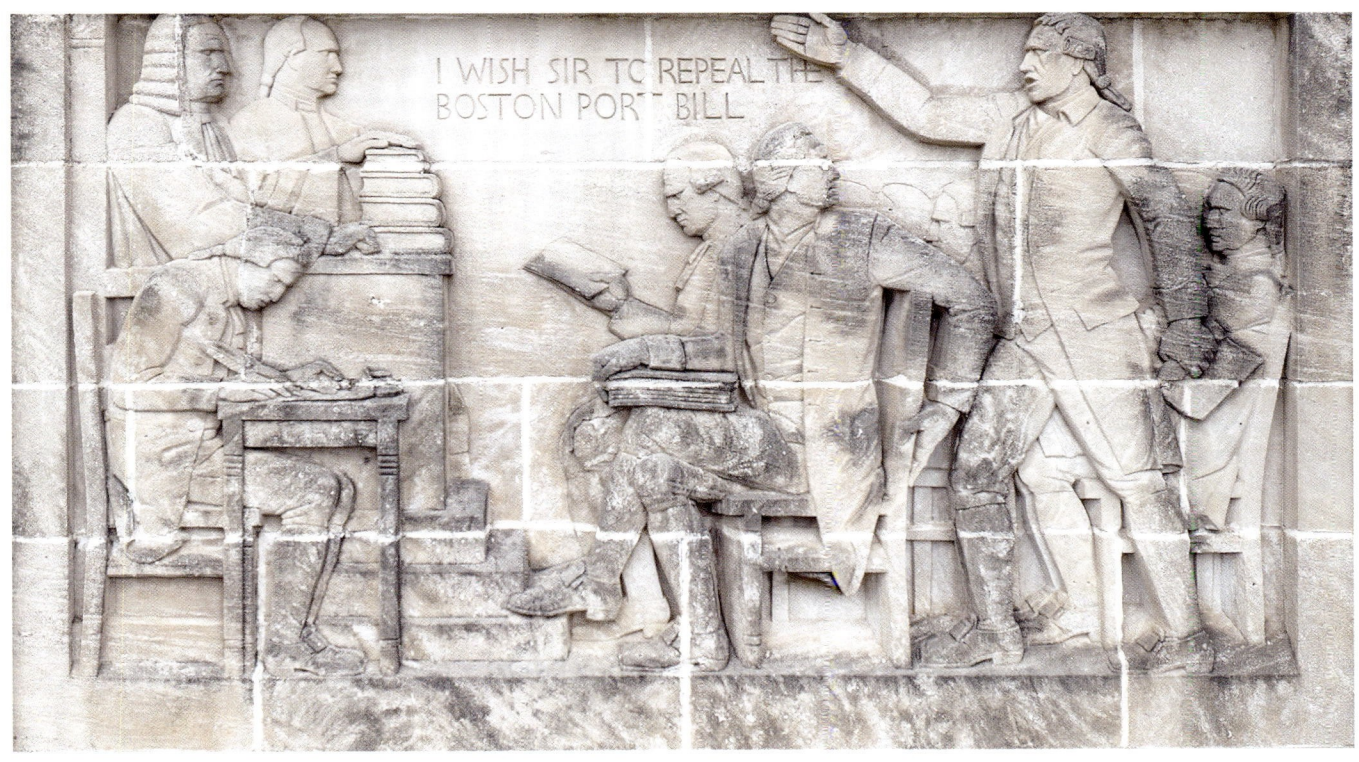

Lee Lawrie
Burke Defends American Colonies in Parliament, c.1932
approx. 6 x 10 feet
Indiana limestone sculpture

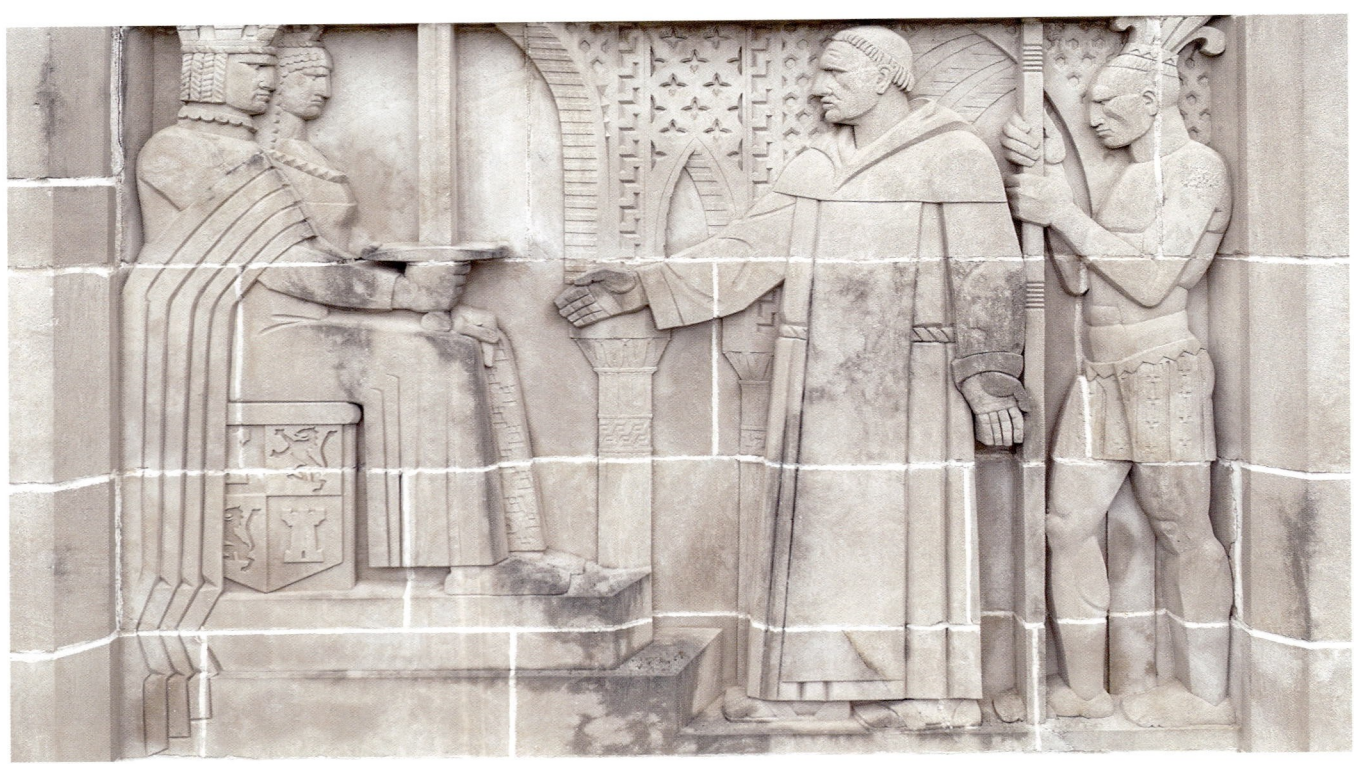

Lee Lawrie
Las Casas Pleads for the Indian, c.1932
approx. 6 x 10 feet
Indiana limestone sculpture

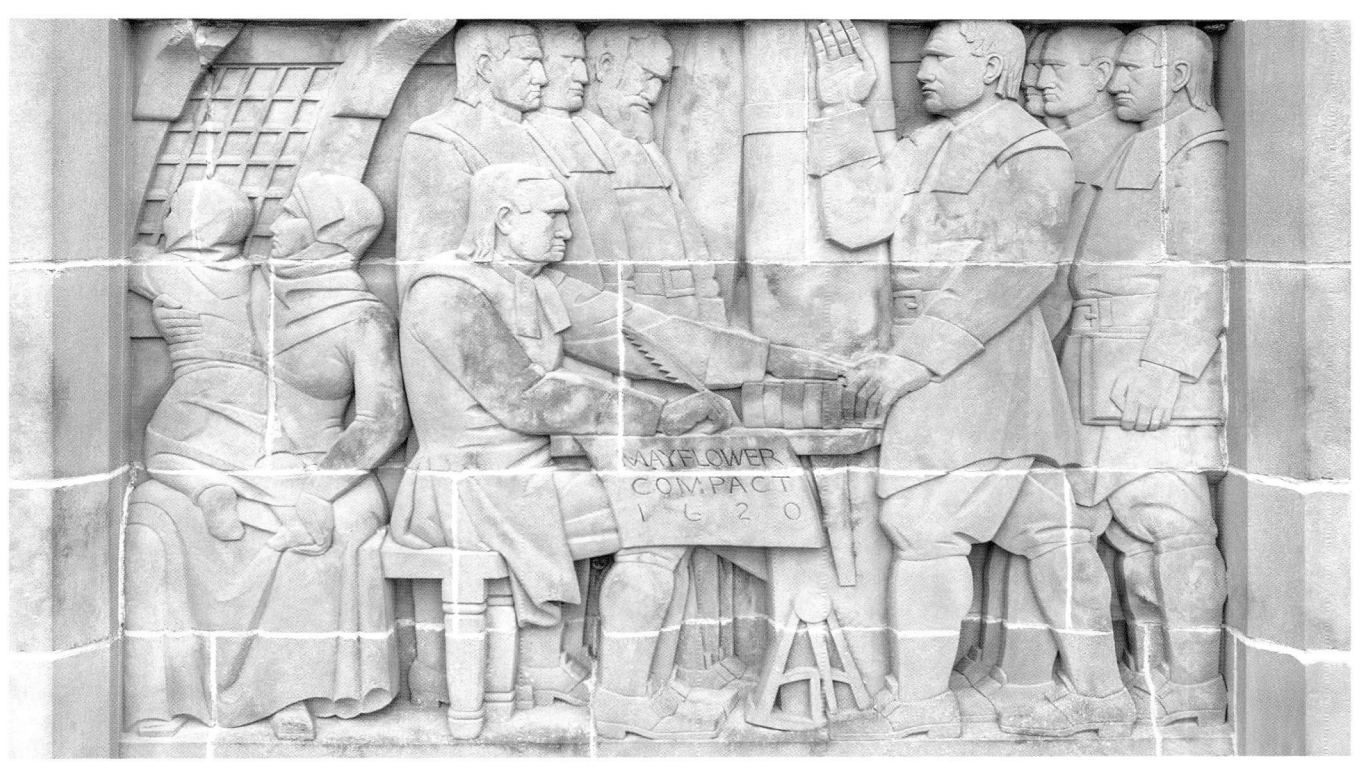

Lee Lawrie
The Signing of the Mayflower Compact, c.1932
approx. 6 x 10 feet
Indiana limestone sculpture

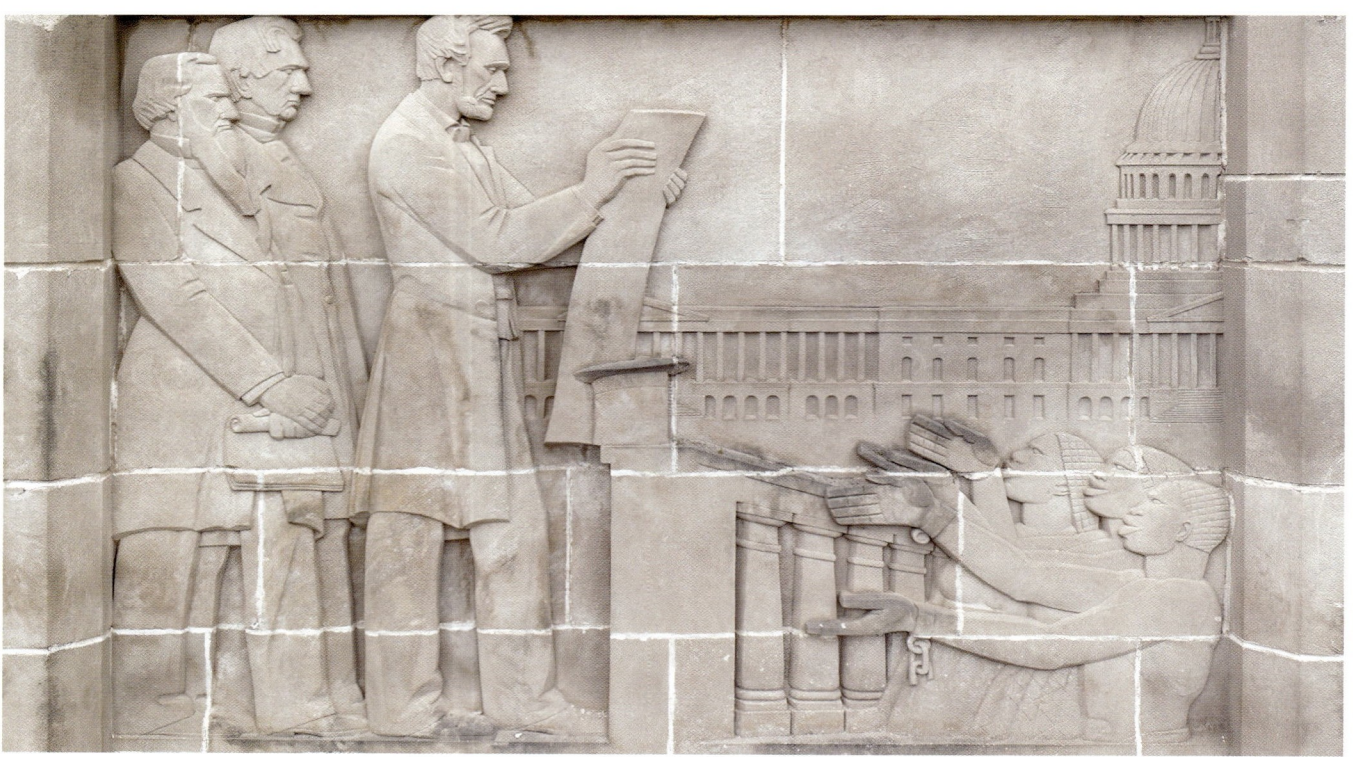

Lee Lawrie
The Emancipation Proclamation, c.1932
approx. 6 x 10 feet
Indiana limestone sculpture

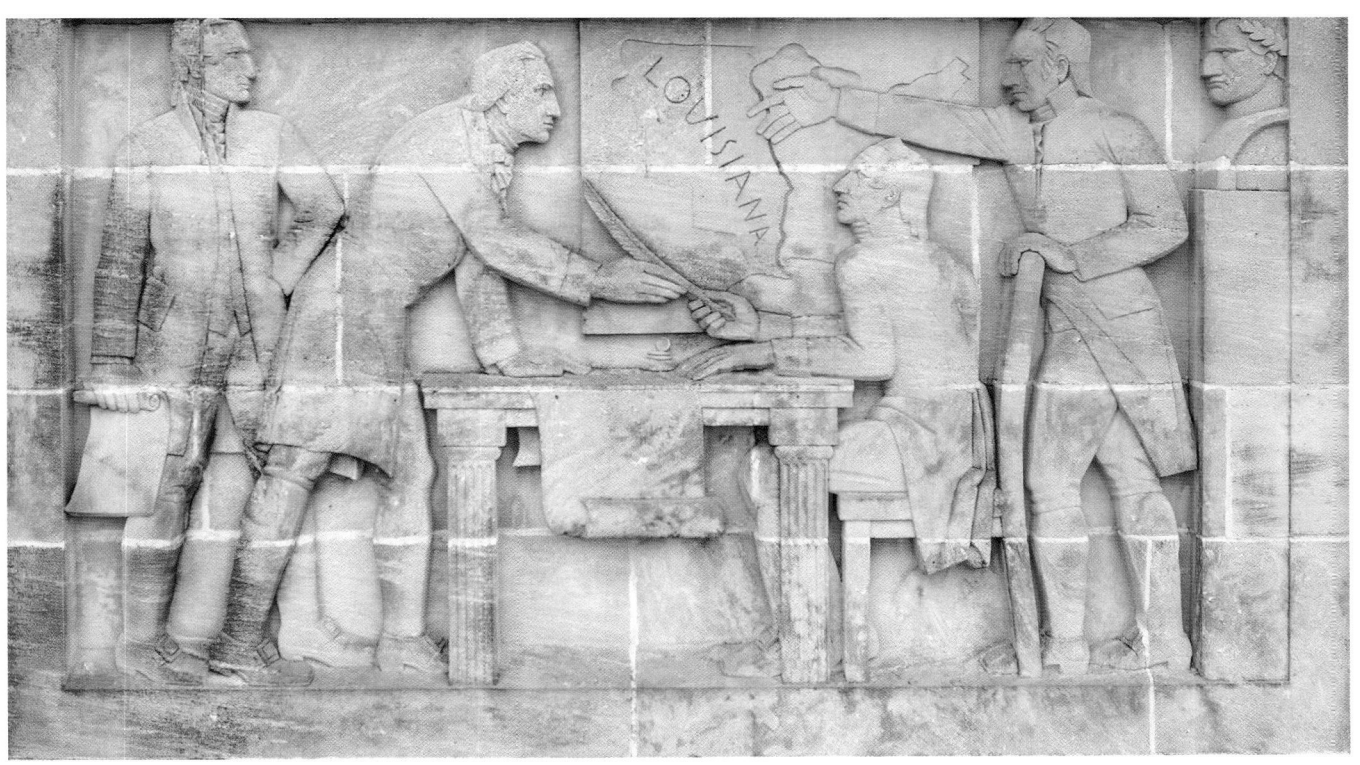

Lee Lawrie
The Louisiana Purchase from Napoleon, c.1932
approx. 6 x 10 feet
Indiana limestone sculpture

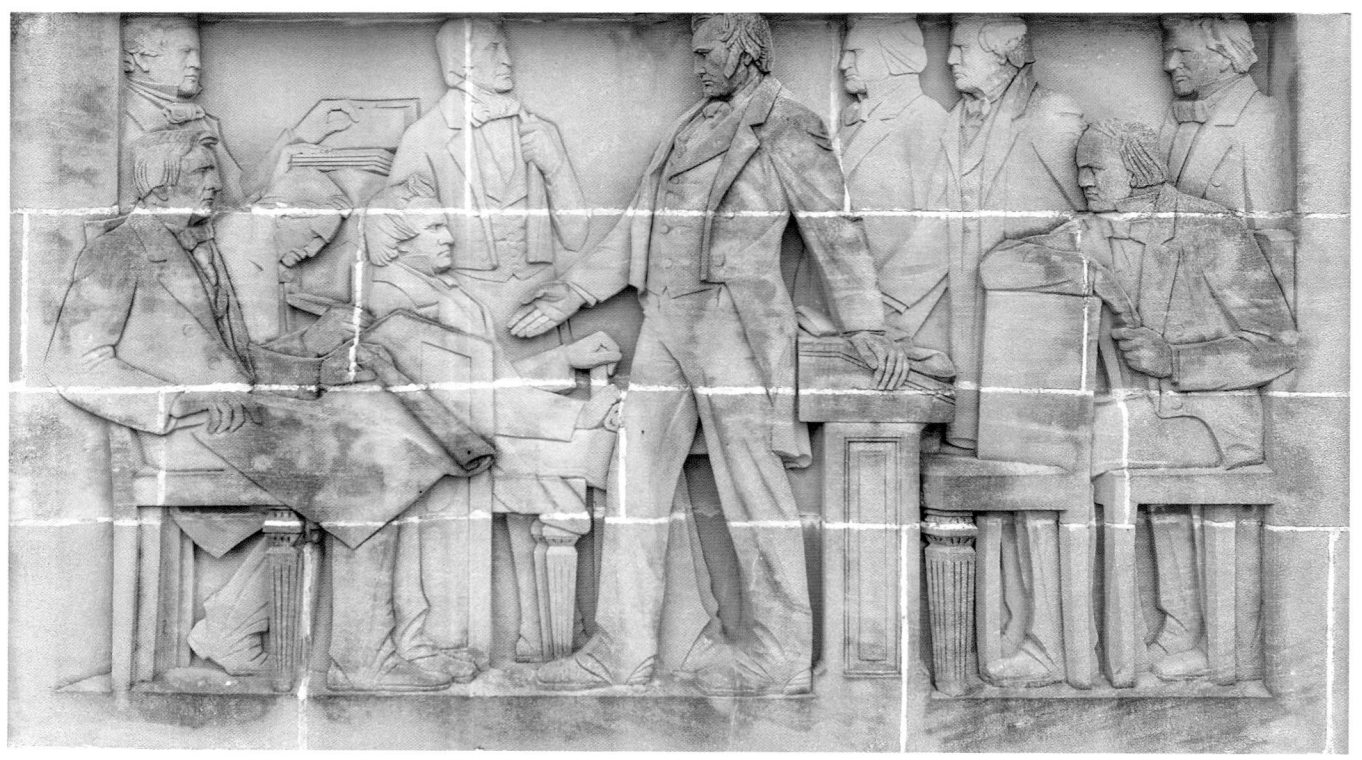

Lee Lawrie
The Nebraska-Kansas Bill, c.1932
approx. 6 x 10 feet
Indiana limestone sculpture

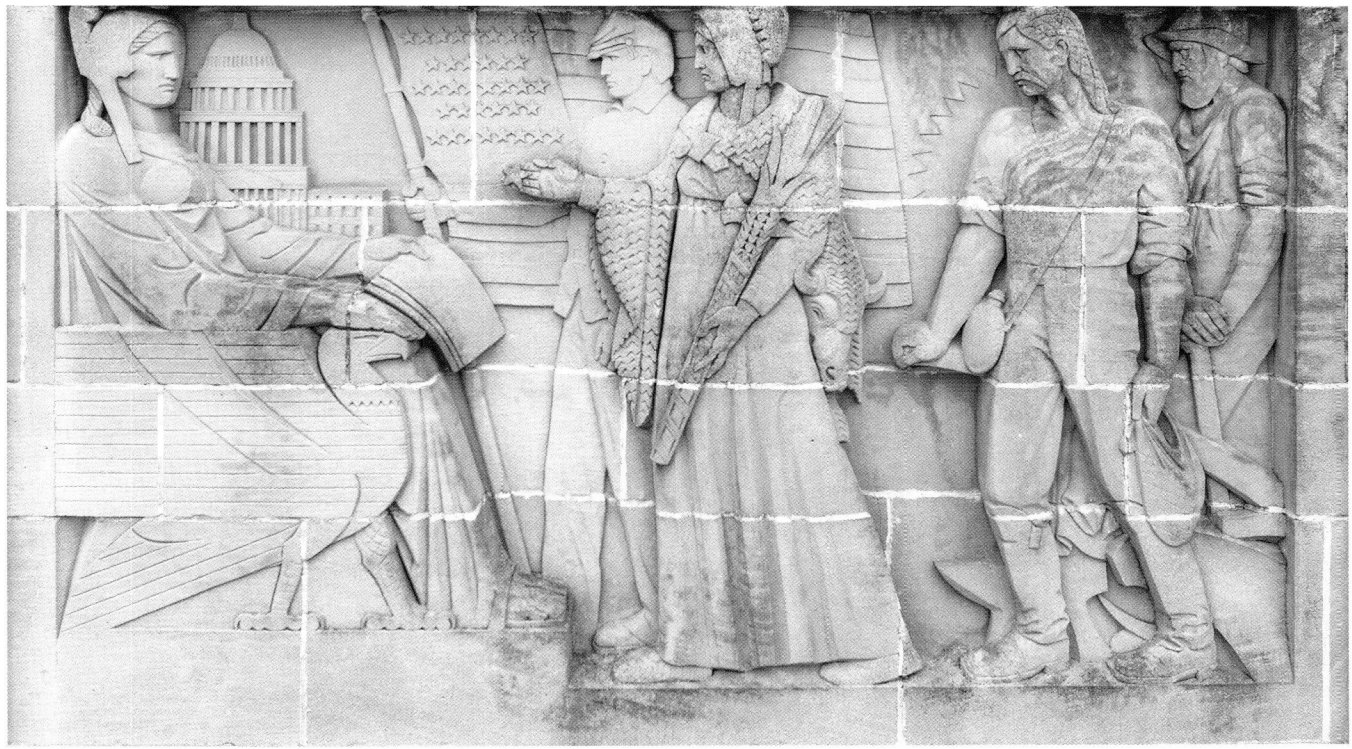

Lee Lawrie
Nebraska Statehood, c.1932
approx. 6 x 10 feet
Indiana limestone sculpture

Nebraska became a state on March 1, 1867, following the end
of the Civil War. In this sculpture, a Civil War veteran carries
the flag with 36 stars. Next to him stands a pioneer woman in a
buffalo robe representing Nebraska. She holds a star to place
on the flag as Nebraska joins the Union as the 37th state.

Lee Lawrie
The Signing of the Declaration of Independence, c.1932
approx. 4.5 x 9 feet
Indiana limestone sculpture

Most of the terrace level carvings portray a chronological history of the law. The south facade, however, breaks from that and tells its own story about the signing of history's most momentous documents detailing the responsibilities of the governed and their government.

Throughout the exterior panels, Lee Lawrie successfully depicted individuals in styles faithful to the period and created recognizable likenesses when possible. In this panel, one of the three separate panels on the south facade, George Washington, Thomas Jefferson, and Benjamin Franklin are easily found.

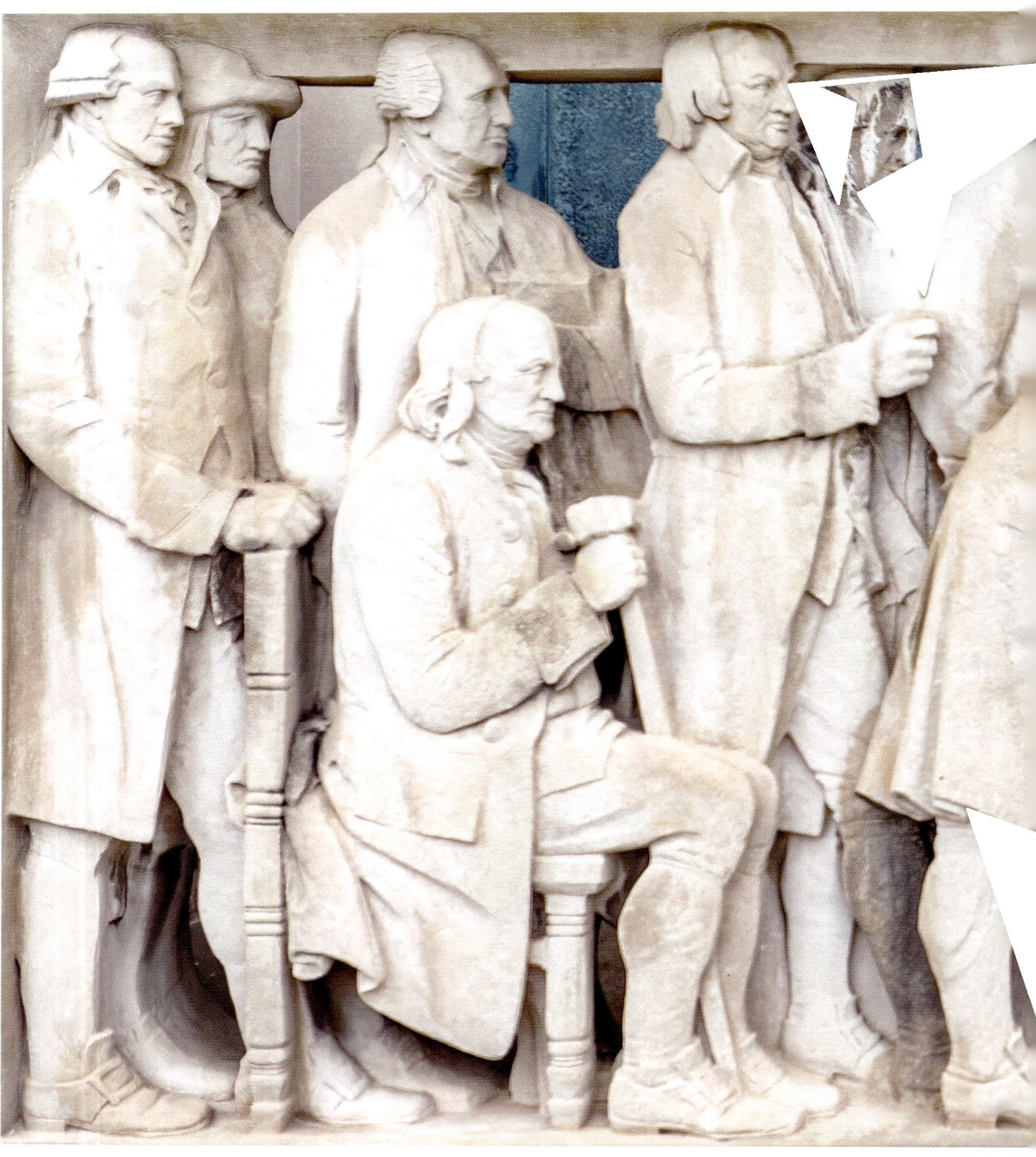

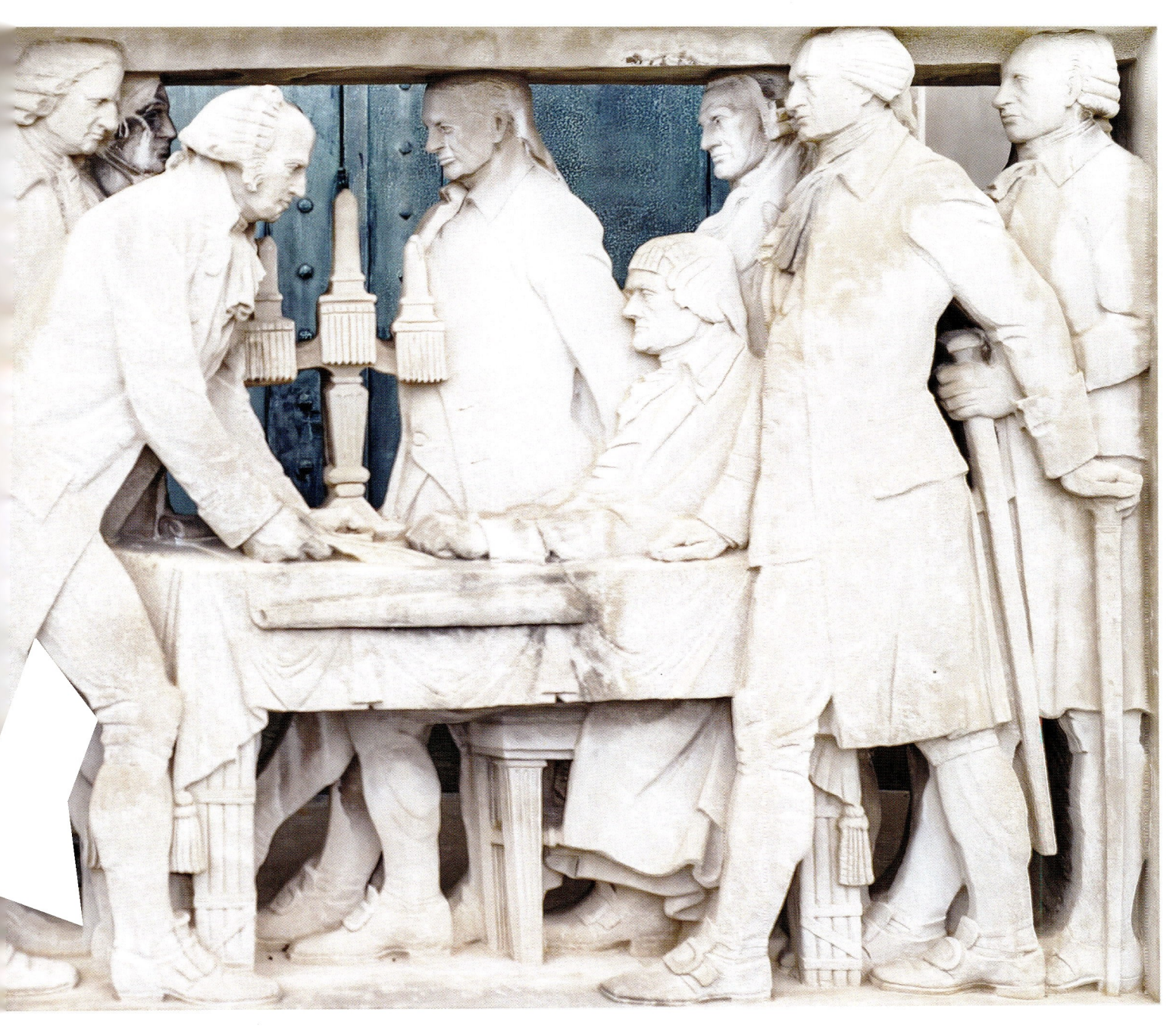

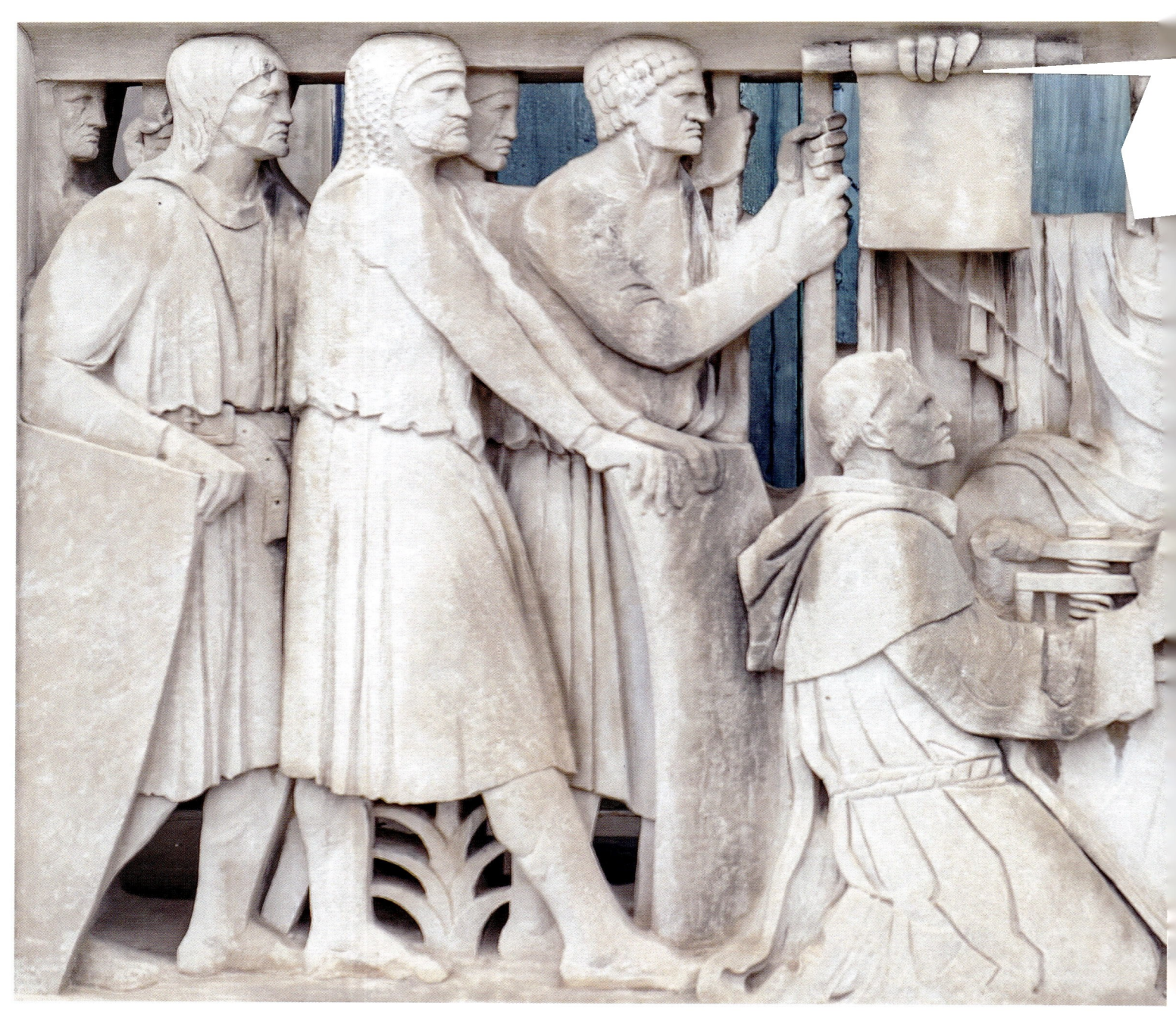

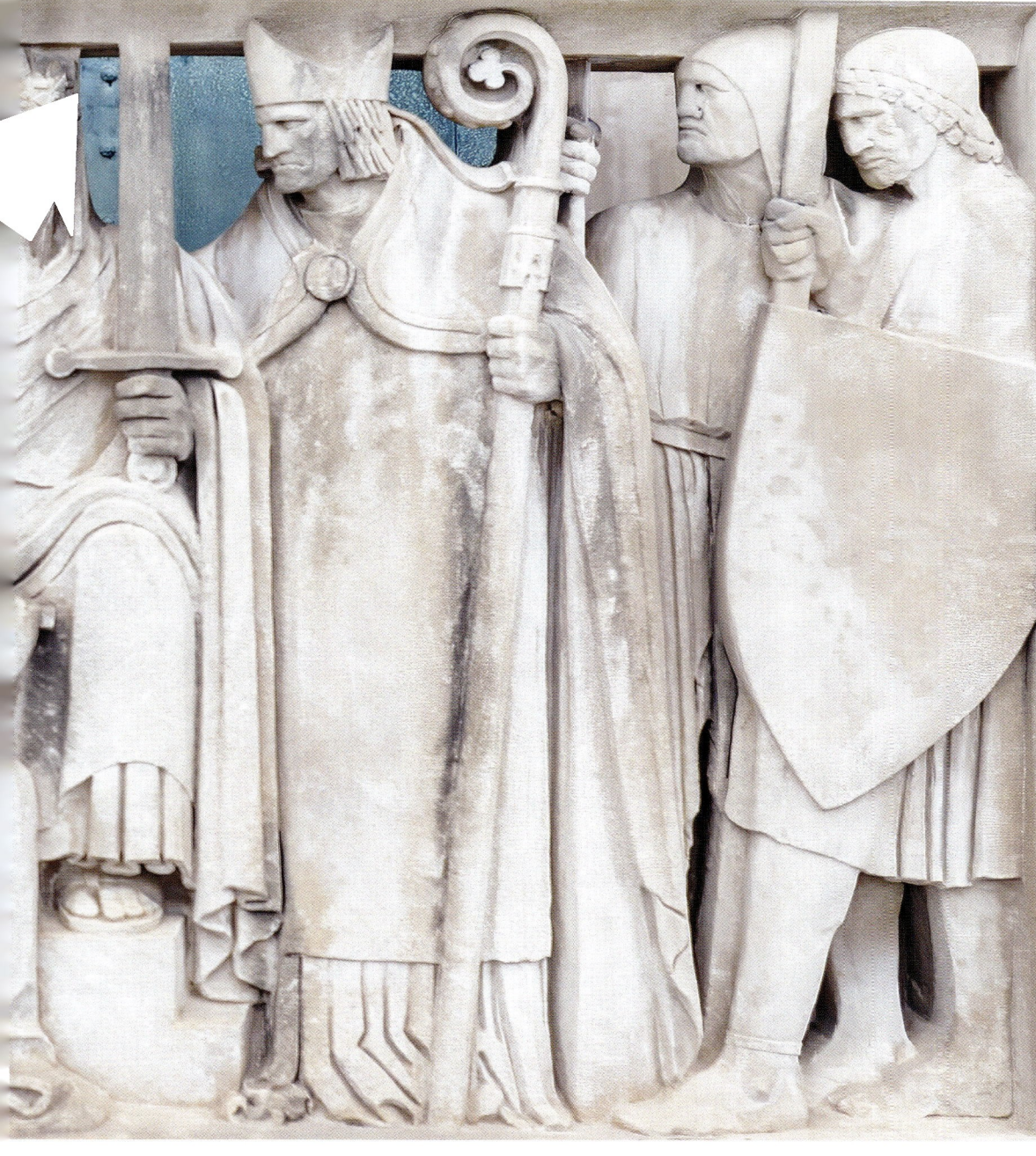

Lee Lawrie
*The Signing of the
Magna Carta*, c.1932
approx. 4.5 x 9 feet
Indiana limestone sculpture

Lee Lawrie
*The Writing of the Constitution
of the United States*, c.1932
approx. 4.5 x 9 feet
Indiana limestone sculpture

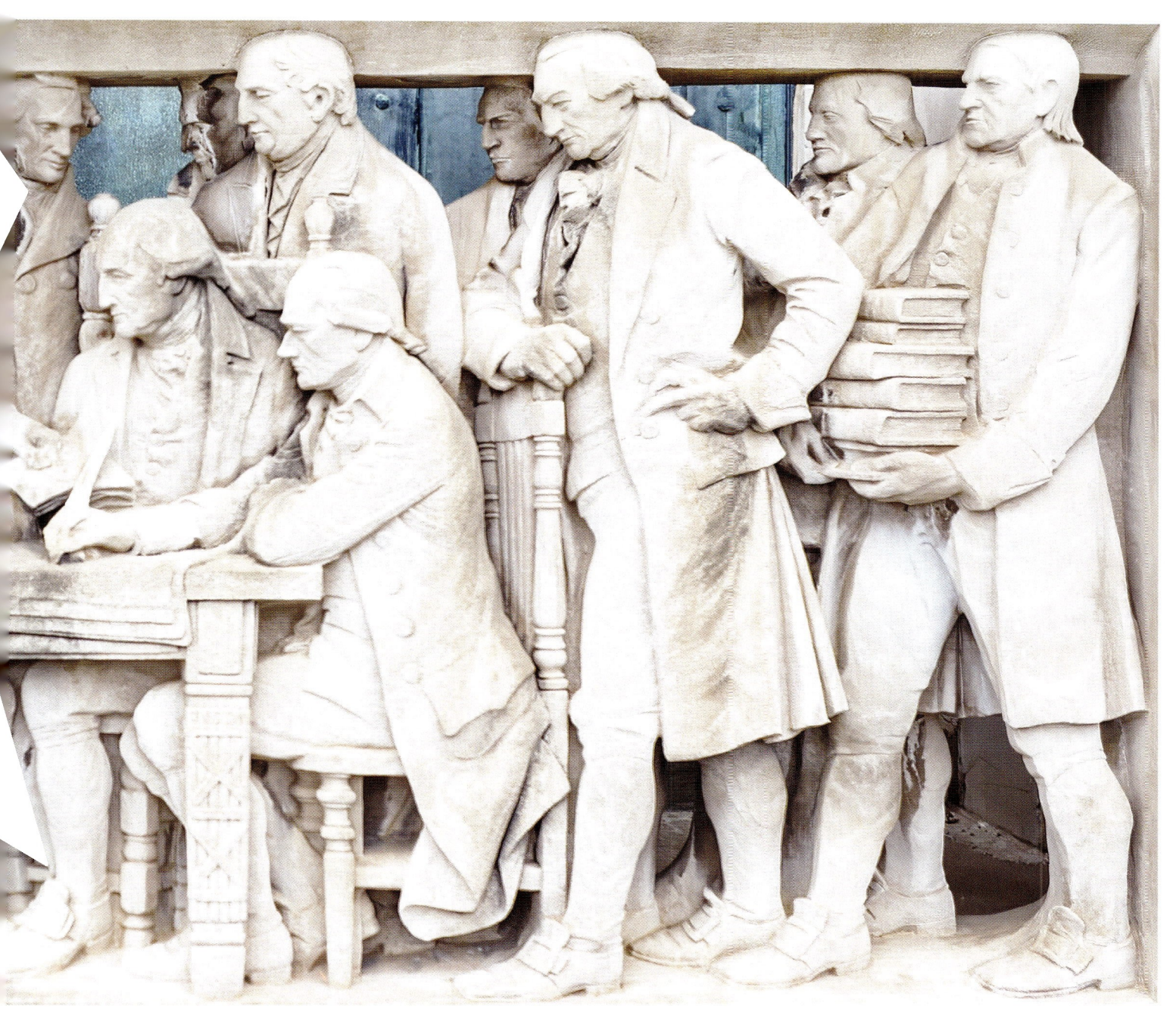

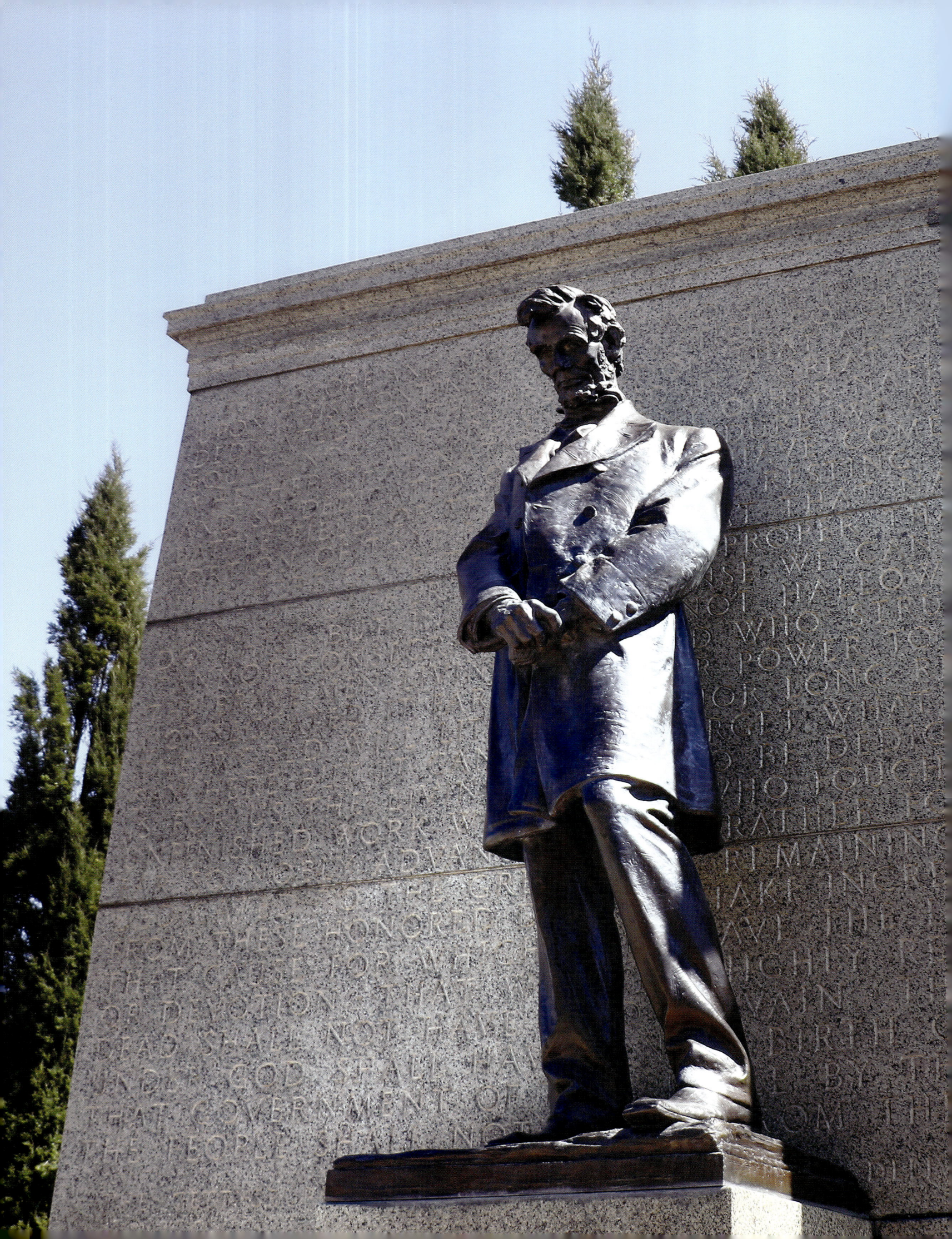

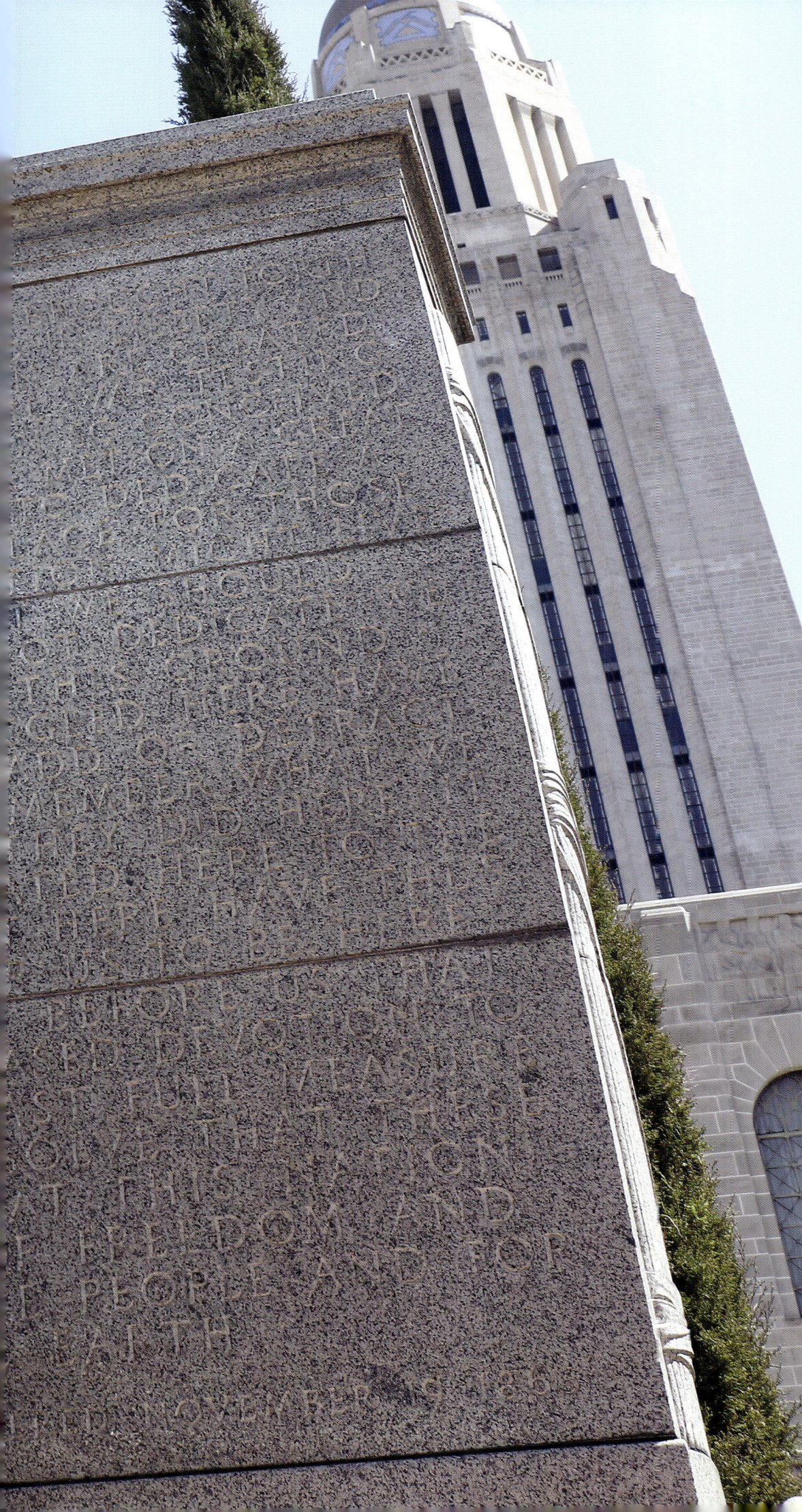

Daniel Chester French
Abraham Lincoln, 1912
Bronze sculpture

Originally commissioned in
1909 and dedicated in 1912, the
bronze statue of Abraham
Lincoln has stood at the west
entrance of the grounds since
the days of the second Capitol.
Daniel French collaborated
with architect Henry Bacon
to create the statue and its
granite pedestal, etched with
the words of the Gettysburg
Address. The two partnered
again to design the Lincoln
Memorial in Washington DC.

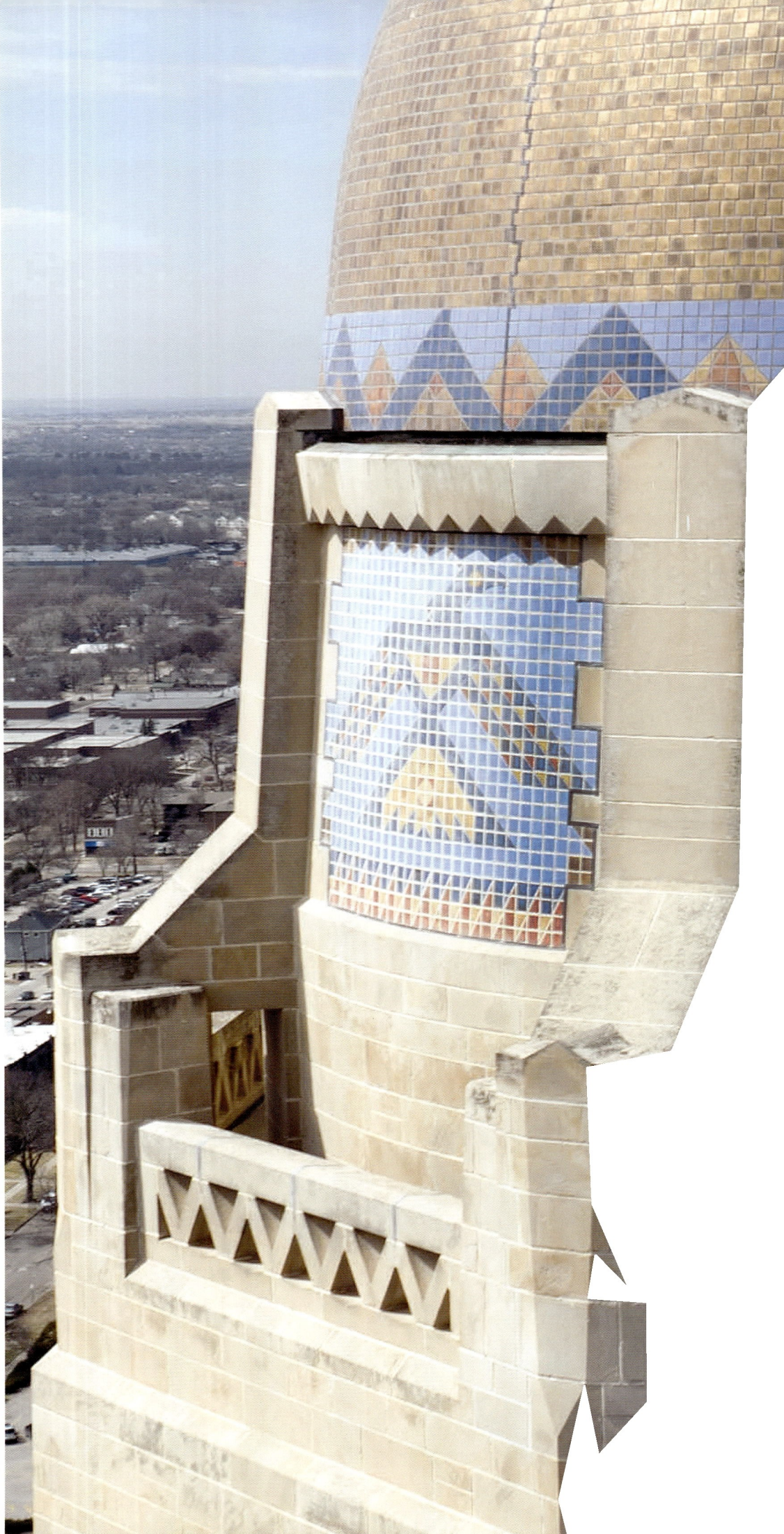

Lee Lawrie
Capitol Tower Dome, c.1932
Glazed tile mosaic

Native American thunderbirds
adorn the gold-tiled dome
of the Capitol tower. The
thunderbird symbolizes rain,
integral to agriculture and life.

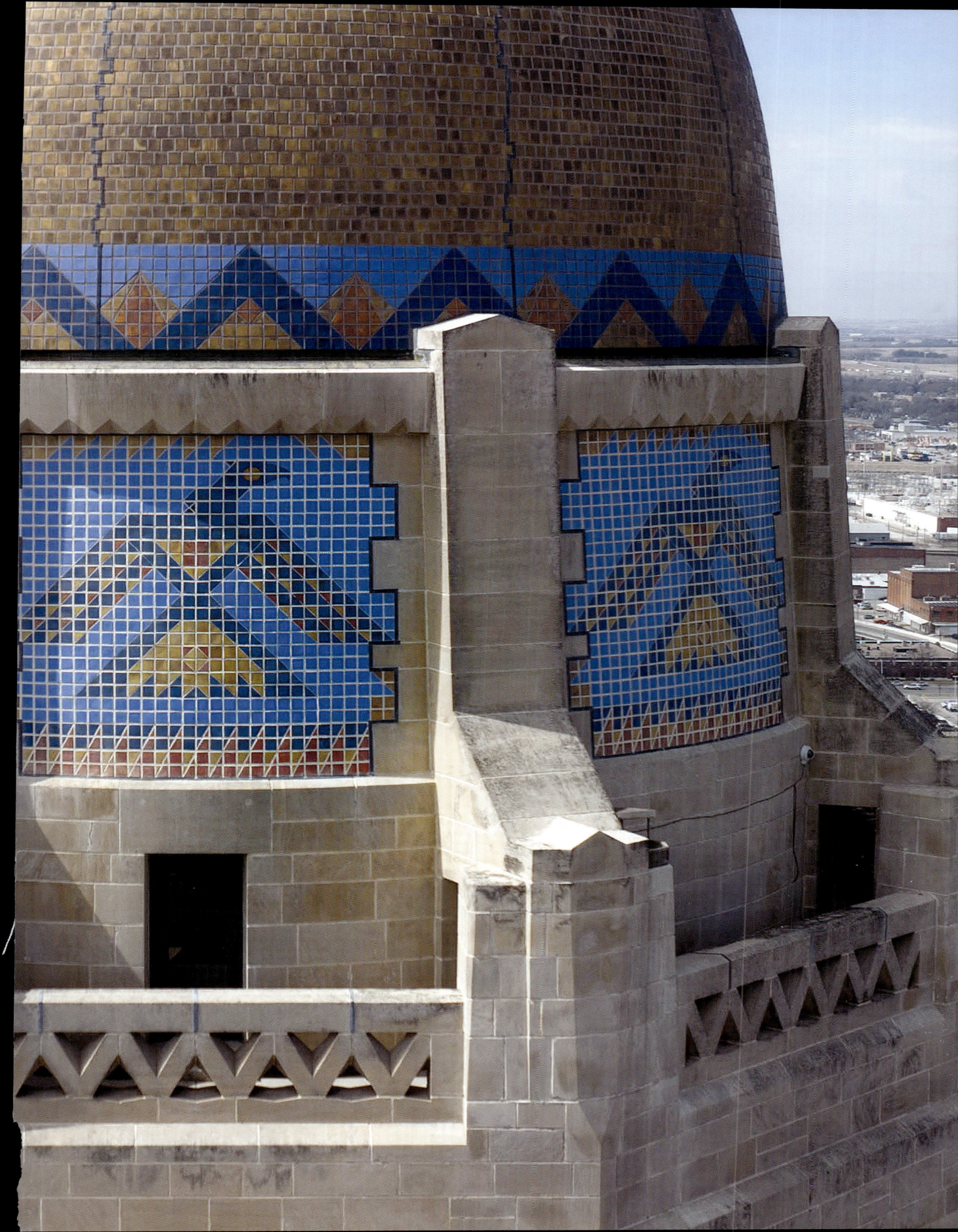

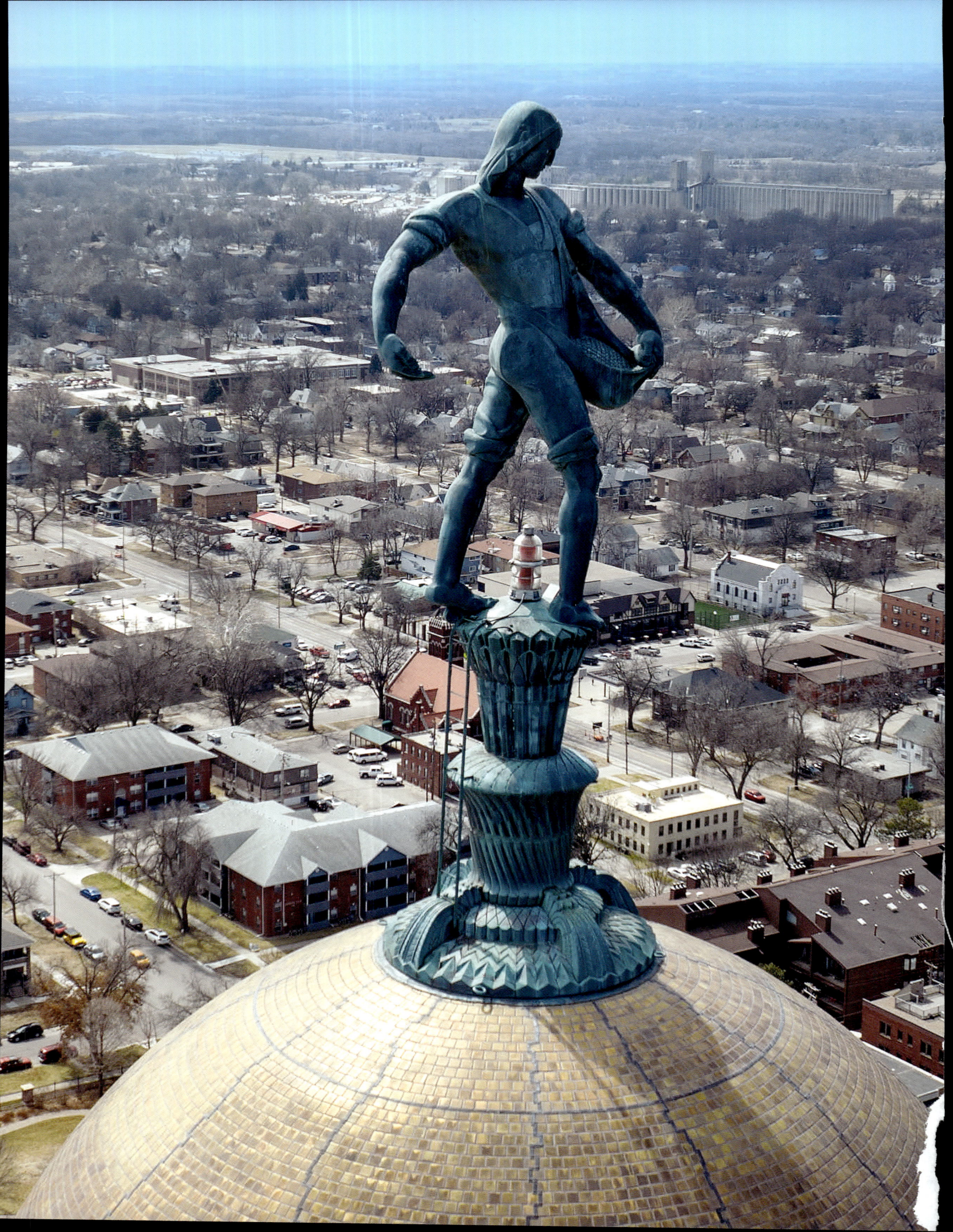

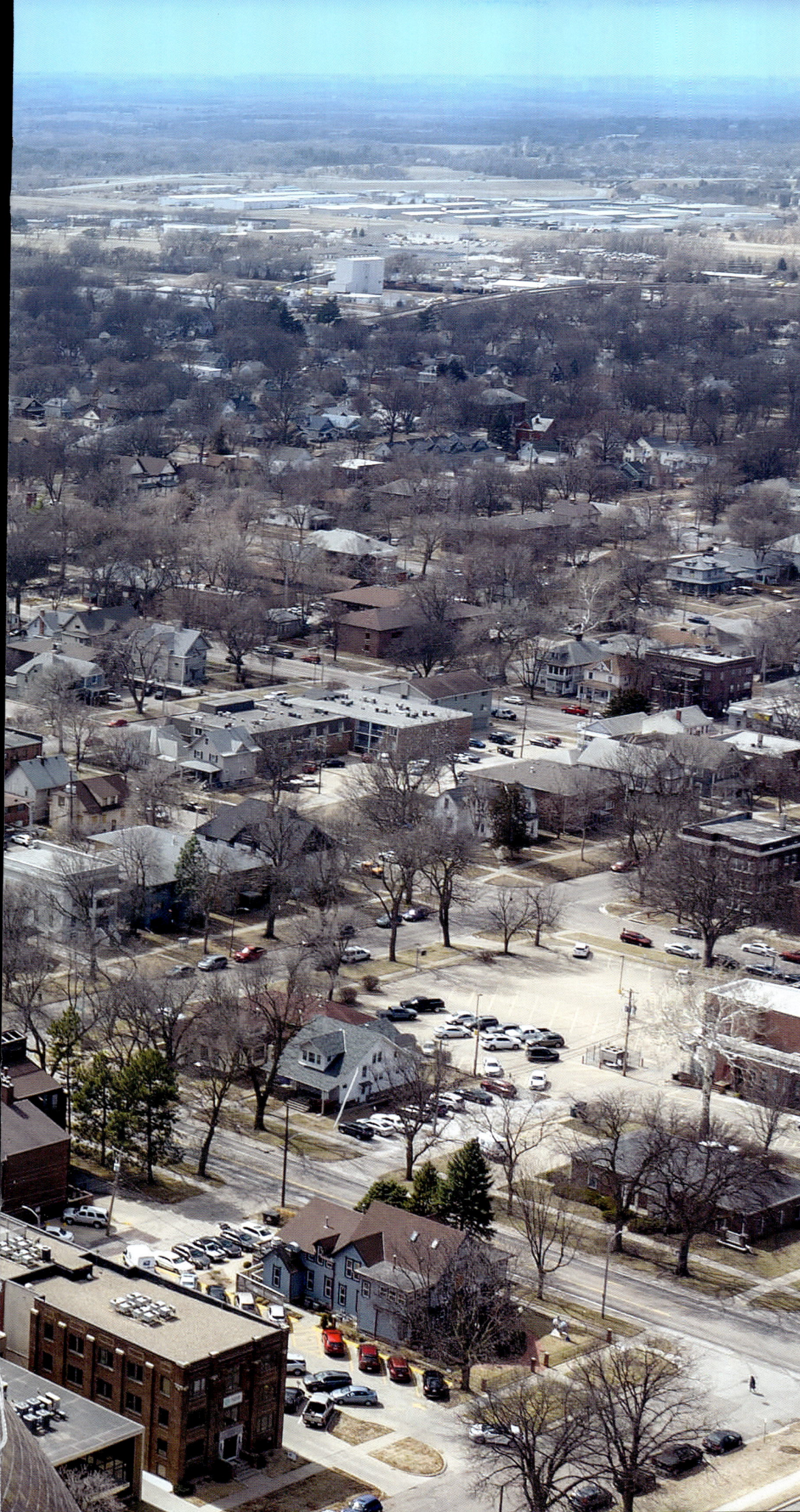

Lee Lawrie
The Sower, c.1932
19 feet tall
Bronze sculpture

Standing atop the Capitol, 400
feet above the ground, the
Sower faces northwest and
casts the seeds of life. The
ancient farmer represents
the great farmers and
families of Nebraska and
signifies the importance of
agriculture to the state and
the world throughout history.

At 19 feet in height, he stands as
Lawrie's tallest human figure.
Though the total sculpture of
his Atlas in Rockefeller Center
stands at 45 feet tall, Atlas
himself is only 15 feet tall.

This is one of at least six sowers
Lawrie is known to have
created, including a female
sower in Rockefeller Center.
In a statement to the Society
of Medalists, Lawrie told of
his fascination. He wrote
that growing up in Illinois,
he watched farmers at work,
spreading grain in the field.

"All of us are sowers and we
should not expect life to yield
much in return for little, or
little for nothing, or anything
at all for the mere wishing."

SELECTED BIBLIOGRAPHY

Prologue and Construction of the Capitol

Bristow, David L. "When Omaha Was the Capital City." *NEBRASKAland Magazine*. March 17, 2022. http://magazine.outdoornebraska.gov/2022/03/when-omaha-was-the-capital-city/.

"Francis Burt." History Nebraska. History Nebraska, n.d. https://history.nebraska.gov/publications_section/francis-burt/.

Luebke, Frederick C. "The Capitals and Capitols of Nebraska." In *A Harmony of the Arts: The Nebraska State Capitol*, edited by Frederick C. Luebke, 1–13. Lincoln: University of Nebraska Press, 1990.

Nebraska State Capitol. "History of the Nebraska Capitol Building," July 13, 2020. https://capitol.nebraska.gov/building/history/.

Hildreth Meière

"Biography of Hildreth Meière - International Hildreth Meière Association Inc." n.d. www.hildrethmeiere.org. https://www.hildrethmeiere.org/bios/hildreth-meiere.

"Walls Speak: The Narrative Art of Hildreth Meiere." 2012. Institute of Classical Architecture & Art. https://www.classicist.org/articles/walls-speak-the-narrative-art-of-hildreth-meiere/.

Bertram Goodhue

"Early History, Design and Construction of the Goodhue Building | Los Angeles Public Library." n.d. www.lapl.org. https://www.lapl.org/branches/central-library/art-architecture/goodhue-building.

"Bertram Grosvenor Goodhue - the Building Team." n.d. Nebraska State Capitol. https://capitol.nebraska.gov/building/history/team/bertram-grosvenor-goodhue/.

Reinhold Marxhausen

The LCMS. 2011. "Artist Reinhold Marxhausen Dies." April 26, 2011. https://reporter.lcms.org/2011/artist-reinhold-marxhausen-dies/.

"Marxhausen Gallery of Art." n.d. Concordia University, Nebraska. https://www.cune.edu/arts/visual-arts/art/marxhausen-gallery-art.

"Reinhold Marxhausen." n.d. Kiechel Fine Art. https://kiechelart.com/artist/reinhold-marxhausen/.

Kenneth Evett

"About the Artist." n.d. Kenneth Evett. https://www.kennethevett.com/about-the-artist.

"Noted Watercolorist and Cornell Art Professor Kenneth Evett Dies at 91." 2005. *Cornell Chronicle*. https://news.cornell.edu/stories/2005/06/noted-watercolorist-and-cornell-art-professor-kenneth-evett-dies-91.

Hartley Alexander

"Alexander, Hartley Burr." n.d. History Nebraska. https://history.nebraska.gov/publications_section/alexander-hartley-burr/.

Alexander, Thomas M. 2008. "Hartley Burr Alexander: Humanistic Personalism and Pluralism." *The Pluralist* 3 (1): 89–127. https://doi.org/10.2307/20708925.

"Hartley Burr Alexander." n.d. Nebraska State Capitol. https://capitol.nebraska.gov/building/history/team/hartley-burr-alexander/.

Unicameral

"Nebraska Legislature - History of the Unicameral." n.d. Nebraskalegislature.gov. https://nebraskalegislature.gov/about/history_unicameral.php.

"Unicameral History | Nebraska Council of School Administrators (NCSA) Legislative News." n.d. Legislative.ncsa.org. https://legislative.ncsa.org/nebraska-unicameral/unicameral-history.

Augustus Tack

Luebke, Frederick C. 1995. Review of The Progressive Context of the Nebraska Capitol: The Collaboration of Goodhue and Tack. *Great Plains Quarterly*. https://digitalcommons.unl.edu/greatplainsquarterly/993/.

Elizabeth Dolan

"Elizabeth Dolan." n.d. Kiechel Fine Art. https://kiechelart.com/artist/elizabeth-dolan/.

McKee, Jim. n.d. "Jim McKee: Well-Known Painter Is Little-Known Lincolnite." *Lincoln Journal Star*. https://journalstar.com/news/local/jim-mckee-well-known-painter-is-little-known-lincolnite/article_59cc692c-beaa-11ed-ab7a-a3febcc559bd.html.

Stephen Cornelius Roberts

Baker, Kamrin. 2018. "Omaha's Own Da Vinci." *Omaha Magazine*. https://www.omahamagazine.com/2018/09/22/301681/omaha-s-own-da-vinci.

"Steven Cornelius Roberts." n.d. Kiechel Fine Art. https://kiechelart.com/artist/steven-cornelius-roberts/.

Lee Lawrie

Haller, Robert. 1993. "The Drama of Law in the Nebraska State Capitol: Sculpture and Inscriptions." *Great Plains Quarterly* 13 (1): 3–20. https://www.jstor.org/stable/23531469.

Ursch, Blake. 2016. "Lee Lawrie, Creator of the Sower, 'Flew under the Radar of Art History.'" *Omaha World-Herald*. https://omaha.com/lifestyles/lee-lawrie-creator-of-the-sower-flew-under-the-radar-of-art-history/article_018f2b06-b0b7-58e5-8dc9-ad434c973a19.html.

ILLUSTRATION CREDITS

All artwork images in the book: Nebraska Capitol Collections; Nebraska Impact Collection.

Sower (page 2): Nebraska Capitol Collections; John Spence, photographer.

Historical capitol photos (pages 13–15): Nebraska State Historical Society; Nebraska State Capitol.

Rotunda floor background image (pages 16–17): Hildreth Meière Dunn.

Hildreth Meière (page 17): F.S. Lincoln. Photograph of work depicting Notre Dame by Hildreth Meiere, circa 1924. Hildreth Meière papers, 1901–2011. Archives of American Art, Smithsonian Institution.

Bertram Goodhue (page 43): Nebraska Capitol Collections.

Reinhold Marxhausen (page 63): *Lincoln Journal Star*; 1977 LJS photo of Reinhold Marxhausen.

Kenneth Evett (page 89): Kenneth Evett papers, #15-2-3481. Division of Rare and Manuscript Collections, Cornell University Library.

Hartley Alexander (page 107): Nebraska State Historical Society; Pound Family.

First Unicameral (page 119): Nebraska State Historical Society; Nebraska State Capitol.

Augustus Tack (page 129): The Phillips Collection.

Stephen Cornelius Roberts (page 157): Michael Malone.

Lee Lawrie (page 175): Smutny, R. V., photographer. Sculptor Lee Lawrie, 1925. Photograph. https://www.loc.gov/item/2015650847/.